FILM &
LITERATURE

10/05

FILM &
LITERATURE
An Introduction

LONGMAN
New York
London

MORRIS BEJA
Ohio State University

FILM AND LITERATURE
An Introduction

Longman Inc., New York
Associated companies, branches, and representatives
throughout the world.

Developmental Editor: Gordon T. R. Anderson
Editorial and Design Supervisor: Linda Salmonson
Design: Antler & Baldwin, Inc.
Manufacturing and Production Supervisor: Louis Gaber
Composition: Book Composition Services
Printing and Binding: The Murray Printing Company

Library of Congress Cataloging in Publication Data

Beja, Morris.
    Film & literature, an introduction.

    Bibliography: p.
    1. Moving-pictures and literature. 2. Film
adaptations. 3. Moving-pictures—History. I. Title.
PN1995.3.B4   791.43′0909′23   78-26167
ISBN 0-582-28094-X

Manufactured in the United States of America

To all I loved in the Bronx:
above all my family, Nancy,
the Loew's 167th Street,
the Zenith, and the Shakespeare Avenue branch
of the New York Public Library.

Acknowledgments

AMONG the friends who have helped me during the time I have worked on this book, I would particularly like to thank Ron and Carol Castell for lending me their extensive library of film books—and never once asking me when they might get the books back. For advice, readings, and various sorts of assistance, I am grateful to Mark Auburn, Dennis Bingham, Thomas Cooley, Edward P. J. Corbett, Marlene Longenecker, Susan Lorsch, Judith Mayne, Arnold Shapiro, Charles Wheeler, and Christian Zacher—and especially to Richard Finholt, Kathy Greenwood, James Griffith, James Naremore, and Pamela Transue. Carol K. Corey and Mary Corliss of the Film Stills Archive of the Museum of Modern Art, and Kathleen Ware of the Teaching Aids Laboratory at Ohio State University, were very helpful.

The Department of English and the College of Humanities of the Ohio State University—in particular John Gabel, Julian Markels, and Arthur Adams—were always encouraging of my "interdisciplinary" efforts and even of my insistence that those efforts weren't really "interdisciplinary" at all. I would also like to thank the many people who responded to a questionnaire about this volume, especially but not only about the films selected for part 2. Sometimes the respondents' interest led to lengthy replies and correspondence which I hope have improved this book. Certainly it has improved as a result of the counsel and encouragement given me by Gordon T. R. Anderson of Longman.

Both personally and professionally, I must express my gratitude to all the students in my film and literature courses who have been eager to ponder with me many of the issues raised here. And finally, my thanks go to Nancy, Drew, and Eleni for their patience.

vi

Contents

The Twenty-Five Films

ALPHABETICALLY BY DIRECTOR

ADAPTATIONS AND ORIGINAL SCREENPLAYS

Films from Novels or Stories

ALPHABETICALLY BY AUTHORS OF ADAPTED WORKS

Introduction

THIS book is designed for undergraduate courses in film, in literature, or in film *and* literature; its goals are to explore two of the most important art forms of our time, and the relationships between them, while demonstrating and preserving the integrity of each. The focus is neither on film nor on written literature, but on understanding and appreciating each form on its own *and* in relation to the other. The premise behind the entire book—like that of most of the courses for which it is intended—is that there is great value in looking at the two genres together; such a pairing enables us to get a sense of all that they share, to be sure, but also of all the traits that they do not, so that one may grasp as well what is unique about each form.

Inevitably, in such an approach, a good deal of attention is occasionally paid to "adaptations," and for good reason. People interested in any art form constantly find themselves referring to other forms: students of literature, for example, continually perceive parallels and distinctions between prose fiction, say, and poetry, drama, music, or painting. The frequency with which literary works become the bases for films provides an added degree of appropriateness to such comparisons. Rarely can we find in other forms examples that purport to tell the same "story" as a given novel or short story; but in the realm of film such resources are extraordinarily common.

While examining examples of such dual "versions" has obvious advantages, however, it is clearly not the only way in which studying film and written literature together can produce an extremely enlightening confrontation. For as this book will attempt to show, their relationships are much more fundamental, pervasive, and significant than is indicated merely by the fact that many movies are adaptations of books. It may be, for example, that a director of adaptations of "classic" novels will seem less genuinely in tune with (or, perhaps, influenced by) literary techniques and approaches than one who does not make adaptations, or who does so rarely, like Fellini or Antonioni. (Griffith's assertions that he was influenced by Dickens are both convincing and illuminating—despite the fact that he never made a movie based on any of Dickens' books: the very real and essential relationships between their works are not dependent on that sort of thing at all.) Similarly, a novelist whose books have all been made into films or who has even worked in Hollywood may seem less genuinely in tune with (or, again, influenced by) cinematic techniques and approaches than one who has had little if anything to do with the movies, like Joyce or Camus.

This book concentrates on the art of *narrative,* the realm in which written literature and film are most intimately connected. Indeed, it will examine the possibility that written stories (for example novels) and filmed stories (what people mean by "the movies") are really two forms of a single art—the art of narrative literature.

Part 1 of the book confronts literature, film, and their relationships in four chapters. Chapter 1, "Narrative Literature," distinguishes briefly among various forms of written narrative (especially prose fiction) and the way we experience them, and it defines and discusses such concepts as story, plot, theme, character, point of view, and prose. Some of the concepts are further pursued in chapter 2, "Narrative Film," which explores the experience of film as well as its creation; it also discusses such concepts as the *auteur* principle, *mise en scène,* montage, and various terms such as shot, aspect ratio, cut, fade, dissolve, and many others. Chapter 3, "Film and Literature," directly confronts the relationships, comparisons, and contrasts between the two forms. And chapter 4, "Adaptations," tackles sometimes similar but ultimately distinct issues— among them, the central question of what the relationships between a film and a work upon which it may be based ought to be.

Part 2 provides aids for appreciating and studying twenty-five films. For each film there are various kinds of background information: for example on the director, the screenwriter, and the cinematographer and their other work; if the film is an adaptation, on the original work and its author; and perhaps on historical contexts as well. Then comes a series of topics to think or write about, including questions, excerpts from reviews or criticism, quotations from the original novel, story, or play which has been adapted, or from the dialogue of the film, or from interviews with an author or a director. Each section ends with a bibliography of further readings. Whenever a film or work of written literature included in part 2 is mentioned elsewhere in the book, its title is preceded by an asterisk: e.g., *Citizen Kane.*

The films in part 2 include some of the most important movies in cinema history, but obviously no attempt is made to lock any course into some particular set of selections. It is true that most courses dealing with film and literature will in fact probably include at least two or three—perhaps more—of the movies covered. But the aim of the section is also to provide students with detailed *examples* of the sorts of directions in which a study of other films might also move. The selection of films to be covered was based in large part on the results of an extensive survey seeking to determine which films have been most frequently and successfully included in film-and-literature courses; instructors from colleges and universities all over the country responded in large numbers, often with very helpful and detailed comments.

The volume ends with a glossary and bibliography covering both film and literature, and a list of major distributors of 16mm films, with their addresses.

A book such as this—like any work of criticism, for that matter—succeeds only to the extent that it helps bring together in a fruitful way a reader and, in this case, literary and cinematic works of art. It cannot concentrate solely on the art and pay no attention to the experience of the audience; but in the world of art the reader of a book and the spectator.of a film are not in themselves sacred either. What matters is what happens when art and audience (book and reader, film and spectator) beautifully come together, or against one another: when they *relate.*

That can take place on all kinds of levels, but it is my conviction that it happens most valuably in a context of wonder so intense that we feel the need to explore our experience and to understand more fully the art and the work that impelled it. At such times the "book addict" or the "movie fan"—either one a fine thing to be—becomes as well a student of literature, or of film, or of both. Surely at least as. fine a thing to be.

Part

1

The Surrounding Vision

To arrest, for the space of a breath, the hands busy about the work of the earth, and compel men entranced by the sight of distant goals to glance for a moment at the surrounding vision of form and color, of sunshine and shadows; to make them pause for a look, for a sigh, for a smile—such is the aim, difficult and evanescent, and reserved only for a very few to achieve.

Joseph Conrad

CHAPTER 1
Narrative Literature

LITERATURE

Sometimes, the term *literature* simply refers to anything that is written or printed: so a travel agent stocks tourist "literature" (time-tables, brochures, and so on), while laboratory researchers familiarize themselves with the experimental "literature" of the particular field they are exploring. But an even more common and equally legitimate sense of the term *literature* reserves it for works which are meant or felt to have interest, pleasure, and value in themselves, beyond their immediate or utilitarian function, and which are appreciated for form and for skill in presentation as well as for their content. A manual on photographic dark-room techniques should no doubt be well-written, but the purposes for which we go to it—and the effects produced by it—will be enormously different from those associated with an imaginative work of literary art, even one in which such dark-room techniques may be significant elements, as in Julio Cortázar's short story *"Blow-Up," or for that matter in Michelangelo Antonioni's film "adaptation" of that story. Clearly, moreover, Cortázar's short story is less like the work also produced in its medium, written prose (the photography manual) than it is like the work in a different medium, film (Antonioni's "adaptation"). In the same way, a story by Edgar Allan Poe will probably strike us as having more in common with poems by Robert Browning or some of the films of Alfred Hitchcock than with almost any prose account of a case study in psychopathology printed in the *American Journal of Psychotherapy*. And Chaucer's poetic account of greed for gold, *The Pardoner's Tale*, has more affinities with B. Traven's prose novel **The Treasure of the Sierra*

Madre or John Huston's film based on that novel than any of these works would have with the entry on "gold" in the Encyclopaedia Britannica.

NARRATIVE

In this chapter, we shall concern ourselves particularly with some of the more prominent written forms of literature by which humanity has fulfilled its universal need for *narrative*. "In the beginning . . ." "There was this traveling salesman . . ." "A funny thing happened to me on the way over here today . . ." "Once upon a time . . ." The varieties of narrative are so numerous that we may well find ourselves agreeing with Gertrude Stein's contention that narrative is no less than "what anybody has to say in any way about anything that can happen has happened will happen in any way." But let us attempt a step toward clarification by saying that a narrative is any work which recounts a *story*.

A story: a sequence of events in time. If the epic poem, the novel, the short story and the ballad are forms of narrative, and if all narratives tell a story, then we cannot have a novel, say—not even the most advanced, subtle novel imaginable—without that primitive element, the "story." The novelist E. M. Forster laments this embarrassing predicament for the sophisticated and ambitious literary artist in his study *Aspects of the Novel:* "Yes—oh dear yes—the novel tells a story. That is the fundamental aspect without which it could not exist. That is the highest factor common to all novels, and I wish that it was not so, that it could be something different—melody, or perception of the truth, not this low atavistic form." [1] Forster tries to escape his semi-ironic plight by pursuing a distinction between story and *plot*. Not all readers will agree that we can distinguish between them, or that we ought to bother, and not all those who agree about the possibility or desirability will agree with Forster's own mode of making the distinction, although it is probably the most common way.

Forster asserts that while story emphasizes chronology, plot stresses causality. He provides some short examples to show what he means: "The king died and then the queen died" is a story, while "The king died, and then the queen died of grief" is a plot. We may still have the time sequence but it is no longer the controlling factor it was in the original, "story" version; "the sense of causality overshadows it." And

---

1. Bibliographical information for works cited may be found in the Bibliography at the end of this book.

then ("and then" is a key phrase in Forster's concept of the story, while "why?" is a key word in his notion of plot) he provides a third version: "The queen died, no one knew why; until it was discovered that it was through grief at the death of the king." This, says Forster, "is a plot with a mystery in it, a form capable of high development."

Illuminating and charming as Forster's examples are, there are difficulties in his fundamental distinction—as perhaps suggested by his third version, in which the mystery is resolved, the causes discovered. Especially nowadays, an equally respectable version might read, "The queen died, no one knew why—or ever found out." Or, "The queen died, having allegedly been assassinated by the court jester, although there was no discernible motive." Many writers are distrustful of simple assumptions about causality—the sorts of assumptions Forster would never be caught making in his own novels. Writers who view the world as absurd (there are no causes and effects, or no rational ones) or mysterious (causes and effects cannot be determined) may base their plots on factors other than causality. Consequently, some readers and critics distinguish plot from story by saying that if story is temporal sequence, plot is the sequence presented or arranged by the teller of the story— whether the result is organized on principles that are causal, temporal, thematic, psychological, or whatever.

In that sense, plot tends to become for all practical purposes indistinguishable from *structure:* the disposition or arrangement of the materials of the story with which we are presented, the shape or pattern into which the author has transmuted them. In traditional stories, the structure often follows a logical and time-honored order, containing such elements as:

Exposition, in which we are given the background information we may need (as when a Western novel informs us that "Big Luke and Badlands Jake had known for a long time that one day their paths would cross, and that there would have to be a showdown between them").

Development, in which the situation is pursued ("One day, Big Luke rode into Dry Gulch, suspecting that Badlands Jake would be waiting for him"—clearly, some plots need less complex development than others).

Conflict, in which we see the element of opposition, in which forces come against one another (often, of course, the good guys against the bad guys: "Standing in the middle of the town road, Badlands Jake sneered at Luke and snarled, 'This town ain't big enough for the two of us' ").

Digression, where our attention is temporarily diverted from the main points of the narrative ("Lindabelle Sue, the pretty young school-teacher, pleaded with the two men to avoid violence").

Climax, the high point of tension or decisive moment toward which everything else seems to have been leading ("Interrupting Lindabelle Sue in the midst of her pleas, and roughly pushing her to the ground, Badlands Jake reached for his six-shooter").

Resolution or *denouement* (the "unknotting" or "unraveling"), wherein if we are lucky the conflicts or mysteries are resolved ("But Luke was too fast on the draw for Badlands Jake, who bit the dust after one blast from Luke's shooting-iron. Stepping over Jake's lifeless body, Luke gently took Lindabelle Sue's arm, and together they rode off into the sunset").

Perhaps another breakdown will help to clarify each term; this time consider a science-fiction plot:

Exposition. Intergalactic scientists were concerned that the solar system seemed to be dying, as the sun was displaying on their boraxic monitors signs of losing its energy.

Development. Kurt Candle, the brilliant young bio-physico-ecologist from Earth-Two, was assigned to the galactical task force investigating the source of that decline.

Conflict. But Candle found his investigations hampered by his fellow officers, until he began to suspect that they were part of a gigantic extra-terrestrial conspiracy, the aim of which was nothing less than the destruction of the solar system and of civilization as we know it. He rushed from the Milky Way to Mars, to report his findings to his commander, Peter Paul.

Digression. The spaceship in which Candle sped was one of the new series with polymorphous engines powered by Nexelsior, its interior decorated by unisex Plutonians to achieve optimum desterility.

Climax. Peter Paul turned out to be Chief of C.E.S.S. (Conspiracy to End the Solar System), and he issued orders to have Candle thrown into the diabolical C.E.S.S. pool, containing a special acid which slowly burnt Candle at both ends.

Resolution. The solar system was now free to be destroyed, and the leaders of C.E.S.S. turned their attention to the rest of the universe—and beyond.

The parodic examples I have provided refer to "formula" plots; similar examples could easily be devised for the detective novel, the gothic romance, or the Novel of Alienated Sensitive Youth in a Cruel World of Adults. But like most oversimplifications, such formulas are as misleading as they are clear, for while the elements I have described will be present in most literary works, in many they will not necessarily be in that order, and in few will they be so obviously delineated. Indeed, many writers will avoid such traditional patterns as assiduously as they can. For example, a novelist may wish to convey the impression that the narrative structure is merely the patternless flow of a character's or narrator's thoughts or "stream of consciousness." This is not an exclusively modern ploy, incidentally. Over two hundred years ago Laurence Sterne had his narrator, Tristram Shandy, boast that his mode of composition was "the best—I'm sure it is the most religious—for I begin with writing the first sentence—and trusting to Almighty God for the second."

As the number of possible variations in structure would suggest, there are many ways in which writers may "treat" their *theme*—the idea or thesis (or ideas or theses) underpinning a work, which is sometimes called simplistically the "message." The choices of theme are even more numerous. And the conceivable subjects through which the themes may be approached are innumerable if not infinite. A work of narrative literature may be "about" anything or anyone the writer wishes it to be about: the journey of an Oklahoma farm family to California; the snipping of a beautiful lady's lock of hair; a bank executive put on trial on obscure charges by mysterious authorities; the tale an ancient mariner somehow compels a wedding guest to hear; some boys marooned on an uninhabited island. It need not even be about "people"; it can be about farm animals or a roan stallion or a dung beetle or leprechauns or extraterrestrial beings or rabbits. Yet even then it almost always seems to be essentially concerned with *character*.

In our context, a character is a person (or personified animal, god, or other sort of figure) depicted in a literary work. Such a creation is of course never a "real person," even when based on a historical or actual human being. Once, after the Irish novelist James Joyce's death, some broadcasters sought to interview a certain Richard I. Best, whose name and personality Joyce had used for a minor character in one of his novels. One of the broadcasters explained their request by remarking, "After all, you're a character in *Ulysses*." Best is reported to have replied—with full justice and, one imagines, righteous annoyance—"I am not a character in fiction. I am a living being." He was right of course. The living being was the product of forces we need not go into here; the character in *Ulysses* was the product of *characterization:* the artistic presentation of a person within a literary work. The Richard I. Best created by Joyce may not be a "living being" in a literal sense, but he does exist, obviously; he exists within the world that Joyce has created. How much we may feel compelled to attribute to such a figure the aura or force of a living being will largely depend upon the talent—or, perhaps, even genius—that the writer brings to characterization. Especially for many dramatists, novelists, and short story writers, to create convincing, illuminating, and moving characters has been a primary goal in their art, or even the fundamental impulse behind it. The British novelist Virginia Woolf has expressed her belief "that men and women write novels because they are lured on to create some character"; and when she asked herself "what demon whispered in my ear and urged me to my doom"— that of becoming a novelist—"a little figure rose before me—the figure of a man, or of a woman, who said, 'My name is Brown. Catch me if you can.'"

Yet "What is character but the determination of incident? What is incident but the illustration of character?" So asked Henry James, like Forster and Woolf a major novelist who wrote illuminatingly about the craft he practiced. Indeed it may be that to concentrate on fine distinctions between story and plot, or between both of them and other aspects of narrative, is to be overly concerned with (or even to be confused by) terminology. As James once observed with some impatience, in an essay entitled "The Art of Fiction," "I cannot see what is meant by talking as if there were a part of a novel which is the story and part of it which for mystical reasons is not." For it is by no means easy to mark off the various aspects of narrative fiction, and to say that A and B are parts of the story, while C and D are elements of the plot, and E and F aspects of characterization; with James, it is hard to "conceive, in any novel worth discussing at all, of a passage of description that is not in its intention narrative, a passage of dialogue that is not in its intention descriptive."

James's assertion implies that there is nothing in a narrative that is not story, nothing that is not plot, and in the sense in which he means that he is indisputably correct. Yet from another perspective, it can be just as essential to refrain from too easily equating the "story" of a narrative (the sequence of events in time related to us) with the entire experience of that narrative. An analogy may be made with a film, in which the acting and the words inform us about what is going on: but other elements are also controlling forces in getting the "story" and its effect across to us. For a "story" is largely determined by *how* it is conveyed—in a film, by the skill or imagination with which cameras are used, by the "theme music" we hear, by whether the film is in black and white or technicolor, by whether the male lead is played by Robert Redford or Mel Brooks, the female lead by Audrey Hepburn or Raquel Welch. If such details did not matter, we could simply read a review of a film and save ourselves a good deal of time and expense. Occasionally it can be enjoyable to hear someone describe a film we have not seen—or to read a screenplay, for that matter. They are just not the same thing as going to the movies.

Drama, too, is a form of narrative meant to be performed, not read: specifically, in the case of drama, to be staged before an audience by actors. The word *drama* derives from the Greek word for "action," although in his extremely influential commentary on tragedy, Aristotle listed a total of six elements of a play: action (or plot), character, thought, language (or diction), music (or song), and spectacle. A central distinction between drama and other forms of narrative is seen in Aristotle's emphasis on drama as an *imitation* of the action: instead of the story being "told" to us, it is "acted out" for us.

Point of View

In either written narratives or performed actions, one of the most important determining factors in the nature of the story will be its "point of view." In narrative, *point of view* refers to the angle of vision or perspective from which a story is conveyed. Too often, the only sorts of distinction made in regard to point of view are such crude ones as whether a written narration is presented in the first person ("I saw," "I said") or the third person ("she saw," "he said"). But the possibilities in point of view are extremely varied; it is important to remember that, but it is even more essential to understand how totally the choice of focus controls both the writer's presentation of a work of narrative and our perception of it. There are many questions which can be asked in regard to the point of view of any work of literature, but perhaps it would help to list some of the most basic ones.

Is there an identifiable narrator? If so, who is it? These two questions bring out, incidentally, one of the primary dangers faced by a reader of literature: confusing the narrator with the author. Few adult readers will mistake the narrator Huckleberry Finn for the author Mark Twain. To realize or keep in mind the full implications of the fact that J. Alfred Prufrock is not T. S. Eliot, or that Pip in *Great Expectations* is not Charles Dickens (that he is not the author even while he is the narrator) takes a bit more sophistication. The further recognition that Jane Austen, Thomas Mann, Dashiell Hammett, and William Faulkner are not to be confused with the unpersonified narrative voices they have created in *Pride and Prejudice*, *Death in Venice*, *The Maltese Falcon*, and *Light in August* is less immediate but ultimately no less crucial.

From what perspective is the narrator telling the story? For example, if a "third person" narration is used, are we nevertheless restricted to what is known or learned by a single character, or by a limited number of characters? Or are no such limitations set on what we are told? Indeed, could we go so far as to describe the narrator as "omniscient"?

What sources of information are available to the narrator or to us, or to both? From what sources are we excluded?

If the narrator is a participant in the events of the story—or one who has personally observed them—how much does that color our reaction to the version of the events that we get?

How reliable does the narrator seem to be? Do we wonder if we ought to react to the narrative with suspicion rather than with full acceptance? An author may very well arrange to have a narrator give us "false" information, as least temporarily. Or perhaps we are meant to recognize all along that our perceptions are quite different from those of the narrator who presents us with everything upon which we base our perceptions.

So important are these and other questions that no aspect of narrative fiction has received more attention from modern critics than has point of view. Much of the consequent discussion has been valuable, although at times evangelical zeal has led critics to extol one approach to point of view at the expense of all others. Yet there seems to be nothing inherent in, say, the "limited" point of view filtered through one observer that makes it invariably preferable to a "multiple" point of view which enters into the minds of several different characters. Rather, the author must try to determine how a given set of characters, and a particular story, subject, or theme, can best be viewed; the writer will obviously write from the viewpoint or combination of viewpoints which seems most likely to produce the effects on the reader that he or she is striving to evoke.

Suppose, for example, you were writing a detective or mystery novel about a murder. Would you want your reader to know the story through the eyes of the killer? Or of the victim? Or would you keep both killer and victim hidden, or in the distance, providing us only with the viewpoint of a detective assigned to the case? Or would you remove us even further from the center of the action by giving us the perspective of a detached spectator, one interested in the murder but not directly involved? Would you so restrict yourself to one such view as to have a single character narrate the entire story? Or would you go from the murderer's thoughts as he eludes exposure to the thoughts of the detective as he feels frustration—or as he closes in?

The elements of crime and detection tend to enhance our immediate awareness of the importance of the choice of point of view, but readers of *Gulliver's Travels, Wuthering Heights, *The Trial, *Lolita, The Stranger,* and many other works will find themselves confronting questions in regard to point of view which are often much more subtle and complex than those we have raised, but at least as central.

The Written Word

A film has to be seen, a meal has to be eaten, a concert has to be heard—and a book has to be read. There is no getting around that if we want to have the *experience* of a book. But for many centuries before there were any printed books, oral narratives (some of them longer than most novels) provided humanity with the stories it so universally seems to need. In such circumstances, a narrative becomes part of a *public* occasion. The act of reading, in contrast, is quite private. Even if we are in a large library reading room with hundreds of other people, each of us is reading alone.

The medium of printed books is language; that of written narratives is the written word. In traditional epics or in ballads, the words are in *poetry:* that is, they are chosen and arranged with special attention to such considerations as their rhythmical and metrical patterns, or their figurative qualities, or perhaps even rhyme. (In poetry such formal matters are so absolutely central that the poet Robert Frost once defined poetry as what is lost in translation.) In novels and short stories, the written words are in *prose,* "ordinary" language (the word *prose* comes from the Latin *prosa,* for "straightforward") in the sense that it usually has no predetermined rhythm or metrical regularity, as most poetry traditionally has.

Obviously, the terms *poetry* and *prose* are much more complex than the above capsule descriptions can indicate; but if both words still sound a bit vague, there is probably even greater ambiguity in the next term we shall consider in our attempt to distinguish among various modes of narrative: *fiction.*

Fiction is what is not true, what someone has imagined or conjured up—"made up" (the word comes from the Latin *fingere,* to make, to fashion, or to form). Yet it probably does not demand an especially cynical turn of mind to be uncomfortable with terms which lead us to refer to the contents of the *Congressional Record* (or even *Time* or *Newsweek*) as "the truth," while *The Iliad,* *Hamlet, Faust, A Portrait of the Artist as a Young Man,* and *1984* become "not the truth." Those fictions prevaricate but do not deceive; they beguile but do not distort. Artists fabricate, but they do not necessarily misrepresent. A failure to realize this distinction has occasionally created in some serious-minded people a sense of discomfort with imaginative literature. They feel that sitting down with a biography or a volume of history or a treatise on world population is obviously a worthwhile pursuit, while reading a novel, say, or going to a movie, is at best merely a distraction: not to be condemned, perhaps, but hardly to be encouraged. Long ago the narrative voice in one of Jane Austen's novels, *Northanger Abbey,* bristled at such an attitude:

> "And what are you reading, Miss—?" "Oh! it is only a novel!" replies the young lady; while she lays down her book with affected indifference, or momentary shame.— . . . in short, only some work in which the greatest powers of the mind are displayed, in which the most thorough knowledge of human nature, the happiest delineation of its varieties, the liveliest effusions of wit and humour, are conveyed to the world in the best chosen language.

Facts of course may be liberating, but so indeed may non-facts. Our awareness of the "facts" of life may not always lead more profoundly to the *truth* of life than our receptivity to make-believe; as Herman Melville recognized, "you must have plenty of sea-room to tell the Truth in."

It is a commonplace to say that in reading a good story we "lose ourselves" in the work, and often that is true; but even when we become so absorbed in the imaginary world we are reading about that we can say that has happened, it has occurred because we have been willing to let it. And ultimately a part of us remains quite aware of what is going on; it is only when we are totally *unaware* that fictions are fictions that they hurt us. When the narrator of Jane Austen's *Pride and Prejudice* informs us that it is a truth universally acknowledged that a single man in possession of a good fortune must be in want of a wife, or when Herman Melville's narrator tells us to call him Ishmael, or when Franz Kafka's narrator tells us that someone must have traduced Joseph K., for without having done anything wrong he was arrested one fine morning, or when the speaker of an old ballad tells us that there lived a wife at Usher's Well, or when Dashiell Hammett's narrator tells us that Samuel Spade's jaw was long and bony, his chin a jutting v, or when Edgar Allan Poe's narrator describes how, on a dull, dark, and soundless day in the autumn of the year, he found himself within view of the melancholy House of Usher—when we are told any of those things, we are being lied to, and we know it, and we love every minute of it.

In literature, as in all art, we play "let's pretend." It is something we

do together with the artist; we both of course know that we are pretending, though we may go so far as to pretend that we are not. (We must not
actually forget that we are pretending, at least not for long; that is almost
as dangerous as never playing "let's pretend" at all.) If we as readers thus
actively cooperate, and if the writer is effective, we become that writer's
accomplice, and are as guilty of—as *involved* in—the artifice as the artist
is. No doubt there are many complex reasons why we let that happen,
but a primary one is our realization that although, as Pablo Picasso
observed, "art is a lie," it is—as he went on—"a lie that leads to the truth."

Forms of Prose Fiction

The most popular forms of written literature the world has ever
known have been the short story and, especially, the novel. Indeed, they
were the first major forms of written literature ever made available to a
mass audience, the original examples of what is now known as "popular
culture." We have come far enough in our discussion of narrative literature to say that the novel and the short story are both fictitious written
narratives in prose, although that does not help us tell one from the
other. Actually, of course, no one has any trouble distinguishing between
a short story that is obviously short and a novel that is obviously long.
The problems arise in the mid-world called the "short novel" (sometimes
also called "novella" and "novelette," but those terms carry with them
historical and other connotations that are probably not fully relevant
here). When does a short story become long enough to be considered a
short novel?

There is no universal agreement on this question, but a frequent
and practical answer is that a narrative is generally not considered a
short story if it is unlikely to be read at a single sitting. That is clearly not
a very precise formulation, dependent as it is on so many relative factors:
interruptions can prevent us from finishing even the briefest of stories,
while—more happily—we can become so engrossed with a short novel
that contrary to our expectations we "can't put it down." To Poe, who
was one of the first to make such a distinction, the outside limit for the
time it should ordinarily take to read a "short prose narrative" is two
hours. In terms of the number of words, the dividing point between the
short story and the short novel is often given as somewhere around
15,000 words. Distinctions between the short novel and the "full-length"
novel are even less clear. Certainly the term *full-length* is itself misleading, insofar as it seems to imply that anything shorter than that is partial,
not "full"—not so much "short" as curtailed. Still, the term short novel is

probably a useful one, and the upper limit for the genre is usually given as around 50,000 words.

Let us then consider the following definitions:

> Novel: a long fictitious written narrative in prose.
> Short Story: A brief fictitious written narrative in prose.

No one is likely to claim that these definitions are either exciting or entirely satisfactory, and one would love to be able to make them fuller and more detailed. The trouble is, as soon as we try to do that we run into more ambiguities and difficulties than we had to begin with.

For example, basing the distinction between the short story and the novel on length goes against one's feeling that significant differences in length are bound to entail other differences and will tend to produce divergent sorts of effects, as well as contrasting sorts of intentions and approaches even within a single writer. There is no denying that. But hazards arise as soon as we try to pinpoint particular tendencies within short or long fiction and claim them as defining features. To attempt that may even lead us to suggest that there is some orthodox or standard way of writing one or the other; and such an approach can be deadly.

Sometimes the claim is that the short story concentrates on a single incident and a single character, while the novel is free to roam more widely. The chief problem with this distinction is that it is demonstrably inaccurate: many short stories range over the entire lives of several characters, while many novels keep us with one or two characters for only a day or so. To say, however, as Poe did in a famous review of Nathaniel Hawthorne's *Twice-Told Tales,* that "if wise" the writer of a short prose narrative will restrict it to "a certain unique or single *effect* to be wrought out," is more vague, perhaps, but also more useful, since it is more often true. But it is not so universally true that it enables us to distinguish all short stories from all novels.

Individual artists, after all, have individual aims: perhaps to analyze society, or to urge us to reform it (or accept it, or overthrow it); perhaps to "entertain" us, to make us laugh (or cry); perhaps to excite us (a term broad enough to encompass both tales of adventure and pornography); for many writers, as we have seen, a prime goal is the creation and exploration of human character. My list is deliberately short, and it could not be exhaustive. The novel especially is often felt to be, as Joseph Conrad characterized it, "the most elusive of all creative arts." To seize upon one aim or tendency as the proper one for the novel—and to say in consequence that this or that work lies within the great tradition of the novel, while another work with another approach is outside the legitimate realm of the genre—is to be coercive and arrogant, or at best ineffectual. As the narrative voice in a novel by Thomas Pynchon observes, "when laws of heredity are laid down, mutants will be born." But if we are careful not to lay down laws, looking at heredity may be enlightening.

THE NARRATIVE TRADITION

Actually, to speak of the "heritage" of the novel may be a bit pretentious, since as literary genres go, it is still fairly new as a major form. True, if any long fictitious written narrative in prose is a novel, then the novel has been around a long time, and in examples well worth reading at least since the first century and the *Satyricon* of Petronius. But for centuries drama and poetry attracted most of the audiences and artists—certainly almost all the artists of interest to today's non-scholarly readers. Perhaps a sense of the relative historical time periods involved can be reached by a chronological experiment or game.[2]

Let us assume that the earliest major examples of narrative literature as we know it in the Western world are the works of Homer, and let us further assume that they date from 800 B.C. (Both assumptions are admittedly debatable, but similar results would be obtained from any date scholars would be likely to choose.) Then, let us imagine all the time since then until the publication of the book you are now reading as the equivalent of a single "year"—that is, 800 B.C. corresponds to January 1. In that case, Christ was born in "mid-April." *Beowulf,* the Anglo-Saxon epic poem that is one of the earliest examples of what we can call "English" literature, was probably composed during the second week of July (that is, around the late eighth century A.D.). But we had to wait until November 12 for the appearance of *Macbeth* and *Don Quixote* (in 1605). December 1 was the publication date for Fielding's *Tom Jones* (1749). T. S. Eliot's *The Waste Land* and James Joyce's *Ulysses* (1922) did not appear until December 23, while William Butler Yeats died on December 26 (the equivalent of 1939) and Vladimir Nabokov on New Year's Eve (1977). In this imaginary time scheme, films all came during the last two

2. The idea for my game of literary history comes from the "cosmic calendar" (with January 1 as the origin of the universe in a Big Bang) in Carl Sagan's *The Dragons of Eden: Speculations on the Evolution of Human Intelligence* (New York: Random House, 1977), pp. 11–17.

weeks of the "year": Edison's Kinetograph was invented on December 19 (in 1891); two days later we saw *The Great Train Robbery* (1903), and *The Birth of a Nation* (1915) the day after that. *The Jazz Singer* (1927) appeared on Christmas Eve; both *Citizen Kane* and *The Maltese Falcon* (1941) came out on December 26, the same day as Yeats's death but several hours later. Just a few days ago we first saw *Psycho* and *L'avventura* (December 28, i.e., 1960). *2001: A Space Odyssey* (1968) was released around 4:50 P.M. on December 29.

The form of the novel did not begin to thrive until the late Renaissance (around the third week in November), and it did not become a major form until the eighteenth century (late November and early December), when a widespread awareness first developed of its value, uniqueness, and tremendous artistic possibilities. Indeed, the genre seemed so different from what writers and readers of English had been accustomed to that they felt a need for a new word by which to describe it; and the one they ultimately settled on was fortunate, as Ian Watt has shown in his study *The Rise of the Novel:*

> Previous literary forms had reflected the general tendency of their cultures to make conformity to traditional practice the major test of truth: the plots of classical and renaissance epic, for example, were based on past history or fable, and the merits of the author's treatment were judged largely according to a view of literary decorum derived from the accepted models in the genre. This literary traditionalism was first and most fully challenged by the novel, whose primary criterion was truth to individual experience—individual experience which is always unique and therefore new. The novel is thus the logical literary vehicle of a culture which, in the last few centuries, has set an unprecedented value on originality, on the novel; and it is therefore well named.

The emergence of the novel as an important literary form in the West only began a little over two hundred years ago—not much time, as our imaginary calendar suggests, when set against the entire span of literary history, but enough for it to become so dominant that to D. H. Lawrence as to others it could be considered "the one bright book of life."

The world welcomed the different genre because the world had changed too, and was receptive to—*needed*—new narrative forms, and was able to produce them in quantity. For that to happen, at least three revolutions had to occur: the technological one of the printing press, which turned out what was probably the first genuine article of mass production, the printed book; the economic revolution of the ability to market ("mass-market," as we would now say) new products for large numbers of consumers able to pay for them; and the social revolution of the interest generated by those new consumers in literary characters more or less like themselves—individual middle-class people.

The epics and medieval romances had dealt with chivalric heroes and heroines, kings and queens, knights and grand ladies; it is no accident that the book which some people like to call (stretching a point, no doubt) the "first" novel, *Don Quixote,* was a satire on the age of chivalry. As Don Quixote himself demonstrates, interest in courtly heroes and heroines did not die, and it never has. But the new bourgeois readers who bought the new books also wanted to hear about men like Robinson Crusoe, who for all his exotic adventures is as bourgeois a hero as the literature of the world has ever produced, a good middle-class Englishman determined to transform his tropical island into a little bit of Britain. Ancient Greek tragedy tended to reflect what we now regard as the "classical" ideals; medieval romances reflected aristocratic, feudal ideals; the new long fictitious written narratives in prose inevitably tended to reflect the new audience's ideals of bourgeois individualism, and its interest in down-to-earth reality.

Indeed, the traditional connection between the novel and realism has been so strong that some readers and critics have felt that works which are not "realistic" but fantastic or larger than life—or mythic, or epic—are best called "romances" rather than "novels." A frequent distinction holds that a romance is particularly "symbolic." On the other hand, if in simplest terms a *symbol* is something that stands for something else, then all literature uses "symbolism," including all fictitious written narratives in prose. Indeed, it would be impossible to exaggerate the importance of symbols in the lives of all of us at any particular moment; and in order to realize that we need not think only of such clearly emotionally packed symbols as the flag, or the Christian cross, or a raised clenched fist. Even a traffic light is a symbol, a sign conveying a meaning beyond what it is merely in itself. Recent linguistic studies—notably those associated with "semiology" or "semiotics," the study of systems of "signs" and their signification (or meaning)—have explored the deep affinities among the "language systems" not merely of the spoken and written word but also of others such as those of dress, of computers, of forms of courtesy, of painting, or of chess.

All such language systems are symbolic. Words for example are all signs; mere sounds in themselves, or black marks on white paper, they take on meaning for us only because they represent concepts or things beyond themselves. If all language is symbolic, it follows that all linguistic art is too. Still, some literature is obviously more symbolic than other literature—just as, for that matter, some symbols are more complex than others. (In some contexts, a Cadillac can be used to symbolize a life-style, but it will not usually bring with it as many references and complexities as will ordinarily be associated with a Star of David, or a swastika, or—after Melville—a white whale.)

As early as 1691, in his preface to *Incognita,* William Congreve expressed his sense of the difference between a novel and a romance by saying that while novels are of a "familiar nature," romances "give more of Wonder." The two terms persisted, and over a century and a half later Nathaniel Hawthorne wrote in the preface to *The House of the Seven Gables* (1851):

> When a writer calls his work a Romance, it need hardly be observed that he wishes to claim a certain latitude, both as to its fashion and material, which he would not have felt himself entitled to assume, had he professed to be writing a novel. The latter form of composition is presumed to aim at a very minute fidelity, not merely to the possible, but to the probable and ordinary course of man's experience. The former—while, as a work of art, it must rigidly subject itself to laws, and while it sins unpardonably, so far as it may swerve aside from the truth of the human heart—has fairly a right to present that truth under circumstances, to a great extent, of the writer's own choosing or creation.

As Hawthorne's words indicate, the terms *novel* and *romance* are not necessarily value terms; nor, for that matter, is the term *realistic* in itself such a term. *Realism* does not imply greater reality, merely more verisimilitude: not greater revelation of truth, not greater cogency or power, but simply a closer correlation to the everyday world as most of us usually see it around us.

Each reader will decide whether the distinction between novel and romance is useful and worth keeping. For many, the differences between them—like, indeed, those between realism and fantasy—are so blurred that they feel with Henry James that the only distinction with any "meaning" is that between "bad novels and good novels." Most readers and critics seem to have concluded that while realism may thrive in the novel, it is not a necessary feature of it. We may in fact feel that *no* particular approach is "necessary" to the novel. After all and above all, the novel is extremely *free*—arguably, the freest of all written narrative forms.

The Short Story

The emergence of the short story as we know it is an even more recent phenomenon in Western literature than that of the novel. This is genuinely paradoxical, for the short narrative seems to be as old as humanity itself. Originally, of course, it took oral forms—in folklore, myths, fairy tales, fables, parables. But in print—and despite the popularity of longer prose narratives—the short story did not become truly popular until the nineteenth century. Various practitioners figure importantly here: in the first half of the nineteenth century there were, especially, Nikolai Gogol in Russia, E. T. A. Hoffmann in Germany, and, in America, Edgar Allan Poe, whose critical writings set forth a number of concepts which influenced the subsequent development of the form. During the second half of the nineteenth century, more and more writers were attracted to the short story—notably such figures as Guy de Maupassant, Anton Chekhov, and Henry James—until by the early twentieth century an impressive number of writers had become masters of the form.

To Poe, as we have seen, the ideal short story concentrates on "a certain unique or single *effect*," and the final product must be tightly controlled: "In the whole composition there should be no word written, of which the tendency, direct or indirect, is not to the one pre-established design." Not all effective modern stories follow Poe's demands, of course, but many do; in other ways, however, they often depart quite far from the sorts of tales of mystery, horror, and the supernatural for which Poe is so famous. At least since Chekhov in Russia and Joyce in Ireland, many short stories have seemed to be "slices of life" rather than the records of outwardly exciting events forming clear "plots" found in, say, fables or folk tales. But there are inwardly exciting events as well as outwardly exciting ones; and if writers of modern stories seem at times to be recording mere fragments, those fragments frequently turn out to be fully wrought creations, and their creators no less capable of conjuring within us powerful reactions than story-tellers have always been.

CHAPTER *2*
Narrative Film

ONE can speak of film as either a medium (an instrument or means) or an end result (a product—indeed, perhaps an artistic product). If one is speaking of "the art of film," then presumably the analogy is with, say, written literature (the novel, or poetry, and so on); if one is thinking of film as a medium, then the appropriate analogy is to *print*. It is not a question of one analogy being more legitimate than the other, for film is in fact *both* an art and a medium. As a medium, it records and presents the *art* of film (or at times the art of ballet or opera, if film is being used to record performances in those arts).

THE MEDIUM OF FILM

To discuss film as a medium with true thoroughness would require a more technical approach than is proper for a book such as this one. But it is necessary to discuss the physical and technical aspects of films in ways that are unnecessary when we talk about literature. In chapter 1, we mentioned the historical importance of the invention of the printing press, but while novels cannot be *distributed* efficiently without being printed, all one theoretically needs (besides genius) in order to write a book like *David Copperfield* or *Lord Jim* is paper and a pen or pencil—or nowadays that product of advanced technology, a typewriter. The physical equipment needed to make even the simplest film, however, is much more technologically complicated, if not indeed, for most of us, ultimately mysterious.

Photography

For example, we call what we see "movies," or the "motion picture"—or "cinema," a word that comes from the Greek for motion (as in the word "kinetic"). Yet when we look at the screen, what we see is not really a "moving" picture at all, but a series of frozen ones, *still* pictures, one followed so immediately by another ever-so-slightly different still picture that we do not perceive a shift. There is, then, a basic similarity between a still camera and a movie camera (or between a slide projector and a movie projector): both the still and movie cameras employ a lens to record light on a section of "film," with the light causing certain chemical reactions which, when other chemical processes are employed, cause the film to become a record of a frozen visual image. For all practical purposes, the earliest examples of such images were those made by the Frenchman Louis Jacques Mandé Daguerre in 1839 on his "daguerreotypes"—single plates so primitive that exposures took fifteen minutes.

The Motion Picture

By the 1880s, however, the American George Eastman had produced celluloid rolls of film, and new techniques made possible exposures of fractions of a second. From then until now, the movie camera and most still cameras—from the simplest Instamatic to the fanciest 35mm Single Lens Reflex—have shared the basic process of recording different images on different areas of a single, continuous roll of film. The major mechanical differences are that in the movie camera the roll is much longer, and the shift from one area ("frame") to the next must be accomplished both automatically and with great speed: the film transport problem was a major hurdle in the early development of the cinema. The intermittent motion mechanism making cinema possible was developed in the 1890s, when Thomas Edison experimented with the Kinetograph (a camera) and Kinetoscope (a peep-show viewing machine for one person). Edison had already developed the phonograph, and his new experiments were part of a conscious attempt to "do for the eye what the phonograph does for the ear." (Indeed he even looked forward to the day when "motion and sound could be recorded and reproduced simultaneously"; but of course many problems had to be resolved before the introduction of sound.) At around the same time, in France, Louis and Auguste Lumière were working on the system that was to determine the future of the motion picture, for it entailed projection not for an individual, as did the Kinetoscope, but for a group of people in a theater. The two brothers showed their first films (shots of workers leaving a factory at the end of the working day, a train arriving in a railway station, and similar scenes) to a paying audience in the basement of a café on December 28, 1895.

Solving the problem of film transport had been especially complicated because the motion is not continuous, as in a tape recorder, but intermittent, for the roll consists of a series of still photographs which must be taken and eventually projected one at a time. In a projector, after one frame is shown, a shutter blacks out the screen while the film is moved and then held still again. This happens twenty-four times each second, producing, in effect, twenty-four still photographs every second (or 1,440 every minute and 86,400 for each hour of film). During the silent film era, the rate was only sixteen times per second, a fact which in part accounts for the effect of flickering (of "the flicks") we perceive when we see old movies on modern equipment.

At a film, then, we see not "movement" but a series of separate photographs; what makes it possible for us to be pleasantly deluded into thinking we see motion is the phenomenon of eyesight known as "persistence of vision" (or the "phi phenomenon"). The retina retains an impression of a visual image just long enough after the image is gone for us to blend it with the next image shown to us while the screen is actually blacked out for less than a twenty-fourth of a second. We do not "see" the split second of darkness between each image.

The Narrative Film: "The Movies"

Obviously, it is possible to define film as the perforated strip of coated celluloid which records the visual images projected on the screen. But that would be no more helpful than defining a novel as a book—that is, a physical object consisting of sheets of paper bound together. Rather, we are concerned here with attempting to describe what most people mean when they think of "the movies": the narrative or story film. That is not the only important film form by any means; there are many films that do not tell stories, at least not fictional ones, such as documentaries, news films, educational films, experimental abstract films, and so on. Still, it is the story film that has been at not merely the economic but the artistic heart of the film world. And the fusion of story and cinema places film art in the continuing tradition of such narrative forms as myth, the folktale, the epic, and the novel.

In chapter 1, we defined the novel as "a long fictitious written narrative in prose." We can define what most people mean by a movie, and the type of film we concentrate on in this book—from *The Birth of a Nation* through *Gone with the Wind* or *The Bicycle Thief* to *Close Encounters of the Third Kind*—as "a long fictitious narrative on film."

Film as Visual Art

Such a definition would not please film critics who dislike any stress on the story-telling aspect of film and emphasize, instead, its role as a *visual* art, more comparable to painting than to either the theater or the novel. And certainly we cannot and should not forget the central importance of what we *see* in a film. Nothing in *Citizen Kane* that either Kane or anyone else explicitly says conveys an awareness of the futility and emptiness of his last years as much as the visual effects of the vast rooms in which we catch glimpses of him living out that life. (See figure 1.) In Rouben Mamoulian's version of *Dr. Jekyll and Mr. Hyde,* Jekyll's first transformation into the "monster" Hyde is followed by our seeing him rush out into the night. It is raining, and as he goes out the door he pauses in glee and removes his top hat in order to let the rain pour over him, as if the water were baptizing him into life. That image conveys to us a much more powerful sense of Hyde's ecstasy in his release than the

FIG. 1. *Citizen Kane*   The Museum of Modern Art/Film Stills Archive. Courtesy RKO.

FIG. 2. *The Collector*   Copyright © 1975 Columbia Pictures Industries, Inc.

first words he had spoken while still in the laboratory—the clichéd "Free! Free at last!" A more subtly frightening figure—Clegg, in William Wyler's adaptation of John Fowles's novel *The Collector*—is given a comparable scene in the rain while he dances with joy after having kidnapped and imprisoned a beautiful young girl. During his romp in the rain he says nothing—and in fact the scene comes after we are almost twenty minutes into the movie and there has been a near total lack of dialogue. Yet we have not merely been able to keep up with what has been going on; we have been gripped by it. The motif of the rain becomes intensified at a later climax of the film, again one without dialogue, when his victim's escape attempt fails and he drags her back to her prison—in a pouring rain. (See figure 2.)

Some critics, however, stress the role of the visual image in film to such an extent that they feel that anything which detracts from its centrality is intrusive, so that Erwin Panofsky will go so far as to say, in his extremely influential essay "Style and Medium in the Motion Pictures" that whenever such elements as "a poetic emotion, a musical outburst, or a literary conceit (even, I am grieved to say, some of the wisecracks of

Groucho Marx) entirely lose contact with visible movement, they strike the sensitive spectator as, literally, out of place."

Color

Others, in their desire to preserve their sense of the "purity" of the visual image, have regretted the increasing use of color, as being too naturalistic—too distractingly "real." It is true that economic pressures (the desire to find ways to compete with television in the 1950s and 1960s, when it was primarily a black and white medium) and technical advances (the improved color films available since the 1960s) have led to the present situation where almost all story films are now made in color, but financial and technological considerations are hardly new factors in the history of film or any other art. No doubt certain effects are lost when almost all films are in color, but it is possible to argue that by and large much more is gained, and in any case there is no turning back. Those who have seen pen and ink drawings by Michelangelo or Van Gogh can admire them without feeling regret that those artists also chose to work with paint and color.

A critic once remarked to Jean-Luc Godard that his film *Pierrot le Fou* has "a good deal of blood"; "not blood—red," Godard replied. His answer suggests the independent value that color can bring to a film, but its cleverness will not make anyone forget all that color can do to enhance film's "dramatic" and "narrative" as well as "visual" effects, insofar as those can be broken down into separate categories. Few filmmakers have made more imaginative use of color or made more visually superb movies than Michelangelo Antonioni, but he is not alone in claiming that "it is the story which fascinates me most. The images are the medium through which a story can be understood." Much earlier, D. W. Griffith had distinguished the filmmakers who invite you to *"see* a great experience" from those with whom he associated himself—those who invite you to *"have* a great experience." The dichotomy is not strict or absolute, of course, but most people would probably agree that beautiful or ingenious visual images are not enough to make a movie worth seeing—or worth seeing again. A good many filmed television commercials are virtuoso performances in regard to visual techniques, but in the end they are usually slick visual pap (and, frequently enough, deceptive and manipulative pap at that).

Sound

Another form of esthetic nostalgia holds that films have gone downhill ever since the introduction of sound. Such a view was especially prominent in the decade or so after sound was introduced with *The Jazz Singer* in 1927. But as late as 1943, no less a critic than the brilliant James Agee could react to "the American addiction to word-dominated films" by asserting, half-seriously, that the "greatest service" words can do a film is "withdrawal," and in 1949 he could say that "the only thing wrong with screen comedy today is that it takes place on a screen which talks." It is true that the early "talkies" were often little *but* talkies: static portrayals of wooden people in what seemed endless bouts of dialogue. In 1928, the Russian filmmakers Sergei M. Eisenstein, Grigori Alexandrov, and V. I. Pudovkin reacted to the inevitable onslaught of sound by enunciating a principle that was to be very influential in film criticism in the coming decades: that what we see should not simply illustrate what we hear, that filmmakers should strive for "nonsynchronization" rather than duplication in combining visual and aural images. An extreme, even apparently crude example of how sight and sound which seem to work "against" each other can be skillfully combined to produce an overall desired effect is found in a scene in Woody Allen's *Annie Hall*. The characters played by Allen and Diane Keaton have recently met and find themselves attracted to each other. They carry on a conversation during which, while we hear what they are saying, we also see—as if we were watching a foreign film—subtitles at the bottom of the screen "translating" what they are saying aloud into what they actually mean or are thinking.

A more harrowing example of the way what we hear can contrast with what we see occurs in Stanley Kubrick's adaptation of Anthony Burgess' *A Clockwork Orange*. The brutal young Alex and his friends break into a home and beat up a husband and wife. As his friends look on, Alex kicks the man and prepares to rape the woman, while doing a dance to his own rendition of "Singin' in the Rain." (He is "ready for love," with a smile on his face.) The scene looks forward to a later sequence in which Alex himself is brutally beaten by the same friends who (like us) have earlier watched him as he beat the man and woman. Now it is actually raining, and we see him have to crawl, not dance—in the rain, not singing—to the same house where he had brutalized his own victims. Still later, at the end of the movie, Alex's fortunes have been restored in a cynical turn of the plot; and at the very end, we get no visual images other than the credits, but we do *hear* something: the voice of Gene Kelly himself singing "Singin' in the Rain."

Words

Film, then, is not simply or totally a visual art, for sound too can be an extremely powerful element in the total film experience. Among the types of sounds at the disposal of a filmmaker are music, sound effects—and dialogue. Words, of all things. For although some critics who emphasize film as a visual art are still reluctant to acknowledge it, the fact is, films *talk:* dialogue, after all, is no more forbidden to a filmmaker than to a dramatist. True, there are risks: no less a master of language than F. Scott Fitzgerald once warned—in a lecture on movies published in Sheilah Graham's *College of One*—that while "a writer's instinct is to think in words," the words must be turned "into visual images for the camera . . . for on the screen, *seeing* is believing, no matter what the characters say." Ernest Hemingway expressed something similar in much more negative and exasperated terms, when he said that when a writer goes to Hollywood, "they get you writing as though you were looking through a camera lens. All you think about is pictures when you ought to be thinking about people." If that is a danger, it is not one

FIG. 3. *Lolita*   The Museum of Modern Art/Film Stills Archive. Copyright © 1962 Metro-Goldwyn-Mayer Inc.

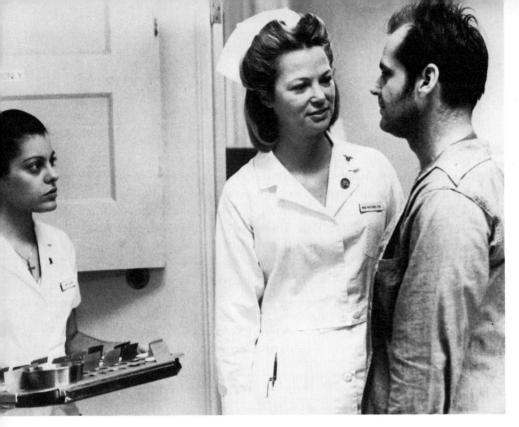

FIG. 4. *One Flew Over the Cuckoo's Nest*   The Museum of Modern Art/Film Stills Archive. Copyright © 1975 Fantasy Films and United Artists Corporation, all rights reserved.

without analogy in written literature: a defender of films could reply that it is surely no less dangerous for some writers to think about *words* when they ought to be thinking about people—if, again, that is a danger at all. It will seem so to those who believe that both films and novels deal above all with *character*.

In a film, of course, what we see when we look at the people in it may determine our impression of them more forcefully than what those people say. In Kubrick's version of Vladimir Nabokov's *Lolita, constant references are made to Lolita—for whom the middle-aged Humbert Humbert has an obsessive passion—as a child, but the actress playing Lolita is Sue Lyon, a beautiful teen-ager, and it is that image rather than the words that describe or refer to her that controls our sense of the character's age. Louise Fletcher as Nurse Ratched in Miloš Forman's adaptation of Ken Kesey's *One Flew Over the Cuckoo's Nest* constantly assures her patients of her solicitous feelings, but the actress's marvelously expressive face tells us otherwise; in the same way, Rod Steiger's performance as Sol Nazerman in Sidney Lumet's film of Edward Lewis Wallant's *The Pawnbroker* belies his bitter claims of total indifference to the world's suffering. (See figures 3 and 4.)

Yet Fitzgerald's words are overstated; even in the examples cited, it is not quite true to say that seeing is believing "no matter what the characters say," for we are also inevitably affected by the words we hear even if we do not "believe" them. Moreover, in films like Akira Kurosawa's *Rashomon and Alain Resnais' *Last Year at Marienbad it is not clear if we are meant to believe anything that we either hear *or* see, and at least in certain sequences during *Marienbad* we seem to be encouraged to grant (even) less credibility to what we are shown than to what we hear people saying.

So while film is, as some people claim, like painting (or still photography) in that it presents us with visual images in a two-dimensional form, it is also, as other people claim, like the novel in presenting us with a story unfolded in words. But it is also like drama in a theater, insofar as those words are conveyed to us through performances by actors. And it is like opera in combining the elements of drama with those of music, and perhaps dance as well. In fact it not only uses dance, it is also *like* dance, in that it relies largely on our visual perception of movement. The ideal filmgoer, then, like the "ideal film critic" that John Simon describes in "A Critical Credo" in *Private Screenings,* "would have to be conversant with cinematography, literature, acting techniques, painting and sculpture (form and composition), music, dance (film musicals), and in view of the generally poor subtitles, as many foreign languages as possible."

FILM PRODUCTION

The Screenplay

After a preliminary prose *treatment,* which summarizes the plot and how the screenwriter foresees various problems will be handled, the first major attempt at predicting or outlining how all the elements will come together in the completed film is the *screenplay,* or script. But it merely predicts, for it is only one step in the process of filmmaking—indeed, according to Ingmar Bergman in the Introduction to his own *Four Screenplays* (1960), "the script is a very imperfect *technical* basis for a film." A later Bergman volume is called in English *Four Stories* (1976), and after noting again in a foreword that "a filmscript is always a half-finished product, a pale and uncertain reflection," Bergman presents for our reading four works which do not resemble screenplays at all, but rather short novels. Their brilliance, moreover, suggests that Bergman's terms—"imperfect," "pale"—are unduly harsh on his own scripts, as well as on the work of screenwriters in general, whose contributions are too frequently overlooked or played down while directors and stars get all the attention.

In contrast, Béla Balázs claims in *Theory of the Film* that the script is "not a mere outline of a work of art, but a complete work of art in itself":

> True, the script puts on paper scenes and dialogues which later are to be turned into a film; but so does the drama put on paper the stage performance. And yet the latter is regarded as a literary form superior to the former.
>
> Written music is only a symbol of the music to be produced by the instruments, but nevertheless no one would call a Beethoven sonata "unfinished" or a "sketch" because of this.

The Director

The analogy with musical composition is a valuable one, and it has often been repeated; but it becomes suspect if extended so as to equate the film director with the orchestra conductor, who is much more severely limited to "interpreting" someone else's creation. The director's role is more fundamentally creative than such a comparison allows. Even the director who does not actually compose (that is, write the script) does more than simply conduct; at the very least, he or she also orchestrates.

It is the director who is in control during the obviously crucial stage of actually shooting the film, and who before and after that as well will often be responsible for innumerable major and minor decisions affecting the finished product. The Italian director Michelangelo Antonioni (in an interview published together with the script of *Blow-Up*, on which he collaborated) has said that "only one person has the film clearly in mind, insofar as that is possible: the director. Only one person fuses in his mind the various elements involved in a film; only one person is in a position to predict the result of this fusion: the director."

The Auteur Principle

Such claims bring up a question that has fascinated many critics, especially in the last two or three decades: if film is an art, as it is, who is the artist? When we talk about a book, we realize that there are publishers and editors and designers and printers and proofreaders and so on, and that the contributions of some of them can be both important and creative, but we still do not hesitate to speak of the "author" as the only true ultimate maker of the book. Can we be that precise with a film?

No we can't—not fully, anyway. Inevitably, a film is much more a cooperative—indeed a corporate—effort, involving producers, directors, writers, actors, cinematographers, composers, musicians, set designers and costume designers, sound technicians, editors, and often hundreds of others as well. No one person could possibly "do it all."

Yet it is also true that there are individual filmmakers who nevertheless manage to put their personal stamp on just about every movie they work on. To accommodate that fact, in the 1950s a number of writers connected with the French journal *Cahiers du Cinéma* devised what they called the *auteur* principle (*"la politique des auteurs,"* literally "the policy of authors," with overtones of "politics" as well): among those critics were a number who went on to become important directors in their own right, such as François Truffaut, Jean-Luc Godard, Eric Rohmer, and Claude Chabrol. (The *auteur* principle was popularized in the United States by the critic Andrew Sarris, who has remained its most outspoken and devoted champion.)

Auteur criticism holds that there *is* someone who can be called the "author" of many films, and almost invariably (indeed invariably according to the original French critics) that person is the director. With some directors, it is easier to see the control they have exerted than with others, since they often produce and write their own films as well as direct them (such as Bergman and Kubrick, or the French directors mentioned above); even when the director is not credited with the screenplay, he or she must have overall supervision of the script, to be a true *"auteur"*—as is the case with the prime example for the *Cahiers* critics, Alfred Hitchcock. In some cases, the director who is also the screenwriter and producer will act and perhaps even star in a given film, like Charlie Chaplin, Jean Renoir, Orson Welles, or Woody Allen.

Auteur criticism has helped to bring home some important but frequently ignored truths, but it has sometimes been seen as indulging in excesses that have caused it to be attacked by the unconverted. Its most notable contribution—its rescue from snobbism of a number of worthy Hollywood directors of the 1930s and 1940s—was connected to what some people came to regard as its greatest excess: its glorification of some directors simply because they had a recognizable style of their own. Even Andrew Sarris bemusedly had to observe, in "Notes on the Auteur Theory in 1962," that "ironically, most of the original supporters of the *auteur* theory have now abandoned it. . . . (The handwriting was already on the wall when Truffaut remarked recently that, whereas he and his colleagues had 'discovered' *auteurs,* his successors have 'invented' them.)"

But perhaps the most troubling aspect of *auteur* criticism has been a naggingly persistent belief that except in a very few cases (and maybe not in them either), to speak of a single *auteur* in regard to a film is more metaphorical than real. There are simply too many skills and arts involved in the art of film. In a book pointedly entitled *Talking Pictures,* Richard Corliss writes a spirited defense of the role of the screenwriter in the "collaborative vision" that is a film, and as an example of his point he asks who the *auteur* of *Ninotchka* is: the director, Ernst Lubitsch, the screenwriting team of Charles Brackett, Billy Wilder, and Walter Reisch, or the star, Greta Garbo? "Obviously, all of them," Corliss replies.

The Star System

Mentioning Garbo does remind us that while many directors have stamped all their films with their personality, so have many stars: it would be simplistic to condemn as merely ignorant the generations of filmgoers who have felt that when they go out, it is to "a Greta Garbo movie," or "a Cary Grant movie," or "a Marx Brothers movie," or "a Fred Astaire movie," or "a Jane Fonda movie." Relatively few stars have been able to impress themselves so intensely on the public, at least for more than just a few years. Among those who have, notably unusual acting ability has mattered less than a distinctive or forceful personality, and a beautiful face less than one which, as the director Howard Hawks used to say, "the camera likes." Those who attain genuine stardom pay a price: they tend to be type-cast on the one hand, or on the other they may meet audience resistance if they try to break loose from the bounds put upon them by their own "image." In a review of *The Treasure of the Sierra Madre,* for example, James Agee praised Humphrey Bogart's portrayal of Fred C. Dobbs as "a wonderful job"—but then had to say that "the only trouble is that one cannot quite forget that this is Bogart putting on an unbelievably good act." Seen from this light, the "star system" limits our vision in serious ways. Humphrey Bogart, for all his adaptability and his willingness to take chances in unexpected roles, would probably have been impossible for an audience to accept in, say, the costume and court of Elizabethan England, or in a Roman toga. Even his few very early ventures into Westerns were embarrassing and have been happily forgotten. Years of "Bogart roles"—if not genes and chromosomes—seem to have given him a face that somehow had the twentieth century written all over it.

Yet not all the results of the star system are so negative, by any means. As it has worked, our vision has been narrowed in some ways, to be sure, but in others it has been expanded. As we watch Marlon Brando in role after role over the years, from the muscular young man of *A Streetcar Named Desire* or *On the Waterfront* to the middle-aged paunchy figure of *Last Tango in Paris* or *The Godfather,* our knowledge—our inevitable knowledge—of the early roles does not so much detract from the effectiveness of the later ones as add to it undeniable dimensions. In a more obvious way, when John Wayne in *The Shootist* plays an aging gunfighter, what might have been just another Western takes on whatever interest it has precisely because it self-consciously plays on our awareness that John Wayne is bringing the John Wayne persona a bit further along.

Indeed, Bogart's portrayal of Fred C. Dobbs greedily protecting his "goods" in *The Treasure of the Sierra Madre* may be as effective as it is in large part *because* we "cannot quite forget that this is Bogart" working against our assumptions and expectations about the Bogart persona. *Treasure* appeared in 1948; it had been only five years before, in 1943, that he had appeared in the film that came to seem to present the quintessential Bogart role: *Casablanca,* with its lone, tough-minded, cynical but deep down surprisingly moral and vulnerable figure of Rick Blaine, who was himself so much like the lone, tough-minded, cynical but moral and vulnerable figure of Sam Spade in *The Maltese Falcon* of 1941. It was this Bogart that was "Bogie," the Bogart who became a cult figure and who formed the model for the Jean-Paul Belmondo character in Godard's *Breathless,* released in 1960, three years after Bogart's death. Behind every role that he played, enhancing that portrayal, were the figures of Sam Spade, Rick Blaine, Philip Marlowe, and all his other enbodiments of that lone, tough-minded, cynical but vulnerable antihero; and as we watch any Bogart film, it is that role that we inevitably have in mind, and we cannot help but expect that, so to speak, Bogart will play it again.

ELEMENTS OF FILM

The Frame

It is probably accurate to say that the most basic element of film is what is called the *frame,* although by that term we can mean either of two things: (1) the single "still" photograph on the strip of celluloid, representing a fraction less than one-twenty-fourth of a second in screen time; or (2) what we see on the screen—that is, the image outlined or encompassed by the screen as distinct from the darkness of the rest of the

FIG. 5. The Screen Image: Common Aspect Ratios

5(a) 1.33:1   35mm   "Standard" or "Academy"   (Also, Television)

5(b) 1.66:1   35mm   European Standard Wide   Screen (Masked)

5(c) 1.85:1   35mm   American Standard Wide   Screen (Masked); VistaVision (Unmasked)

5(d) 2.2:1   65mm and 70mm   Todd-AO

5(e) 2.35:1   35mm Anamorphic; CinemaScope, Panavision
If 70mm, Non-Anamorphic: Super Panavision)

5(f) 2.75:1   70mm Anamorphic; Ultra-Panavision

theater. Obviously, the very shape of the frame will enormously affect its *composition*—that is, it will determine the decisions made while shooting about what we are to be shown within the frame and how what we are shown will be arranged (what will be left or right, or near or far, and so on).

Inevitably, if one is dealing with the screen image which was standard for decades, and which was almost but not quite square (its ratio was 1.33:1, or 4 to 3, width to height), composition will be different from what it will be when working with a more definitely rectangular shape, as with wide screen processes. The aspect ratio is the proportional relation between the width and height of the projected image. Figure 5 illustrates to scale the most common "aspect ratios."

The 1.33:1 ratio was devised by Thomas Edison in his early experiments and was the most common aspect ratio from the earliest films until the 1950s. It is called the "Academy" ratio because it was made standard by the Academy of Motion Picture Arts and Sciences. It also became the standard shape for television, and that fact—rather than any esthetic dissatisfaction with the Academy ratio—caused filmmakers in the 1950s to abandon the old ratio; they felt they had to compete with television by coming up with enticements such as "wide screen" films that would go beyond what the television screen could offer. Various systems were devised, including those that utilized more than one camera; notably successful for a time was the Cinerama process involving three cameras and three projectors and a huge, deeply curved screen. But the multi-camera process was so complicated and unwieldy that it has given way to single-lens systems.

The simplest system is also the least satisfactory, since it means that a great deal of film space is wasted: the top and bottom of the frame are simply masked off, so that, in the standard American wide screen process yielding an aspect ratio of 1.85:1, more than a third of the available film frame is not used, causing inevitable loss of image quality when the usable area is projected. Long before the 1950s, Henri Chrétien in France had devised a system which projected a wide screen image while retaining use of the entire 35mm frame. He did so by developing anamorphic lenses—that is, lenses which "squeeze" the image horizontally (the height remains the same) in order to fit a wider image onto the frame, and which then reverse the process by unsqueezing the image during projection. Although he had patented it in 1927, Chrétien's anamorphic process was not developed commercially until the Hollywood studio Twentieth Century–Fox bought rights to it in 1952, refined it and re-named it CinemaScope, and released the financially successful *The Robe* the next year. Still other anamorphic processes were developed, as were systems using larger film stocks—65mm and 70mm—such as Todd-AO and Super Panavision. Despite the financial importance of these new systems, many filmmakers at first did not take the artistic possibilities of wide screens seriously. Jean Cocteau—a poet as well as a director—is said to have remarked in response to CinemaScope that "next time I write a poem, I shall use a wider piece of paper." But like sound and then color, both of which had also been resisted, the wide screen gained acceptance and is now dominant in contemporary filmmaking (although there has been a backing away from the more extreme systems and the widest screens). Sometimes the dominance of the wider frame has led to abuses, as when older films are re-released and an attempt is made to dress them up as new ones, "adapting" them for wide screens by brutally cutting off the tops and bottoms, thus butchering the original composition of the frame. The opposite sort of distortion occurs when a movie originally shot for a wide screen process is shown on television and its squarish screen. Even the best intentions in the world, and the special telecine projectors which the networks often use for sweeping from one part of the screen image to another as needed, cannot prevent a serious distortion of the original composition, or of the *mise en scène*.

Mise en Scène

A French phrase literally if awkwardly translated as placing-in-the-scene, and originally a theatrical term for the staging or placement of scenery, properties, and actors in a play, *mise en scène* has come to be a common but complex, ambiguous, and sometimes almost mystically important term in film criticism. Fundamentally it refers to the arrangement of the space within the frame: the setting, the lighting, the placement of the actors and the direction of their movements, the perspective of the camera, and generally the interrelationships of all the components making up the visual image in the frame. That image may be complex (an aerial panoramic view of a battlefield and two opposing armies, for example) or simple (a single person in a given setting, perhaps). But the simplicity may be deceptive. In Alfred Hitchcock's *Psycho,* a young man and woman played by Anthony Perkins and Janet Leigh are having a conversation in the parlor behind the office of a motel, and among the things they talk about is Perkins' relationship with his mother. In a number of shots during that scene, the camera looks up from a low angle at Perkins' face while we see behind him a stuffed owl—and at one point Perkins says of his mother that "she's as harmless as one of those stuffed birds." The full significance of the words and of the *mise en scène* is not realized by the viewer until the end of the film. An equally subtle use of *mise en scène* can occur if a viewer *is* aware of the significance of one of its elements. In Henri-Georges Clouzot's thriller, *Les Diaboliques* (1955), a wife has been planning with another woman to kill her husband in a plot that involves his drinking some drugged whiskey. In a scene in which the husband and wife both appear and in which various things are talked about in the dialogue, the bottle—of Johnnie Walker scotch—is on a table. Sometimes it is in the center of the frame, sometimes off to the side, or not even in focus, but it is always there for us to see and be aware of, as the suspense intensifies. Years before, Alfred Hitchcock, again, had made even more emphatic visual use of two glasses of drugged wine, in *The Lady Vanishes* (1938); and Laurence Olivier similarly used our awareness of a chalice of poisoned wine in a number of shots during the climactic fencing scene in *Hamlet* (1948).

Point of View

Thinking about *mise en scène* will remind us that a term we discussed in chapter 1 in regard to narrative literature, "point of view," is in fact a visual metaphor, and that the concept of point of view is no less important in film than in prose fiction. Certainly it controls the *mise en scène;* for, as Béla Balázs puts it, "every picture shows not only a piece of reality, but a point of view as well." Indeed, film and theater differ in their presentation of *mise en scène* above all in the way in which the camera eye so ruthlessly and completely controls what *our* eyes see. When we are in a theater watching a stage play, our eyes can be guided, but they cannot be controlled so absolutely as when we are in a theater watching a film; still, it is when we are outside either kind of theater—in the "real world"— that we are truly in control and are faced with innumerable decisions about what we shall look at or not, turn toward or away from, keep in or out of focus. Paradoxically, however, despite this multiplicity of choice, in our everyday lives our point of view is always single. Although the human eye is an immensely adaptable instrument, our own eyes are the only ones each of us has and provide the only perspective we are granted. In contrast, although film is limited to the camera eye at all times, procedures of cutting and editing (which we shall shortly discuss) permit that eye to shift its perspective with a frequency, completeness, and suddenness no human eye can match.

A corollary of that adaptability, however, is that because film so rarely restricts its vision solely to what one person actually sees, an apparent total blend of narration and perspective is much more difficult to achieve in film than in the novel, say; the first person narration that often seems so straightforward in literature never seems so in film. Or almost never: the one prolonged attempt at a totally subjective camera perspective is Robert Montgomery's *The Lady in the Lake* (1946), in which the hero's eye is that of the camera—so that, for example, he is never seen except when he is looking in a mirror. The attempt was more interesting than successful, and no one has tried it again. But even before that, in 1940, Orson Welles had thought of making a film adaptation of Conrad's *Heart of Darkness* using such a technique. Instead, he went to the less narrowly conceived but brilliantly effective use of point of view in **Citizen Kane* (where various aspects of Kane's life come to us filtered through the perceptions—although not precisely the visual perspectives—of different people who knew him) and his adaptation of

FIG. 6. Deep Focus in *Citizen Kane*   The Museum of Modern Art/Film Stills Archive. Courtesy RKO.

FIG. 7. Shallow Focus in *Blow-Up* The Museum of Modern Art/Film Stills Archive. Courtesy MGM.

FIG. 8. Deep Focus in *Blow-Up* The Museum of Modern Art/Film Stills Archive. Courtesy MGM.

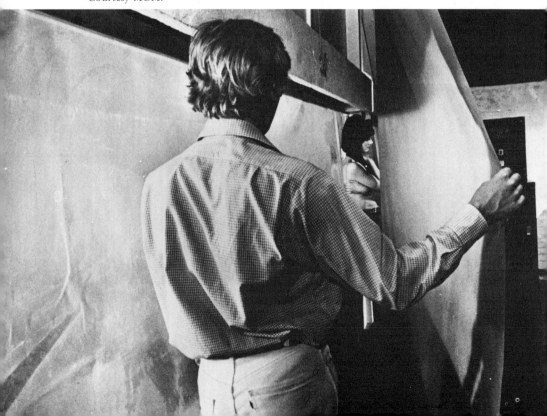

Franz Kafka's *The Trial* (where we feel *as if* we are limited to the consciousness of Joseph K., the protagonist).

Welles is also famous for his pioneering use of variations in *focus*— another element of the visual image which is under the control of the filmmaker, while in our daily lives our decisions as to what we shall focus on (that is, keep in sharp definition) are our own, insofar as those decisions are conscious and willed. The camera can easily make us look at one element in the frame by means of *shallow focus:* that is, by keeping that element sharp while blurring everything else; and the focus can be switched back and forth between, say, two people talking, by means of *selective focus.* A contrast to such methods is *deep focus,* in which objects or persons in the frame are clear whether they are in the foreground or the background, so that our attention is not restricted solely to one area of the *mise en scène.* (See figures 6 through 8.)

The *depth of field*—the range or zone of distance with acceptably sharp focus—is determined by the *f* stop (the size of the opening of the *diaphragm,* the adjustable aperture that controls how much light passes through the lens to the film) and by the focal length of the lens. The *focal length* is the distance between the outer surface of the lens and the film. For 35mm film, a "normal" focal length (that is, one giving a sense of approximating normal human vision) is 50mm. A shorter focal length takes in a wider area (thus a 28mm lens is called a "wide angle" lens) and also allows a larger depth of field; a lens with a longer focal length (such as a 135mm or 500mm "telephoto") has both a narrow angle of view and a very restricted depth of field. The various focal lengths have other effects as well. For example, the longer a telephoto lens is, the more it will flatten depth perception and make elements of the frame seem more "crowded" than when seen by the naked eye, while a wide angle lens will have the reverse effect and make the elements seem further away from one another. (See figures 9 through 12.)

A lens with a variable focal length is called a *zoom,* and it can change from a wide angle to a telephoto within a single shot. This ability to move us toward and away from any object in the frame brings us back to the heart of the difference between still photography and the cinema: *movement.* The motion picture camera records movement—including its own.

Camera Movement

There are two basic types of camera movement: either the camera revolves or pivots as it remains in the same spot, or it moves from place

FIG. 9. Wide Angle Lens (35mm)

FIG. 10. "Normal" Lens (50mm)

FIG. 11. Moderate Telephoto Lens (100mm)

FIG. 12. Telephoto Lens (135mm)

to place. The first type includes the *pan* (in which the camera pivots on a horizontal plane, from left to right or right to left; the word derives from "panorama") and the *tilt* (in which the camera pivots on a vertical plane, pointing up or down), although sometimes the term *pan* is used to refer to any camera movement in which the camera itself is not transported from one place to another.

The general term for movements that do cause the camera to change its location is *tracking*, a term derived from the fact that the movements are often made smoother by means of special tracks over which a wheeled platform carrying the camera rides. Sometimes tracking is synonymous with words like *dollying, trucking,* and *craning,* but occasionally more specific references are intended by those terms: then, to *dolly* is to move toward or away from a subject, or to keep up with it as it moves forward or backward, with the camera either behind or in front of it. (The effect is similar to that of zooming, but not identical, since in a dolly shot the focal length of the lens remains constant; when the two effects are combined, the results can be extraordinary, as in some notable shots in Hitchcock's *Vertigo* which convey the sensation of the title word.) The "dolly" itself is a small truck or wheeled platform upon which the camera is mounted. *Trucking* refers to moving horizontally or keeping up with a moving object, alongside of it. A *crane* shot involves vertical movement, or a combination of vertical and horizontal movements, in which the camera is mounted on a "crane" or "boom," a mechanical device resembling less the crane found on a construction site than the flexible arm used by telephone line workers.

The Shot

I have been using the word *shot:* that term refers to the unedited strip of film resulting from a single running of the camera, whether the basic contents of the frame remain constant or change as a result of camera movement or because objects come in and out of the camera's angle of view. Conceivably, the shot can be as short as a single frame of the film strip (that is, about one twenty-fourth of a second) or as long as the strip of film a camera can hold, which is usually about ten minutes' worth; in practice, of course, most shots are nowhere near those two extremes. The length of the various shots in a scene will largely determine our sense of tempo. A quick series of short shots will produce a much more hectic tempo than a single prolonged shot of basically the same *mise en scène.*

Shots may be distinguished spatially as well as temporally, according to the distance between the camera and the objects being filmed. In a *long shot,* for example, the objects are in the distance; if they are far enough away—as when they are people in an outdoor setting who can just about be discerned as people—we use the term *extreme long shot.* Often, a long shot is used as an *establishing shot:* one which orients us at the start of a scene by letting us see enough of its elements for us to have a notion of the overall context before we get more detailed shots: a city street scene before we go into a particular apartment, or a shot of a crowded ball before we get closer views of some of the people in the room. A *full shot* is one close enough for the object or objects being filmed to fill the frame, although not so close that we cannot see, for example, the full body of a person. A *medium shot* is closer (we see a person from the knees or waist up), but not as much as a *close shot,* where we see a person from the shoulders up: we are near, but usually far enough away for other elements of the setting to be glimpsed. That is what makes a close shot different from a *close-up,* in which the object fills much or almost all of the frame; generally, a close-up of a person includes only the face. In an *extreme close-up* (also called a *detail shot*), we are unusually close to the object—so that we see, for example, only a person's lips, or a single eye.

Sometimes, during filming, a shot does not work out right, or a number of different variations on it are made so that one or two can be selected and used in the finished movie. Each version of that shot is called a *take.* For each shot that we see in a finished feature film, there have probably been at least five or six different takes, often a dozen or more; that same feature film will often contain as many as a thousand different shots.

The simplest mode of switching from one shot to another—and therefore from one image or continuous set of images to another—is the *cut,* by which two strips of film are spliced, or joined, so that the transition between shots is instantaneous. The *direct cut* preserves our sense of the continuity between two shots; others may or may not, depending on how they are handled. For example, a *jump cut* is one in which a segment of a shot has been removed—as when we see a man crossing the street and then reaching the other side of it before enough time has elapsed for him actually to have gotten there. But the jump cut can be handled so that the audience will not usually notice that fact; or, in contrast, it will not be disguised, and the *purpose* of the jump cut will be to disorient us or to stress the abruptness of the transition, as in many cuts in Godard's *Breathless* and Richard Lester's *A Hard Day's Night.* In a *match cut,* the two shots are made to seem parallel—often in visual composition, although perhaps in terms of theme, action, or subject matter. Among the most famous match cuts in film history is Stanley Kubrick's near the start of *2001: A Space Odyssey, when the ape-man throws toward the sky a bone he has been using as a weapon—a tool of sorts—and we get a match cut to a space station floating in outer space. Sometimes a film will use match cuts so extensively and elaborately as to make them seem its primary mode of transition, as in Laszlo Benedek's version of Arthur Miller's *Death of a Salesman,* Stanley Donen's *Two for the Road,* and George Roy Hill's adaptation of Kurt Vonnegut's *Slaughterhouse Five.*

A less abrupt mode of transition between shots is the *fade.* In the *fade-out,* the image on the screen gradually disappears into darkness; then the darkness gradually gives way to the visual images of the next shot, in the *fade-in;* usually similar adjustments are simultaneously being made in the level of the sound. When the old shot gradually fades as the new shot is coming in, so that for a time the two visual images are superimposed on the screen, we have a *dissolve.* The effect is one of greater continuity between the two shots than is the case with the fade, in which the moments of darkness have created a break in the action, however brief. Another device that suggests a connection of some sort between the two scenes is the *wipe*—an optical effect in which a line or soft edge sweeps across the screen, wiping away the old shot as it brings in the new one. A common wipe is that imitating the movement of a windshield wiper, but there are also many other possibilities, ranging from a simple straight vertically or horizontally moving line to such complex patterns as spirals, flips, and clockwise swirls. Wipes were once very common but are now rare; as a result, when they are used it will often be in order to create a deliberately old-fashioned or nostalgic atmosphere. The same is true of the transition effect known as the *iris;* in the *iris-out,* the screen gradually turns to black by having a circle of darkness around the edges cause the image to get smaller and smaller; then, in the *iris-in,* the blackness gradually disappears as a pinhole image of the new shot gets larger and larger until it fills the screen. Long almost totally associated with silent movies, the iris has been used to evoke their aura in modern films as different from each other as François Truffaut's *The Wild Child* and Peter Bogdanovich's *Nickelodeon.*

Two vague but common terms relevant to any discussion of shots are *scene* and *sequence. Scene* is occasionally used as a synonym for shot; in a more frequent use it refers to a series of shots which occur in the same locale and are part of the same general action; or it may refer to any

CHAPTER 3

Film and Literature

THE RELATIONSHIP BETWEEN FILM AND LITERATURE

Ever since film arose as a story-telling art, there has been a tendency by filmmakers, writers, critics, and audiences alike to associate it with literature, as well as an insistence by many people that the association is false or perhaps deceptive; not the least fascinating aspect of making such a connection is that it is so controversial. The assumption behind this book—that there are fundamental relationships between narrative film and written narrative literature that are worth pursuing—is not one that everyone shares, certainly not every filmmaker or writer. Ingmar Bergman, for example, claims that "film has nothing to do with literature; the character and substance of the two art forms are usually in conflict," while according to Norman Mailer, "film and literature are as far apart as, say, cave painting and a song." Yet numerous filmmakers from Griffith and Eisenstein to Resnais and Fellini have talked about the literary ramifications of their films, and many writers have either openly acknowledged their attempts to adapt cinematic approaches or techniques to their own work or have agreed with the novelist Graham Greene that "there is no need to regard the cinema as a completely new art; in its fictional form it has the same purpose as the novel, just as the novel has the same purpose as the drama." And the influential media critic Marshall McLuhan asserts that "the close relation . . . between the reel world of film and the private fantasy experience of the printed word is indispensable to our Western acceptance of the film form. . . . Film, both in its reel form and in its scenario or script form, is completely involved with book culture."

Both print and film surround us every day of our lives and can hardly be avoided in modern society; as a result, they are tremendously important forces in our culture. Their role can indeed be dangerous, since they can communicate lies and distortions as easily as truth and wisdom. But while print, for example, can be a potentially malign force, it can also be a major liberating one, for literacy and the popularity of literature have been among the most significant democratic and egalitarian forces in the history of humanity in the last five or six centuries. Film, which does not even demand that its audience have so complex a skill as the ability to read, is even more anti-elitist.

Of course many filmmakers and writers have wanted little more than to *be* popular (and thereby financially successful), a goal which in itself is obviously not reprehensible, and in the pursuit of which many works of genuine and enduring value have been created. But artists have also had less tangible goals. Among the most famous words ever uttered about the aims of art are those of Joseph Conrad, in the Preface to *The Nigger of the "Narcissus,"* a novel he published in 1896: "To arrest, for the space of a breath, the hands busy about the work of the earth, and compel men entranced by the sight of distant goals to glance for a moment at the surrounding vision of form and color, of sunshine and shadows; to make them pause for a look, for a sigh, for a smile—such is the aim, difficult and evanescent, and reserved only for a very few to achieve." The visual stress of Conrad's terms makes the aims he cites seem as appropriate to a filmmaker as a novelist, and in fact a passage earlier in his essay is one that is often quoted in comparisons of film and literature: "My task which I am trying to achieve is, by the power of the written word, to make you hear, to make you feel—it is, before all, to make you *see*. That—and no more, and it is everything." This passage is cited in studies of film and literature because it closely—if, apparently, coincidentally—parallels a remark made almost two decades later by D. W. Griffith: "The task I'm trying to achieve is above all to make you see."

Obviously, Griffith's sense of what it would be to make us see—truly see—encompasses more than showing us pretty pictures on a screen; Sergei M. Eisenstein made the same point in an essay in his *Film Form* comparing Griffith's techniques to those of Charles Dickens:

Let Dickens and the whole ancestral array, going back as far as the Greeks and Shakespeare, be superfluous reminders that both

Griffith and our cinema prove our origins to be not solely as of Edison and his fellow inventors, but as based on an enormous cultured past; each part of this past in its own moment of world history has moved forward the great art of cinematography. Let this past be a reproach to those thoughtless people who have displayed arrogance in reference to literature, which has contributed so much to this apparently unprecedented art and is, in the first and most important place: the art of viewing—not only the *eye,* but *viewing*—both meanings being embraced in this term.

Yet it is important to remember that, in talking about film hardly less than in talking about literature, to speak of making you "see" is to be metaphorical, and such metaphors should not be used to make identifications between art forms that cannot hold up.

Film as Literature

Still, terminology—and labels—can help us to arrive at a greater understanding of substance. For example, asking whether film *is* literature, or a form of it, entails asking some basic questions and raising some fundamental issues. The title of the present chapter, "Film *and* Literature," should not be taken as necessarily assuming that two entirely different entities are being referred to—anymore than would be the case in a title like "Painting and Art," or "Automobiles and Transportation." In a book with a reverse title, *Literature and Film,* Robert Richardson makes the interesting and valid point that when we think of a historical period such as the Renaissance, we generally agree that its "literature" includes "works on theology, philosophy, education, science, history, biography, journalism, manners, morals, and navigation, in addition to poems, plays, and works of fiction," yet for some reason we act as if "twentieth century literature is inexplicably confined to poems, plays, and novels." Moreover, if we go further back than Richardson does, we will include works that are not written or printed: everyone agrees that the Homeric epics are literature, yet it was not until centuries after they were composed that anyone ever wrote them down. Had movies somehow existed in ancient Greece—or during the Renaissance—we would surely now be studying them as works of literature.

If, instead of stressing writing or print, we were to argue that it is best to regard literature as a purely linguistic art, one that uses words alone, then no doubt we would have to exclude film—along with the plays of Shakespeare, Sophocles, Shaw, and O'Neill, to be sure. Like drama, film is not exclusively a linguistic art; indeed it is not even primarily so. But when some critics argue that it is exclusively a "visual" art and not *at all* an art of words, one can only wonder when was the last time they went to a movie.

The "literary" art with which film is most often associated, by far, is not the drama, as one might at first expect, but the novel; and the reason for this near universal tendency is above all that both are forms of telling stories, and their modes of telling those stories are comparably open. So basic indeed are these similarities that they overshadow many of the differences. The French film critic Christian Metz even claims, in his discussion of what he calls "the total invasion of the cinema by novel-esque fiction," that "the rule of the 'story' is so powerful that the image, which is said to be the major constituent of film, vanishes behind the plot it has woven . . . so that the cinema is only in theory the art of images." (In the previous chapter, we saw Michelangelo Antonioni assert that "it is the story which fascinates me most. The images are the medium through which a story can be understood.")

Verbal and Cinematic "Language"

But if narrative literature and film share, indeed by defintion, the basic element of the story, they do not "tell" the story in the same way or in the same "language." Many critics have gotten round that fact by in a sense denying it, through elaborate comparisons of verbal and cinematic language. They point out that the basic components of verbal language—that is, of course, what most people think of as language—are words (vocabulary) and the ways in which they are put together (grammar and syntax). The comparable elements in film, say these critics, are the frame or the photographed image (which is parallel to the word) and the editing of the images (parallel to grammar and syntax). Sometimes, just as the word is seen as the equivalent of the frame, so the sentence is compared to the shot, the paragraph to the scene, and the chapter to the sequence.

Such one-to-one analogies, at first glance perhaps intriguing, are in fact basically misleading. If editing is syntax, how do we know when a particular example of a "sentence" (or shot) is "ungrammatical" or "nonstandard"? If frames are words, how can a dictionary be compiled which will "define" each image? Moreover, a fundamental problem in such analogies is that by describing film in terminology which is suitable to verbal language, they inevitably make film seem cruder by comparison; film is not being examined on its *own* terms.

A more fruitful approach has been the newer one associated with semiotics, the study of systems of signs and meanings, which has sought to describe *cinematic* language. According to this approach, film *is* a language, but it is one that is quite different from verbal language. Film is language in the most general sense—it is a mode of communication—not in the more particular sense by which we mean "language" to refer to such highly systematized codes as "the English language," or Italian, or German. Christian Metz, who has been doing important work in this field, has pursued numerous associations and distinctions between film language and verbal language. For example, he points out that the total number of *words* is large but finite, while the number of possible *statements* using those words is infinite; a film image or frame is in that sense like a statement and unlike a word, since the number of possible images is also infinite. Each visual image is comparable to a full sentence in other ways as well. An image of a man and woman kissing each other is the equivalent not of any single word—for example, "kiss"—but, even at the crudest level, of a full sentence, "The man and woman are kissing each other." In addition, words already exist, but at least theoretically each writer creates a statement for the first time. (The words *whose, woods, these, are,* and so on are part of the vocabulary for all of us; the statement "Whose woods these are I think I know" is the creation of Robert Frost.) Each film image is also, again at least theoretically, a new invention.

Moreover, the relationship between each "signifier" (the word or statement on the one hand and the visual image or shot on the other) and what is "signified" is very different. A photograph of a bird has a relationship to the "real" bird which seems closer or more direct than does the word *bird.* Yet the photograph is *not* a bird; it is a picture (a sign, a symbol, a representation of birdness). It is unlike the word in that it is universally recognizable as signifying a bird and because it is *specifically* representational (of a cardinal rather than an eagle, say). Still, neither the word nor the picture will fly, so to speak.

Words and Movies

The fact that the relation between signifier and signified in a picture seems undeniably more direct than in the case of a word may remind us that, as everyone knows, one picture is worth a thousand words. But what everyone knows need not always be true. In this case, sometimes it is (indeed, if anything, it is often an understatement), but sometimes it is not. It *is* true when the given conception is best comprehended in visual terms. We shall explore this question of which realms may seem more ideally suited to each art, but first it is important to recognize the possibility of a hidden assumption in asking whether one picture is worth a thousand words in the context of a discussion of film and literature. It is in fact an assumption made by numerous critics: that film employs one rather than the other, pictures rather than words. The problem with the assumption is that, as we have already seen, it is false. Film today is not a "purely" visual medium, but an *audio-visual* one. If one doubts that, one can ask a number of people to name some of the most memorable film moments they can think of. Even excluding musical numbers—indeed, even those not in musicals as such, like Jeanne Moreau singing "Le Tourbillon" in *Jules and Jim*—or such nonverbal moments as the devastating one in *The Blue Angel* when Emil Jannings crows like a rooster, an extraordinary number will center on famous lines: Peter Sellers at the end of *Dr. Strangelove* exulting, "Mein Führer, I can walk!"; Al Pacino and Marlon Brando in *The Godfather* referring to offers that can't be refused, or an earlier Brando in *On the Waterfront* claiming to Rod Steiger that he could have been a contender; Lauren Bacall telling Humphrey Bogart in *To Have and Have Not* that if he needs her, he can just whistle; or Bogart himself assuring us in several films that he sticks his neck out for nobody (sometimes the line need not be one actually uttered: "Play it again, Sam"); James Cagney at the end of *White Heat* shouting "Top of the world, Ma!"; or Paul Muni at the end of *I Am a Fugitive from a Chain Gang* whispering "I steal!"

The lines are all short, and they do not come from long speeches, and even as one feels that there is no need to exclude words from the tools at a filmmaker's disposal, one can recognize the artistic dangers in being *too* reliant on words alone, or on too many of them. The novelist Virgina Woolf argued in her essay "The Cinema" that although film "has within its grasp innumerable symbols for emotions that have so far failed to find expression," all "which is accessible to words and to words alone, the cinema must avoid."

The Limits of Genre

Woolf's essay was written in 1926, before the advent of the sound film, but one could still agree that there is little point in a film attempting what can *only* be done in words; however, there will be less universal agreement about what we are thinking of when we talk that way, or about which areas are in fact "accessible to words and to words alone." To put the question in more general terms, can we determine which realms in the artistic depiction of human existence are more or less suited to the genre of film than to other genres? Are there aspects of human experience that are better or worse served by written literature than by film?

In practice, attempts to answer these questions seem invariably to talk about the limitations of film, and about what is either "cinematic" or "uncinematic": one rarely hears claims that a given topic is unsuited to print, or that it is either "literary" or "unliterary." Probably the most common distinction is one that sees the novel as more appropriate to the presentation of *inner* mental states, while the film is seen as being better able to show what people do and say than what they think or imagine. The reason is that film depicts what is external and visible, physical and material. In the essay from which we have already quoted, Virginia Woolf contemplates a film adaptation of Tolstoy: "The eye says 'Here is Anna Karenina.' A voluptuous lady in black velvet wearing pearls comes before us. But the brain says, 'That is no more Anna Karenina than it is Queen Victoria.' For the brain knows Anna almost entirely by the inside of her mind—her charm, her passion, her despair. All the emphasis is laid by the cinema upon her teeth, her pearls, and her velvet."

George Bluestone begins his *Novels into Film* by saying that "between the percept of the visual image and the concept of the mental image lies the root difference between the two media," and throughout his valuable book he stresses his conviction that "the rendition of mental states— memory, dream, imagination—cannot be as adequately represented by film as by language," since "the film, having only arrangements of space to work with, cannot render thought, for the moment thought is externalized it is no longer thought." But it could be countered that written literature itself has only words on pages to work with, and that putting them there is also an act of externalization—and that, in any case, thought is less exclusively "verbal" than Bluestone's distinction seems to imply.

As a matter of fact, a number of major filmmakers have not been willing to yield their right to the depiction of psychological states so easily. In an essay called "Words and Movies," Stanley Kubrick explains his preference for adapting novels concentrating on a character's inner life by saying that it is easier to invent external action which will be—and here he borrows T. S. Eliot's term—an "objective correlative of the book's psychological content" than it is to invent a character and a motivation for action plots lacking them. Much earlier, in 1930, Sergei M. Eisenstein sought out James Joyce, whose *Ulysses* he greatly admired. The two men discussed what Joyce had done in his novel to represent inner thought processes by means of the *interior monologue,* a device or technique used to record the *stream of consciousness*—that is, the current of associations going on uninterruptedly in our minds, the flux of thoughts, sensations, and feelings that we all experience, the direction of which is determined by associative rather than "logical" channels. Contrary to the usual assumption, Eisenstein believed that film, even more forcefully than literature, could make such mental processes accessible, comprehensible, and vivid. Joyce was sufficiently impressed by Eisenstein's ideas to remark to a friend that he could imagine Eisenstein succeeding in his wish to adapt *Ulysses* into film.

When Joseph Strick adapted that novel more than thirty years later, in 1966, his chief device for depicting inner thoughts was the *voice-over*, a term for the use of an off-screen voice heard "over" the scene we are seeing; the voice may be that of a narrator, or that of a character who is in the scene but not talking aloud. Laurence Olivier's *Hamlet* presents a number of soliloquies in this way, and Robert Bresson uses a voice-over to give us the journal entries of the protagonist in *Diary of a Country Priest*. But of course films can also use visual as well as verbal correlatives for mental states: Bergman's *Wild Strawberries* makes extensive use of the voice-over, but we *see* the flashbacks and silent dreams of its protagonist, Isak Borg; the visual world of Wiene's *The Cabinet of Dr. Caligari* seems entirely controlled by the intensely subjective mental perspective of its ambiguously disturbed hero.

Often, verbal means such as the voice-over, narration, and dialogue are used to get round a fundamental limitation within the visual image: it cannot easily and immediately convey abstract concepts. It can show a person in pain, but not the general notion of "pain." It can show a woman and a child, but there is no single visual image equivalent to the word "mother." Nor are there specific yet general visual signs for "love," or "hatred," or "sex," or "violence," or "religion." Such abstractions are of course not completely beyond the capabilities of film so long as film uses words; nevertheless, it does seem true that ideas are more economically treated in written literature than in film.

So much is widely acknowledged; many people believe that a corollary is that while literature is a more "intellectual" medium, film is the more emotional; according to Ingmar Bergman, the reason film has more in common with music than with literature is that both film and music "affect our emotions directly, not via the intellect."

Sometimes a similar but actually quite different generalization says that film is a simple rather than a complex medium (in content, not execution). Such a view is expressed with special frequency by people who have worked as both novelists and screenwriters, such as Budd Schulberg, who says that the film

. . . has no time for what I call the essential digression. The "digression" of complicated, contradictory character. The "digression" of social background. The film must go from significant episode to more significant episode in a constantly mounting pattern. It's an exciting form. But it pays a price for this excitement. It cannot wander as life wanders, or pause as life always pauses, to contemplate the incidental or the unexpected.

Perhaps the most important if obvious source of this difference is in length; the film of two or three or even four hours simply does not have the time to go into all the details which are possible and ordinary in a novel of two or three or four hundred pages. That is one of the reasons for Alfred Hitchcock's conviction that "the nearest art form to the motion picture is . . . the short story. It's the only form where you ask the audience to sit down and read it in one sitting." The drama is also experienced in a single sitting, of course. We shall be comparing drama and film in another context, but in the present one it is surely worth observing that playwrights such as Shakespeare, Chekhov, Shaw, and Beckett have managed to be quite inclusive, subtle, and complex within works encompassing only a few hours.

It is coming to seem, then, as if all the distinctions we have considered between film and other forms of literature are valid, certainly, and yet are not completely so either; they are both revealing and potentially misleading. Pauline Kael speaks for many others in their response to much film criticism and theory when she asks, in regard to Siegfried Kracauer's discussion in *Theory of Film* of subjects that are either "cinematic" or more suitable to the theater: "Who started this divide and conquer game of aesthetics in which the different media are assigned their special domains like salesmen staking out their territories—you stick to the Midwest and I'll take Florida?" It is surely true that, as Kael goes on to say, "what motion picture art shares with other arts is perhaps even more important than what it may, or may *not*, have exclusively." But the key word, perhaps, is *perhaps*. For the differences among art forms can also be extremely revealing, and no doubt the best stance is to be aware of both comparisons and contrasts. For example, it is enlightening to consider distinctions as well as similarities in regard to both the *creation* and *perception* of film and written literature. Let us consider some aspects of the former first.

CREATION AND PRODUCTION

Authorship

As we saw in our discussion of the *auteur* principle in chapter 2, it is much easier to say who controls the creation of a book than a film. Indeed, if one were to be absolute about it, it would be difficult to imagine a film as being exclusively *by* a single person unless it were a single-cast-member film produced and directed and written and photographed and edited by that cast member. Yet that is precisely the situation which any novelist assumes as a matter of course. In his Foreword to his own version of a screenplay for his novel *Lolita (a version quite different from the one that had been filmed by Stanley Kubrick), Vladimir Nabokov says:

> If I had given as much of myself to the stage or the screen as I have
> to the kind of writing which serves a triumphant life sentence
> between the covers of a book, I would have advocated and applied a
> system of total tyranny, directing the play or the picture myself,
> choosing settings and costumes, terrorizing the actors, mingling
> with them in the bit part of guest, or ghost, prompting them, and, in
> a word, pervading the entire show with the will and art of one
> individual—for there is nothing in the world that I loathe more than
> group activity, that communal bath where the hairy and slippery
> mix in a multiplication of mediocrity.

To be sure, there are such tyrants; some "underground" filmmakers go even further and approximate in their achievements that of the single-cast-member film described above. Or at least they create films which involve only a few creative hands—many fewer than do standard feature films. Such films are often extremely interesting and successful, but they are rarely the full-length narrative films on which we are concentrating.

Production and Distribution

For good or bad (and, not surprisingly, it has been for both), feature films are commercial products which depend for their very existence on being able to appeal to a relatively large number of people. Even a film which from its initial conception has been aimed at a limited or sophisticated rather than a mass audience will lose money (and a great deal of it) if it is not seen by a million or so people. If it is, to be sure, the financial risk has become more than worthwhile: the monetary rewards for even a moderately successful feature film are staggering.

Yet in other respects the plight of the serious filmmaker is less enviable when contrasted to that of the novelist, poet, musician, sculptor, or painter. They can practice their arts, even if they cannot make a decent living out of them, with a minimal financial outlay. The traditional image of the misunderstood and unappreciated painter, alone in a garret, who comes to be revered after death as a genius, cannot have a complete parallel in the art of film. The painter can live in utter seclusion and continue to paint; filmmakers cannot continue to make films unless they are supported by a huge paying audience. The reason is simply that just about any narrative film of much length is enormously expensive to make. A writer who can afford to take the time and buy a typewriter and reams of paper can produce a novel as long as *War and Peace;* most writers cannot afford to do that, but some can. For all practical purposes, *no* filmmaker can afford single-handedly to produce and create a major feature film. In fact, no filmmakers can even own all the massive, complicated equipment that they need in order to make such a film; and once we are talking about using other people's equipment, we are talking about a commercial operation. The variety, expense, and complexity of equipment needed to produce a full-length narrative film today are so immense that the relationship between the art of film and the technology that makes it possible becomes vastly different from the relationship between art and technology involved in the creation of written literature.

On the other hand, if the writer who has produced that manuscript the length of *War and Peace* wishes to *publish* it, so that other people will get to read it, we are entering an altogether different realm. Such a writer is up against similar odds then, and one thing certain is that he or she has come upon the world of commercial considerations and questions of profit and loss. If the manuscript were accepted by a publisher, the book would probably lose money, but it could avoid that fate by sales numbering in the tens of thousands. If you were the writer, and even if that manuscript had been rejected by commercial publishers, it would be possible for you to take on the burden of publication yourself, and you could do so for the relatively small sum of a few thousand dollars. You would not be likely to get it distributed, reviewed, sold, and read very widely, but you would have brought out the book. Actually, this happens quite frequently, although it is more common with poetry than novels. But to create and produce a film, even one much less ambitious than the novel we have been contemplating, is to enter into an entirely different financial world; there, costs are almost incomprehensibly enormous, running not into the thousands but into the millions. Even the richest of filmmakers do not carry that risk by themselves, and so they enter into intricately complicated financial deals with corporate "packagers."

And yet . . . we do for some reason talk about a film "by" Orson Welles or Alfred Hitchcock. (Richard Corliss, as an epigraph to the Introduction to his *Talking Pictures,* quotes a remark by the director Burt Kennedy that he "was driving by Otto Preminger's house last night—or is it 'a house by Otto Preminger'?") We are in the long run probably more correct than not to speak that way about Welles and Hitchcock, but we should probably be more cautious in regard to *most* films and *most* directors, for relatively few directors will exert the control over their products that these two—or Francis Ford Coppola, Robert Altman, or, in Europe, François Truffaut, Federico Fellini, or Michelangelo Antonioni—will have. That list could be extended by adding other names as well, but even those names are only partial exceptions which in any case serve to prove the proverbial rule: that a film, unlike a book, is a group endeavor which depends upon hosts of people each doing a specific task. They will design the scenery or the wardrobe; or find the locations; or act in major roles or in bit parts; or be the production manager; or write the original treatment or the final script; or be the director or one of the assistant directors; or create special effects; or supervise the make-up; or act as the property master or the hairdresser; or record, synchronize, or edit the sound; or control the cameras; or edit the film that the cameras have shot—and so on.

Notice that the screenwriter is only one of many such people; obviously his or her role will be much more significant than those of almost all the other people mentioned, but it will nevertheless be nowhere nearly as absolutely controlling as the role of the writer in the production of a novel or a book of poems—the writer who is, to quote the artist-hero of Joyce's *A Portrait of the Artist as a Young Man,* "like the God of the creation." But while any one artist in the making of a film may be hampered by an inevitable dependence on other people, the art itself profits enormously from their varied skills; if the individual artists are bound by the limitations on what they can achieve as individuals, the film form itself enjoys immense mobility, range, flexibility, and freedom.

PERCEPTION AND APPRECIATION

Such freedom is present only on the creative end: the spectator at a film is much less free or flexible than the reader of a novel, and that brings us to various distinctions in regard to the perception and appreciation of film and written literature. Such distinctions may come to seem less pervasive if and when video cassettes or comparable systems become widely distributed and economical, in which case the experiences of a movie and of, say, a novel will seem much less dissimilar than they do now. But, at least for the present, the differences in our sense of control over our experiences of film and written literature are both obvious and important. When we go to a theater to see a film, we are in a real sense trapped. First of all, we must go there when the movie is scheduled, not at three o'clock in the morning if that is when we happen to feel like it. We are prisoners when we get there, too; if we have to go to the rest room during the showing, that is permitted, but no one stops the projector while we do. With a book, in contrast, we make all the decisions, or at least a good many more of them. We pick the book up at our own discretion and put it down with the same freedom. We are also largely in control while we are actively reading; we can skip any parts we find boring, for example. On the other hand, if we find we have been daydreaming, or if we are confused, we can go back and read a page over again. The film, in contrast, moves mercilessly along, with no pity for the distracted or the slow on the uptake—another reason why films will usually tend to be simpler and more direct than novels. These characteristics of the film experience are not necessarily drawbacks, by any means, especially from the viewpoint of an artist. If our only choice is to leave altogether or stick it through, many novelists would love to have us in their power to that extent. When we feel that they do—that we "can't put the book down"—that is a sign indeed of their power. But even the greatest of novelists cannot stop the phone from ringing, or a friend from asking if we want to go out for pizza, or a stewardess from announcing that we are about to land. (Of course, however, if it is a question of having to go to the bathroom, a book is something that we can take with us.)

The simple fact of availability and ease of possession is a fundamental element of distinction in the experience of film or written literature. We buy our own books, or borrow them from libraries; no doubt some day people will customarily do that with films or electronic cassettes, but in the state of the art as it currently exists, matters are very different. Students in a course, for example, can own their own textbooks; but when films are to be shown, elaborate and costly arrangements have to be made. Still, if the students are not sick that day, or if their cars do not break down on the way to campus, they can see the film—and that is all. They will probably not have access to the sorts of equipment that would enable them to review it, or study it. They cannot play back parts at their own whim; nor can they mark up the margins.

On any given day, a person in a moderately sized town with at least one decent bookstore and an average sort of library can walk into one or the other and have an immediate choice from among thousands of different novels. On that same day, that same person will have an absurdly more limited selection when it comes to choosing a movie—from among only one or two in a small town, to perhaps a dozen or two in a small city. Allowing for all the neighborhood theaters running the same bill, even a city like New York will not offer more than a few hundred choices to the most intrepid subway-rider. And if that city-dweller happens to want to see, say, Hitchcock's 1948 film *Rope,* he or she may have to wait for a "Hitchcock Festival" at a downtown theater or museum, or on a television channel. It will be no easier to see just about any other film made that year—Olivier's **Hamlet,* for example, or Ophuls' *Letter from an Unknown Woman.* But if that same person is curious about a novel published that year—perhaps Norman Mailer's *The Naked and the Dead* or William Faulkner's *Intruder in the Dust*—he or she need only go to a good library or bookstore. Nor would there be much more trouble locating a book from one hundred years earlier, 1848 (Thackeray's *Vanity Fair* or Dickens' *Dombey and Son*), or even two hundred years, 1748 (say, Smollett's *Roderick Random*). All the books I have named are currently available in inexpensive paperback editions which could be ordered even if they were not immediately on hand.

There are other ways in which our freedom of choice is more limited with respect to film. While reading a book, we can imagine things quite freely even within the limits set by the description of the writer. Before *Gone with the Wind* was adapted to film, readers could picture Rhett Butler however they wished, although presumably basing that picture on the descriptions provided by Margaret Mitchell. But from the release of that movie on, Rhett Butler will always look like Clark Gable; indeed, that will be hardly less so even for readers who have never seen the film, so famous has that portrayal become. When we read Mary Shelley's novel *Frankenstein,* we may or may not be able to overcome the visual image imposed by all the movie Frankenstein monsters. But when we see the film *Frankenstein,* it is impossible for us to overcome the visual image; that is all there is, it is right in front of us, and we cannot make it any different. Moreover, a film can only show us what can be shown: the eye can only see what can be seen by the eye, a limitation not shared by the mind's eye.

When we examined the creative end of the comparison between film and written literature, we brought up the question of whether each was an individual or group endeavor. In a way, a similar distinction is equally valid in regard to their audiences. As we saw in chapter 1, the act of reading is a private one. We may be with other people as we are reading, but we are *reading* alone; when we read aloud to children, or when we attend a "public reading," something else is going on. At the very least, we know that that is not the way things ordinarily are when we read. In contrast, seeing a film is a group experience. Most people do not usually go to the movies alone; even the preparatory rituals are not private, but rather involve someone else with whom one "takes in a movie." In any case, once we are there we are part of a group. It is true that on rare occasions we may be among only a very few people in the theater, but we know that that is not the way it is *supposed* to be. (And not the way the exhibitor intended it to be.)

That association with a large group is one of the many ways in which film is different from the medium with which it also shares significant similarities: television. The difference can have a major effect on the reaction of a spectator, whose enjoyment of a comedy in a crowded theater filled with laughter may be quite different from his or her experience watching the same comedy alone at home on the late show. Of course, too, there are other differences to compound the distinction between watching a movie in a theater and watching it on television: the size of the screen, the quality of the image and sound, the commercial interruptions—and the fact that in scheduling, television gives an audience even less freedom of choice than films. Moviegoers can often choose to go Tuesday rather than Friday, or to a matinee instead of in the evening; viewers who cannot arrange to see a television program at 9:00 P.M. on a given evening of the year will simply miss it, and they must hope that someday it will be rerun at a more convenient time. Again, to be sure, electronic videotape cassettes could change all that if they catch on.

FILM AND DRAMA

At first glance, the form with which film would seem to have the most intimate similarities would be the drama; in both, a story is performed (rather than told), in one sitting, before an audience. So it is not surprising that an early name for the motion picture was the "photoplay," or that George Bernard Shaw, for example, could assume that the motion picture is simply "filmed theater; it is an extension of the literary art of the stage, with some limitations removed." Moreover, early films owed a great deal to the stage plays of their time, and a number of talented people in film came to it from the world of the theater. That debt has continued, as witnessed by the careers of figures like Orson Welles, Laurence Olivier, Ingmar Bergman, Peter Brook, and Mike Nichols. But for a while a negative consequence of that association was that early filmmakers seemed to be enslaved by the approaches and conventions of drama, and it took time for them fully to comprehend the demands and possibilities inherent in the new medium—the ways in which the close-up called for a mode of acting quite different from that needed on a stage, for example, or all that the mobility of the camera could mean. Before very long, filmmakers began to realize that they could present spectacles which could not be directly presented on a stage, or which could be suggested only in oblique or stylized ways. For example, a stage performance cannot have the wagon train go into a circle while we see it being attacked by hundreds of Indians on horseback; nor can it show us underwater divers looking for treasure or being attacked by sharks. At the other extreme, it cannot show us an ant carrying a crumb of bread, or a human eye shedding a tear.

In his essay "The Art of Fiction," from which we quoted other passages in chapter 1, Henry James asks:

> What is character but the determination of incident? What is
> incident but the illustration of character? What is either a picture or
> a novel that is *not* of character? What else do we seek in it and find
> in it? It is an incident for a woman to stand up with her hand resting
> on a table and look out at you in a certain way; or if it be not an
> incident I think it will be hard to say what it is. At the same time
> it is an expression of character.

In their study of *The Nature of Narrative,* Robert Scholes and Robert Kellogg point out that James's example "would hardly be an incident in a play . . . , would be much more likely in a movie, and would be most likely in a novel."

The incident would be more likely in a movie or a novel in part because a dramatist would have more difficulty controlling our perception of it. When we are members of an audience at a play, and three or four people are on stage, it is possible for us to look at whichever one we happen to choose, and it will not necessarily always be, for example, the one who is talking. A capable director will control the staging and light-ing so that we are likely to look where we are meant to, but that director cannot easily have the degree of control over us that a film director always has. For with the film, we cannot be selective; what we look at has been more or less completely decided for us, and we either look or not. The element of control is clearly a positive force in many ways, but it can also have its limiting side-effects; for one thing, the audience at a film is more passive than the audience at a drama. At a film, more is done *to* and *for* us, and less *by* us, than at a play. In the terms made famous by Marshall McLuhan, that makes drama a "cool" medium and film a "hot" one, visually.

The most obvious difference between film and drama is one we have not yet mentioned: that drama employs "live" (present) actors and ac-tresses, while film employs photographic representations of them. Thus a given cinematic scene is not like its equivalent in a novel (which is unrealized in concrete visual terms, although it is thereby filled with immense visionary potential) or in a play (which is "actually" in front of us while we watch it). The filmed scene is in a mid-realm between those states—neither unrealized nor real. The fact that a play differs from a movie by employing live human beings at the moment of our watching it is so obvious that we may neglect to recognize all that it entails. For example, in a way that is impossible in a film, in a production of a play there is an immediate and constant interaction between the performers and the audience. At a movie, I see and hear an actor; but the actor performing in front of the cameras does not see and hear me, and both of us are affected by our knowing that. I am in a sense both cut off and protected from him, even as I react to the undeniable (though photo-graphed) "reality" of what I am witnessing.

Important developments in contemporary drama have seized on the advantages intrinsic to the possibilities of contact and interrelatonships between audience and performers—in movements with names like the Living Theatre, or Environmental Theatre, or even "Theatre of Cruelty." Such possibilities have long been known; in Shakespeare's time, actors in the Globe Theatre had addressed the audience directly. Occasionally, "audience participation" becomes an active part of the drama. When Peter Pan asks us at a theatrical production to help save Tinker Bell, the reaction of an involved audience produces an effect vastly different from that produced at a movie by a screen image of Peter—and even more different from a televised Peter addressing mil-lions of *isolated* individuals or small groups who cannot hear the shouts of hundreds of others as they would in a theater.

FILM AND THE NOVEL

The presence of live human beings also means that, in the theater, no two performances are ever exactly alike. Even the same cast will not present a play in exactly the same way two nights in a row. That is another of the major reasons for the widespread conviction that film is essentially closer to the novel than to drama. In both film and prose fiction, the finished product is always the same. People who buy a copy of Dickens' *Great Expectations* in the twentieth century get different binding and pages from the person who bought it in the nineteenth century, but they have a right to assume they are getting exactly the same words—the same *novel* if not the same "book." The person who saw John Ford's *The Informer* in the 1930s watched the same film as the person who sees it today—or the person who will see it in the twenty-first century, for that matter. In contrast, every theatrical production of a play—even of an ancient Greek tragedy—is brand-new. It is both fresh and absolutely perishable. The play may be "immortal"; the production is not. For better or worse, novels and films are.

Yet they also age, although they do not always seem to age at the same rate. It is often said that films date much more quickly than novels. And there is little doubt that, for example, Emily Brontë's *Wuthering Heights,* published in 1847, reads today with a freshness that few films produced in 1947 could come near matching. True, the example is hardly a fair one. Readers can still be powerfully moved by *Wuthering Heights;* but there were many novels also published in 1847 which few people aside from literary scholars subject themselves to reading, just as there were mediocre novels published in 1947 which would not seem fresh if read today. Yet such reservations aside, it does seem to be the case that even major film achievements come to seem dated in ways that major prose fiction and poetry do not. The great films of the 1920s and 1930s, although they remain powerful movies, retain their power in spite of (or, perhaps, in part because of) their having an old-fashioned air that is not comparably present in the great novels and poems of the same decades.

A major cause of that difference is the closer connection in films than in written literature between the art and the technology that produces it, a connection we have already discussed in a different context. Throughout the history of films, technological advances have been so frequent and so sweeping that each generation has given film a new *look*. That is one reason why there is a greater market for remakes of classic films than for rewritten versions of classic novels. A re-issue of an old movie looks old; a re-issue of an old book may contain obsolete words and archaic prose, but as a book it *looks* just as new as a contemporary book. The book—the package, as it were—can be given bright new pages, modern type, contemporary graphics for the cover, and so on; there is little one can do with a film that will make it seem *technologically* up-to-date. *The Informer* will still be in black and white, and while modern techniques can do wonders with old sound tracks, the sound will never achieve the quality of a contemporary film; the little that can be done to make the film seem new may involve distortion—such as the abomination of masking the top and bottom of the frame to fit it on to a modern wide screen.

TRENDS

On the other hand, not all conjecture about the relevance of technological advances is so favorable to written literature, either, for it is sometimes felt that, if novels last, the novel will not. As we saw in chapter 1, the novel could never have become so prominent a form had it not been for the development of the printing press. There is in that a possible irony: for while the fictitious written narrative in prose owes its dominance if not its existence to a major technological breakthrough, it is conceivable that it will in its own turn fall victim to still newer technological revolutions—and the movies and television have often been cited as signaling the "death" of the novel. Certainly basic changes have taken place in the way most people "get" their stories. The once common oral tradition of listening to someone relate an extended narrative declined long ago, so that in most parts of our culture it has almost entirely disappeared. Instead, people have tended to read printed stories—while now it is even more common for them to watch the stories being performed. There is then no necessity to believe that the novel, which after all replaced older forms of narrative, is for some reason itself irreplaceable. That people will always recount stories to each other is much more certain than that people will always be writing novels.

But predictions of the death of the novel have been with us almost as long as the novel itself. Although it is useless to predict what will happen centuries from now, when film and television may themselves be archaic, anyone familiar with the realities of publishing in the world today (as distinct from those who glibly use phrases about the rise of the visual image and the consequent decline of the word) will not feel foolhardy in supposing that the novel will remain alive a good deal longer than even the youngest readers of this volume.

It seems less likely that the novel will die in the foreseeable future than that it will change. The ability to adapt has always been one of its strengths. The art of the long fictitious written narrative in prose was not in the eighteenth century what it had been in the sixteenth or seventeenth; it was not in the nineteenth century what it had been in the eighteenth; and it is not today what it was a hundred years ago. That is not to say that change is always "progress," or that the art of the novel

FIG. 13.

Jacob Riis, a journalist writing of the conditions in the New York slums in the 1880s, took the above photograph. Because techniques of reproducing photographs had not yet been perfected, the drawing on page 71 was made by Kenyon Cox to accompany Riis's article "How the Other Half Lives" in *Scribner's Magazine*, in 1889. The drawing is scrupulously faithful, but it cannot convey the desolation of the scene with the force produced by our sense that the photograph is "real." [From *Documentary Photography*, by the editors of Time-Life Books (New York: Time-Life Books, 1972). Courtesy the Jacob A. Riis Collection, Museum of the City of New York.]

has "improved." As Virginia Woolf once observed in an essay called "Modern Fiction," the analogy between literary creation and the manufacture of automobiles "scarcely holds good beyond the first glance. It is doubtful whether in the course of the centuries, though we have learnt much about making machines, we have learnt anything about making literature. We do not come to write better; all that we can be said to do is to keep moving . . ."

Photography and Painting

Comparable predictions used to be made that photography would inevitably destroy the art of painting, but those announcements have also come to seem premature. It is true that photography has largely taken over a task which painters and other graphic artists used to have all to themselves: the documentary representation in visual terms of "reality." (See figures 13 and 14.) Yet it has become a commonplace that far

Lodgers in a Crowded Bayard Street Tenement—"Five cents a spot."

FIG. 14.

from destroying the graphic arts, photography has had the effect of liberating them from tasks and duties for which another art is better suited anyway, so that they have been able to turn toward newer and excitingly creative realms—although in fact that liberation has not been a story of the graphic arts invariably or meekly yielding the representation of reality to photography. Instead, much exciting work has involved meeting the new art on its own grounds.

In an analogous way, by depicting so many exciting stories which could be understood by audiences with minimal cinema literacy and perhaps no reading literacy at all, film clearly cut into the popularity of, for example, "pulp" and adventure fiction, readers of which went over to B-movies (and then television). But that trend can be exaggerated, as indicated by the millions of copies sold annually of Gothic romances, thrillers, westerns, and fantasy novels. Similarly, film was also supposed to mark the death of drama. Instead, drama has been by and large a much livelier and more exciting art in the twentieth century than it was in the nineteenth, although *melodrama* has come to be less important on the stage than on the screen.

The Challenge of New Forms

Paradoxically but undoubtedly, much of the excitement in the worlds of painting, drama, and the novel, as well as all the other arts meeting the magnificent challenge of film in our time, has come about not in spite of that challenge but as a result of it. Moreover, the challenge was reciprocal. To pursue our analogy once more, if photography largely took over from painting the task of documenting the real world, it did not restrict itself to that task but entered the realms of impressionism, expressionism, design, and abstraction which the plastic arts were also exploring. So anyone who wishes to understand the development of modern photography must learn as well about the development of modern painting. The same applies to an understanding of film and, say, the history of the novel. A spectator at a showing of *The Graduate*, which was released in 1967, would profit from an awareness of such earlier examples of movies about the initiation of a young man into adulthood and sex as Preston Sturges' *The Lady Eve* (1941), Orson Welles's *The Magnificent Ambersons* (1942), or even Harold Lloyd's *The Freshman* (1925) and the entire Andy Hardy series that began with *A Family Affair* in 1937. But in the case of *The Graduate*, such a spectator might gain even more from a knowledge of many novels in the same tradition or dealing with similar subjects—from Fielding's *Joseph Andrews* (1742), to Dickens' *Great Expectations* (1861), Lawrence's *Sons and Lovers* (1913), Joyce's *A Portrait of the Artist as a Young Man* (1916), Wolfe's *Look

Homeward, Angel (1929), and Salinger's *The Catcher in the Rye* (1951). Anyone seeing *King Kong* will be helped by knowing about all the earlier and later monster movies, but someone with an awareness of literary tradition will also be able to bring in the Cyclops, Grendel, Moby Dick, and Tolkien's Smaug.

The Influence of Literature on Film

François Truffaut, whose film *Fahrenheit 451* takes on the character of a love story about books, has said, "I don't want to make films for people who don't read." As we have seen earlier in this chapter, Eisenstein takes a similar stance in his essay on Griffith, where he also points out that Griffith claimed that he derived the idea of "parallel action" (cutting back and forth between two different stories, or between two parts of one story) from Dickens; Eisenstein brilliantly analyzes some passages from *Oliver Twist* to show how they are "prototypes" of "Griffith's *montage exposition*," and he pinpoints what he regards as novelistic equivalents of such cinematic devices as fades and dissolves.

Other studies of Griffith have explored the effect on his work of a number of major nineteenth-century literary figures, and for a long time the influence of literature on film was in general manifested in terms of traditional novelists rather than the innovative moderns. But Eisenstein himself became fascinated with the work of the most widely influential modern writer of them all, James Joyce. It was only when he met Joyce, says Eisenstein's biographer Marie Seton, that he "felt himself to be sitting at the feet of any living master." A few years later, in 1934, after a speech by Karl Radek before the Congress of Soviet Writers attacking Joyce as a "hero of contemporary bourgeois literature," Eisenstein told an audience at the Soviet Institute of Cinematography that he was "furious at Radek's speech," and that "we must study Joyce."

Ironically, the speech that made Eisenstein so angry had itself constantly referred to Joyce's work through analogies with film, saying that Joyce "cinematographs the life of his subject with the maximum of minuteness": "A heap of dung, crawling with worms, photographed by a cinema apparatus through a microscope—such is Joyce's work." Radek's comments, although typical of many attacks at the time, were as wrongheaded as they could be, except insofar as he grasped what others have as well: that Joyce's work is relevant to and perhaps directly influenced by the new art form of the film. As a matter of fact, Joyce had opened the first movie theater in Ireland, in 1909, in a business venture that did not succeed. And when the two met, Joyce was so impressed by Eisenstein

that in spite of his near blindness he was eager to see Eisenstein's films
Potemkin and *October.*

The Influence of Film on Literature

The ways in which written literature has affected film are often so
pronounced—as in providing material for adaptations, a topic we shall
pursue in the next chapter—that sometimes the obverse is overlooked:
that film has also exerted its power over the literature of our century.
The first important book of cinema criticism in the United States was *The
Art of the Moving Picture* (1915), by the poet Vachel Lindsay. And even
earlier, in 1908, Tolstoy predicted that "this little clicking contraption
with the revolving handle will make a revolution in our life—in the life of
writers." He felt certain that "we shall have to adapt ourselves to the
shadowy screen and to the cold machine. A new form of writing will be
necessary"—"but," he said, "I rather like it."

Writers have not always been so receptive to the new art; indeed,
even many of those who became directly involved with the film industry
as screenwriters often did so by going to Hollywood merely in order to
take the money and run. A notable example was William Faulkner,
although, actually, much of his fiction is stamped by his awareness of the
possibilities opened up by film. Others have regarded their work on films
very seriously indeed, while remaining primarily committed to their own
literary forms—novelists like John Steinbeck and Graham Greene, for
example, or dramatists like Tennessee Williams and Arthur Miller.
Fewer writers, although still an appreciable number, have considered
their film work to be as fully important and central as their written forms
of expression; this dual commitment has been especially frequent in
France, as exemplified by the careers of Jean Cocteau, Marguerite
Duras, and Alain Robbe-Grillet. To be sure, still other writers have from
the start created their work with an eye on a big sale to the movies—
Irving Wallace and Harold Robbins, for example.

Probably the most profound influences, however, have been those
which have made themselves felt on numerous literary artists whose
direct contact with filmmaking has been nonexistent or minimal, but
who have adapted approaches and techniques which originated or developed in film: John Dos Passos, Ernest Hemingway, Albert Camus,
Lawrence Durrell, John Barth, Thomas Pynchon, and many, many
others—including, again, James Joyce. As early as 1941, in one of the
first general studies of Joyce's work, Harry Levin used "Montage" for the
title of one of his chapters on *Ulysses;* and ever since then the many critics

who have examined the relationship between Joyce's art and film have been especially conscious of his use of something extraordinarily close to what film critics and theorists mean by montage. Actually, a similar technique was used by several novelists even before the advent of film, notably Flaubert in the scene at the fair in *Madame Bovary,* and, as we have seen, Dickens; or one could go further back to the eighteenth-century innovations of Laurence Sterne as well.

Of course, when a cinematic device is adapted for written literature, the effect is often quite dissimilar. A flashback, for example, can be handled in a novel so that we are constantly aware that it is to be seen as an element out of the past; that is harder to accomplish in a film since, as Béla Balázs observes, "pictures have no tenses"—which means that they are, in effect, always in the present tense. As Robbe-Grillet says in the Introduction to his script for *Last Year at Marienbad;* "the essential characteristic of the image is its presentness. Whereas literature has a whole gamut of grammatical tenses . . . by its nature, what we see on the screen *is in the act of happening,* we are given the gesture itself, not an account of it."

To some extent, literary artists have occasionally seemed to be attempting to overcome that difference by striving for "spatial form." In an important essay in modern literary criticism, "Spatial Form in Modern Literature," Joseph Frank has described that attempt as entailing a movement "in the direction of increased spatiality"—"the exact complement in literature . . . to the developments that have taken place in the plastic arts," as if the goal were for the reader to apprehend a work of literature "spatially, in a moment of time, rather than as a sequence." But a novel—like, for that matter, a feature film—cannot truly be apprehended all at once, in the strictly limited sense in which we might say that we can "see" a painting all at once (however much time it may take before we do it justice). Ultimately, as Frank of course recognizes, "since reading is a time-act, the achievement of spatial form is really a physical impossibility." Yet an awareness of the concept of spatial form—and of the beneficial blurring it may produce between what is totally temporal and totally spatial—serves as a valuable counter to the common and oversimplified distinctions between film as essentially a spatial art and literature as almost purely a temporal one.

Any arts so pervasive in modern culture as film and literature are bound to have major repercussions on the way we perceive our world, just as their development in turn will be profoundly affected by any shifts in the ways in which we see. In all the arts—in painting at least since Cézanne; in music at least since Schönberg—there has been a discernible trend away from seeing and representing existence "whole" (as a single, continuous, harmonious entity) and toward seeing it as fragmented—as multiple, discontinuous, discordant, and confusing. Robbe-Grillet connects this view of human thought and existence with all that he and the director Alain Resnais attempted in *Marienbad:* "the total cinema of our mind admits both in alternation and to the same degree the present fragments of reality proposed by sight and hearing, and past fragments, or future fragments, or fragments that are completely phantasmagoric."

In Robbe-Grillet's novels and films, and in those of the modernists who preceded him, a prominent result of such a mode of perception has been an increasing trend away from linear chronological approaches in telling a story, in favor of techniques in which the chronology is disrupted and shifted. The novelist-within-a-novel Pursewarden in Lawrence Durrell's *Balthazar* strives "to escape from the absurd dictates of narrative form in prose." Once, when someone asked Jean-Luc Godard if he didn't agree that films should have "a beginning, a middle, and an end," he replied, "Yes, but not necessarily in that order."

In a comparable remark, Federico Fellini has declared, "I am trying to free my work from certain constrictions—a story with a beginning, a development, an ending. It should be more like a poem, with metre and cadence." His countryman, the director Pier Paolo Pasolini, has also called for a "cinema of poetry" rather than a "cinema of prose." Paradoxically, many modern novelists as well—even while continuing to write prose fiction—have quite consciously moved their work closer and closer toward characteristics and techniques usually associated with poetry. In that as in much else, Joyce, Woolf, Faulkner, Proust, Djuna Barnes, Beckett, Nabokov, and numerous other modern novelists are close in spirit to Fellini, Cocteau, Renoir, Welles, Bergman, Antonioni, and numerous other modern filmmakers. In such realms literature and film meet so intimately that it is difficult or impossible—and perhaps ultimately unimportant—to discern which art "originates" an idea or a technique and which one immediately takes it up for its own ends.

CHAPTER 4

Adaptations

T HE topic we come to now—the "adaptation" for a film of material from another medium (a novel, short story, or play, for example)—is obviously connected to the topics pursued in the previous chapter, the relationships between film and written literature; but it is nevertheless a quite different topic that is very important in its own right. It is arguable that a director like Fellini, few of whose films are adaptations, is much more genuinely in tune with and influenced by literary techniques than most of the directors who have ever put or tried to put famous novels or plays on the screen. Many of Welles's films are adaptations of novels, stories, or plays, but when one thinks of his work as "literary"—as one well may—one thinks of *Citizen Kane* (which does not come from some other source) as much as of his versions of Tarkington's *The Magnificent Ambersons,* Shakespeare's *Macbeth,* or Kafka's *The Trial.*

THE IMPORTANCE OF ADAPTATIONS

Some of the important impulses toward adaptations may not be, strictly speaking, "literary" at all; they are financial, perhaps, or derive from the sheer need to come up with material to be filmed. In any case, the impulses have exerted a major impact on motion picture history, for most movies are adaptations of material from other media, not productions of original screenplays. And far and away the single most important medium has been the novel. Studies have produced varying figures, but it seems probable that for most years, the proportion of American movies based on novels is around 30 percent—sometimes higher, and rarely under 20 percent. Actually, the figures would be a good deal higher if we counted only "major" or "prestige" productions. If the Academy Awards tell us anything about the American film industry or its sense of itself, then it is interesting that (according to my calculations) since their inception in 1927–28, more than three-fourths of the awards for "best picture" have gone to adaptations; and of those, about three-fourths were based on either novels or short stories. The figures would be roughly similar for the New York Film Critics Award for "best motion picture," which began in 1935: about two-thirds have gone to adaptations, and about three-fourths of those were based on novels or stories. The all-time box office successes favor novels even more: of the top twenty money-makers reported by *Variety* as of 1977, sixteen were adaptations—if you count *The Ten Commandments*—fourteen of them based on novels.

These last figures make the interest of filmmakers in works of fiction quite understandable: producers assume that a successful or famous novel will have a substantial audience who will want to see the movie too. (I estimate that in the last fifty years, about 80 percent of the best-selling novels for each year have so far been made into films—about twice the figure for the novels that won the Pulitzer Prize in the same years.) But other considerations also explain that interest. Especially during the days of the prime of the Hollywood studios in the 1930s and 1940s, movies were being turned out by the hundreds each year, and there did not seem to be all that many good original story ideas available—or all that many bad ones, for that matter. As we have seen, the novel is fairly new among literary forms, but it predates film by centuries—long enough to have produced untold numbers of works upon which filmmakers could base movies.

However, motives of profit or rationales in terms of need do not necessarily coincide with questions of artistic value—questions which ask not merely why one might adapt a work of written literature but also whether doing so (or attempting to do so) is either legitimate or worthwhile. ("Sir," Samuel Johnson once remarked of a dog's walking on its hind legs, "it is not done well; but you are surprised to find it done at all.") Those who have argued against the practice include prominent filmmakers (Ingmar Bergman flatly says that "we should avoid making films out of books"), writers (Virginia Woolf: "The alliance is unnatural" and "the results are disastrous") and numerous critics, who cite all the undeniably profound and seemingly insurmountable differences in the media entailed in transferring a given story from one art form to another.

The French director Alain Resnais has said that for him adapting a novel for one of his own films would seem—since the writer of the book has already "completely expressed himself"—"a little like re-heating a meal." But could not a similar comment have been made by a contemporary of Shakespeare's in an attempt to convince him of the impropriety of adapting stories from other media into his plays? Had such an attempt been successful, we would not have *Hamlet, As You Like It, King Lear,* and many others of his plays. When we contemplate all the obstacles to adaptation, we may feel certain that it cannot be done; yet when we place less emphasis on some abstract sense of theoretical proprieties and consider the real world, we cannot avoid the recognition that important filmmakers have in fact adapted novels into films which are themselves valuable and distinguished, and occasionally masterpieces. Presumably, people who decry the practice of adaptation must thereby reject some of the most artistically successful films of some of the foremost filmmakers in movie history: Von Stroheim, De Sica, Ford, Welles, Wyler, Hitchcock, Bresson, Truffaut, Kubrick, and many others. For their part, prominent writers have also worked on attempts either to adapt their own novels (as have Steinbeck, Greene, Fowles, and Nabokov) or to write honorable screenplays based on the works of other novelists (as have Fitzgerald, Huxley, Capote, and Pinter).

Their reasons for doing so are no doubt varied and complex, but surely among them is their sharing with other readers—dare one admit it?—the simple, even crude desire to see, as it were, what the books look like. In the beginning is the word, but we wish to see it made flesh.

If that visceral reaction seems unsophisticated, more intellectual and theoretical defenses have not been lacking. In *Theory of the Film,* for example, Béla Balázs asserts:

> There can be no doubt that it is possible to take the subject, the story, the plot of a novel, turn it into a play or a film and yet produce perfect works of art in each case—the form being in each case adequate to the content. How is this possible? It is possible because, while the subject, or story, of both works is identical, their *content* is nevertheless different. It is this different *content* that is adequately expressed in the changed form resulting from the adaptation.

Not everyone fully agrees that the essential content changes between the two versions, although some transformations will be unavoidable. But the alterations may turn out to be more in "form" than in "content," insofar as they can be distinguished—and it is axiomatic in esthetic criticism that that is not very far. Form and content determine one another, in a sort of artistic version of the Heisenberg Principle in physics. As we saw in chapter 1, for example, it is a mistake to make a total equation between the story within a narrative and the entire experience of that narrative, since the story is largely determined by the way it is conveyed, the form in which it is presented.

Yet Stanley Kubrick makes what seems to be a valid and essential point when he says, in the context of some remarks on one of his own adaptations:

> People have asked me how it is possible to make a film out of *Lolita* when so much of the quality of the book depends on Nabokov's prose style. But to take the prose style as any more than just a part of a great book is simply misunderstanding just what a great book is. . . . Style is what an artist uses to fascinate the beholder in order to convey to him his feelings and emotions and thoughts. These are what have to be dramatised, not the style. The dramatising has to find a style of its own, as it will do if it really grasps the content. . . . It may or may not be as good as the novel; sometimes it may in certain ways be even better.

The passages from Balázs and Kubrick indicate both agreement and disagreement. They disagree on whether an identical "content" can be retained; but the area of their fundamental concurrence is in their mutual conviction that it is possible to create a film adaptation of a written work of art that becomes in itself an admirable artistic achievement.

THE PRINCIPLES OF ADAPTATIONS

If we are willing to assume that adaptations are both possible and at least potentially worthwhile, film criticism and theory can help us answer (and raise) other questions as well: How should a filmmaker go about the process of adapting a work of written literature? Are there guiding principles that we can discover or devise? What relationship should a film have to the original source? Should it be "faithful"? Can it be? To what? Which should be uppermost in a filmmaker's mind: the integrity of the original work, or the integrity of the film to be based on that work? Is there a necessary conflict? What types of changes are permissible?

Desirable? Inevitable? Are some types of works more adaptable than others? The rest of this chapter will attempt to confront these and other questions, although no one will be surprised that I do not claim that we shall arrive at definitive answers.

Yet we can begin with a categorical statement: some changes will be inevitable. Even the most well-intended, literal-minded, indeed slavish adapter will have to *adapt* (change) a book, or a short story, and perhaps even a play; certainly in regard to a novel, the possibility of altering nothing can be dismissed. Disagreement comes only when we discuss the nature and degree of such alteration as will take place, for some modes of alteration will seem "faithful" to a given book, and others will seem a betrayal. "Betrayal" is a strong word, and perhaps needlessly or distractingly moralistic, but in fact it does reflect the way people can feel about seeing a movie based on a book they have read. They resent it if "liberties" are taken, or if a movie "distorts" or "fools around" with a book of which they are fond. There is no doubt that Hollywood has given us cause to be suspicious: instances in which movies have added love interest, tacked on happy endings, or "improved" things to make them more "cinematic" have caused many living authors to squirm in agony or scream in fury, and many dead ones to turn over in their graves. A few writers—like Jerzy Kosinski, or J. D. Salinger after his short story "Uncle Wiggily in Connecticut" was made into *My Foolish Heart* (1949), a slick weepy vehicle for Susan Hayward—flatly refuse to permit any of their works to be made into films. But very few authors indeed can resist the financial temptations involved: a film of *The Catcher in the Rye* could perhaps earn Salinger millions of dollars. (Some authors, like John Updike or Saul Bellow, claim to have had the ideal relationship in those instances in which they have been paid large sums of money for the rights to novels which, however, were never actually made into films.)

Of course, the temptations may be artistic as well as financial, since the results are *not* invariably disastrous—far from it. Even if we assume that, yes, a film should always be faithful to the spirit of the original work, it can do that while making alterations. Indeed it *must*. The only way to be completely and utterly "true" to a novel, say, would be to repeat it, word for word. The ideal "adapter" would be the hero of Jorge Luis Borges' fable, "Pierre Menard, Author of *Don Quixote*," whose work, "possibly the most significant of our time," is "to produce pages which would coincide—word for word and line for line—with those of Miguel de Cervantes": "He did not want to compose another *Don Quixote*— which would be easy—but *the Don Quixote*."

If we may oversimplify for the sake of discussion, there are probably two basic approaches to the whole question of adaptation. The first approach asks that the integrity of the original work—the novel, say—be preserved, and therefore that it should not be tampered with and should in fact be uppermost in the adapter's mind. The second approach feels it proper and in fact necessary to adapt the original work freely, in order to create—in the different medium that is now being employed—a new, different work of art with its own integrity.

Béla Balázs, whom we have quoted in defense of the practice of adaptation, was a very strong adherent of the second approach, urging filmmakers not to be overly reverential toward the works they are adapting. Balázs' views are especially interesting not only because he was among the handful of the most influential of all film theorists, but also because he was himself a novelist, poet, and playwright as well as a filmmaker, whose perceptions were enhanced by both a firm theoretical basis and a working knowledge of the needs of a practicing artist. He argued that if "the artist is a true artist and not a botcher," a filmmaker "may use the existing work of art merely as raw material, regard it from the specific angle of his own art form as if it were raw reality, and pay no attention to the form once already given to the material." The idea that the original book is "raw material" to be worked with, rather than a sacred text to be copied, is a recurrent one in many comments on film adaptations. To Balázs, "nearly every artistically serious and intelligent adaptation" is "a re-interpretation" of that raw material.

A French critic of the next generation, André Bazin, also defended the practice of adaptation, and he too was both an important critic in his own right and a significant influence, especially on younger French critics who themselves went on to become prominent film directors, such as François Truffaut, Jean-Luc Godard, and Claude Chabrol. But in contrast to Balázs, Bazin contended that "it is those who care the least for fidelity in the name of the so-called demands of the screen who betray at one and the same time both literature and the cinema." When filmmakers become so concerned with being absolutely certain that the final film is "cinematic" rather than "literary," the result can all too easily turn out to be films that seem "copies" not of books but of one another: so that a version of a book by Émile Zola seems not much different from one of a book by Stendhal or by André Gide, a version of a novel by Raymond Chandler quite like that of one by Ernest Hemingway. As if in support of this general attitude, John Huston—whose own films include adaptations of such novels as *Moby Dick*, *The Maltese Falcon*, and *The Treasure of the Sierra Madre*—has said: "I don't *seek* to interpret, to put my own stamp on the material. I try to be as faithful to the original material as I can. . . . In fact, it's the fascination that I feel for the original that makes me want to make it into a film."

Some of these controversies are nicely focused in a dispute about the film version of Georges Bernanos' novel *Diary of a Country Priest* (1936). The adaptation by Robert Bresson, released in 1950, was as we say extremely "faithful" to the book, even to the point of including numerous voice-overs of the actor reading from the priest's diary—a practice which was attacked as uncinematic by many critics, including Siegfried Kracauer, who referred to their "obtrusive presence." To Bazin, however, the voice-overs are evidence of Bresson's daring, disposing "once and for all of that commonplace of criticism according to which image and sound should never duplicate one another. The most moving moments in the film are those in which text and image are saying the same thing, each however in its own way."

An even more spirited defense of Bresson came from Bazin's disciple, François Truffaut, who was then in his early twenties and not yet a director. Truffaut took up Bazin's attack on the notion that the need for cinematic "equivalents" allows a filmmaker to ignore the nature and essence of the original work. He criticized two prominent screenwriters, Jean Aurenche and Pierre Bost, who had already collaborated on film adaptations of several famous French novels and had been working on their own version of *Diary of a Country Priest,* which would have been much freer but which was never filmed. Their stated ideal was "inventing without betraying"; but Truffaut demonstrated that their plans would have reflected little invention—it seemed to Truffaut that Aurenche and Bost turned out the same film over and over again no matter how varied their sources—and a great deal of treason. Years later, as if to reiterate his confidence in Bresson's procedure, Truffaut used in his own film *The Wild Child* (1970) a series of voice-overs, in which the figure of Jean Itard (whom he also played) reads us the words of his journal—Itard's actual *Mémoire et rapport sur Victor de l'Aveyron,* upon which the film was based.

Neither Bazin, Truffaut, nor any other serious defender of the practice of adaptation will deny that some changes are necessary from one medium to the other; the controversies arise in regard to what we *make* of that fact, and where we go from it. What types of changes are proper or not, desirable or not? A similar question will ask which changes are arbitrary, or in any case not necessary, and which ones seem inherent in the differences in the media. There is nothing in film form that demands a happy ending, or a nude sex scene. But there is, at least arguably, something that calls for fewer things to be described and more things to be seen. Perhaps the most obvious demands are those dictated by length: when a three-hundred-page novel is made into a two- or three-hour movie, a great deal will have to be sacrificed. Less will be lost in a television serial, to be sure, which may last from eight to ten or even twelve hours, although at least as much will be lost when a novel as long as *Anna Karenina* becomes a ten-hour serial as when relatively short novels like *Of Mice and Men*, *The Maltese Falcon*, *The Third Man*, and *The Fox* become films of less than two hours each. Yet in one respect the quality of the experience in watching a serial television version of a novel will undeniably be closer to reading most novels than a feature film can be: for it will be something we come back to periodically, rather than something we complete in a single sitting.

Often, a comparison is made between a filmmaker's task in adapting a novel like *Anna Karenina*—or *Death in Venice* or *Madame Bovary*—and the task of a translator who must find English counterparts ("equivalents") of Tolstoy's Russian, Mann's German, or Flaubert's French. If we are willing to go along with that analogy and say that a filmmaker adapting a novel is a translator of sorts, then our next question is bound to be: a translator into what? Obviously, that is an immensely complicated question, since the answer must take in everything that makes up what we call a film. At the very least, we can reply, "into film language," or "into sounds and pictures." (*Not* into "reality," by the way. Rod Steiger does not "really" become Sol Nazerman when Edward Lewis Wallant's novel *The Pawnbroker* is made into a film; indeed, by the time the film is shown to us, we do not see the reality of the actor Rod Steiger either, but a photographic representation of him.)

Undoubtedly, some works "translate" more readily or persuasively than others. There is a general agreement that novels are more successfully adaptable than plays usually are, since the play will seem deceptively close in form to the film and may, therefore, be slavishly reproduced; filmmakers adapting a novel, however, will not be able to yield to such a temptation and will be forced at least to try to be creative and imaginative. And they will do so in a form that, as we saw in the previous chapter, in many ways is fundamentally closer to the novel than to drama.

There has been less consensus in regard to what types of novels are likely to make good movies, although it is frequently assumed that a "psychological" novel will adapt less well than one we can loosely call an "action" novel or one which, as Kracauer puts it, avoids "touching on situations, events, and relationships which are not in a measure transparent to physical reality." (The subtitle of Kracauer's *Theory of Film* is *The Redemption of Physical Reality*.) Certainly that attitude seems to have controlled the film industry in determining which novels will be adapted; its dominance has been all the more pronounced as a result of its conveniently matching commercial considerations as well, enabling filmmakers to avoid in good conscience many "serious" novels in favor of popular "entertainment." Yet in the last decade or two Kracauer's criterion has seemed to be less completely in command. And in some important adaptations it seems a difficult gauge to apply with full clarity, whether we are considering a film that is notably stark in its presentation of physical reality (like *Diary of a Country Priest*, or Jack Clayton's *The Innocents*, based on James's *The Turn of the Screw*) or one that is in contrast visually lush (like Visconti's version of Mann's *Death in Venice*, or Kubrick's film of Thackeray's *Barry Lyndon*). Each of these films is a psychological study at least as much as it may be a religious parable, or a mystery, or a love story, or a picaresque.

Except for *Barry Lyndon* (a little-known novel by a major writer), the works upon which those films are based are generally acknowledged to be literary masterpieces. But there is a widespread conviction that, as the novelist Anthony Burgess has said, "the brilliant adaptations are nearly always of fiction of the second or third class." The feeling is that truly first-rate works of written literature will be the most difficult to adapt, since they are the ones in which form and content have already been perfectly matched, so that any attempted disjunction between them is bound to produce problems. As Truffaut once remarked while interviewing Alfred Hitchcock, "Theoretically, a masterpiece is something that has already found its perfection of form, its definitive form"—an especially interesting comment coming from Truffaut, whose own adaptations (as of Henri-Pierre Roché's *Jules and Jim*, or Ray Bradbury's *Fahrenheit 451*) have seemed strikingly "faithful" even as they are consistently "cinematic."

The belief that any "masterpiece" has already found "its definitive form" has led to the odd situation in which many filmmakers and critics agree that the better the original work, the less likely that the film based on it will be a major achievement, and that, consequently, filmmakers should avoid adaptations of major works of literature in favor of less imposing—or indeed even mediocre—ones. In that same conversation with Truffaut, Hitchcock seems to agree that most attempts to film a classic novel "probably wouldn't be any good." Hitchcock's own career provides evidence of what can be done with unexceptional material. Most people who have seen *Strangers on a Train* and **Psycho* and who have also read the novels on which they are based will be struck by the way in which Hitchcock has taken good but fairly standard novels and transformed them into memorable film experiences. In contrast his film *Sabotage,* based on Joseph Conrad's *The Secret Agent,* is not one of Hitchcock's finest, as he himself has acknowledged. In less skilled hands, the results of working with major material can be positively horrific, as in some of the adaptations of novels by Ernest Hemingway and William Faulkner.

Most of us, then, would be willing to say that some films based on mediocre novels are better than some films based on "masterpieces," or, to use less loaded terms, on truly fine literary achievements. But we may be less willing than some knowledgeable people to make that into a universal law—to say as the film critic John Simon does that *"always* either the book or the film is less than absolutely first-rate" (my italics). "Absolutely" makes the statement difficult to argue with, but many people will insist that there have been "first-rate" films based on "first-rate" novels. I have mentioned *Diary of a Country Priest, *The Innocents,* and **Death in Venice;* just a few of the many other possible contenders might be *Greed* (based on Frank Norris's *McTeague*), **The Grapes of Wrath, All the King's Men, *Great Expectations, The Collector, Women in Love, *The Pawnbroker,* or even such a film as Rouben Mamoulian's version of *Dr. Jekyll and Mr. Hyde.* Still, it may be true that these and other successful adaptations of excellent novels are exceptions to a general if not a categorical principle.

Dr. Jekyll and Mr. Hyde is an example—others would be *The Three Musketeers* and *Frankenstein*—of works which are known by many more people in their transmuted form, especially in the movie versions and their innumerable re-makes and sequels, than in their original manifestations. One result is that filmmakers working with such material feel that they have a greater opportunity to maneuver. In a similar way, they feel freer when adapting a mediocre or unknown novel than when handling a widely admired or famous one. Rightly or wrongly, fewer people care what happens when Lionel White's novel *Clean Break* becomes Stanley Kubrick's film *The Killing* than about what David Lean does with Dickens' **Great Expectations,* or how best-sellers like *Jaws* or *The Godfather* are filmed. It is hard to imagine many people getting upset at changes made when a play by Murray Burnett and Jean Alison called *Everyone Came to Rick's,* which died before it reached Broadway, was turned into *Casablanca.* But it will not be only the dour scholarly pedant who will raise an eyebrow when the 1929 film version of *The Taming of the Shrew* carries the credit line, "By William Shakespeare, with additional dialogue by Sam Taylor."

Our expectations, then, are affected not only by whether we know the original but also by our perception and evaluation of it. We can think of what our attitudes would be like were the process reversed—that is, if we encountered that increasing phenomenon of recent years, the "novelization": the book which is based on a film, rather than the reverse. Surely our demands would be largely determined by whether the novel were based on a film that is perhaps an enjoyable entertainment but not widely regarded as a serious achievement—say *The Quiet Man,* or *Hail the Conquering Hero,* or *Butch Cassidy and the Sundance Kid*—or on a film such as **Citizen Kane,* or **Wild Strawberries,* or **8¹/₂.*

Incidentally, adaptations and, more recently, novelizations have been enormously important economic forces in book publishing. It has long been obvious that while books create audiences for movies, movies also create audiences for books—often vast audiences. The film versions of *Wuthering Heights* and *David Copperfield* sent to those novels untold numbers of people who would otherwise never have read them. Ken Kesey's *One Flew Over the Cuckoo's Nest* had been a fairly successful novel before Miloš Forman's film appeared: but it was afterward ("Now a Major Motion Picture!") that the paperback sold over a million copies. Best-sellers like *Jaws* create a great deal of interest in the films that are based on them, but the sales after the film is released are multiplied several-fold. So huge are the numbers involved that often, it is clear, a book is written not for its own sake, or even necessarily with its becoming a best-seller as the primary goal, but rather with the intention that it be sold to the movies. Increasingly, in those cases where there was no book to begin with, publishers and filmmakers (who may be under the same huge corporate conglomerate) will commission a writer to come up with one. That happened with *The Sting* and *Rocky,* for example. The practice is not new: there were novelizations of *The Son of the Sheik* in 1926 and of the original *King Kong* in 1932. But it is now so common that it is rare indeed for any big-budget film (regardless of its success or failure) not to have a counterpart in book form in one way or the other. Of the top twenty box-office successes of all time, the four that were not adaptations have all been turned into novelizations.

Sometimes, the screenwriter will in turn write the novel (as did Richard Seltzer in the case of *The Omen*); or, somewhat doubtfully, the name of the director appears as the novelist (as with Stephen Spielberg for *Close Encounters of the Third Kind*). Occasionally, matters are more complicated, when for one reason or another the original book upon which a film adaptation has been based may not seem suitable for the "media tie-in." Thus the Disney studio may commission its own version of *Mary Poppins* or *Bambi*, which will be closer to the film adaptation than the original book managed to be. Such intricate history is not restricted to children's literature, however. Henri-Georges Clouzot's 1953 film, *The Wages of Fear,* was based on a novel by Georges Arnaud. In 1977, William Friedkin came out with a re-make of the Clouzot film called *Sorcerer,* with a screenplay by Walon Green; at the same time, Warner Books published a novel by that title—not the original Arnaud novel with a new title, but a new novel based on the new screenplay, by a new writer, John Minahan. (All that made for a rather cluttered title page.)

Readers of novelizations usually love them, since they seem to read just like movies. Whether or not the novels succeed as "literature" is to most such readers a matter of not the slightest interest. All too often, readers with a great deal of literary sophistication bring a similar attitude to film adaptations: that is, whether or not a given film based on a cherished novel succeeds *as a film*—as a cinematic work of art—is a matter of not the slightest interest, compared to the question of whether it is "faithful." Most readers and most movie-goers agree that books and films with the same title ought to be virtually identical, and that if they are not, then something unclean has to have happened along the way. In both cases the attitude is wrong-headed but fully understandable and not especially depressing. My point is that at bottom they are the same, and that literary critics who praise or damn an adaptation of *Sons and Lovers, *Death·in Venice, Moby-Dick,* or *Ulysses* solely on the basis of their own sense of how much fidelity each has in relation to the novel are no more (if, to be sure, no less) justified or sophisticated than the reader who brings such criteria to a novelization based on *Carrie*—or, for that matter, on the television series *Happy Days* or *Charlie's Angels.*

Of course what a film takes from a book matters; but so does what it brings to a book. When it brings dedication and talent (or, if we are truly fortunate, genius), the result can be what André Bazin calls "the novel so to speak multiplied by the cinema." The resulting film is then not a betrayal and not a copy, not an illustration and not a departure. It is a work of art that relates to the book from which it derives yet is also independent, an artistic achievement that is in some mysterious way the "same" as the book but also something other: perhaps something less but perhaps something more as well.

Part 2

Twenty-Five Films

Introduction

THIS section presents aids for appreciating and thinking about a large number of major or representative films especially appropriate to the study of film and literature. The basic aim is to provide points of departure helping students to confront and explore each film (and, if applicable, the work upon which it is based).

If the film is an adaptation, the section on it begins with background information on the novel, story, or play, and its author. Similar information is then given for the film itself and those involved in its creation. Fullest attention is paid to the director and screenwriter, but for others as well an attempt is made to go far beyond the usual procedure of providing a bare list of credits. Instead of a compilation of unfamiliar names, I have in most instances given a brief indication of some of the other movies upon which a given cinematographer, designer, editor, or technician has worked, or some of the other pictures in which an actor or actress has appeared. The hope of course is that such information will provide a basis for comparisons and a context for understanding each person's approach and achievement within the film under consideration. Some filmmakers are represented by more than one movie; two films directed by Welles are covered, for example, and three by Kubrick. In order to keep the section on each film independent, I have not avoided some repetition of information. I have given the running time for each film and the distributors from which a 16mm print is available for rental. (The addresses for all the distributors mentioned appear at the end of the volume.)

In the case of some films—*Potemkin,* for example, and *The Grapes of Wrath*—there is an additional section on the historical background.

The background information is followed by Topics to Think About, which are also designed to provide useful and challenging topics for essays and reports. The Topics include questions, excerpts from reviews or criticism, additional information or observations about a book or a film, and various sorts of quotations. The latter include bits of dialogue from the movie, or passages from the work upon which it may be based. The purpose of such quotations is at least dual: to alert one to their significance before one encounters them, or to remind one of their ramifications afterward. Other quotations may be from interviews with, or essays by, the original author or one of the filmmakers, or occasionally from works not directly connected to the film but which I hope will provide a spur to thought about issues raised or techniques employed. In support of the aim of supplying points of departure, there is an annotated selected list of "Further Readings" for each film.

In the case of adaptations, usually there is no necessary assumption that the adapted work will also be read; I assume only that the film either has been or will be seen. Inevitably, however, the original book, story, or play looms larger in some instances than in others: for *Hamlet* or *The Trial,* say, more than for *Psycho* or *Jules and Jim.*

I have tried to present materials and topics that will be helpful to students who in most cases will only be able to view a film once. I assume that most will read or glance at the Background sections before seeing the film or reading the adapted work. The Topics to Think About could also be read beforehand, or they could be postponed until afterward. Realizing that at least some readers will look at them before seeing the film or reading the novel, I have been alert to the possible danger of somehow seeming to "spoil" an esthetic experience by giving away too much. I believe I have avoided that, but in several instances of suspense films—*The Third Man, Psycho,* and *The Innocents*—I found no alternative but emphatically to warn readers away from the Topics until they have either read the book or seen the movie.

As the person responsible for making the ultimate choices, I am the first to realize that the films covered do not constitute some sort of definitive selection; too many of my own favorites are not included for me to have any delusions on that score. Nevertheless, I do not think it necessary to be overly defensive about the inclusions or their balance. Some of the greatest works in movie history are dealt with, to be sure, but the central criteria for selection have centered on their utility, appropriateness, and availability for courses in film and literature. (Most are adaptations, but not all, since, as part 1 has attempted to show, the relationships between literature and film transcend those demonstrated in the process of adaptation.)

To determine which films have in fact been most frequently and successfully included in such courses, a detailed questionnaire was distributed to hundreds of instructors throughout the United States. The responses were gratifying in their numbers and, often, in their thoughtfulness and thoroughness. I am grateful to all those who were tremendously helpful. Although other criteria—notably, of balance—also had to be considered besides frequency of mention, the survey enabled a selection of twenty-five films that will probably include at least two or three of those taught in most courses in film and literature. Certainly no attempt is made to suggest that any single course should be restricted to films covered here. My aim is not to be inclusive, since that would entail the presumption of being exclusive as well. Rather, my goal is to provide through certain important and representative films points of departure serving as detailed examples for studying other films, too.

The films are discussed in the chronological order of their release date. Movie dates are notorious for being given differently in various sources or reference books. In the interests of logic and consistency, I have opted for the date of the first significant showing of each film, not the date of copyright or production. (Similarly, dates indicated for books and stories reflect their publication, not completion.) The films are covered in chronological order because that seems the least restrictive or "loaded" procedure.

Whenever a film or work of written literature to which a section is devoted is mentioned elsewhere, an asterisk (*) precedes its title.

■ ■
THE CABINET
OF DR. CALIGARI
■ ■

BACKGROUND

The date of the release of *The Cabinet of Dr. Caligari* (*Das Kabinett des Dr. Caligari*)—1920—marks the start of a great era of German films,

FIG. 15.   The Museum of Modern Art/Film Stills Archive

which lasted until the assumption of power by the Nazis in 1933. In itself, *Caligari* is an extreme example of the benefits of collaborative efforts in filmmaking—and of the controversies that arise from it.

The idea for the film came from the authors of the basic script, two young men who had never before written anything for the movies: Hans Janowitz, a Czech, and Carl Mayer, an Austrian. Mayer, however, did go on to write several other important screenplays, including *The Last Laugh* (*Der Letzte Mann,* 1924). Both men drew on some of their own traumatic experiences: in a park near a fair in Hamburg, Janowitz had once seen a respectable-looking bourgeois man who, he later believed, may have just committed a murder; Mayer had felt victimized by a military psychiatrist while he was in the army during World War I.

They brought their idea to the German producer, Erich Pommer, who later produced such films as *The Last Laugh* and *The Blue Angel* (*Der Blaue Engel,* 1930). (There have been some claims that the production was really under the charge of Rudolf Meinert, but they are not widely credited.) Pommer liked the idea, and he at first assigned the script to the director Fritz Lang, but when Lang turned out to be too busy with another project, the production was given to Robert Wiene (1881–1938), whose subsequent films have never received anything like the attention given to *Caligari:* they include *Raskolnikoff* (1923; an adaptation of Dostoevsky's *Crime and Punishment*) and *The Hands of Orlac* (*Orlacs Hände,* 1925). A major dispute arose between Wiene and the scriptwriters, Janowitz and Mayer, over the final version of the film. (See below, topic 8.)

The fame of *Caligari* probably owes even more to the set designers than to either the authors or the director, although in fact the writers did envision designs inspired by the artist Alfred Kubin, an exponent of "Expressionism." (See below, topic 2.) Wiene asked three artists to work on the film: Walter Reimann, who was primarily responsible for the costumes, and Hermann Warm and Walter Röhrig, who were primarily responsible for the sets. All three men were connected with an avant-garde group known as *Der Sturm.* Because of severe energy shortages, the studio had very little available electricity, so the artists suggested that the light and shadows be *painted* on the sets. Pommer rejected the idea as absurd, but they persisted—since they also felt that the idea had fascinating esthetic possibilities—and he finally agreed.

The photography was by Willy Hameister.

Werner Krauss, who played Caligari, had worked with Max Reinhardt, the important theatrical producer. After *Caligari,* he was in a number of important German films—including *The Student of Prague* (1926)—but he also starred in a viciously anti-Semitic version of *Jew Süss* (1940) for the Nazis. In contrast, the actor who portrayed Cesare, Conrad Veidt—who had also been with Reinhardt's company—fled Germany in the 1930s and eventually went on to become best known to American audiences for his portrayals of Nazis!—above all, that of Major Strasser in *Casablanca* (1943). But before then he had given notable performances in several major films, including *Der Januskopf* (1920), *The Student of Prague* again with Krauss, and, in Hollywood, *The Man Who Laughs* (1928). Friedrich Feher (Francis) went on to become a director; years later, after Wiene's death, Feher claimed to have directed much of *Caligari.*

Other members of the cast: Lil Dagover as Jane; Hans Heinz von Twardowski as Alan; Rudolf Lettinger as Dr. Olson; Rudolph Klein-Rogge as the criminal-suspect.

The original print of *Caligari* was color tinted, in green, brown, and steel-blue. Wiene's hopes for a sound remake in collaboration with Jean Cocteau were never realized, but in 1962 Roger Kay directed a new version. It had a screenplay by Robert Bloch, the author of the novel upon which Hitchcock's *Psycho* was based, but it drew little attention.

Running time: 75 minutes at 16 frames per second; 53 minutes at sound speed. Prints are available from many distributors, including: Audio Brandon; Kit Parker; Museum of Modern Art; Video Communications. In addition, many universities own their own prints.

TOPICS TO THINK ABOUT

1. In 1922, shortly before he became a director, René Clair wrote in *Reflections on the Cinema:*

> And now, all of a sudden, in the face of that realistic dogma which to nearly all of us seemed unassailable, *Caligari* came to announce that the only interesting truth was the subjective one. . . . From now on we shall have to face it: cerebral cinema exists.

2. *Caligari* came out of—and had a role in—the important artistic movement known as *Expressionism.* Influenced by the French Impressionist painters, the German Expressionist artists sought to express subjective, inner, ordinarily hidden states of being, often through stylized, symbolic, and even grotesque representations. The movement, which in painting dates from the first decade of the century, had a great influence on German literature, drama, and film in the 1920s. Since then, and outside Germany in general, it has continued to exert some influence on important novelists, playwrights, and filmmakers, although it has not been a truly dominant force in either written literature or film.

3. What is your own reaction to seeing light and shadow that are painted—and obviously, not subtly painted—rather than the products of either actual sunlight or artificial lighting? Are the results effective? Ludicrous? Both?

4. Sergei M. Eisenstein called *Caligari* "this barbaric carnival of the destruction of the healthy human infancy of our art, this common grave for normal cinema origins, this combination of silent hysteria, particolored canvases, daubed flats, painted faces, and the unnatural broken gestures and actions of monstrous chimeras." (*Film Form*)

5. Other writers have also attacked *Caligari* as uncinematic: as "theatrical," with a largely static camera, no creative set-ups, few close-ups, and little imaginative editing—and overall as a step backwards in film terms rather than the bold experiment it may at first seem.

In contrast, Arthur Lennig argues that "the film is an exciting and stimulating visual experience (admittedly from *what* is shown, rather than *how*), and by far one of the most interesting and individual works in cinematic history. That it is not in the mainstream of the film's development is not quite saying that it is a retrogression. It is, rather, another aspect." (*The Silent Voice*)

6. In that context, how effective is the use of titles in the film? Do any of them seem unnecessary or intrusive? What is your reaction to the device of Caligari's diary?

7. When and how does Wiene employ the iris effect? (See the discussion of that device on page 46.)

8. The frame story—in which we see Francis and the older man in the garden at the start and then realize where they are at the end—was not part of the original script. It was suggested by Fritz Lang (who was at first to direct the film) and adopted by Wiene over the vehement objections of the writers, Janowitz and Mayer.

They felt that it would be a distortion of their conception and its vision of evil power, and many viewers and critics agree with them. Others, however, believe that the frame story makes the film even more powerful, transforming what might otherwise seem mere gimmickry— the expressionist scenery and so on—into a psychologically meaningful and illuminating achievement. What is your own view?

9. If the justification of the frame story is to make the bulk of the film seem the delusions of a madman, why is the decor at the end also weirdly expressionistic? Is that a mistake?

10. Siegfried Kracauer, in *From Caligari to Hitler:*

> Janowitz and Mayer knew why they raged against the framing story: it perverted, if not reversed, their intrinsic intentions. While the original story exposed the madness inherent in authority, Wiene's *Caligari* glorified authority and convicted its antagonist of madness. A revolutionary film was thus turned into a conformist one— following the much-used pattern of declaring some normal but troublesome individual insane and sending him to a lunatic asylum.

11. As the full title of his book—*From Caligari to Hitler: A Psychological History of the German Film*—suggests, Kracauer argues that the forces leading to the rise of the Nazis can be detected in the films of the same period, and he concludes his study by writing:

> Irretrievably sunk into retrogression, the bulk of the German people could not help submitting to Hitler. Since Germany thus carried out what had been anticipated by her cinema from its very beginning, conspicuous screen characters now came true in life itself. Personified daydreams of minds to whom freedom meant a fatal shock, and adolescence a permanent temptation, these figures filled the arena of Nazi Germany. . . . Self-appointed Caligaris hypnotized innumerable Cesares into murder. . . . It all was as it had been on the screen.

12. In part at least, *Caligari* is a tale of "possession." (In German, "Kabinett" refers not only to a cabinet as in modern English, but—as in an older English usage of "cabinet"—also to a collection, usually of valuables, or to the room in a museum where such a collection is kept.) Who possesses whom?

What is suggested by the writing in the vision Caligari has during the flashback: "DU MUSST CALIGARI WERDEN" ("You must become Caligari")?

13. Are there any sexual undertones, do you think, in the relationship between Caligari and Cesare, in such scenes as the one in which Caligari feeds him, or when he first sees him, or in his grief at seeing Cesare's dead body?

14. What is the motivation, if any, for the murder of Alan?

15. "The difference between *The Cabinet of Dr. Caligari* and American productions, remarked Will Rogers, was that the former was frankly about the ravings of two maniacs while the latter was the result of the ravings of director and star." (Lewis Jacobs, *The Rise of the American Film*)

How many "maniacs" are there in *Caligari*?

16. Compare and contrast Dr. Caligari as presented within Francis' tale to countless examples of "obsessed" or "mad" scientists: Faust, Frankenstein, Hawthorne's Aylmer (in "The Birthmark") or Rappaccini (in "Rappaccini's Daughter"), Dr. Jekyll, Dr. Strangelove, and several of the James Bond villains.

17. *Caligari* is frequently compared to the work of a writer who, like his contemporary Hans Janowitz, came from Prague and wrote in German: Franz Kafka. If you know some of Kafka's work, what does one gain in understanding by such a connection? Are there any ways in which the comparison seems to you misdirected?

Another major German writer active at the time was Thomas Mann. In a story published in 1929, "Mario and the Magician," he presents an outwardly realistic but ultimately strange and evocative tale of hypnotism and power, with numerous political as well as psychological overtones. You may wish to set *Caligari* off against this tale, or such works as Kafka's "A Report to an Academy" (1927) or "In the Penal Colony" (1919). (Mann's *Death in Venice* and Kafka's *The Trial* are discussed on pages 303 and 250, respectively.)

18. If you know either the novel or film version of *One Flew Over the Cuckoo's Nest,* compare and contrast the presentation and plight of McMurphy with those of Francis in *Caligari.*

19. At several key points in the film the audience is confused and misled: the garden turns out to be on the grounds of an insane asylum and Francis to be one of its patients; we see Cesare both in his cabinet and elsewhere at the same time; at the end we see a doctor who may or may not be Caligari.

What is real or unreal in this tale? Can we always distinguish between them? If we can, which is which—and when? If we cannot, why—and what does that suggest?

20. At the end, the Director says that at last he understands the nature of his patient's madness. Do you?

Further Readings

CLARENS, CARLOS. *An Illustrated History of the Horror Film.* New York: Capricorn, 1968.

EISNER, LOTTE. *The Haunted Screen: Expressionism in the German Cinema and the Influence of Max Reinhardt.* Trans. Roger Greaves. Berkeley: University of California Press, 1969.

KRACAUER, SIEGFRIED. *From Caligari to Hitler: A Psychological History of the German Film.* Princeton: Princeton University Press, 1947.

LENNIG, ARTHUR. *The Silent Voice.* Troy, N.Y.: Snyder, 1969.

SOLOMON, STANLEY J., ed. *The Classic Cinema: Essays in Criticism.* New York: Harcourt Brace Jovanovich, 1973. Reprints excerpts from the books by Eisner, Lennig, and Kracauer, above.

WIENE, ROBERT, CARL MAYER, and HANS JANOWITZ. *The Cabinet of Dr. Caligari: A Film.* Trans. and described by R. V. Adkinson. New York: Simon and Schuster, 1972. A detailed description, with some stills. Also reprints the chapter on *Caligari* from Kracauer, above, and short pieces by Erich Pommer and Paul Rotha.

■ ■ ■ ■ ■ ■ ■ ■ ■ ■ ■ ■ ■ ■ ■ ■ ■ ■ ■ ■

POTEMKIN

■ ■ ■ ■ ■ ■ ■ ■ ■ ■ ■ ■ ■ ■ ■ ■ ■ ■ ■

BACKGROUND

On the Film

Potemkin (in Russian, *Bronenosets Potyomkin*) is often called in English *The Battleship Potemkin,* or occasionally *Armored Cruiser Potemkin.* It was first shown in December 1925, in the Bolshoi Theatre in Moscow, and it was released for public showings in January 1926. The film was an immediate success, although it perhaps made its fullest impact abroad; it has universally been regarded as one of the most important films in cinema history. At the Brussels World's Fair of 1958, it was chosen the "best film of all time."

Potemkin was directed by Sergei M. Eisenstein (1898–1948), who also wrote the script, based on some broader concepts he had been working on with Nina Agadzhanova-Shutko. After studying architecture, Eisenstein joined the Red Army in 1918. He planned to study Japanese culture after the war but became employed in a Moscow theater, and he eventually began directing; his first film, *Gloumov's Diary* (1923), was a five-minute short intended as an interlude during the production of a play. He shot his first major film the next year—*Strike* (*Stachka,* released 1925). When he made *Potemkin* in 1925, he was only twenty-seven years old. It was a time of major pioneering efforts in Soviet film. V. I. Pudovkin, whose *Mother* was also released in 1926, was only five years Eisenstein's senior. Both men, like several other early Soviet filmmakers, were active in film theory as well as production.

Eisenstein's next film, *October* (*Oktiabr,* sometimes called *Ten Days That Shook the World*), was about the October Revolution of 1917; but problems arose when Leon Trotsky was expelled from the Communist Party in 1927, and the important role he was depicted as having in the Revolution had to be edited out of the film, which was not released until 1928. On several occasions during the rest of his life, Eisenstein's work ran into trouble with Soviet authorities, especially when its experimental qualities were deemed to go against the demands of socialist realism. *Alexander Nevsky* (1938), a story of Russian heroism in repelling Teutonic invaders, was suppressed when the Soviet Union signed a pact with Nazi Germany in 1939; it was not released until after the German invasion.

FIG. 16.   The Museum of Modern Art/Film Stills Archive

Ivan the Terrible (*Ivan Groznyi*) was an ambitious project planned in three parts: the first appeared in 1944, but Stalin disapproved of the second, and it was not released until 1958—ten years after the death of Eisenstein, who never completed the trilogy. Other projects he never finished included an adaptation of Theodore Dreiser's novel *An American Tragedy,* which he planned during a trip to Hollywood in 1930, and *Que Viva Mexico!;* he shot a great deal of film for the latter, some of which was edited without his approval and released as *Thunder Over Mexico* (1933).

Eisenstein's cameraman for *Potemkin* and throughout his career was Edward Tisse, one of the finest cinematographers in film history: Eisenstein's biographer Marie Seton refers to Tisse as acting "in the capacity of a third eye." He deserves much of the credit for the effectiveness especially of the Odessa steps sequence, and it was his idea—during a stroll in the former Czarist palace at Alupka—to create a montage out of three statues of lions past which he and Eisenstein were walking.

Eisenstein edited the film himself. His assistant director was Grigory Alexandrov, who had also worked with him on *Strike* and who went on to direct his own films (such as *Jazz Comedy*, 1934); he also appears in the cast of *Potemkin* as the Commander's aide, Lieutenant Guiliarovsky. Other assistants included Maxim Strauch, Mikhail Gomorov (who also plays Matoushenko), A. Levshin, and Alexander Antonov (who plays Vakulinchuk). The art director was Vassili Rakhails. Other members of the cast included Vladimir Barsky as Commander Golikov and anonymous nonprofessionals as the doctor and the priest. (There was long a false rumor that the priest was played by Eisenstein himself.) Extras were played by sailors of the Soviet Navy and citizens of Odessa, as well as members of the Proletkult acting troupe.

The most complete version of the original *Potemkin* is available from the Museum of Modern Art in New York: running time, 86 minutes at 18 frames per second. Various other prints are distributed by many firms; most have English titles and an added musical sound track, with a running time on modern 16mm projectors of 67 minutes.

Historical Background

The year 1905 marked the disastrous end for Russia of the Russo-Japanese War and a series of revolutionary disturbances following an incident in January when a peaceful crowd at the Czar's palace in St. Petersburg was fired upon. There were strikes, demonstrations, peasant riots, and mutinies in both the army and the navy. After the revolutionary movement failed, pogroms against Jews occurred in many parts of Russia, including Odessa, especially after many of its citizens sympathized with the mutinying sailors of the Potemkin.

After the success of the October Revolution of 1917, many—including Lenin—looked back on 1905 as a dress rehearsal of what was to come. Eisenstein was commissioned to create a film called *The Year 1905*, as one of a series of films (including Pudovkin's *Mother*) to commemorate the twentieth anniversary of the 1905 Revolution. He and Nina Agadzhanova-Shutko worked on a script which covered many of the most important incidents in the entire eventful year, and shooting began; but they ran into a number of problems, including poor weather. It was on a visit to Odessa, a port on the Black Sea, that Eisenstein suddenly decided—when he first saw the great steps leading to the bay—to discard all that had been done and concentrate on the Potemkin mutiny.

TOPICS TO THINK ABOUT

1. In his *Notes of a Film Director,* Eisenstein says that the scene in which the condemned sailors are covered with a tarpaulin was his own invention, but he justifies his departure from strict documentary accuracy by citing "Goethe's statement that 'for the sake of truthfulness one can afford to defy the truth.' "

2. A more important departure from strict accuracy results from the impression of triumph with which the film ends: the crew of the actual Potemkin sailed to Constanta, a Rumanian port on the Black Sea, where they abandoned the ship. Many escaped, but not all; Matoushenko, for example, was hanged. "But," Eisenstein says, "we were quite justified in ending the film with the historical battleship victorious. Because the 1905 Revolution itself, though drowned in blood, has gone down in history as an objectively victorious episode, the harbinger of the triumph of the October Revolution." (*Notes of a Film Director*)

Do you agree, in principle? Do you see any difference in the handling of the two shifts from strictly accurate history—that of the incident with the tarpaulin and that of the immediate consequences of the mutiny?

3. Eisenstein, in *Film Form:*

Potemkin looks like a chronicle (or newsreel) of an event, but it functions as a drama.
     The secret of this lies in the fact that the chronicle pace of the event is fitted to a severely tragic composition. And furthermore, to tragic composition in its most canonic form—the five-act tragedy.

4. When Eisenstein speaks of the composition of *Potemkin* as that of a "five-act tragedy," he is assuming an awareness of the division of the film into five parts; but since not all available prints retain the division titles, here is Eisenstein's own summary of "the contents of the five acts":

Part I—"Men and Maggots." Exposition of the action. Milieu of the battleship. Maggoty meat. Discontent ferments among the sailors.

Part II—"Drama on the Quarterdeck." "All hands on deck!" Refusal of the wormy soup. Scene with the tarpaulin. "Brothers!" Refusal to fire. Mutiny. Revenge on the officers.

Part III—"Appeal from the Dead." Mist. The body of Vakulinchuk is brought into Odessa port. Mourning over the body. Indignation. Demonstration. Raising the red flag.

Part IV—"The Odessa Steps." Fraternization of shore and battleship. Yawls with provisions. Shooting on the Odessa steps. The battleship fires on the "generals' staff."

Part V—"Meeting the Squadron." Night of expectation. Meeting the squadron. Engines. "Brothers!" The squadron refuses to fire. The battleship passes victoriously through the squadron. (*Film Form*)

5. In *Theory of Film,* Siegfried Kracauer refers to Eisenstein's claim that *Potemkin* is a tragedy and asserts that "no definition of this film could be more misleading": "*Potemkin* is a real-life episode told in pictures."

6. Stanley Kauffmann, in "Eisenstein's *Potemkin*":

Clearly, he felt that a new society meant a new kind of *vision;* that the way people saw things must be altered; that it was insufficient to put new material before old eyes. Anyone anywhere could tell a story of heroic resistance in traditional style; Eisenstein believed . . . that it was his duty as a revolutionary artist to find an aesthetically revolutionary way to tell a politically revolutionary story.

7. "At its most obvious level, *Potemkin* was regarded as propaganda for the Revolution; at a deeper level it was a highly complex work of art which Eisenstein thought would affect every man who beheld it, from the humblest to the most learned." (Marie Seton, *Sergei M. Eisenstein*)

8. David Thomson, in *A Biographical Dictionary of Film:*

The propagandist purpose in Eisenstein's films diminishes the human beings dressed up as authority, just as uncompromisingly as the authorities are supposed to oppress the workers.

In short, the Soviet attitude to art was as narrow and totalitarian as its political history proved. One is less moved by the Odessa massacre in *Potemkin* than excited by it: the frenzied pictorial dynamism and the pulsing montage refute the message that cruelty is destructive.

9. Stanley Kubrick, in an interview in *Sight and Sound,* 1972:

You could say that Chaplin was no style and all content. On the other hand, the opposite can be seen in Eisenstein's films, who is all style and no content or, depending on how generous you want to be, little content. Many of Eisenstein's films are really quite silly; but they are so beautifully made, so brilliantly cinematic, that, despite their heavily propagandistic simplemindedness, they become important.

10. Dwight Macdonald, on Eisenstein: "He was, in short, an artist before he was a Communist, and he felt guilty about it."

11. For a number of Eisenstein's comments on the relationships between film and literature, see part 1 (especially chapter 3, page 52). But: "It was probably the link between painting and literature—both seen plastically—that I became aware of first." (Eisenstein, "The Close-up," in *The Complete Films of Eisenstein*)

12. In *Film Form* Eisenstein cites "the pince-nez of the surgeon in *Potemkin*" as an example of "that most popular of artistic methods, the so-called *pars pro toto*" (the part for the whole). Can you think of other examples? What effects do they have?

13. Two of the concepts for which Eisenstein is well known are *typage* and of course *montage*. Typage refers to the use as actors of non-professionals who exemplify in their appearance the characteristics being depicted in the various roles in a film; two decades after the release of *Potemkin,* typage became notably important in the films of the Italian neo-realists, such as Roberto Rossellini and Vittorio De Sica. Montage and Eisenstein's ideas about it are discussed in chapter 2, page 47.

14. The scene on the Odessa steps is one of the most famous in film history. Although one may not immediately realize it on first viewing, the scene is not "realistically" presented. For one thing, its duration is un-naturally prolonged; it takes much longer than it "really" would for the soldiers to go down the steps, or for the baby carriage to roll down. In part, that is the result of repetition: the soldiers go down the same steps several times over, the carriage starts its descent three times (just as, earlier, we twice saw the sailor break the plate with the inscription "Give us this day our daily bread").

15. Still another source of the visual power of the scene on the steps is the use of striking contrasts—for example, the machine-like precision of the soldiers as against the panic of their victims; or the way in which all the descending forces are contrasted by the upward movement of the crazed woman carrying her dead child.

16. How valid or compelling an example of montage is the use of the stone lions when the guns of the ship begin to fire?

17. What is the effect of the shots of the rotating pistons when the Potemkin meets the squadron?

18. In contrast, there have also been "quiet" shots, sometimes unexpectedly placid ones: the sailors in their hammocks, the empty mess tables, the life preserver after the officer has ordered the firing squad to fire. What are the effects of such shots?

19. Notice the parallels between early and later parts of the film—for example, the physician's pince-nez and that of the woman whose eye is slashed by the officer's sabre on the steps; or the shout "Brothers!"

20. Léon Moussinac quotes what he calls an "apocryphal" remark attributed to Samuel Goldwyn during Eisenstein's stay in Hollywood: "I've seen your film *Potemkin* and admire it very much. What I would like is for you to do something of the same kind, but a little cheaper, for Ronald Colman." (*Sergei Eisenstein*)

Further Readings

BARNA, YON. *Eisenstein.* Bloomington: Indiana University Press, 1973.

EISENSTEIN, SERGEI M. *The Complete Films of Eisenstein.* Trans. John Hetherington. New York: Dutton, 1974. Shot-by-shot summaries of each film, with stills.

_____. *Film Form: Essays in Film Theory.* Ed. and trans. Jay Leyda. New York: Harcourt Brace Jovanovich, 1949.

_____. *The Film Sense.* Ed. and trans. Jay Leyda. New York: Harcourt Brace Jovanovich, 1969.

_____. *Notes of a Film Director.* Trans. X. Danko. London: Lawrence and Wishart, 1959.

_____. *Potemkin.* Described by David Mayer. New York: Grossman, 1972. Detailed "shot-by-shot presentation," with some stills.

_____. *Potemkin: A Film.* Trans. Gillon R. Aitken. New York: Simon and Schuster, 1968. A description, with some stills. Prints part of a chapter from *Film Form* as an "Introduction."

KAUFFMANN, STANLEY. "Eisenstein's *Potemkin.*" *Horizon* 15 (Spring 1973): 110–17.

MOUSSINAC, LÉON. *Sergei Eisenstein.* Trans. D. Sandy Petry. New York: Crown, 1970.

SETON, MARIE. *Sergei M. Eisenstein: A Biography.* New York: Grove, 1960.

THE GRAPES OF WRATH

BACKGROUND

On the Novel

When it appeared in 1939, *The Grapes of Wrath* was an immediate popular and critical success, but because of its descriptions of conditions in both Oklahoma and California, it was also widely attacked as false, distorted, radical, "Communist," and obscene. But if many of the attacks on the novel were politically rather than artistically inspired, so was much of the praise. In this respect its reception and impact on the American public have often been compared to those of Harriet Beecher Stowe's *Uncle Tom's Cabin,* perhaps the only novel in American literary history to have created an even greater social furor. *The Grapes of Wrath* was banned in various communities and burned in others. In Congress, Representative Lyle Boren—speaking "as a citizen of Oklahoma . . . for the great state of Oklahoma"—denounced the book as "a lie, a black, infernal creation of a twisted, distorted mind." Steinbeck received the Pulitzer Prize for the novel in 1940.

John Steinbeck (1902–1968) was born and educated in California. His first book, *Cup of Gold* (1929), did not receive much attention; a later novel, *In Dubious Battle* (1936), looked forward to *The Grapes of Wrath* in telling of a strike by migratory workers in the California apple orchards. But *The Grapes of Wrath* was his first major success.

For the rest of his life, Steinbeck's books usually enjoyed great sales, and a number of them are still popular today. His critical reputation has been less steady; it declined for a time, partly as a result of a critical reaction against the political literature of the 1930s. But in 1962 Steinbeck received the Nobel Prize, and interest in his work has since increased. Most critics believe that *The Grapes of Wrath* remains his major achievement; but other important books include *Of Mice and Men* and *The Pearl* (both 1937), *East of Eden* (1952)—probably his most ambitious novel—and *The Winter of Our Discontent* (1961), as well as works of nonfiction, such as *Travels with Charley* (1962). Several of his novels became major films, and he also worked as a screenwriter, notably on Elia Kazan's *Viva Zapata!* (1952).

FIG. 17. The Museum of Modern Art/Film Stills Archive. Courtesy 20th Century-Fox.

On the Film

Because of the notoriety of the novel, the film of *The Grapes of Wrath* (1940) also aroused controversy, even before it appeared. Various Chambers of Commerce and farm groups attacked the proposed production, for example, while on the other hand many people were vocal in their fears that the studio, Twentieth Century–Fox, would yield to pressures and cancel the project. So that production could proceed without incident, the script was kept a close secret, and shooting was done under a false title, *Highway 66*. But on release the film immediately received a critical and popular acclaim rivaling that of the book.

The Grapes of Wrath is probably the most famous of all the films of John Ford (1895–1973), yet in some ways it is not typical of his career. He is best known for his Westerns, and while he has also made other types of films, relatively few of them have touched directly on contemporary social issues, with *The Informer* (1935), *Tobacco Road*, and *How Green Was My Valley* (both 1941) as the partial exceptions. Yet in other ways the theme of *The Grapes of Wrath* is an important one in Ford's films: when the French critic Jean Mitry asked him in an interview about his recurrent "theme of a small group of people thrust by chance into dramatic or tragic circumstances," Ford replied that "it enables me to make individuals aware of each other by bringing them face to face with something bigger than themselves. The situation, the tragic moment, forces men to reveal themselves, and to become aware of what they truly are. The device allows me to find the exceptional in the commonplace."

Ford received the Academy Award as best director for *The Grapes of Wrath*, as he did for *The Informer, How Green Was My Valley,* and *The Quiet Man* (1952). He received many other honors throughout his career, including the first Life Achievement Award of the American Film Institute, in 1973. He had begun as a bit player and performer of various odd jobs in silent films, and he directed his first movie in 1917; he had already directed several dozen when he made his first important one, *The Iron Horse* (1924), a major Western and the longest movie Ford ever made. His first sound Western, however, did not come until *Stagecoach* (1939), which made John Wayne a star. Other Ford-Wayne films include *She Wore a Yellow Ribbon* (1949), *The Quiet Man,* and *The Searchers* (1956).

The producer of *The Grapes of Wrath* was Darryl F. Zanuck, one of the legendary Hollywood "moguls" and long the head of Twentieth Century–Fox. He also served as producer for several other Ford films, as well as for *Gentleman's Agreement* (1948), *Viva Zapata!,* and *The Longest Day* (1962).

Nunnally Johnson served as the associate producer and also wrote the screenplay; his other scripts include those for Ford's *Tobacco Road* and Fritz Lang's *The Woman in the Window* (1944), as well as some for films he directed himself, such as *The Man in the Grey Flannel Suit* (1956) and *The Three Faces of Eve* (1957).

The cinematography was by Gregg Toland, who was to work with Orson Welles on **Citizen Kane* (1941) and with Ford again both on *The Long Voyage Home* (1940) and on films for the Navy during World War II. Of *The Grapes of Wrath* Ford said to Peter Bogdanovich during an interview: "Gregg Toland did a great job of photography there—absolutely nothing but nothing to photograph, not *one* beautiful thing in there—just sheer good photography." For his "documentary" style, Toland seems clearly to have been influenced by two pioneering films of Pare Lorentz: *The Plow That Broke the Plains* (1936) and *The River* (1937).

Alfred Newman has been musical director for numerous dramatic films, such as *Wuthering Heights* (1939) and *The Robe* (1953), as well as for many lush musicals, like *Call Me Madam* (1953) and *The King and I* (1956); but in *The Grapes of Wrath* he kept the music evocatively simple, restricting it to the traditional song "Red River Valley" played solely on the accordion by Dan Borzage.

Other credits: assistant director, Edward O'Fearna (Ford's brother); art directors, Richard Day (who received an Academy Award the next year for *How Green Was My Valley*) and Mark Lee Kirk; set decorator, Thomas Little; editor, Robert Simpson; sound directors, George Leverett and Roger Heman; sound effects director, Robert Parrish.

Henry Fonda, who played Tom Joad, had already been in two Ford films, *Young Mr. Lincoln* and *Drums Along the Mohawk* (both 1939), and he went on to appear in others as well: *My Darling Clementine* (1946) and *The Fugitive* (1947), an adaptation of Graham Greene's *The Power and the Glory*. He has of course also appeared in many other films, and he received the Life Achievement Award of the American Film Institute in 1978.

Jane Darwell received the Academy Award for best supporting actress for her portrayal of Ma Joad. John Carradine (Casy) has appeared in many horror films, but in a number of Ford movies as well, including *Stagecoach* and *Cheyenne Autumn* (1964).

Other members of the cast: John Qualen as Muley Graves; Russell Simpson as Pa Joad; Charley Grapewin as Grampa; Zeffie Tilbury as Granma; O. Z. Whitehead as Al; Dorris Bowden as Rosasharn; Eddie Quillan as Connie; Frank Darien as Uncle John; Grant Mitchell as the manager of the government camp; Paul Guilfoyle as Floyd, the man who challenges the agent and the deputy sheriff; Shirley Mills as Ruthie; Darryl Hickman as Winfield; Adrian Morris as the agent; Charles D. Brown as Wilkie; Kitty McHugh as Mae; Harry Tyler as Bert.

Running time: 115 minutes. Distributor: Films Inc. (Some universities own their own prints.)

Historical Background

Compounding the economic hardships of the Great Depression of the early 1930s for many farmers was the decline of the system of tenant farming, largely as a result of mechanization that made small plots of land economically "obsolete." Since 1930, for example, the total farm area of Oklahoma has increased, but the number of individual farms has been greatly reduced; and even more drastically reduced has been the number of tenant farmers, who had been especially numerous in cotton producing areas. Starting especially in the 1930s, farming came to seem less and less a function of individual families working a small piece of land and increasingly a corporate enterprise, impersonal and anonymous. (In the film, Muley asks in desperation, "Who *do* we shoot?")

Adding immeasurably to the troubles the small farmers already had were the "dusters." In 1934, one of the worst droughts in American history turned the Great Plains into what came to be called the "Dust Bowl," which was plagued by devastating dust storms.

In the novel, the reply of "the owner men" to the farmers' question about where they can go when they are kicked off the land is, "Maybe you can go on relief. Why don't you go on west to California?" (chapter 5). Many people did in fact emigrate from the Plains region, becoming "migrants." (Relatively early in the novel, a symbolic indication of the Joads' new life is provided when we are told, "The family met at the most important place, near the truck. The house was dead, and the fields were dead; but this truck was the active thing, the living principle"—chapter 10.)

But in California, as the novel and film show, conditions were also dismal. In a letter of February 1938, John Steinbeck described the situation to his literary agent, Elizabeth Otis:

> I must go over to the interior valleys. There are about five thousand families starving to death over there, not just hungry but actually starving. The government is trying to feed them and get medical attention to them with the fascist group of utilities and banks and huge growers sabotaging the thing all along the line and yelling for a balanced budget. In one tent there are twenty people quarantined for smallpox and two of the women are to have babies in that tent this week. I've tied into the thing from the first and I must get down there and see it and see if I can't do something to help knock these murderers on the heads. Do you know what they're afraid of? They think that if these people are allowed to live in camps with proper sanitary facilities, they will organize and that is the bugbear of the large landowner and the corporation farmer. The states and counties will give them nothing because they are outsiders. But the crops of any part of this state could not be harvested without these outsiders. I'm pretty mad about it.

Things did not appreciably improve until forces took over that had nothing to do with Oklahoma, California, or the people or administrations of either state: World War II began. Even before the United States entered the war at the end of 1941, the nation had been preparing for it, and the Okies and other migrants were finding jobs in industry and in shipyards, or joining the armed services. Many of them and their descendants settled in California, and they have often prospered; in fact, because of the resulting scarcity of native migrant laborers, the new "Okies" are often illegal aliens from Mexico, called "wetbacks." Problems, disputes, and controversies remain, as indicated by the difficulties and resistance encountered in organizing California farm workers since major efforts to do so began to receive widespread notice during the 1960s.

TOPICS TO THINK ABOUT

1. Grampa, in the novel: "Well, sir . . . we'll be a-startin' 'fore long now. An', by God, they's grapes out there, just a-hangin' over inta the road. Know what I'm a-gonna do? I'm gonna pick me a wash tub full a grapes, an' I'm gonna set in 'em, an' scrooge aroun', an' let the juice run down my pants." (Chapter 10)

The narrative voice: "The people come with nets to fish for potatoes in the river, and the guards hold them back; they come in rattling cars to get the dumped oranges, but the kerosene is sprayed . . . and in the eyes of the hungry there is a growing wrath. In the souls of the people the grapes of wrath are filling and growing heavy, growing heavy for the vintage." (Chapter 25)

2. "One other thing—I am not writing a satisfying story. I've done my damndest to rip a reader's nerves to rags, I don't want him satisfied." (Steinbeck, letter, January 16, 1939)

3. Does the novel *The Grapes of Wrath* somehow seem especially appropriate to adaptation as a film? A number of critics have argued that it does, and that, as the literary critic Edmund Wilson put it in 1941, "*The Grapes of Wrath* went on the screen as easily as if it had been written in the studios, and was probably the only serious story on record that seemed equally effective as a film and as a book." (*The Boys in the Back Room*)

Similarly, Siegfried Kracauer explains what he regards as the contrast between the success of this film—"a classic of the screen as well as a faithful adaptation from the Steinbeck novel"—and the relative failure of the great director Jean Renoir's adaptation of Gustave Flaubert's *Madame Bovary* by pointing to "a difference inherent in the adapted novels themselves":

First, Steinbeck's novel deals in human groups rather than individuals. But, as compared with the possible experiences of an isolated person, those of the group are relatively primitive; and they exceed the former in visibility because they must manifest themselves in terms of group behavior. Are not crowds a cinematic subject par excellence? Through his very emphasis on collective misery, collective fears and hopes, Steinbeck meets the cinema more than halfway. Second, his novel exposes the predicament of the migratory farm workers, thus revealing and stigmatizing abuses in our society. This too falls into line with the peculiar potentialities of film. In recording and exploring physical reality, the cinema virtually challenges us to confront that reality with the notions we commonly entertain about it—notions which keep us from perceiving it. Perhaps part of the medium's significance lies in its revealing power. (*Theory of Film*)

Do you regard this passage as accurate in its characterization of the novel, or the movie, or the "peculiar potentialities of film"?

4. In his chapter on *The Grapes of Wrath* in *Novels into Film*, George Bluestone reports that John Ford once remarked to him, "I never read the book." But in his *John Ford,* Peter Bogdanovich records Ford's reply to a question about what had attracted him to the project:

I'd read the book—it was a good story—and Darryl Zanuck had a good script on it. The whole thing appealed to me—being about simple people—and the story was similar to the famine in Ireland, when they threw the people off the land and left them wandering on the roads to starve. That may have had something to do with it—part of my Irish tradition—but I liked the idea of this family going out and trying to find their way in the world. It was a timely story.

5. "You don't 'compose' a film on the set; you put a predesigned composition on film. It is wrong to liken a director to an author. He is more like an architect, if he is creative." (Ford, interview with Jean Mitry)

6. John Steinbeck, in a letter of December 15, 1939, after seeing the film for the first time: "Zanuck has more than kept his word. He has a hard, straight picture in which the actors are submerged so completely that it looks and feels like a documentary film and certainly it has a hard, truthful ring. No punches were pulled—in fact, with descriptive matter removed, it is a harsher thing than the book, by far."

7. In contrast, some critics feel that the film is fundamentally unfaithful to the novel. Warren French, for example, argues that "despite their use of similar characters, settings, and situations, they are very different works, expounding different philosophies." The antagonism, French believes, lies in the film's being less political and revolutionary: "The final point of the movie is exactly the opposite of the novel's. It is an insistence that survival depends not upon changing and dynamically accommodating one's self to new challenges, but rather upon passively accepting one's lot and keeping plodding along." (*Filmguide to The Grapes of Wrath*)

8. George Bluestone agrees that in the film the "political implications" are muted, but he argues that as a result the film *is* faithful to the novel after all: "If the film's conclusion withdraws from a leftist commitment, it is because the novel does also. If the film vaporizes radical sociology, the novel withdraws from it, too, with Rose of Sharon's final act." (*Novels into Film*)

9. What is the effect in the film of the refrain of the tune of "Red River Valley"?

10. Slightly more than half the chapters—the ratio is sixteen to fourteen—are what critics have come to call "intercalary" chapters: ones in which neither the Joads nor any of the other important characters appear. What function do they serve? Are they successful? How does the film go about incorporating some of the elements in those chapters? Does it do so effectively?

11. Claude-Edmonde Magny, in *The Age of the American Novel:*

Historically, Steinbeck is a realistic novelist of the Depression era. He did not, however, live through the economic crisis . . . in the implacable, inorganic world of the big cities, but among the gentle landscapes of the "long valley," in the mild California climate and amid the peace of its vast orchards. This is what is responsible for the note of serenity that is never absent from his stories, regardless of the objective bleakness of the events he recounts. It is impossible for him to achieve a realism as sordid, a despair as absolute, as that which marks, for example, James T. Farrell's novels about the corrupt, urban childhood of young Lonigan.

12. Compare the opening scene between the truck driver and the waitress, shortly before Tom gets his lift, and what Tom then says about what a good guy does even when "some rich bastard" ("some heel" in the film) makes him put stickers on his truck, to the later scene between the two truck drivers and the waitress who lies about the price of the candy.

13. From Steinbeck's Preface to *The Forgotten Village* (1941), a book that came out of a documentary film about Mexico for which he had written the script:

A great many documentary films have used the generalized method, that is, the showing of a condition or an event as it affects a group of people. The audience can then have a personalized reaction from imagining one member of that group. I have felt that this is the more difficult observation from the audience's viewpoint. It means very little to know that a million Chinese are starving unless you know one Chinese who is starving. In *The Forgotten Village* we reversed the usual process. Our story centered on one family in one small village.

In an article he published in 1928, John Ford wrote that "the quality of universality in pictures is in itself a pitfall," and that "the picture likely to attain great and wide success must have its theme of universal appeal but its people vivid."

The Joads are clearly meant to seem "representative" in at least some ways; do they nevertheless also remain vivid, as individuals? Or do they seem to you to become *merely* representative or "symbolic"?

14. One character whom a number of critics—following in particular the studies by Peter Lisca and Martin Staples Shockley—have regarded as symbolic yet successfully presented is Jim Casy, who is often felt to be "a Christ figure." They point to: his initials; his early comment to Tom that he has "been in the hills, thinkin', almost you might say like Jesus went into the wilderness" (chapter 8); the way he later sacrifices himself for Tom ("Somebody got to take the blame"—chapter 20); and his last words before he is killed, "You fellas don' know what you're doin' " ("Jesus, George," one of the men says after Casy has been struck down, "I think you killed him"—chapter 26).

Most of these signs, if such you agree they are, remain in the film. To what effect? In such a Biblical allegory, what would Tom Joad's role be?

15. In lines repeated almost word for word in the film, Casy says: "There ain't no sin and there ain't no virtue. There's just stuff people do. It's all part of the same thing. And some of the things folks do is nice, and some ain't nice, but that's as far as any got a right to say." (Chapter 4)

16. In a letter of November 20, 1958, to Henry Fonda, Steinbeck wrote of having recently seen the film again: "It's a wonderful picture, just as good as it ever was. It doesn't look dated . . ."

Andrew Sarris regards John Ford as one of the few truly great filmmakers (a "pantheon director"), but he asserts about this film that its "New Dealish propaganda . . . has dated badly, as has John Steinbeck's literary reputation." (*The American Cinema*)

Leaving aside the question of Steinbeck's "reputation," how do the novel and the film respectively hold up with the passage of time?

17. A notable change between the novel and the movie is the reversal of the order of the episodes at the government camp and in the field employing strikebreakers; in the film, the latter comes before the former, which is thereby the last important episode before Tom leaves as a fugitive. Why do you think the filmmakers made that switch?

18. Tom's last conversation with Ma in the film follows very closely the passage in the book:

> Tom laughed uneasily, "Well maybe like Casy says, a fella ain't got a soul of his own, but on'y a piece of a big one—and then—"
> "Then what, Tom?"
> "Then it don' matter. Then I'll be all aroun' in the dark. I'll be ever'where—wherever you look. Wherever they's a fight so hungry people can eat, I'll be there. Wherever they's a cop beatin' up a guy, I'll be there. If Casy knowed, why, I'll be in the way guys yell when they're mad an'—I'll be in the way kids laugh when they're hungry an' they know supper's ready. An' when our folks eat the stuff they raise an' live in the houses they build—why, I'll be there." (Chapter 28)

19. Ma Joad's last speech in the film is based on a remark she has made much earlier in the novel: "Why Tom, we're the people that live. They ain't gonna wipe us out. Why, we're the people—we go on." (Chapter 20)

20. "This you may say of man—when theories change and crash, when schools, philosophies, when narrow dark alleys of thought, national, religious, economic, grow and disintegrate, man reaches, stumbles forward, painfully, mistakenly sometimes. Having stepped forward, he may slip back, but only half a step, never the full step back." (Chapter 14)

Further Readings

BLUESTONE, GEORGE. *"The Grapes of Wrath."* In his *Novels into Film.* Berkeley: University of California Press, 1957, pp. 147–69.

BOGDANOVICH, PETER. *John Ford.* Berkeley: University of California Press, 1968. Extensive interviews with the director.

DAVIS, ROBERT MURRAY, ed. *Steinbeck: A Collection of Critical Essays.* Englewood Cliffs, N.J.: Prentice-Hall, 1972.

FORD, JOHN. "Veteran Producer Muses." In *Hollywood Directors: 1914–1940.* Ed. Richard Koszarski. New York: Oxford University Press,

1976, pp. 198–204. Originally published in *The New York Times,* June 10, 1928.

FRENCH, WARREN, ed. *A Companion to The Grapes of Wrath.* New York: Viking, 1963. A collection of critical essays and material dealing with the historical background of the novel.

———. *Filmguide to The Grapes of Wrath.* Bloomington: Indiana University Press, 1973. The most detailed analysis available of the film and its relation to the novel.

———. *John Steinbeck.* New York: Twayne, 1961. An introductory study.

JOHNSON, NUNNALLY. *The Grapes of Wrath.* In *Twenty Best Film Plays.* Ed. John Gassner and Dudley Nichols. New York: Crown, 1943. The original screenplay, which differs in some respects from the final film. The changes are noted and described in French's *Filmguide,* above; see especially the appendix, pp. 73–87.

LEVANT, HOWARD. *The Novels of John Steinbeck: A Critical Study.* Columbia: University of Missouri Press, 1974.

LISCA, PETER. *The Wide World of John Steinbeck.* New Brunswick, N.J.: Rutgers University Press, 1958.

MAGNY, CLAUDE-EDMONDE. "Steinbeck, or the Limits of the Impersonal Novel." In her *The Age of the American Novel: The Film Aesthetic of Fiction Between the Two Wars.* Trans. Eleanor Hochman. New York: Ungar, 1972.

MITRY, JEAN. "John Ford." Trans. Andrew Sarris. In *Interviews with Film Directors.* Ed. Andrew Sarris. New York: Avon, 1969, pp. 193–201. Originally published in *Cahiers du Cinéma* 45 (March 1955).

STEINBECK, ELAINE, and ROBERT WALLSTEN, eds. *Steinbeck: A Life in Letters.* New York: Viking, 1975.

STEINBECK, JOHN. *The Grapes of Wrath.* Ed. Peter Lisca. New York: Viking, 1972. Contains the full text of the novel, as well as critical and historical essays.

———, with photographs by Rosa Harvan Kline and Alexander Hackensmid. *The Forgotten Village.* New York: Viking, 1941.

TEDLOCK, E. W., JR., and C. V. WICKER, eds. *Steinbeck and His Critics: A Record of Twenty-Five Years.* Albuquerque: University of New Mexico Press, 1957. Contains essays on *The Grapes of Wrath* by Joseph Warren Beach, Frederic I. Carpenter, and Martin Staples Shockley.

CITIZEN KANE

BACKGROUND

Citizen Kane (1941) is probably the most widely praised film in movie history. In polls attempting to determine the ten best films ever made, *Citizen Kane* often comes out in first place, as it did in those taken by the film journal *Sight and Sound* in both 1962 and 1972. (But it took time for full recognition to come about: in the 1952 poll, eleven years after its release, *Kane* did not make the top ten.) Even those who might not rate it quite that high—or who, perhaps, do not believe in such rankings in the first place—recognize it as one of the two or three most *influential* films of all time. When it appeared, Orson Welles was twenty-five years old.

Moreover, he was already famous—indeed notorious. Born in Wisconsin in 1915, Welles came to films from the theater and radio. At the age of sixteen, he somehow convinced the directors of the Gate Theatre in Dublin, Ireland, that he was already a star, and played with that important group for a year. Back in the United States, he directed productions of Shakespeare (*Macbeth* with an all-black cast, *Julius Caesar* in modern dress) which received widespread attention and praise. With his Mercury Theater, which he had founded in 1937 with John Houseman, he also did pioneering work in radio drama—including the famous broadcast in 1938 of *The War of the Worlds,* which caused some panic and made Welles a sensation.

The RKO studio then invited Welles to Hollywood to make a film, giving him unprecedented control over the production. As his first project, he and scriptwriter Herman J. Mankiewicz (1898–1953) decided to make a movie based in part on the life of newspaper magnate William Randolph Hearst (1863–1951). Many correspondences between the lives of Hearst and Charles Foster Kane are quite close: Hearst also bought his first newspaper as a young man; his mastery of sensational ("yellow") journalism enabled him to form an "empire" of thirty newspapers; and he often used his power unscrupulously—as when, for example, he fomented the Spanish-American War of 1898. (Kane's cable to Wheeler is very close to an infamous one Hearst had sent to Frederic Remington: "Please remain. You furnish the pictures and I'll furnish the war.") Other associations are more loosely handled, notably in the character of

Fig. 18. The Museum of Modern Art/Film Stills Archive. Courtesy RKO.

Susan Alexander, who was modeled on Marion Davies (1897–1961). Davies was Hearst's mistress for many years, and he did vigorously promote her career (in films, not opera), but unlike Susan Alexander she was actually fairly successful and talented; she retired in 1936 and stayed with Hearst loyally until his death.

The Hearst interests were successful in assuring that the distribution of *Citizen Kane* was more restricted than it would otherwise have been, and a timid industry made it difficult for RKO to exhibit the film in theaters controlled by other Hollywood studios. When RKO showed the film in its own and leased theaters, Hearst newspapers refused to carry reviews of—or even ads for—any RKO pictures. However, reviews in other newspapers and magazines were generally enthusiastic. And nothing could stop the public image of William Randolph Hearst from being permanently influenced by this film: the major biography by W. A. Swanberg, published in 1961, is called *Citizen Hearst*. Nevertheless, the film did not do especially well at the box office, and it was eventually withdrawn from general circulation and not released again until the 1950s.

Another controversy has centered on the authorship of the screenplay, for which Welles and Herman J. Mankiewicz shared an Academy Award. In a 1971 essay published in *The New Yorker* entitled "Raising Kane" (subsequently reprinted with two versions of the film script in *The Citizen Kane Book*), Pauline Kael charged that Welles had little to do with the creation of the script ("Orson Welles wasn't around when *Citizen Kane* was written, early in 1940"), and even that he at first intended to keep Mankiewicz's role secret and only gave him screen credit when "forced to." A number of people have come to Welles's defense, including some who were involved in the actual production—an important development given the fact that, as Peter Bogdanovich claimed in an *Esquire* article called "The Kane Mutiny," "there is nothing to show that Miss Kael interviewed anyone of real importance associated with the actual making of the film."

The consensus now seems to be that it was just and proper for Kael to bring attention to the role of Mankiewicz, but that she was less convincing in her denigration of Welles. While the script of *Citizen Kane,* it seems clear, was primarily written by Mankiewicz, in the end it was sufficiently changed for it to be honestly termed a collaborative effort; in any case, after one has said that about the script, one may also say that as a whole *Citizen Kane* is a film by Orson Welles. (Even Kael observes that "Welles had a vitalizing, spellbinding talent; he was the man who brought out the best in others and knew how to use it.")

One of the most convincing ways of stressing Welles's importance in the creation of *Citizen Kane* is to look at Mankiewicz's other credits; it becomes difficult to name many (out of the dozens of screenplays that he worked on) that remain memorable: he did contribute to two Marx Brothers movies without being credited (*Monkey Business,* 1931, and *Horse Feathers,* 1932); he received credit for *Dinner at Eight* (1933), for example, and, after *Kane,* for *The Pride of the Yankees* (1942). As George Coulouris (the actor who played Thatcher) says about Mankiewicz in an interview attacking Kael's thesis, "It's hard to connect any of the stuff he wrote with *Citizen Kane.* Most of it is superficial, shallow entertainment." In the same interview Bernard Herrmann, who composed the music for *Kane,* said: "I think the greatest thing that ever happened to Herman Mankiewicz, whatever his contribution, was that he met Welles, not the other way round. . . . Mankiewicz's credits don't show any other remarkable scripts. His only moment in the sun was when he came across Orson Welles."

Some critics see *Citizen Kane* as a film not only by Orson Welles but, as if prophetically, *about* him as well; they discuss what they see as parallels between Kane's "self-destructive" tendencies and those they see in Welles himself, and notice correspondences between the careers of the two men after great youthful promise. Yet although none of his later work has seemed to most people to match *Citizen Kane,* he has in fact made some fine, important films. Movies he has directed include *The Magnificent Ambersons* (1942), *The Lady from Shanghai* and *Macbeth* (both 1948), *Othello* (1951), *Confidential Report* (or *Mr. Arkadin,* 1955; based on his own novel, *Mr. Arkadin*), *Touch of Evil* (1958), **The Trial* (1962), *Chimes at Midnight/Falstaff* (1966), and *F for Fake* (1973). He has of course also been very active as an actor in other directors' films; aside from Kane, probably his most famous role was that of Harry Lime in **The Third Man* (1949). He received the Life Achievement Award of the American Film Institute in 1975.

The photography for *Citizen Kane* was by Gregg Toland, whom Welles has called "the best director of photography that ever existed." Welles eloquently expressed his gratitude to Toland by sharing with him his own credit title at the end of the picture. Toland had already worked on *Dead End* (1937), *Wuthering Heights* (1939), for which he won an Academy Award, and **The Grapes of Wrath* (1940); his credits after *Kane* include *The Best Years of Our Lives* (1946).

The editors were Robert Wise and (uncredited) Mark Robson, both of whom went on to direct: Wise's films include *The Set-Up* (1949) and *The Sound of Music* (1965); Robson's *Champion* (1949) and *Earthquake* (1974).

Bernard Herrmann composed the music, including the aria Susan Alexander sings in the made-up opera *Salammbô*. Herrmann had already worked with Welles at CBS radio. Later credits include *The Magnificent Ambersons,* **Psycho* (1960), and *Taxi Driver* (1976).

Other credits: art direction, Van Nest Polglase and Perry Ferguson; costumes, Edward Stevenson; decors, Darrell Silvera; special effects, Vernon L. Walker; sound recording, Bailey Fesler and James G. Stewart.

The chief members of the cast came from Welles's Mercury Theater, with two exceptions: Dorothy Comingore as Susan Alexander Kane and Ruth Warrick as Emily Norton Kane. Joseph Cotten, who played Jedediah Leland, also helped to write parts of the screenplay; he has appeared in many films, including *The Magnificent Ambersons*—and as a foil for Welles again in **The Third Man.* Everett Sloane (Mr. Bernstein) was later brilliant in a vastly different and menacing role in Welles's *The Lady from Shanghai.*

Other members of the cast: George Coulouris as Walter Parks Thatcher (a figure modeled in part on the financier J. P. Morgan); William Alland as both Thompson, the reporter, and the voice in the opening newsreel; Agnes Moorehead as Kane's mother; Ray Collins as Boss Jim Gettys; Paul Stewart as Raymond, the butler; Fortunio Bonanova as Matisti; Erskine Sanford as Mr. Carter; and Buddy Swann as the boy Kane.

Running time: 119 minutes. Distributors include: Audio Brandon; Films Inc.; University of Washington.

TOPICS TO THINK ABOUT

1. The review by novelist John O'Hara in *Newsweek,* published in March 1941, before the general release of the film and reflecting the anticipated difficulties in distribution, begins:

> It is with exceeding regret that your faithful bystander reports
> that he has just seen a picture which he thinks must be the best
> picture he ever saw.
>   With no less regret he reports that he has just seen the best actor
> in the history of acting.
>   Name of picture: *Citizen Kane.*
>   Name of actor: Orson Welles.
>   Reason for regret: you, my dear, may never see the picture.

2. ". . . *Citizen Kane* is far and away the most surprising and cinematically exciting motion picture to be seen here in many a moon. As a matter of fact, it comes close to being the most sensational film ever made in Hollywood." (Bosley Crowther, review in *The New York Times*)

3. Welles came to Hollywood with youth and inexperience, but with an eagerness to learn and a determination to experiment, and he was willing alternately to listen and to bully. ("I don't know how to run a newspaper," Kane tells Thatcher, "I just try everything I can think of.") The surprising result is a film that is not merely a fine achievement in character portrayal and narrative but also a cinematic and technical tour de force—and that rare thing, a work of both youthful innovation and mature accomplishment.

Welles showed his technical boldness in, for example: the lighting; the camera angles (especially those in which Kane is seen from below); the use of sound (to which Welles's background in radio contributed); and perhaps above all his use of *deep focus* (for a brief discussion of which, see page 41). Actually, none of these techniques were really "new"—but they became new in Welles's hands.

4. Peter Bogdanovich reports that in answer to "an elementary question: why did you *want* so much depth-of-focus?" Welles replied with what seems an equally elementary answer: "Well, in life you see everything in focus at the same time, so why not in the movies?" Years before, the director of photography Gregg Toland had written, in *Popular Photography* magazine:

> The normal human eye sees everything before it (within reasonable distance) clearly and sharply. There is no special or single center of visual sharpness in real life. But the Hollywood cameras focus on a center of interest, and allow the other components of a scene to "fuzz out" in those regions before and beyond the focal point.
>
> The attainment of an approximate human-eye focus was one of our fundamental aims in *Citizen Kane*.

5. "*Citizen Kane* can never be too highly praised. Thanks to the depth of field, whole scenes are covered in one take, the camera remaining motionless. Dramatic effects for which we had formerly relied on montage were created out of the movements of the actors within a fixed framework. Of course Welles did not invent the in-depth shot any more than Griffith invented the close-up." (André Bazin, *What Is Cinema?*)

6. In Welles, a predilection toward deep focus has often meant a reluctance to employ close-ups. As he said in a 1965 interview, "I find it marvelous that the public may choose, with its eyes, what it wants to see of a shot. I don't like to force it, and the use of the close-up amounts to forcing it: you can see nothing else. In *Kane,* for example, you must have seen that there were very few close-ups, hardly any."

7. David Bordwell, in *"Citizen Kane"*:

> Welles' *mise-en-scène* modulates the drama's flow with great subtlety, using angle to indicate patterns of domination. Recall the climactic scene when Kane confronts Boss Jim Gettys in Susan's apartment. Gettys' entrance is as thunderous as a kettledrum roll: Kane, Emily, and Susan are on the staircase, light is pouring out of the doorway, and quietly Gettys' silhouette steps into the shot; for once someone has the upper hand over Kane; Nemesis has caught up with the hero. . . . Inside Susan's bedroom, the angles crisply build the tension. First, a shot frames Emily in the foreground, Susan in the middle ground, and Gettys and Kane facing each other deep in the shot. But as Gettys explains the power he has over Kane, he advances to the foreground, dwarfing his rival; Emily says that

apparently Kane's decision has been made for him; Kane, in the distance, seems overpowered by circumstance. But when Kane decides to assert his will, the shot cuts to an opposite angle: he dominates the foreground, and Gettys, Susan, and Emily taper off into the background. Then, a head-on shot, with Kane in the center, Susan on the left and Gettys on the right, capsulizes his choice: he can save his mistress or fight his opponent. Welles' arrangement of actors in the frame and his timing of the cuts brilliantly articulate the drama of the scene. The material seems to be objectively observed (no close-ups or first-person points-of-view), but the structure of each shot and the pacing of the editing inject subjective attitudes.

8. In the sequence presenting the several breakfast scenes, how do editing, camera movement, and *mise en scène* work together to present a brief condensed history of a marriage?

9. At the start of "News on the March," we see a title quoting the first two lines of Samuel Taylor Coleridge's poem, "Kubla Khan": "In Xanadu did Kubla Khan/ A stately pleasure dome decree . . ."; you may of course wish to look at the entire poem (which was written around 1797–98), but in any case here is the last stanza:

> A damsel with a dulcimer
> In a vision once I saw:
> It was an Abyssinian maid,
> And on her dulcimer she played,
> Singing of Mount Abora.
> Could I revive within me
> Her symphony and song,
> To such deep delight 'twould win me,
> That with music loud and long,
> I would build that dome in air,
> That sunny dome! those caves of ice!
> And all who heard should see them there,
> And all should cry, Beware! Beware!
> His flashing eyes, his floating hair!
> Weave a circle round him thrice,
> And close your eyes with holy dread,
> For he on honeydew hath fed,
> And drunk the milk of Paradise.

10. Another title on the screen during "News on the March" quotes Kane as having said, "I Am, Have Been, And Will Be Only One Thing—An American." The original title for this film was to have been, in fact, *American.* What effect would such a title have had on our experience of the film?

Is Kane correct? What does your agreement or disagreement with him say about his life (or, perhaps, about being an "American")?

11. In an essay entitled *"Citizen Kane, The Great Gatsby,* and Some Conventions of American Narrative," Robert L. Carringer discusses what he regards as similarities between the personalities and lives of Kane and F. Scott Fitzgerald's Gatsby. If you know Fitzgerald's novel, you may wish to examine Carringer's argument—or to consider possible comparisons on your own. Carringer writes:

> Unlike, say, [Henry Fielding's] Tom Jones or [James Joyce's]
> Stephen Dedalus, whose stories involve the search for a father as the
> search for an identity, Gatsby and Kane proceed in the Emersonian
> mode, creating themselves in their own best images. . . . And
> while the European protagonist starts from the premise "What place
> am I to occupy?" American protagonists start (like Gatsby and Kane)
> from the premise "What world am I to conquer?"

12. What is the effect of beginning and ending the film with shots of a sign that proclaims "NO TRESPASSING"?

13. How much or how little do we come to know Charles Foster Kane? In his book on Welles, Charles Higham complains that we know "too little," and that as a result "we see only a dazzlingly illuminated cartoon figure." Do you agree? Or might you argue that in this case ambiguity is a strength?

14. Welles, in *"Citizen Kane* Is Not About Louella Parsons' Boss" (i.e., Hearst), an article he wrote before the release of the film:

> Kane, we are told, loved only his mother—only his newspaper—only
> his second wife—only himself. Maybe he loved all of these, or none.
> It is for the audience to judge. Kane was selfish and selfless, an
> idealist, a scoundrel, a very big man and a very little one. It depends
> on who's talking about him. He is never judged with the objectivity
> of an author, and the point of the picture is not so much the solution
> of the problem as its presentation.

15. KANE: "You know, Mr. Bernstein, if I hadn't been very rich, I might have been a really great man."

Do you think so?

16. Consider the narrative technique of *Citizen Kane* in light of the discussions of narrative structure, plot, and story in chapter 1.

17. What is accomplished by our getting an overview of Kane's life in "News on the March" so early in the film? Is anything lost by this device?

18. The use of multiple points of view in order to search for a measure of truth about someone has reminded many people of some of the writings of Joseph Conrad, and in fact Welles's original intention in Hollywood was to adapt Conrad's *Heart of Darkness*. If you know Conrad's tale—or, perhaps, a novel such as *Lord Jim*—compare and contrast it with *Citizen Kane* in regard to such aspects as narrative technique, theme, and characterization.

19. Why does Thompson, the reporter, remain so visually indistinct throughout the film?

20. In *Confidential Report,* Mr. Arkadin, the character played by Welles, tells a little fable which Welles also frequently likes to tell, for example on television talk shows. A scorpion is unable to cross a stream and asks a frog to carry him across on his back. The frog refuses, since he fears the scorpion might sting him. But when the scorpion points out that if he were to sting the frog, he would drown and die too, the frog admits the logic of that and agrees—but, halfway across the stream, the scorpion stings the frog after all. As they are both drowning, the frog cries, "Is that logic?" The scorpion admits it isn't: "But I can't help it. It's my character."

Does that tale at all illuminate Kane's character?

21. Leland, now an old man, says about Kane: "Love . . . that's why he did everything." Then in one of the flashbacks we see Kane drink "a toast, Jedediah, to love on my terms. Those are the only terms anybody ever knows, his own." What are Kane's terms?

22. Kane and others at the banquet sing:

> Who buys the food, who buys the food
> Who buys the drinks, who buys the drinks
> Who thinks that dough was made to spend
> And acts the way he thinks?

Much is made in the film about all that Kane *buys,* owns, and collects. Why?

Leland claims that Kane "never gave anything away. He just left you a tip." Does that seem just?

23. LELAND: "Bernstein, am I a stuffed shirt? Am I a horse-faced hypocrite? Am I a New England schoolmarm?"

BERNSTEIN: "Yes."

Kane surely loses some of our sympathy as he compromises his ideals (his "Declaration of Principles"); does Leland ever lose some of our sympathy as he steadfastly refuses to compromise his?

24. What is the role of the paperweight depicting the snow scene? It occurs at several key points in the film and is in Susan's room when she and Kane first meet—on that evening when, he says, "I was on my way to the Western Manhattan Warehouse, in search of my youth." (Presumably, one of the things in the warehouse is Rosebud.) Does that explain Susan's attraction for Kane?

25. Thompson says at the end, "Maybe Rosebud was something he couldn't get or something he lost. Anyway, it wouldn't have explained anything. I don't think any word can explain a man's life."

How much *does* Rosebud "explain"? Do you agree with those who attack it as an unfortunate, sentimental gimmick? Or are sentimentality and ultimate superficiality somehow part of the point?

26. Pauline Kael, on *Citizen Kane:* "It is a shallow work, a *shallow* masterpiece. Those who try to account for its stature as a film by claiming it to be profound are simply dodging the problem—or maybe they don't recognize that there is one."

How might one defend or attack this evaluation?

27. Is Kane what you might be willing to call a "tragic hero"? Is his story a tragedy? (See the brief discussions of tragedy in the section on *Hamlet, topics 3 to 5, pages 160–61.)

28. From a 1965 interview, a question on *Citizen Kane:*

> Q.—*During the shooting, did you have the sensation of making such an important film?*
> WELLES—I never doubted it for a single instant.

Further Readings

BAZIN, ANDRÉ. *Orson Welles: A Critical View.* Trans. Jonathan Rosenbaum. New York: Harper and Row, 1978.

BOGDANOVICH, PETER. "The Kane Mutiny." *Esquire* 78 (October 1972): 99–105, 180–90.

BORDWELL, DAVID. *"Citizen Kane." Film Comment* 7 (Summer 1971): 38–47. Reprinted in Solomon, below.

CARRINGER, ROBERT L. *"Citizen Kane, The Great Gatsby,* and Some Conventions of American Narrative." *Critical Inquiry* 2 (Winter 1975): 307–25.

COBOS, JUAN, MIGUEL RUBIO, and JOSÉ ANTONIO PRUNEDA. "Orson Welles." Trans. Rose Kaplin. In *Interviews with Film Directors.* Ed. Andrew Sarris. New York: Avon, 1969, pp. 528–57. Originally published in *Cahiers du Cinéma* 165 (April 1965).

COULOURIS, GEORGE, BERNARD HERRMANN, and TED GILLING. *"The Citizen Kane Book." Sight and Sound* 41 (Spring 1972): 71–73.

COWIE, PETER. *A Ribbon of Dreams: The Cinema of Orson Welles.* South Brunswick, N.J.: A. S. Barnes, 1973. An intelligent and useful general study.

GOTTESMAN, RONALD J., ed. *Focus on Citizen Kane.* Englewood Cliffs, N.J.: Prentice-Hall, 1971. A very useful collection of early reviews, articles by Welles, Herrmann, and Toland, and essays by various critics. Also contains a "Content Outline" of the film.

HIGHAM, CHARLES. *The Films of Orson Welles.* Berkeley: University of California Press, 1970. Often surprisingly negative in its evaluations.

KAEL, PAULINE. "Raising Kane." In *The Citizen Kane Book* (see under Mankiewicz, below). Originally published in *The New Yorker* (1971).

MANKIEWICZ, HERMAN J., and ORSON WELLES. *Citizen Kane.* In *The Citizen Kane Book.* New York: Bantam, 1971. Prints both the shooting script and the "cutting continuity" (i.e., the transcription of the final version of the film). Also reprints Kael (above).

NAREMORE, JAMES. *The Magic World of Orson Welles.* New York: Oxford University Press, 1978. Excellent.

SOLOMON, STANLEY J., ed. *The Classic Cinema: Essays in Criticism.* New York: Harcourt Brace Jovanovich, 1973. Reprints the essay by Bordwell and excerpts from Higham and Kael, above.

WELLES, ORSON. *"Citizen Kane* Is Not About Louella Parsons' Boss." *Friday* 2 (February 14, 1941): 9. Reprinted in Gottesman (above).

THE MALTESE FALCON

BACKGROUND

On the Novel

The Maltese Falcon (1930) was the third novel by Dashiell Hammett (1894–1961), who is often credited with "inventing" the genre of the tough private detective and who in any case certainly had a major influence on others who wrote in that form, notably for example Raymond Chandler. Earlier novels had been *Red Harvest* and *The Dain Curse* (both 1929); he later wrote *The Glass Key* (1931) and *The Thin Man* (1932)—the latter having as its hero the antitheses of Samuel Spade in the debonair and charming Nick and Nora Charles, characters who appeared in a successful series of films starring William Powell and Myrna Loy.

Hammett had himself been, like Spade, a private detective in San Francisco (for the Pinkerton Agency) before he began writing his stories and novels, many of which were published in the magazine *Black Mask*.

On the Film

John Huston's *The Maltese Falcon* (1941) was actually the third film version of the novel. A film by the same name appeared in 1931, directed by Roy del Ruth and starring Ricardo Cortez as Spade and Bebe Daniels as Brigid O'Shaughnessy. This version was largely played for laughs, but it was otherwise fairly faithful to the original plot line. That was not true of the 1936 version, called *Satan Met a Lady* and directed by William Dieterle, in which for example the Fat Man became the Fat Lady (played by Alison Skipworth); Warren William and Bette Davis starred.

John Huston (b. 1906) had been having a successful career as a screenwriter, working on such films as *Juarez* (1939) and *Sergeant York* (1941), when—to keep him happy, Huston says—the Warner Brothers studio agreed to let him try directing. They stipulated that he choose a relatively inexpensive project, and Warners still owned the rights to *The Maltese Falcon*. At first there was pressure to cast George Raft as Spade. Raft had turned down *High Sierra*, which Huston had helped to write, because he did not want to play a character who dies at the end, thus enabling Humphrey Bogart to break out of the type-cast bad-guy secondary roles he had been restricted to for years. Raft did not want

FIG. 19.   The Museum of Modern Art/Film Stills Archive. Courtesy Warner Bros.

to take chances with a new and inexperienced director, so he turned down *The Maltese Falcon* too. Bogart thus played the role that made him a major star—and he remained one for the rest of his life, just as Huston has remained a major director, if an often controversial and not always successful one.

Huston made important documentaries during World War II, and his first postwar film starred, again, Bogart: *The Treasure of the Sierra Madre* (1948). His other films include *Key Largo* (1948) and *The African Queen* (1951), both also with Bogart, and *The Asphalt Jungle* (1950), *The Red Badge of Courage* (1951), *Moby Dick* (1956), *The Misfits* (1961), and *The Man Who Would Be King* (1975), as well as some films that caused his reputation to decline somewhat, such as *The Bible* (1966) and *The Mackintosh Man* (1973). In any case, *The Maltese Falcon* is almost universally admired and is indeed regarded by many people as the greatest of all detective films; for that matter, it was immediately greeted as such upon its release.

Huston wrote the screenplay in addition to directing the film. The producer was Hal Wallis, then head of production for Warner Brothers; he also produced *Little Caesar* (1930), *Casablanca* (1943), and many other films. Henry Blanke (who went on to produce *The Treasure of the Sierra Madre*) served as the associate producer. The director of photography was Arthur Edeson, whose previous work included *All Quiet on the Western Front* (1930), *Mutiny on the Bounty* (1935), and *Satan Met a Lady*, the earlier version of *The Maltese Falcon.* He would later photograph Bogart, Sydney Greenstreet, and Peter Lorre again in *Casablanca.*

Other credits: music, Adolphe Deutsch; editor, Thomas Richards; dialogue director, Robert Foulk; assistant director, Claude Archer; art director, Robert Haas; sound recorder, Oliver S. Garretson; make-up, Perc Westmore.

Looking back at *The Maltese Falcon* over thirty years and thirty films later, Huston once said, "I've never had a better cast"—and that remark came from someone who is widely regarded as especially good at directing actors. Humphrey Bogart (1899–1957) of course was Sam Spade; for a discussion of the Bogart persona, see chapter 2, pages 32–33. Other films besides those mentioned above for which he is especially remembered include *To Have and Have Not* (1945), *The Big Sleep* (1946), and *The Caine Mutiny* (1954). He won an Academy Award for his performance in *The African Queen* (1951).

Mary Astor (Brigid O'Shaughnessy) received an Academy Award for best supporting actress in 1941, but for her role in *The Great Lie* (1941) rather than for *The Maltese Falcon.* She went on to play understanding mothers in *Meet Me in St. Louis* (1944) and *Little Women* (1949). Sydney Greenstreet was Kasper Gutman, the Fat Man: he was a British actor who had worked in the American theater for many years, and this was his first film role (at the age of sixty-one). He made many other films for Warner Brothers, including *Casablanca* and *The Mask of Dimitrios* (1944), both of which also featured Peter Lorre. Lorre (Joel Cairo) had become famous in the role of a psychopathic murderer in Fritz Lang's *M* (1931). He had also appeared in *Mad Love* (1935) and as Raskolnikov in an adaptation of Dostoevsky's *Crime and Punishment* (1935). Elisha Cook, Jr. (Wilmer) later appeared in such films as *The Big Sleep* and *Shane* (1953).

Other members of the cast: Ward Bond as Detective Tom Polhaus; Barton MacLane as Lieutenant Dundy; Lee Patrick as Effie Perine; Gladys George as Iva Archer; Jerome Cowan as Miles Archer; James Burke as Luke; Murray Alper as Frank Richman; John Hamilton as District Attorney Bryan; and, without a screen credit, Walter Huston (John Huston's father) in the cameo role of Captain Jacobi.

Running time: 100 minutes. Distributor: United Artists (which also distributes the 1931 and 1936 versions).

TOPICS TO THINK ABOUT

1. John Huston, in an interview with Gideon Bachman:

The directing of a film, to me, is simply an extension of the process of writing. It's the process of rendering the thing you have written. . . .
. . . What goes for film also goes for literature, for any form of art; the originality of Joyce is in no way to be divorced from what he was saying. There's no separation between style and subject matter, between style and intention, between style and . . . the idea.

2. Raymond Chandler, the author of the Philip Marlowe detective novels, such as *The Big Sleep* and *Farewell, My Lovely:*

How original a writer Hammett really was it isn't easy to decide now, even if it mattered. He was one of a group—the only one who achieved critical recognition—who wrote or tried to write realistic mystery fiction. . . .
Hammett wrote . . . for people with a sharp, aggressive attitude to life. They were not afraid of the seamy side of things; they lived there. Violence did not dismay them; it was right down their street. Hammett gave murder back to the kind of people that commit it for reasons, not just to provide a corpse; and with the means at hand, not hand-wrought dueling pistols, curare and tropical fish. He put these people down on paper as they were, and he made them talk and think in the language they customarily used for these purposes.
. . . *The Maltese Falcon* may or may not be a work of genius, but an art which is capable of it is not "by hypothesis" incapable of anything. (*The Simple Art of Murder*)

3. Stanley Solomon, in a discussion of "The Private Detective Myth":

Of all the major American film categories, only the private investigator film has a recurring mythic dimension that is present in almost all the notable works within it. The Western closely resembles it in the thematic and tonal thrust of a myth pattern, but the numerous categories of the Western prove that there is no one central myth present in all films of that genre. . . . [The world of the Western] is sometimes rural America but usually the uncharted desert and mountains where a man dependent on his inner strength must make his way. The private detective's world is urban America, where conflicts and passions are hidden beneath a veneer of sophistication. It is an indoor world where the worst traits of people, primarily greed, are depicted in intricate, sometimes almost indescribable plots. (*Beyond Formula: American Film Genres*)

4. "I work a great deal from novels perhaps because there is much less difference between the cinema and the novel than the cinema and the threatre." (Huston, in Gerald Pratley, *The Cinema of John Huston*)

5. Few adaptations stick so close to an original source as this film does to the novel. Nevertheless, there are changes, some of which are mentioned below; but the dialogue for example is amazingly close to Hammett's.

Indeed, *The Maltese Falcon* is an unusually "talky" film, and occasionally it calls our attention to that fact if we have not noticed it—as when Spade, realizing that he has been saying a great deal very quickly, asks the District Attorney's stenographer, "You getting this all right, son, or am I going too fast for you?" (a line which itself comes out of the novel).

Is the film *too* talky? Is it insufficiently visual?

6. "I attempted to transpose Hammett's highly individual style into camera terms with sharp photography, geographically exact camera movements, and striking but not shocking set-ups." (Huston, in Pratley, *Cinema of John Huston*)

Did he succeed? Consider the shot in which Spade has shown what Gutman calls "a most violent temper" and stalks out after threatening Wilmer—and, in the hall, grins silently at his shaking hand. Or consider the scene in which Wilmer wakes up and we cut from his face to Gutman's, back to Wilmer's, then to Cairo's, then back to Wilmer's, then Spade's, and back to Wilmer's as he realizes where he stands and what has been decided.

7. Andrew Sarris, who does not think much of Huston's career, argues that even his successful films "owe more to casting coups than to directorial acumen. *Falcon*, particularly, is an uncanny match-up of Dashiell Hammett's literary characters with their visual doubles. . . ." (*The American Cinema*)

Is that accurate? Examine the descriptions we are given in the novel of the various characters—such as that of Spade in the first two pages.

8. As stated above, the film, however close to the novel it is in many details, does make some changes. Which ones strike you as especially notable?

9. The novel is much more explicit than the film about sexual matters: Spade and Brigid clearly go to bed together; Spade makes her strip to be certain she hasn't taken the $1,000; and Cairo's homosexuality and his feelings for Wilmer are treated more openly.

How much is the explicitness needed? In the novel, Brigid asks Spade, "Can I buy you with my body?" In the film, her words are, "What else is there I can buy you with?" Is her meaning less clear?

How much is lost if we do assume that the various sexual relationships are more ambiguous in the film? Is anything gained?

10. The importance of point of view in both written literature and film is discussed in chapters 1 and 2 of this volume (pages 9–11 and 38–41). Huston has observed: "The book was told entirely from the standpoint of Sam Spade, and so too, is the picture, with Spade in every scene except the murder of his partner. The audience knows no more and no less than he does. All the other characters are introduced only as they meet Spade, and upon their appearance I attempted to photograph them through his eyes." (In Pratley, *Cinema of John Huston*)

Do you think a great deal is gained from this limited point of view? Are there any disadvantages? Should the insertion of the shot of Archer's murder—in which we see the change of expression in his face—have been avoided? (A sharp eye might detect another small exception or two—as when we see Cairo get out of the elevator but Spade does not notice him. Are such shots unfortunate?)

11. Notice how Spade frequently puts the relationship between himself and others on the level of a contest; like Gutman, he seems to take almost equal pleasure in being outwitted as in outwitting someone else. In the film, he smiles when Cairo says he will search the office after all, and he smiles when he eludes Wilmer's tail—and when he admiringly tells Brigid, "You're good," and later, "You're good, you're very good."

12. What *is* Sam Spade's relationship to the world and other people? To his partner? To the police? To the criminals? To women?

13. In words similar to those she uses in the novel, Effie says to Spade about Brigid, in the film, "She's all right. Oh, maybe it's her own fault for being in whatever the trouble is, but she's all right, if that's what you mean."

Gutman later warns Spade to "be careful" of Brigid: "Dangerous?" Spade asks. "Very," Gutman replies. (In the novel, the word is "bad" instead of "dangerous.")

Who is correct? Is it possible there is no discrepancy?

14. Brigid has lied to Spade all along ("I've always been a liar," she admits). Do we feel that she is probably still lying to him in their last scene together?

15. Does Spade's moral stance at the end ("Don't be too sure I'm as crooked as I'm supposed to be") come as a surprise?

16. How do you react to Spade's final decision and his speech to Brigid?

17. In the novel, Effie says, "Sam, if that girl's in trouble and you let her down, or take advantage of it to bleed her, I'll never forgive you, never have any respect for you, as long as I live." (Chapter 4)

By those standards, how does Spade stand up? Effie's role as a conscience for Spade seems clearer or more emphatic throughout the novel, and in a short final scene which does not appear in the film, she says to him, "I know—I know you're right. You're right. But don't touch me now—not now."

18. What is the significance of what we see in our final visual glimpse of Brigid?

19. James Naremore, in "John Huston and *The Maltese Falcon*":

> The very choice of *Falcon* was consistent with the personality Huston would convey in nearly all his subsequent work—perhaps *Falcon* even determined that personality to some degree. Notice how neatly it fits into the Huston canon: most of his good films—*Treasure of the Sierra Madre, Key Largo, We Were Strangers, The Asphalt Jungle, The Roots of Heaven, Beat the Devil, The Misfits, Fat City*—have depended on simple visual symbolism and sharp contrasts of character. They are all quasi-allegorical adventures about groups of exotic, eccentric people, and, as several commentators have observed, they usually end on a note of great, ironic failure.

20. Of the object that Gutman has called the *"rara avis"* (rare bird), Spade—in one of the few major lines in the film not to be found in the novel—says that it is the "stuff that dreams are made of." James Naremore feels that the remark is "corny" and a "blemish on the film." Do you agree?

21. Gutman's fate differs in the film—perhaps because Warner Brothers contemplated a sequel in which Huston would once again direct Bogart, Astor, Greenstreet, and Lorre. (All except Lorre were teamed again in *Across the Pacific,* 1942; all except Astor in *Casablanca,* 1943.) The sequel was never made, although a comedy about Sam Spade's son (played by George Segal), David Giler's *The Black Bird,* appeared in 1975, attracting little notice. (Despite that attempt, and despite the earlier versions, one can paraphrase Kasper Gutman in another context and observe that "there's only one *Maltese Falcon.*")

Further Readings

BACHMAN, GIDEON. "John Huston." In *Interviews with Film Directors*. Ed. Andrew Sarris. New York: Avon, 1969, pp. 253–73. Originally published in *Film Quarterly* 19 (Fall 1965): 3–13.

CHANDLER, RAYMOND. *The Simple Art of Murder*. New York: Ballantine, 1972.

EVERSON, WILLIAM K. *The Detective in Film*. Secaucus, N.J.: Citadel, 1972. Illustrated.

HAMMETT, DASHIELL. *The Adventures of Sam Spade and Other Stories*. New York: World, 1946.

―――. *The Maltese Falcon*. New York: Vintage, 1972.

―――. *The Novels of Dashiell Hammett*. New York: Knopf, 1965.

HUSTON, JOHN. *The Maltese Falcon*. Ed. Richard J. Anobile. New York: Avon, 1974. Valuable shot-by-shot record of the film; over 1400 frame stills.

KAMINSKY, STUART. *John Huston: Maker of Magic*. Boston: Houghton Mifflin, 1978.

NAREMORE, JAMES. "John Huston and *The Maltese Falcon*." *Literature/Film Quarterly* 1 (July 1973): 239–49.

NOLAN, WILLIAM F. *John Huston: King Rebel*. Los Angeles: Sherbourne, 1965. A biography.

PRATLEY, GERALD. *The Cinema of John Huston*. South Brunswick, N.J.: A. S. Barnes, 1977. Consists chiefly of comments by Huston, in some general chapters and in discussions of individual films. Pratley summarizes the story of each film.

HENRY V

BACKGROUND

On the Play

William Shakespeare (1564–1616) was born in Stratford-upon-Avon; he married in 1582, but relatively little else is known about his life until 1592, by which time he had settled in London. He probably began his work in the theater as an actor, eventually becoming connected with

FIG. 20.   The Museum of Modern Art/Film Stills Archive. Courtesy Two Cities.

one of the most prominent dramatic companies of his day, the Lord
Chamberlain's Men (later called the King's Men).

The Life of Henry V was almost certainly written in 1599 and was
probably first produced at the Globe Theatre in 1600 (as indicated by the
playbill at the start of the film), with Richard Burbage in the title role. It
was one of a long series of "chronicle" plays or "histories," a genre which
was especially popular during the 1590s; others by Shakespeare include
plays about the reigns of King John, Richard II, Henry IV, Henry VI,
and Richard III. Henry V was the last for which Shakespeare was completely responsible, although later in his career he is believed to have
collaborated on one about Henry VIII.

In Richard II, Henry Bolingbroke usurps the throne of Richard, an
inefficient and unpopular king, and becomes Henry IV. After Richard's
murder by Sir Pierce of Exton, a man of Henry's party, there is a rebel-
lion against Henry, which forms the core of the situation of Henry IV,
Part I. In that play, we meet Hal, the Prince of Wales and the future
Henry V, who has been leading a wild, undisciplined life which greatly
troubles his father. Among those encouraging Hal's dissolute ways is Sir
John Falstaff, one of the greatest of all comic creations. Hal promises to

reform, and at the battle of Shrewsbury kills Hotspur—a leader of the opposing forces—in single combat. The army of Henry IV wins the battle as well, but rebellions continue to trouble his reign in *Henry IV, Part II*. By the time Hal's father dies and he becomes Henry V, he has repudiated his old way of life, and at his coronation he rejects Falstaff as well, in lines Olivier has inserted as a voice-over during the scene depicting Falstaff's death:

> I know thee not, old man. Fall to thy prayers.
> How ill white hairs become a fool and jester!
> I have long dreamed of such a kind of man,
> So surfeit-swelled, so old, and so profane,
> But being awaked, I do despise my dream. . . .
> Presume not that I am the thing I was,
> For God doth know, so shall the world perceive,
> That I have turned away my former self.
> So will I those that kept me company. (Act V, scene v)

In the Epilogue, Shakespeare promises to "continue the story, with Sir John in it," but as we see in *Henry V* he changed his mind, perhaps because he found that the figure of Falstaff would be too dominant or distracting in a play about the monarch who came to seem to later generations of the English people as—in the words of the Chorus in *Henry V*—"the mirror of all Christian kings." (Act II)

On the Film

Henry V (1944) is widely regarded as the first truly successful adaptation of a Shakespeare play for the movies, and many people regard it as still unsurpassed. Upon its American release in 1946, Olivier received a special Academy Award for his work as producer, director, and actor, and he also received the New York Film Critics Award as the best actor for that year.

The idea for the film began with a proposal in the late 1930s by Dallas Bower that a production of the play be undertaken for British television, then in its infancy. Nothing came of that plan, nor of talks Bower had with Olivier about a possible film that would fit the patriotic mood of an England in the midst of World War II, until the rights to a treatment Bower had devised were bought by Filipo Del Giudice, who was then head of Two Cities Films and who urged Olivier to take on the project.

Even by then, many people regarded Laurence Olivier (b. 1907) as perhaps the greatest Shakespearean actor of the century. He was a movie star as well, having been in such American films as *Wuthering Heights* (1939, as Heathcliff) and *Rebecca* (1940), although his chief interest was and has remained the theater. Nevertheless, he has also directed and starred in two other major Shakespeare films: **Hamlet* (1948) and *Richard III* (1955). He had already played Orlando in Paul Czinner's film of *As You Like It* (1936); and a film of his stage performance in *Othello* for the National Theatre was made in 1965. He has directed only one film aside from the three adaptations of Shakespeare: *The Prince and the Showgirl* (1957), which co-starred Marilyn Monroe, unless we also count his *Three Sisters* (1970), a film record of his production of Chekhov's play. Other major film roles include those in *The Entertainer* (1960) and *Sleuth* (1972). He became Sir Laurence Olivier in 1947 and Lord Olivier in 1971.

Olivier offered the film of *Henry V* to several directors, including William Wyler, who had directed him in *Wuthering Heights* and who, it is said, first convinced him that movies could be taken seriously. It was only after they had turned him down that he decided to take on the job himself. He wrote his own adaptation with Reginald Beck, who also edited the film. (Bower became the associate producer.) Beck and Olivier worked on the script with Alan Dent, a drama critic with a special interest in Shakespeare, who served as "text editor." Olivier, Beck, and Dent worked together again on *Hamlet*. The shooting of *Henry V* faced numerous obstacles created by wartime conditions; because of numerous aircraft in England, for example, the outdoor battle scenes were shot in neutral Ireland.

Henry V was one of the first films for which Robert Krasker directed the photography, and his first film in color; he later won an Academy Award for **The Third Man* (1949) and also photographed Castellani's *Romeo and Juliet* (1954), Ustinov's *Billy Budd* (1962), and Wyler's *The Collector* (1965). The camera was operated by Jack Hildyard, who later became a director of photography, receiving an Academy Award for *The Bridge on the River Kwai* (1957).

The music was by William Walton, whose other film scores include those for *Hamlet* and *Richard III*. Others who also worked on *Hamlet* include art director Paul Sheriff and his assistant Carmen Dillon, and costume designer Roger Furse, here assisted by Margaret Furse.

Other credits: assistant director, Vincent Permane; special effects, Percy Day; sound, John Dennis and Desmond Dew; make-up, Tony Sforzini.

Leslie Banks, who played the Chorus, had appeared in *The Most Dangerous Game* (1932) and Hitchcock's first version of *The Man Who Knew Too Much* (1934). Robert Newton (Pistol) played Bill Sykes in Lean's *Oliver Twist* (1948) but is most remembered for his role of Long John Silver in *Treasure Island* (1950).

Leo Genn (the Constable of France) has also been in *The Snake Pit* (1948) and *Moby Dick* (1956). Renee Asherson (Katharine) came from a background in theater. Harcourt Williams (King Charles VI of France) was later the Chief Player in *Hamlet*. Felix Aylmer (the Archbishop of Canterbury) had acted with Olivier in *As You Like It* and played Polonius in *Hamlet*. Freda Jackson (Mistress Quickly) played Mrs. Gargery in Lean's **Great Expectations* (1946). The role of Falstaff, who of course does not appear in the play but is shown in the film, went to George Robey, a famous music-hall comedian. The Dauphin was played by Max Adrian, a stage actor whose other films include *The Pickwick Papers* (1953) and *The Devils* (1971). Robert Helpmann (the Bishop of Ely) is a ballet dancer whose most famous films are *The Red Shoes* (1948) and *Tales of Hoffman* (1950).

Other members of the cast: Esmond Knight (Bernardo in *Hamlet*) as Fluellen; Ralph Truman as Montjoy, the French Herald; Michael Shepley as Gower; John Laurie as Jamy; Niall MacGinnis as Macmorris; Jimmy Hanley as Michael Williams; Michael Warre as Gloucester; Nicholas Hannen as Exeter; Griffith Jones as Salisbury; Gerald Case as Westmoreland; Morland Graham as Erpingham; Brian Nissen as Court; Frederick Cooper as Nym; Roy Emerton as Bardolph; Ivy St. Helier as Lady Alice; Janet Burnell as Queen Isabel of France; Valentine Dyall as Burgundy; Russell Thorndike as Bourbon; Francis Lister as Orleans; and George Cole as the Boy.

Running time: 137 minutes. Distributors include: Audio Brandon; Budget; Twyman; Walter Reade.

Historical Background

Henry V (1387–1422) acceded to the throne in 1413; the legends of his profligate youth that came down to Shakespeare's time may have had little basis in truth. Taking advantage of disunity in France, he invaded that country in 1415. The town of Harfleur fell in September, but at the cost of about half of Henry's men. Nevertheless, against overwhelming odds (the French had from 20,000 to 30,000 men, mostly in heavy armor, to Henry's 6,000, most of them archers), the English were victorious at the battle of Agincourt in October. The French probably lost between 7,000 and 10,000 men; Shakespeare gives the loss of Englishmen at only twenty-nine, but even historical estimates rarely go above 500.

Shakespeare treats Agincourt as the culminating battle, but campaigns lasted until 1420 and the signing of the Treaty of Troyes and the marriage of Henry and Katharine, the daughter of King Charles VI and Isabel of France. Even then, wars continued against the dauphin. Henry died in 1422, succeeded by his son, Henry VI, whose disastrous reign is predicted by the Chorus at the end of the play (in a passage left out of the film).

TOPICS TO THINK ABOUT

1. James Agee, in his review for *Time:*

The movies have produced one of their rare great works of art. . . .
   Henry V is one of the great experiences in the history of motion pictures. It is not, to be sure, the greatest: the creation of new dramatic poetry is more important than the recreation of old. For such new poetry, movies offer the richest opportunity since Shakespeare's time, and some of them have made inspired use of the chance. But *Henry V* is a major achievement—this perfect marriage of great dramatic poetry with the greatest contemporary medium for expressing it.

2. At the start of the film, a crane shot takes us from an aerial view of London (a large model, fifty by seventy feet, based on a seventeenth-century map by J. C. Visscher), down to the Globe—the wooden O—where we eventually hear the words of the Chorus:

> Can this cockpit hold
> The vasty fields of France? Or may we cram
> Within this wooden O the very casques
> That did affright the air at Agincourt? . . .
> On your imaginary forces work. (Act I)

In the play, the Chorus seems in part defensive and in part proud or even boastful, recognizing that we cannot be shown scenes which are impossible to reproduce on a stage—but that we shall "see" them anyway:

>Thus with imagined wing our swift scene flies,
>In motion of no less celerity
>Than that of thought. . . .
>Work, work your thoughts, and therein see a siege: . . .
>   . . . Still be kind,
>And eke out our performance with your mind. (Act III)

What is the effect of our hearing these words in a film which then goes on actually to *show* us depictions of the scenes? Is the effect a celebration of the art of film, or perhaps somehow the reverse?

 3. In either the play or the film, does the Chorus come to seem like a "narrator" of sorts? In the film, does he seem more like a narrator once we no longer see him but only hear his words in a voice-over? (See the discussion of narration in chapter 2, and of voice-overs in chapter 3, page 58.)

 4. A major innovation of this film is to treat the soliloquies as, basically, interior monologues. Voice-overs carry the words for a "silent" character, except when someone suddenly speaks a thought aloud, giving the words thus uttered a special emphasis or significance. (See the discussion in chapter 3, pages 57–58, of the depiction of the interior monologue—and of mental states in general—in film and written literature.)

 5. What are the functions of the framing device in the film, by which the scenes in the Globe give way to those in the "real" world, only to have us return at the end?

 6. In the film, how "real" is the world we see outside the Globe? Most of it of course is by no means realisitically *depicted*. Indeed, the locations are clearly, even ostentatiously, stylized, with painted backdrops and flattened perspectives, until the major thrust into a naturalistic world for the battle scenes. But after that we return, by stages, through a theatrical-cinematic world, finally back to the Globe and its totally theatrical production (a "totally theatrical production" which, to be sure, we are shown cinematically).

 7. There has been a great deal of disagreement about the wisdom of this mixture of styles. According to the entry on *Henry V* in the *Oxford Companion to Film,* for example, "stylization and naturalism are uneasily mated." In contrast, Siegfried Kracauer asserts in *Theory of Film* that "the whole arrangement does credit to Olivier's film sense," while William Bayer writes in *The Great Movies:*

The effect is something like a dream, as if we have become so wrapped up in the performance of a play upon the stage that our minds have been stolen into a world where fantasy becomes reality; and then, as the dream recedes, Olivier gently leads us back to our seats. It is an amazing accomplishment, something never quite done before.

What is your own view: is the film an unfortunate hodgepodge or a masterful counterpoint of approaches—or something in between?

8. Ernest Lindgren: *"Henry V* was a very fine filmed version of the play, but . . . what is required is poetry *of* the film, instead of poetry *in* the film." (*The Art of the Film*)

9. Does *Henry V* succeed as a film, as distinct from what Richard Griffith calls a "photographed play"?:

Laurence Olivier's *Henry V* (1944) was probably the first instance of a legitimately photographed play, inasmuch as its structure was designed constantly to remind the spectator of the fact that it was a play and not a film. When the action moved out of the Globe Theatre, it moved into fairyland, not actuality, and thus avoided that conflict between poetic speech and three-dimensional reality that has set all previous versions of Shakespeare at nought. (In "The Film Since Then," in Paul Rotha, *The Film Till Now*)

10. If you know **The Cabinet of Dr. Caligari* (1920), compare and contrast its use of obviously painted backdrops to that of *Henry V*.

11. Do you discern any shifts in the acting styles—Olivier's in particular—comparable to the various visual, cinematic, and theatrical styles in the different parts of the film?

12. The film of *Henry V* leaves out a great many lines of the play, but since almost all productions of Shakespeare, stage or screen, are abridgments, the major question is not so much whether any deletions are justified as whether the particular cuts or other changes seem proper and effective. Do they in this instance? How do they affect how we react to the people and events we see? Is the resulting adaptation "faithful" to Shakespeare's original play? How essential is it that it should be?

13. In his war, Henry is the underdog; is he nevertheless also the aggressor and even an imperialist? How much are we affected by our own historical perspective as we see or read Shakespeare's play?

Does Olivier's interpretation of the play and especially of its hero make both seem more "modern"?

14. Are deletions, performances, and the camera used to make Olivier's Henry more sympathetic to a modern audience than Shakespeare's Henry? If so, are the manipulations proper, or perhaps even inevitable? Or do they strike you as distortions?

15. Mark Van Doren, in *Shakespeare* (on the play, not the film):

> The figure whom he has groomed to be the ideal English king, all plumes and smiles and decorated courage, collapses here into a mere good fellow, a hearty undergraduate with enormous initials on his chest. The reasons must be that Shakespeare has little interest in the ideal English king. He has done what rhetoric could do to give us a young heart whole in honor, but his imagination has already sped forward to Brutus and Hamlet: to a kind of hero who is no less honorable than Henry but who will tread on thorns as he takes the path of duty—itself unclear, and crossed by other paths of no man's making. Henry is Shakespeare's last attempt at the great man who is also simple. Henceforth he will show greatness as either perplexing or perplexed; and Hamlet will be both.

If Van Doren is correct, is Olivier's Henry even less complex than Shakespeare's? Or has Olivier managed to distill the essence of "the ideal English king" in a convincing, stirring way?

16. Harry M. Geduld analyzes the *mise en scène* of the shots of Henry courting Katharine:

> The movements of Henry and Katharine in relation to the stylized setting effectively underscore the scene's dramatic developments. Thus, when Henry begins his wooing, the couple appear divided, in different panels—that is, an ornamental post stands between them. As Henry becomes more ardent, he moves into Katharine's panel. After Henry has offended Katharine by kissing her hand, the princess and Lady Alice retreat from him until they stand framed in separate windows; Henry joins them to stand in a third window so that the group forms an ornamental triptych rather than a natural arrangement. Then, Henry takes Katharine's hand, leads her away from the windows and panels that suggest their division and kisses her again, this time in the open set where nothing can separate them. (*Filmguide to Henry V*)

17. Keep alert to the ways in which low-angle, high-angle, and eye-level shots determine our perspectives on certain figures, notably of Henry at various points in the film.

18. What are the effects of the use of point of view and camera motion as Henry walks among the troops the night before the battle?

19. For the most part, there is little use of striking montage in this film, and Olivier relies more heavily on camera movement and *mise en scène* to achieve his desired effects. But a major exception is the sequence of the battle of Agincourt—which, incidentally, was greatly influenced by Eisenstein's editing and use of music in the battle sequence in *Alexander Nevsky* (1938).

20. "There is more cinema, and great cinema at that, in *Henry V* alone than in 90 percent of original scripts." (André Bazin, *What Is Cinema?*)

Further Readings

BARKER, FELIX. *The Oliviers.* Philadelphia: Lippincott, 1953.

ECKERT, CHARLES W., ed. *Focus on Shakespearean Films.* Englewood Cliffs, N.J.: Prentice-Hall, 1972. Reprinted essays and reviews of various critics on fourteen films.

GEDULD, HARRY M. *Filmguide to Henry V.* Bloomington: Indiana University Press, 1973. The most detailed analysis of the film, and an excellent one.

HUTTON, C. CLAYTON. *The Making of Henry V.* London: Ernest J. Day, 1945.

JORGENS, JACK J. *Shakespeare on Film.* Bloomington: Indiana University Press, 1977. A good, judicious study.

Literature/Film Quarterly. Occasionally has a special issue entirely devoted to "Shakespeare on Film"; see Fall 1973, Spring 1976, Fall 1977.

MANVELL, ROGER. *Shakespeare and the Film.* New York: Praeger, 1971. Helpful. Dedicated to Olivier.

MORRIS, PETER. *Shakespeare on Film: An Index to William Shakespeare's Plays on Film.* Ottawa: Canadian Film Institute, 1972. A chronological, annotated list, 1929–71.

OLIVIER, LAURENCE, and REGINALD BECK. *Screenplay for Henry V.* In *Film Scripts One.* Eds. George P. Garrett, O. B. Hardison, Jr., and Jane R. Gelfman. New York: Appleton-Century-Crofts, 1971.

VAN DOREN, MARK. *Shakespeare.* Garden City, N.Y.: Anchor, 1954.

WHITEHEAD, PETER, and ROBIN BEAN, eds. *Olivier-Shakespeare.* London: Lorrimer, 1966.

GREAT EXPECTATIONS

BACKGROUND

On the Novel

Great Expectations was published as a book in 1861, after having appeared as a serial starting the previous year. It was a late work by one of the most important English novelists of all time, and certainly the most popular: Charles Dickens (1812–1870).

Dickens was born to a middle-class but financially troubled family (his father formed a model for the plucky but hapless Mr. Micawber of the partially autobiographical *David Copperfield*); at an early age his education was interrupted while he was employed in a factory, and for a time the family even lived with the father in debtors' prison. Dickens became a clerk while an adolescent, and he eventually began to publish prose sketches in various magazines: one group of them, *The Pickwick Papers* (published as a book in 1837) was hugely successful, and from then on he was enormously popular. Among his most well-known works are: *Oliver Twist* (1838), *A Christmas Carol* (1843), *Dombey and Son* (1848), *David Copperfield* (1850), *Bleak House* (1852), *Hard Times* (1854), *A Tale of Two Cities* (1859), *Our Mutual Friend* (1865), and *The Mystery of Edwin Drood*, which he left unfinished at his death in 1870.

On the Film

All the Dickens works mentioned above have been adapted for films, some of them many times. Indeed, probably no other novelist in history has written so many works which have been made into so many movies—in Dickens' case, over seventy films, thirteen of them adaptations of *Oliver Twist* alone. (The runners up are *A Christmas Carol* with ten and *David Copperfield* with seven.)

The most widely respected Dickens adaptation of all is the one we are considering here: David Lean's 1946 *Great Expectations*. But there have been at least five other film versions of that novel. Two of them were silent: an American film of 1917 starring Jack Pickford as Pip, and a Danish one of 1921 directed by A. W. Sandberg. The first sound version was an American one, again, directed by Stuart Walker and starring Phillips Holmes as Pip, Jane Wyatt as Estella, and Henry Hull as

Magwitch. The first British version was Lean's. In 1971, a Swiss production was directed by Leopold H. Ginner, and in 1974 another British
adaptation was directed by Joseph Hardy, starring Michael York as Pip,
Sarah Miles as Estella, James Mason as Magwitch, and Margaret
Leighton as Miss Havisham; it was released as a theatrical motion picture
in Europe but appeared only as a television movie in the United States,
although it is now available for rental (from Swank: running time, 90
minutes).

   David Lean (b. 1908) had a strict upbringing as a boy, during which
he was not permitted to go to the movies; nevertheless, he had his first
job at a studio at the age of nineteen. He went through various technical
jobs and then became a widely respected film editor (one of his most
important and creative asuignments was *Pygmalion,* 1938). He served as
co-director with Noel Coward on *In Which We Serve* (1942), and he has
been a director ever since. His film of Coward's script for *Brief Encounter*
(1945) was widely praised. Then came two Dickens projects, for both of
which Lean collaborated on the screenplay: *Great Expectations* in 1946

and *Oliver Twist* in 1948. Other notable films since then have been *The Bridge on the River Kwai* (1957), *Lawrence of Arabia* (1962), *Dr. Zhivago* (1965), and *Ryan's Daughter* (1970). Lean makes few films, devoting years of careful preparation to each one. Alec Guinness has testified that Lean is "easily the most meticulous artist in motion pictures, the most painstaking in every department" (quoted in Gerald Pratley, *The Cinema of David Lean*).

In *Great Expectations,* Lean used again many of the talented people who had worked with him during the war on *In Which We Serve.* Ronald Neame, who had done the photography for it, now worked as the producer and as co-author of the screenplay; he later became a director himself, his films including *Tunes of Glory* (1960), *Scrooge* (1970; a musical version of *A Christmas Carol*), and *The Poseidon Adventure* (1972).

The executive producer, Anthony Havelock-Allan, has been credited with contributing to the screenplay as well. He had been associate producer for *In Which We Serve,* on which Guy Green, the cinematographer, had also worked; Green received an Academy Award for *Great Expectations.* Green's other films include *Oliver Twist, The Mark* (1960), and *The Magus* (1968).

Also receiving Academy Awards for this film were Wilfred Shingleton for set decoration and John Bryan for art direction; Bryan later became a producer as well, for example of *The Horse's Mouth* (1958).

Other credits: editor, Jack Harris; costumes, Sophia Harris and Margaret Furse; music, Walter Goehr; sound, Stanley Lambourne; assistant director, George Pollock (later a director, for example of *Murder She Said,* 1963).

The adult Pip was John Mills, who had been in films since the early 1930s but first attracted wide attention in *In Which We Serve;* he has had a long career and been in many films, directing one (*Sky West and Crooked,* 1966). He received an Academy Award for his supporting role in Lean's *Ryan's Daughter.* Pip as a child was Anthony Wager, who has since worked in Australian television.

Valerie Hobson played the adult Estella; her other films include *The Bride of Frankenstein* (1935) and *Kind Hearts and Coronets* (1949). Jean Simmons (the child Estella) went on to play Ophelia in Olivier's **Hamlet* (1948) and to star in many other films, including *The Robe* (1953), *Guys and Dolls* (1955) and *Elmer Gantry* (1960).

Herbert Pocket was Alec Guinness, one of the most impressively versatile actors in the history of British films. He followed this role with that of Fagin in Lean's *Oliver Twist,* his first part to use the elaborate facial disguises that for a time became something of a trademark. He received an Academy Award for his role in Lean's *The Bridge on the River Kwai;* his films since then have included *Lawrence of Arabia, Dr. Zhivago,* and *Star Wars* (1977). He wrote the script for his role in *The Horse's Mouth* (1958). Earlier, he had written a play based on *Great Expectations* (1938), in which he and Martita Hunt played Pocket and Miss Havisham, as they then did in the film. Hunt had been in films since the 1930s; her later movies include *Anastasia* (1959). Finlay Currie was in his late sixties when he played Magwitch, yet two decades later he was still appearing in films such as *Bunny Lake Is Missing* (1965).

Other members of the cast: Bernard Miles as Joe Gargery; Francis L. Sullivan as Jaggers (repeating the role he played in the 1934 American adaptation); Ivor Bernard as Wemmick; Freda Jackson (Mistress Quickly in Olivier's **Henry V,* 1944) as Mrs. Gargery; Torin Thatcher as Bentley Drummle; Eileen Erskine as Biddy; Hay Petrie as Uncle Pumblechook; George Hayes as Compeyson; Richard George as the Sergeant; Everly Gregg as Sarah Pocket; John Burch and Grace Denbigh-Russell as Mr. and Mrs. Wopsle; and O. B. Clarence as the Aged Parent.

Running time: 118 minutes. Distributors include: Audio Brandon; Budget; Twyman; University of California Extension Media Center; Walter Reade.

TOPICS TO THINK ABOUT

1. *Great Expectations* is generally regarded as one of the two or three finest novels by a writer who is frequently compared to Shakespeare as a creator of vivid and complex worlds and characters. The comparison is so often made in terms of the highest praise that it is perhaps worthwhile to quote what the young James Joyce wrote in 1912 (for an examination he was taking), before he had published any of his own novels:

> The influence which Dickens has exercised on the English language (second perhaps to that of Shakespeare alone) depends to a large extent on the popular character of his work. Examined from the standpoint of literary art or even from that of literary craftsmanship he hardly deserves a place among the highest. The form he chose to write in, diffuse, overloaded with minute and often irrelevant observation, carefully relieved at regular intervals by the

unfailing humorous note, is not the form of the novel which can carry the greatest conviction. (*James Joyce in Padua*)

Is such criticism accurate? Does it seem to you relevant? How could one expand upon it? How might a defender of Dickens counter it? (Incidentally, if you know any of Joyce's novels, you may wish to consider them in light of his description of Dickens' work.)

2. Perhaps appropriately (given the frequency of the comparison between Dickens and Shakespeare), this film is often compared to the best adaptations of Shakespeare's plays. When it appeared, a number of reviewers observed that, in the words of James Agee, "*Great Expectations* does for Dickens about what *Henry V* did for Shakespeare. That is, it indicates a sound method for translating him from print to film." But Agee moderated his praise by continuing: "The method is not one of the most exciting that could be imagined, nor in its own terms is it used as excitingly as could be imagined; but the film is almost never less than graceful, tasteful, and intelligent, and some of it is better than that."

3. Lean spoke, during an interview with Gerald Pratley, about "this writing of a film script of these great big novels": "Years and years ago I did two Dickens films: one, *Great Expectations;* and the other, *Oliver Twist.* And people who hadn't read the book for some time thought they were seeing the book. In fact, they weren't. They were seeing, as it were, a synopsis of the book."

How good is the synopsis in this case? By definition, a synopsis must leave things out. What is left out here that seems to you of special significance?

4. Lean has called Dickens "the perfect screenwriter," asserting especially that his "dialogue is perfect for the screen." A few years before the appearance of this film, the Russian director and film theorist Sergei M. Eisenstein wrote an essay, "Dickens, Griffith, and the Film Today," which is quoted in important contexts in chapter 3 of the present volume. Eisenstein claims that "Dickens's nearness to the characteristics of cinema in method, style, and especially in viewpoint and exposition, is indeed amazing." Of what in particular might Eisenstein be thinking? (You may of course wish to go to his essay itself to find out!)

5. Eisenstein also quotes someone who remembered D. W. Griffith once proposing an idea for a sequence of scenes that led to his being asked, "How can you tell a story jumping about like that?" Griffith asked in return, "Well, . . . doesn't Dickens write that way?" To the reply, "Yes, but that's Dickens; that's novel writing; that's different," Griffith countered, "Oh, not so much, these are picture stories; not so different."

Eisenstein adds that, "to speak quite frankly, all astonishment on this subject and the apparent unexpectedness of such statements can be ascribed only to our—ignorance of Dickens."

6. Dramatic versions of Dickens' novels were produced during his lifetime. And late in his career—but several years before he wrote *Great Expectations*—he began giving hugely successful dramatic readings of his own works. Do you detect any possible ways in which *Great Expectations* might have been influenced by those facts?

7. According to the writer J. B. Priestley, "to understand what Dickens meant to his time, we have to forget writers altogether and to remember a man who achieved world fame in a different medium—Charles Chaplin. In the breadth and scope of his appeal, in his mixture of farce and pathos, even though he had not the depth of Dickens's genius, Chaplin of all twentieth-century figures comes nearest to Dickens." ("The Great Inimitable")

8. We have seen Dickens' work compared to both Griffith and Chaplin, and at one time or another numerous other directors, including such disparate ones as Eisenstein, Fellini, Welles, Bergman, and Truffaut, have been called "Dickensian." In cinematic terms (or, indeed, in novelistic ones), what might such an epithet mean? If you were willing to use it yourself, to which filmmaker would you apply it, and what would *you* mean by it?

9. Pip of course narrates both the novel and the film (see the discussions of point of view in written literature and in film in chapters 1 and 2, pages 9–11 and 38–41). Relatively how much importance does Pip's being the narrator have in each version? How reliable does he seem? How much is that question connected to how honest and truthful he is, and how much is it not?

Does Lean find visual cinematic equivalents for the constantly subjective viewpoint of the novel? If so, do they work?

10. In a letter to John Forster in October, 1860, Dickens mentioned that he was beginning a new book: "The name is, GREAT EXPECTATIONS. I think a good name?"

Others have agreed. Indeed, the contemporary American novelist John Irving has observed, "That title, 'Great Expectations,' is what every novelist wishes was still an available title. 'The Great Gatsby' could more simply have been called 'Great Expectations'; and 'The Sun Also Rises' and 'Jacob's Room' and 'To the Lighthouse,' 'The Mayor of Casterbridge,' 'Moby Dick' and 'The Good Soldier'—all great expectations. I'm just beginning work on another novel, whose working title is 'Great Expectations.' " (*The New York Times Book Review,* June 4, 1978)

11. At least in part, obviously, the title is "ironic." Critics use the term *irony* to mean numerous things, but there are three especially prominent traditional usages.

Verbal irony refers to language with dual meanings, when the actual statement is undercut or even negated by what is suggested, or in which the explicit statement employs hyperbole or understatement—or, perhaps, an uncertain mixture of both, as can be argued is present in the title *Great Expectations.* Similarly, affirmation and negation complicate our responses to Antony's reiterations in Shakespeare's *Julius Caesar* that "Brutus is an honorable man."

Dramatic irony, or *irony of situation,* occurs when a reader or an audience perceives that the truth is extraordinarily different from what it seems to be to fictional characters. The most famous example is that of Oedipus, who insists on searching out the truth of a crime only to discover that he himself is guilty of it, as well as of crimes he had not imagined.

Irony of fate produces paradoxical or even seemingly perverse twists in the expectations or situations of the characters; it is thereby clearly allied to dramatic irony—as suggested by the example of Oedipus above—but need not be totally identified with it. In *Pride and Prejudice,* Elizabeth realizes she loves Darcy only after she has rejected his proposal; in *Citizen Kane,* it is "Rosebud" that Kane recalls on his deathbed; in *Psycho,* the $40,000 turns out to seem an irrelevance. Here in *Great Expectations,* Pip believes that his benefactor is Miss Havisham, when in effect her intention is to make his life one of misery; and the act which Pip regards as one of his rare selfless deeds—his setting Pocket up in business—turns out to be his financial salvation.

12. Pip: "All other swindlers upon earth are nothing to the self-swindlers, and with such pretences did I cheat myself. Surely a curious thing." (Chapter 28)

13. When the facts about Magwitch's role in his life come out, what else does Pip learn—about his situation, his expectations, his life, other people, and himself? What has he yet to learn?

14. In the novel and the film, as Pip's knowlege of the true facts comes to seem more in line with reality, *our* perceptions also change. What happens for example to our view of him, his life, and his character—and to our perspectives on the people whom we have been seeing, all along, through his eyes, such as Estella, Miss Havisham, Jaggers, and Magwitch?

15. "Everybody should know his own business," asserts Jaggers, and then he repeats, "every man ought to know his own business best"; and still again he says, in regard to Miss Havisham, that *"she* ought to know her own business best." (Chapter 51)

Consider the view of society and human existence implied here; presumably, it is not easy to be wholly "for" or "against" Jaggers' insistent opinion. Toward which direction does the novel and the film seem to lean? Consider Jaggers' life and career as an example, or those of Miss Havisham, Estella, Magwitch, and Pip.

16. Examine the roles allotted to males and females, and the ways those roles seem to be defined and determined, in the novel and the film.

17. Miss Havisham, to Pip: "Until you spoke to her [Estella] the other day, and until I saw in you a looking-glass that showed me what I once felt myself, I did not know what I had done. What have I done! What have I done!" (Chapter 49)

How might you answer this question that has no question mark?

18. George Orwell, in "Charles Dickens":

Psychologically the latter part of *Great Expectations* is about the best thing Dickens ever did; throughout this part of the book one feels "Yes, that is just how Pip would have behaved." But the point is that in the matter of Magwitch, Dickens identifies with Pip, and his attitude is at bottom snobbish. The result is that Magwitch belongs to the same queer class of characters as Falstaff and, probably, Don Quixote—characters who are more pathetic than the author intended.

19. George Bernard Shaw, in his Foreword to an edition of *Great Expectations:* "Dickens never regarded himself as a revolutionist, though he certainly was one."

Edgar Johnson, in *Charles Dickens: His Tragedy and Triumph:*

There is a layer of criticism . . . in *Great Expectations* still deeper than . . . personal triumph over false social values. It pierces to the very core of the leisure-class ideal that lurks in the heart of a pecuniary society. This is symbolized in Pip's dream of becoming a gentleman living in decorative grandeur on money he has done nothing to earn, supported entirely by the labors of others. It was the dream of nineteenth-century society, willing to base its hopes of comfort and ostentation on the toil of the laboring classes. Pip's "great expectations" were the great expectations of Victorian society, visions of a parasitic opulence of future wealth and glory, a materialistic paradise of walnut, plush, gilt mirrors, and heavy dinners.

Do you agree that social and political implications are important in the novel? Do they appear in the film?

20. Lean has been quoted as saying of *Great Expectations* that "to a certain extent we had a fantasy on our hands. The characters were larger and more highly colored than in life: and we deliberately kept them that way, because it was part of our intention to make a fairy tale." (*The New York Times,* June 29, 1947)

Is the intention successfully carried out? If so, is the film thereby "faithful" to the novel?

A. L. Zambrano argues that it is: "What Lean saw in *Great Expectations* was the fanciful fairy tale quality prevalent in Victorian pantomimes which Dickens had drawn on in creating his novel. Dickens took traditional elements like the fairy godmother, the beautiful princess who must be won, and the ogre who impedes the way, and through a transformation of their familiar roles yoked them to Pip's fanciful interpretations of his experience." (*Dickens and Film*)

21. George Bernard Shaw, on the novel: "Its beginning is unhappy; its middle is unhappy; and the conventional happy ending is an outrage on it."

22. As it turns out, Dickens' original ending was quite different, but he was persuaded by a friend (the novelist Edward Bulwer Lytton) to change it. The original version ends with a chance encounter in London between Pip and Estella, who has remarried after Drummle's death. The meeting is cordial but brief, and the last words of the novel are: "I was very glad afterwards to have had the interview; for in her face and in her voice, and in her touch, she gave me the assurance, that suffering had been stronger than Miss Havisham's teaching, and had given her a heart to understand what my heart used to be."

Was Dickens wise to make the change, or should he have kept the first version?

23. Still another ending to the story of Pip and Estella is the one in the film. What is your reaction to the climactic scene in Miss Havisham's home? It has sometimes been accused of being too "melodramatic." Do you agree, or is it effective?

24. "And we're a very, very young art. I'm flattered that you say it's an art. I think it's coming up that way a little . . . pieces of certain films are, I suppose, art, but I think we've got quite a way to go. We're a very young toddler at the moment." (Lean, interview with Gerald Pratley)

Further Readings

DICKENS, CHARLES. *Great Expectations.* There are many editions, of course. Two convenient ones which print both versions of the ending are those published by New American Library (with an afterword by Angus Wilson: New York, 1963) and Penguin (ed. Angus Calder: Baltimore, 1965).

DYSON, A. E. *The Inimitable Dickens: A Reading of the Novels.* London: Macmillan, 1970.

EISENSTEIN, SERGEI M. "Dickens, Griffith, and the Film Today." In his *Film Form: Essays in Film Theory.* Ed. and trans. Jay Leyda. New York: Harcourt Brace Jovanovich, 1949. Frequently reprinted in anthologies of film criticism.

JOHNSON, EDGAR. *Charles Dickens: His Tragedy and Triumph.* 2 vols. New York: Simon and Schuster, 1952. The major biography, now also available in a one-volume version (New York: Viking, 1977).

MILLER, J. HILLIS. *Charles Dickens: The World of His Novels.* Cambridge, Mass.: Harvard University Press, 1958.

ORWELL, GEORGE. "Charles Dickens." In his *An Age Like This, 1920–1940.* Vol. I of *The Collected Essays, Journalism and Letters of George Orwell.* Ed. Sonia Orwell and Ian Angus. New York: Harcourt Brace Jovanovich, 1968, pp. 413–60.

PRATLEY, GERALD. *The Cinema of David Lean.* South Brunswick, N.J.: A. S. Barnes, 1974.

———. "David Lean." In *Interviews with Film Directors.* Ed. Andrew Sarris. New York: Avon, 1969, pp. 316–21. Conducted in 1965 for the Canadian Broadcasting Company.

TOMLIN, E. W. F., ed. *Charles Dickens 1812–1870: A Centennial Volume.* New York: Simon and Schuster, 1970. Includes J. B. Priestley's "The Great Inimitable," quoted above, and Harry Stone's "The Genesis of a Novel: *Great Expectations.*"

WALL, STEPHEN, ed. *Charles Dickens: A Critical Anthology.* Baltimore: Penguin, 1970. Includes letters from Dickens, early reviews, and critical essays.

ZAMBRANO, A. L. *Dickens and Film.* New York: Gordon, 1977. Carefully researched, and occasionally quotes from unpublished or not easily available sources.

HAMLET

BACKGROUND

On the Play

More has been written about William Shakespeare (1564–1616) than about any other author in history, and more about *Hamlet* than any of Shakespeare's other works. The play is fascinating for any number of reasons, not the least of which are its ability to arouse dispute and its tendency to yield interpretations which often do not so much reveal complete solutions as suggest further questions and the need for more profound and complex answers. And while of course our major reasons for interest in Shakespeare himself center on his works and a desire to know more about the genius who produced them, another is probably our sense of mystery arising from our knowing so little about him— although in fact we know more than many people assume. Nevertheless, aside from his having been born in Stratford-upon-Avon, having married in 1582 Ann Hathaway (a woman eight years older than he), and having become an actor in London by the early 1590s, facts are especially scarce in regard to his life before his thirties.

Hamlet was probably written around 1600 or 1601. It seems to have been based on a now lost older play (the so-called *Ur-Hamlet,* dating back at least to the 1580s), and perhaps on a French translation of the Latin *Historia Danica* by the Danish historian of the twelfth to thirteenth centuries, Saxo Grammaticus. We know that the play was produced by 1602.

On the Film

Laurence Olivier (b. 1907) followed the success of **Henry V* with a very different Shakespearean project—*Hamlet* (1948), which received the International Grand Prize at the Venice Film Festival and the Academy Award for best picture and best actor. For many people, it solidified Olivier's standing as the foremost Shakespearean actor, producer, and director of his time.

Olivier had acted the role of Orlando in Paul Czinner's film of *As You Like It* (1936) and had starred in films throughout the thirties, but his first memorable roles were those in *Wuthering Heights* (1939, as Heathcliff), *Rebecca,* and *Pride and Prejudice* (both 1940). All along, he was also

FIG. 22. The Museum of Modern Art/Film Stills Archive. Courtesy Two Cities.

active in the theater, which has always been his primary interest (he served as director of the National Theatre from 1963 to 1973). *Henry V* was his first film as a director, and *Hamlet* his second. His only other two—unless one counts the film record of his production of Chekhov's play *Three Sisters* (1970)—were another Shakespeare film, *Richard III* (1955), and *The Prince and the Showgirl* (1957), in which he co-starred with Marilyn Monroe. He has been in many other films, including *Carrie* (1952; an adaptation of Theodore Dreiser's *Sister Carrie* in which Olivier played Hurstwood), *The Entertainer* (1960), and *Marathon Man* (1976); he also appeared in a film of his performance in a stage production of *Othello* (1965). He was knighted in 1947 and became a life peer (Lord Olivier) in 1971.

Many of the people who worked with Olivier on *Hamlet* had also been involved in the making of *Henry V*. For example, he and Alan Dent—whose credit title is "text editor"—worked together again on the screenplay. And Filipo Del Giudice was once again involved in the early stages of setting up the production. Reginald Beck, who had co-written the screenplay for *Henry V*, worked here as associate producer; he has said that his function "could best be described as technical adviser to Laurence Olivier" (in Brenda Cross, ed., *The Film Hamlet*). The assistant producer was Anthony Bushell, who also worked on Richard III; an actor as well, he has an interesting short essay in Cross's *The Film Hamlet* on selecting the cast.

Desmond Dickinson received the award for best photography at the Venice Film Festival; his other work includes *The History of Mr. Polly* (1949) and *The Importance of Being Earnest* (1952). Ray Sturgess operated the camera. The music was by William Walton, who also wrote the score for *As You Like It,* and both *Henry V* and *Richard III.*

Roger Furse, who had designed costumes for *Henry V,* received an Academy Award for his work here, and he and Carmen Dillon (the assistant art director for the earlier film) shared another one for art direction and set decoration; they also worked together later on *Richard III.* The editor (in close consultation with both Olivier and Reginald Beck) was Helga Cranston, who also edited *Richard III.*

Other credits: production manager, John Gossage; sound, John W. Mitchell and L. E. Overton; sound editor, Harry Miller; assistant director, Peter Bolton; special effects, Paul Sheriff (the art director for *Henry V*), Henry Harris, and Jack Whitehead; mime play, David Paltenghi; sword play, Denis Loraine; make-up, Tony Sforzini.

In addition to playing Hamlet, Olivier recorded the voice of the Ghost, slowing down the tape to produce an eerie effect. Gertrude was Eileen Herlie, who has also been in *Freud* (1962) and *The Seagull* (1968); although she played Olivier's mother, she was actually a dozen years younger than he. Basil Sydney (Claudius) was in *Caesar and Cleopatra* (1945), *The Man Within* (1947), and *Treasure Island* (1950).

Jean Simmons received the award for best actress at the Venice Film Festival for her portrayal of Ophelia; Olivier had chosen her after seeing her performance as the child Estella in Lean's **Great Expectations* (1946). Her many other roles include those in *Young Bess* (1953), *Guys and Dolls* (1955), and *Spartacus* and *Elmer Gantry* (both 1960).

Felix Aylmer (Polonius) was the Archbishop of Canterbury in *Henry V* (playing him rather like Polonius); he was also in *Separate Tables* (1958) and *Becket* (1964). Horatio was Norman Wooland's first film role; he later played in Castellani's *Romeo and Juliet* (1954) and Olivier's *Richard III.* Terence Morgan (Laertes) was later in such films as *They Can't Hang Me* (1955) and *The Curse of the Mummy's Tomb* (1964).

Stanley Holloway (the gravedigger) is best remembered for his performance as Mr. Doolittle in the Broadway production of *My Fair Lady,* which he repeated for the film (1964). Peter Cushing (Osric) went on to make a specialty of horror films such as *The Curse of Frankenstein* (1957) and *Tales from the Crypt* (1972), although he was also villainous in *Star Wars* (1977).

Other members of the cast: Esmond Knight (Fluellen in *Henry V*) as Bernardo; Anthony Quayle (later a prominent stage actor, also in many films) as Marcellus; Harcourt Williams (the King of France in *Henry V*) as the Chief Player; John Laurie as Francisco; Niall MacGinnis as the sea captain; and Patric Troughton and Tony Tarver as the Player King and Queen.

There have been many other film adaptations of *Hamlet* besides Olivier's; those readily available for rental in 16mm prints are:

1. Franz Peter Wirth's version in German, starring Maximilian Schell (1960). This is an interesting film, although it is inevitably marred by dubbing in the English version.

2. Grigori Kozintsev's Russian version in a translation by Boris Pasternak (author of *Dr. Zhivago*), starring Innokenti Smakhtunovski and with music by Dmitri Shostakovich (1964). Kozintsev's film has been widely admired; the English subtitles employ Shakespeare's original lines.

3. Tony Richardson's version starring Nicol Williamson (1969). Actually, this is a record of their stage production of the same year, even using most of the same sets, but it was distributed and is available as a feature film.

Running time for the Olivier film: 152 minutes. Prints are available from many distributors, including: Audio Brandon; Budget; Twyman; Walter Reade.

TOPICS TO THINK ABOUT

1. Charles Lamb, in "On the Tragedies of Shakspeare, Considered with Reference to Their Fitness for Stage Representation" (1811):

> It may seem a paradox, but I cannot help being of opinion that the plays of Shakspeare are less calculated for performance on a stage, than those of almost any other dramatist whatever. Their distinguishing excellence is a reason that they should be so. There is so much in them, which comes not under the province of acting, with which eye, and tone, and gesture, have nothing to do.

What is your reaction to Lamb's claim? From such a perspective, are Shakespeare's plays equally unsuited to the screen? More so? Less so?

2. *Hamlet* is an example of a genre that was extremely popular in Shakespeare's time, the "revenge play." Revenge plots lend themselves to embellishment, since the *basic* plot structure is fairly standard: the hero plans and presumably carries out revenge.

One mode of embellishment is the use of irony, in particular what literary critics term *irony of fate,* which involves unexpected or even perverse twists in the situations of a character or characters (see the discussion of various types of irony in the section on **Great Expectations,* Topic 11, page 152): a villain in a James Bond film who sends victims to their deaths in a pool filled with piranha will surely be dumped in that pool himself in the last reel; the Maltese falcon for which various characters have committed murder turns out to be valueless; or, perhaps, poisoned wine a villain has meant for the hero will be drunk instead by the woman for whose sake he committed his crimes in the first place—or perhaps the drink will in fact be forced down his own throat as well.

What other examples of such irony can you see in *Hamlet?*

3. Of course it is as a *tragedy*—not a revenge play—that *Hamlet* is famous. There is probably little point in asking whether that fame is justified in terms of its actually being a tragedy, since there is just about universal agreement on the fact that it is, but it may be valuable to pursue what makes it one.

The most ancient and still the most well-known and influential concept of tragedy is Aristotle's, according to which a tragedy is in the first place "an imitation of an action." That is, it is a drama (see the summary of Aristotle's concept of drama in chapter 1, page 9): it is "in the form of dramatic action, not of narrative." A tragedy depicts the downfall of a hero in an action that is "serious, complete, and of a certain magnitude," and its language is "embellished with every kind of artistic ornament." And "through pity and fear" it effects the proper "purgation" (or "catharsis") of those emotions—that is, of pity and fear.

Of course, Aristotle develops upon this basic definition. Notably, he describes the hero of a tragedy as someone who is neither perfectly virtuous nor truly evil and villainous, but rather "the character between these two extremes—that of a man who is not extraordinarily good and just, yet whose misfortune is brought about not by vice or depravity, but by some error of judgment or frailty."

4. How well do *Hamlet* the play and Hamlet its hero fit Aristotle's criteria? Keep in mind that the question is not necessarily an evaluative one. As Alexander Pope remarked in 1737, to judge Shakespeare "by Aristotle's rules, is like trying a man by the laws of one Country, who acted under those of another." But setting Aristotle and *Hamlet* off against one another may help to illuminate both.

5. There are innumerable theories of tragedy—much too many to mention—besides Aristotle's. But in order to provide at least a partial context for his, we may refer here to one that was especially influential in the first half of the twentieth century: A. C. Bradley's expansion upon the theories of the German philosopher Hegel.

According to this view, "the essentially tragic fact is the self-division and intestinal warfare of the ethical substance, not so much the war of good with evil as the war of good with good. . . . The family claims what the state refuses, love requires what honour forbids." To Bradley, when such a conflict is tragic it leads to "a division of spirit involving conflict and waste":

> And it may well be that, other things being equal (as they never are), the tragedy in which the hero is, as we say, a good man, is more tragic than that in which he is, as we say, a bad one. The more spiritual value, the more tragedy in conflict and waste. The death of Hamlet or Othello is, so far, more tragic than that of Macbeth, that of Macbeth than that of Richard.

Does this concept of tragedy seem to you a helpful or satisfactory one? Does it match or illuminate *Hamlet?*

6. What are the central conflicts in *Hamlet?*

7. In Goethe's novel *Wilhelm Meister* (1795), the story of Hamlet is described as one in which "a beautiful, pure, noble and most moral nature, without the strength of nerve which makes the hero, sinks beneath a burden which it can neither bear nor throw off."

8. In Aristotle's terms, what might Hamlet's "error of judgment or frailty" be (his so-called "tragic flaw")?

9. Olivier's film begins with his voice-over of a cut and simplified version of Hamlet's lines to Horatio while they are waiting for the Ghost:

> So oft it chances in particular men
> That [through] some vicious mole of nature in them . . .
> By the o'ergrowth of some complexion
> Oft breaking down the pales and forts of reason,
> Or by some habit [grown] too much . . .
>   . . . that these men—
> Carrying, I say, the stamp of one defect . . .
> Their virtues else—be they as pure as grace . . .

> Shall in the general censure take corruption
> From that particular fault. (Act I, Scene iv)

Then, as we see a tableau of the soldiers bearing Hamlet's body as they will at the end, Olivier says in another voice-over, "This is the tragedy of a man who could not make up his mind."

How do you react both to this interpretation of *Hamlet* and to its being announced so explicitly?

Not all viewers believe that Olivier's film and portrayal actually match that announced stress on Hamlet's indecisiveness. Do you?

10. Olivier's explicit interpretation of Hamlet as indecisive and hesitant is certainly a traditional one—and, perhaps, an especially "romantic" one, as in the quotation above from Goethe, or Samuel Taylor Coleridge's remark that in Hamlet "we see a great, an almost enormous, intellectual activity, and a proportionate aversion to real action." Yet long before that, too, Samuel Johnson had written that Hamlet "is, through the whole play, rather an instrument than an agent." Is that accurate?

11. If Hamlet delays and hesitates too long, what are the possible alternatives and how are they demonstrated? Are they those we see in Laertes ("To hell allegiance, vows to the blackest devil,/ Conscience and grace to the profoundest pit!"—IV, v) and Claudius ("That we would do/ We should do when we would . . ."—IV, vii)? What of Fortinbras, the figure who is entirely left out of the film?

12. In explaining why he at first intended only to direct the film and not star in it, Olivier has said: "I feel that my style of acting is more suited to stronger character roles, such as Hotspur and Henry V, rather than to the lyrical, poetical role of Hamlet." ("An Essay in Hamlet")

What sense of the character of Hamlet do these words indicate? Is it one you share?

13. According to Aristotle, "character determines men's qualities, but it is by their actions that they are happy or the reverse. The purpose of dramatic action in tragedy, therefore, is not the representation of character: character comes in for the sake of the action. . . . The plot, then, is the first principle and, as it were, the soul of a tragedy: character holds the second place."

Is that true of the tragedy *Hamlet*?

14. One of the sources of the difficulty we may have in feeling confident that we truly understand Hamlet's character is the fact that he seems constantly to be playing a part: he is one person with Claudius, another with Gertrude, still another with Ophelia, and so on. Only with Horatio does he seem to try to act himself, and at first he hides even from him the full story of what the Ghost had said. Despite such complexity, do you believe that we can determine the chief features of Hamlet's character? What would they be?

15. Is madness one of the roles Hamlet plays? T. S. Eliot has said that "it is less than madness and more than feigned." ("Hamlet and His Problems")

What might he mean, and would you agree?

16. *Hamlet* is Shakespeare's longest play, and uncut productions are extremely rare, even on the stage; but while deletions are common, of course one always asks whether the particular cuts made by a given production seem wisely chosen. Do they seem so in Olivier's film? Is his adaptation a "faithful" one? Do you regard it as essential that it should be?

17. Olivier, in "An Essay in Hamlet":

> From my experience on 'Henry V,' I had learnt that in dealing with 'Hamlet,' the only real way to solve the problem of adaptation for the screen was to be ruthlessly bold in adapting the original play. . . .
> There are so many jewels in 'Hamlet' that it is impossible to make cuts in the play without sacrifice. Amongst other characters who play a continuous part in Shakespeare's 'Hamlet,' we have taken out altogether Rosencrantz and Gildenstern, and also Fortinbras. This is a radical approach to adaptation, and because it is so much more than mere condensation, I feel that the film 'Hamlet' should be regarded as an 'Essay in Hamlet,' and not as a film version of a necessarily abridged classic.

18. What is lost from the play (and from the tragedy) without Fortinbras?

19. You may wish to look at Tom Stoppard's *Rosencrantz and Guildenstern Are Dead* (1967), a fascinating modern play about the two men whom Olivier omits from his film, and about their frightening and ludicrous role on the periphery of a great drama they do not and cannot comprehend.

20. In the context of an essay on Kurosawa's *Throne of Blood,* an adaptation of *Macbeth,* J. Blumenthal asks, "Are there certain types of character that are not really fit for film narrative?"—and he concludes that "no film-maker could help but grossly distort or over-simplify a character such as Hamlet's."

His point is apparently different from that of Charles Lamb as quoted above in topic 1, since Blumenthal stresses that he is not talking about the problems of "a theatrical performance of the role, but about those that would be involved in trying to create the character filmically. . . . Hamlet would be untranslatable because of the verbality of his experience."

What are the assumptions here about Hamlet, drama, and film? Do you share them? Is *Hamlet* unadaptable to film?

21. Does Olivier's film of *Hamlet* succeed as a film, rather than as, say, a photographed play?

22. "I determined not to let the beautiful medium of black and white be shuffled out of existence by the popular ascendancy of colour on the screen, until I had explored as thoroughly as possible the beauties and advantages of black and white, so rarely used for a great subject in recent years." (Olivier, "An Essay in Hamlet")

23. Given the quality of color stock at the time, the decision to film in black and white meant that certain possibilities were available that would not have been possible in color—notably, the use of *deep focus,* which is in fact greatly stressed throughout the film. On deep focus, see chapter 2, page 41. And see as well the section on **Citizen Kane,* topics 4 and 5 (page 123): Desmond Dickinson, the cinematographer for *Hamlet,* has acknowledged the influence of Gregg Toland's work in *Kane.* (Olivier had worked with Toland on *Wuthering Heights.*)

24. One effect of the reliance on deep focus within *Hamlet* is a corresponding stress on *mise en scène.* As Jack J. Jorgens notes in *Shakespeare on Film:*

> Montage between shots is hardly used, save for a few blatant examples such as the dissolve from Gertrude's bed to Claudius swilling wine. Rather, meaning is generated *within* shots: the head of Hamlet's shadow falls upon Yorick's skull (foreshadowing death, and linking him with the role of fool), the ghost seems to rise out of Hamlet's head as it reveals the murder, Claudius and Gertrude slowly ascend stairs to separate rooms while reading Hamlet's letters, signalling his success in parting them.

25. There is in fact a relative absence of striking cuts in the film; Jorgens mentions one exception above. Can you think of others?

In any case, as we saw in chapter 2, camera movement can produce shifts in *mise en scène* which produce effects very much like those of montage; and *Hamlet* uses a great many tracking shots—for example, as the camera explores the vast labyrinthine sets of the castle of Elsinore. Some critics indeed have argued that such shots are tiresomely overdone. Would you?

26. Occasionally, a scene which is only described by someone in the play is *shown* to us in the film, while we also hear the words of description in a voice-over. For example, the Ghost describes the murder, and we see it acted out; or Ophelia tells of Hamlet's strange behavior, and we see it in mime; or Ophelia drowns, and we hear Gertrude's words.

Does the combination of sight and sound seem in this case redundant? Or do they reinforce one another? (See the discussion of voice-overs in chapter 3, page 58, and see chapter 2, page 26, for a brief account of the manifesto on "non-synchronization" of visual and aural images, issued by Eisenstein, Alexandrov, and Pudovkin in 1928.)

27. This film continues Olivier's innovative treatment of the soliloquies in *Henry V,* by presenting them as voice-overs rather than as direct speech, except when certain passages are given special emphasis or significance by suddenly being uttered aloud. How effective is that device here? (See the discussion in chapter 3, pages 57–58, of the depiction of mental states and of the interior monologue in film and written literature.)

28. "*Hamlet* is a remarkable, if quixotic, effort to instill cinematic life into an outspoken dialogue film. But you cannot eat your cake and have it." (Siegfried Kracauer, *Theory of Film*)

How might one counter or support that assertion?

29. Olivier, in "An Essay in Hamlet":

> 'Hamlet,' the greatest of all plays, which has kept commentators enthralled for four centuries, was the first to be created by an author with the courage to give his audience a hero with none of the usual excursions of heroism. Perhaps he was the first pacifist, perhaps Dr. [Ernest] Jones is sound in his diagnosis of the Oedipus complex, perhaps there is justification in the many other complexes that have been foisted on to him—perhaps he just thought too much, that is, if a man can think too much. . . . I prefer to think of him as a nearly great man—damned by lack of resolution, as all but one in a hundred are.

Although Olivier here mentions the interpretations stressing the Oedipus complex as only one among all the possible views of *Hamlet,* many viewers feel that in fact it receives major emphasis in the film. Is that so, do you think? If it is, does that mean that the film distorts the play?

30. Of course, the term "Oedipus complex" derives its name from the mythical figure who unknowingly ("unconsciously," as it were) married his mother after having killed his father, in a myth embodying what Sigmund Freud (in his *Complete Introductory Lectures on Psychoanalysis*) calls "the two extreme wishes that arise from the son's situation—to kill his father and take his mother to wife." In Freud's view, then, the relationship between a male child and his mother is fundamentally a sexual one, thereby entailing as well ambivalent feelings of envy and jealousy—in addition to love—in regard to the father, the rival whom the child would like to dispose of. All boys experience such feelings, according to Freud, but most outgrow them and achieve "normal," "healthy" relationships with other women.

31. The first person to look at *Hamlet* in light of the above views was Freud himself, in *The Interpretation of Dreams* (1900):

> The plot of the drama shows us . . . that Hamlet is far from being represented as a person incapable of taking any action. . . . What is it, then, that inhibits him in fulfilling the task set him by his father's ghost? The answer . . . is that it is the peculiar nature of the task. Hamlet is able to do anything—except take vengeance on the man who did away with his father and took that father's place with his mother, the man who shows him the repressed wishes of his own childhood realized. Thus the loathing which should drive him on to revenge is replaced in him by self-reproaches, by scruples of conscience, which remind him that he himself is literally no better than the sinner whom he is to punish.

32. Freud's views were expanded upon by his disciple, Ernest Jones, in *Hamlet and Oedipus,* where for example he argued:

> When sexual repression is highly pronounced, as with Hamlet, then both types of women are felt to be hostile: the pure one out of resentment at her repulses, the sensual one out of the temptation she offers to plunge into guiltiness. Misogyny, as in the play, is the inevitable result.
>
> The intensity of Hamlet's repulsion against women in general, and Ophelia in particular, is a measure of the powerful "repression" to which his sexual feelings are being subjected.

Do you in fact sense this degree of misogyny and sexual repression in the play and the film?

33. Haines, a character in James Joyce's novel *Ulysses,* on *Hamlet:* "I read a theological interpretation of it somewhere. . . . The Father and the Son idea. The Son striving to be atoned with the Father."

The ninth chapter of *Ulysses* contains a fascinating conversation in which various characters—notably Stephen Dedalus—discuss Shakespeare's play, art, and life.

34. From Vladimir Nabokov's novel *Bend Sinister,* on Shakespeare: "Who is he? . . . The person who said (not for the first time) that the glory of God is to hide a thing, and the glory of man is to find it."

Further Readings

ASHWORTH, JOHN. "Olivier, Freud, Hamlet." *Atlantic Monthly* 183 (May 1949): 30–33. A vehement attack on the "Freudianism" of the movie.

BARKER, FELIX. *The Oliviers.* Philadelphia: Lippincott, 1953.

BLUMENTHAL, J. " 'Macbeth' into 'Throne of Blood.' " In *Film and the Liberal Arts.* Ed. T. J. Ross. New York: Holt, Rinehart and Winston, 1970, pp. 122–35. Not on *Hamlet,* but quoted above in topic 20.

BRADLEY, A. C. "Hegel's Theory of Tragedy." In his *Oxford Lectures on Poetry.* New York: Macmillan, 1909. Reprinted in *Criticism: The Foundations of Modern Literary Judgment.* Ed. Mark Schorer et al. New York: Harcourt Brace Jovanovich, 1948, pp. 55–66.

———. *Shakespearean Tragedy.* New York: Meridian, 1955.

CROSS, BRENDA, ed. *The Film Hamlet: A Record of Its Production.* London: Saturn Press, 1948. An extremely valuable short book, with essays by a number of people involved in the film; includes Olivier's "An Essay in Hamlet."

DENT, ALAN, ed. *Hamlet: The Film and the Play.* London: World Film Publications, 1948. The screenplay.

ECKERT, CHARLES W., ed. *Focus on Shakespearean Films.* Englewood Cliffs, N.J.: Prentice-Hall, 1972. Reprinted essays and reviews by various critics on fourteen films.

ELIOT, T. S. "Hamlet and His Problems." In his *Selected Essays.* New York: Harcourt Brace Jovanovich, 1960.

JONES, ERNEST. *Hamlet and Oedipus.* New York: Norton, 1949.

JORGENS, JACK J. *Shakespeare on Film.* Bloomington: Indiana University Press, 1977. A good, judicious study.

KOZINTSEV, GRIGORI. *Shakespeare: Time and Conscience.* Trans. Joyce Vining. New York: Hill and Wang, 1966. By the director of the Russian film of *Hamlet.*

Literature/Film Quarterly. Occasionally has a special issue entirely devoted to "Shakespeare on Film"; see Fall 1973, Spring 1976, Fall 1977.

MANVELL, ROGER. *Shakespeare and the Film.* New York: Praeger, 1971. Helpful. Dedicated to Olivier.

MORRIS, PETER. *Shakespeare on Film: An Index to William Shakespeare's Plays on Film.* Ottawa: Canadian Film Institute, 1972. A chronological, annotated list, 1929–71.

OLIVIER, LAURENCE. "An Essay in Hamlet." In Cross (above).

WHITEHEAD, PETER, and ROBIN BEAN, eds. *Olivier-Shakespeare.* London: Lorrimer, 1966.

■■■■■■■■■■■■■■■■■■■

THE TREASURE OF THE SIERRA MADRE

■■■■■■■■■■■■■■■■■■■

BACKGROUND

On the Novel

B. Traven, the author of the novel *The Treasure of the Sierra Madre,* is a mysterious figure who guarded his privacy and insisted that, as he once said, "my life belongs to me, my work to the public." Consequently, little is known about his life with any certainty, but a few things seem probable: that he was born around 1890 in the United States, perhaps in the Chicago area; that he went to Germany in childhood or adolescence, and there received much of his education; that he was known for a time early in the 1900s under the name of Ret Marut, an actor and radical journalist who escaped from almost certain execution by a German military court in 1919; that he went to Mexico in the 1920s, when writings began to appear under the name of B. Traven; that he also went by the names of Traven Torsvan and Hal Croves; that he died in Mexico in 1969. The mysteries have encouraged conjectures: for a time at least it was widely believed, especially in Germany, that he was the illegitimate son of Kaiser Wilhelm II. A seriously held theory which has some scholarly supporters is that *two* men were actually responsible for the works of "B. Traven."

The Treasure of the Sierra Madre was first published in German (as *Der Schatz der Sierra Madre*) in 1927. Apparently it was only afterward that

FIG. 23.   The Museum of Modern Art/Film Stills Archive. Courtesy Warner Bros.

Traven wrote the English version (which was published in the United States in 1935; a translation by someone else had appeared in England in 1934). But Traven always claimed that he wrote his work first in English, which does in any case seem to have been his original native language. Other novels include *The Death Ship* (1926) and *The Bridge in the Jungle* (1929), and he continued publishing novels and stories into the 1950s and 1960s, including *The Night Visitor and Other Stories* in 1966; but none of his other works was as popular or as generally respected as *The Treasure of the Sierra Madre*.

On the Film

The Treasure of the Sierra Madre (1948) is one of the most widely praised films in Hollywood history. John Huston (b. 1906) had already directed Humphrey Bogart in **The Maltese Falcon* (1941); they made several other films together as well, such as *Key Largo* (1948) and *The African Queen* (1951). Other Huston films include *The Asphalt Jungle*

(1950), *The Red Badge of Courage* (1951), *Moby Dick* (1956), *The Misfits* (1961), and *The Man Who Would Be King* (1975). In recent years he has been increasingly active as an actor (he has a bit part as the man in the white suit at the start of *The Treasure of the Sierra Madre*); he played in a 1970 version of another Traven novel, *The Bridge in the Jungle,* directed by Pancho Kohner. Huston also wrote the screenplay for *The Treasure of the Sierra Madre,* winning an Academy Award for that as well as for his direction.

This film was one of the first major Hollywood productions to go "on location" outside the United States, and Huston had to plead with Warner Brothers to let him do so; one of the reasons for his interest in the novel was in fact that he knew Mexico well, having served in the Mexican cavalry for two years while a young man. He had learned the importance of authentic locations while filming documentaries during World War II.

The Treasure of the Sierra Madre was Huston's first major project after the war. He wrote a screenplay and mailed it to Traven, who sent a letter in reply. They agreed to meet in Mexico City, but Traven did not show up; instead, a man came to Huston in the middle of the night and introduced himself as Hal Croves, a friend of Traven's. Huston hired him as a "technical adviser," suspecting (almost certainly correctly) that Croves was in fact Traven. A rumor to that effect spread during shooting, and Croves left the set. Later, someone showed Humphrey Bogart one of the few verifiable photographs of Traven, and Bogart identified him as Croves. When that story came out in *Life* magazine, Croves wrote an angry letter of denial. Huston's response was, "personally, I would deplore any definite proof that Croves and Traven are one. Traven has worked very hard at being mysterious . . . in a world where too much is known about too many."

The director of photography was Ted McCord, who also worked on *East of Eden* (1955), *The Sound of Music* (1965), and *A Fine Madness* (1966). The music by Max Steiner, who had composed scores for *King Kong* (1933) and *Gone with the Wind* (1939), received the award for best music at the Venice Film Festival.

Other credits: producer, Henry Blanke (associate producer for **The Maltese Falcon*); art direction, John Hughes; musical director, Leo F. Forbstein; editor, Owen Marks; set decorations; Fred M. MacLean; special effects, William McGann and H. F. Koenekamp; assistant director, Dick Mayberry; make-up, Perc Westmore; sound recording, Robert B. Lee; orchestration, Murray Cutter.

Heading the cast was Humphrey Bogart (1899–1957) as Fred C. Dobbs. (See chapter 2, pages 32–33, for a discussion of the Bogart persona, and especially of our awareness of it as we watch his performance as Dobbs.) Other films in addition to those he made with Huston mentioned above include *The Petrified Forest* (1936), *Casablanca* (1943), *The Big Sleep* (1946), *The African Queen* (1951), for which he received an Academy Award, and *The Caine Mutiny* (1954).

Walter Huston, John Huston's father, won an Academy Award for supporting actor for his role as Howard. He came to Hollywood from Broadway in his mid-forties, and one of his early roles was the title one in D. W. Griffith's *Abraham Lincoln* (1930). His many other films include *Rain* (1932), *All That Money Can Buy* (1941), and *Duel in the Sun* (1946).

Tim Holt (Curtin) appeared in a large number of low-budget Westerns throughout his career, but he is probably best remembered for his leading role in Welles's *The Magnificent Ambersons* (1942). (His father, Jack Holt, who had been in action movies since the silents, was one of the flophouse men in this film.) Bruce Bennett, who played Cody (the name given to the Lacaud of the novel), started in movies under the name of Herman Brix, playing Tarzan in 1935. Barton MacLane (McCormick) was tough-looking in a great many films, including *The Maltese Falcon.*

Other members of the cast: Alfonso Bedoya as "Gold Hat" (or El Jefe, the bandit chief); A. Soto Rangel as the Presidente; Jose Torvay and Margarito Luna as Pablo and Pancho; Jacqueline Dalya as McCormick's girl. The boy selling the lottery tickets is Bobby Blake—the Robert Blake of *In Cold Blood* (1967) and the television series *Baretta.*

Running time: 126 minutes. Distributor: United Artists.

TOPICS TO THINK ABOUT

1. In a "Declaration of Independence from Personal Publicity," which he gave, instead of biographical information, to a reporter for the Mexican magazine *Siempre!* in 1966, Traven declared:

> My work is important, I am not; I am only a common, ordinary worker. The God of nature granted me the gift of writing books, therefore I am obliged to write books instead of baking bread. In making them, I am no more important than the typographer of my books, than the worker who labors in the factory that makes the paper for my books; I am no more important than the binder of my books or the woman who wraps them or the sweeper of the floors in

the office that handles my books. . . . Nevertheless, I have never heard of the reader of a good book having asked for the autograph of the typographer, the printer, or the binder.

Do you see a comparable attitude toward work and workers in the novel *The Treasure of the Sierra Madre?*

2. Hal Croves (that is, Traven) said, in an interview published in *Ramparts* in 1967, that Traven "always wanted to write *books*. They came out to be novels perhaps more accidentally." What do you suppose he meant?

3. Hans Koningsberger, whose novel *A Walk with Love and Death* John Huston adapted in 1969, has said:

> It was my good fortune as a writer that Huston is a man who believes in books. Real books are seldom seen circulating in the movie world; its dealings are with story *outlines,* as if what mattered in literature was really and only what the personages ended up doing to each other, and the rest just decoration—a parallel to saying, never mind whether this painting is a Vermeer or a Picasso or a Smith; just tell me its subject.

4. Huston, in an interview with Gideon Bachmann: "The most important element to me is always the idea that I'm trying to express, and everything technical is only a method to make the idea into clear form. I'm always working on the idea: whether I am writing, directing, choosing music or cutting."

5. Do you see any evidence in the prose of the novel for its possible German-language origin?

6. How do you react to the long interspersed stories within the main narrative of the novel? Was Huston wise to omit them all?

7. In what sense is gold a "value" in the novel and/or the film, and in what sense is it not? What *is* seen as having special value?

8. Compare the treatment of the theme of greed in the novel and the film.

9. "Since they now owned certain riches, their worries about how to protect them had started. The world no longer looked to them as it had a few weeks ago. They had become members of the minority of mankind." (*The Treasure of the Sierra Madre*, chapter 6)

10. Compare the changes we see Dobbs's character undergo as they are presented within the novel and within the film.

11. According to Howard, "most people are only afraid of getting

caught, and that makes them, not better, but only more careful and more hypocritical." (Chapter 7)

12. "If Howard is the character we wish to emulate, Dobbs is the one we fear we might become." (Donald O. Chankin, *Anonymity and Death*)

13. Why is it Dobbs who does what he does, rather than Curtin or Howard?

14. In the film, Dobbs's final confrontation is with El Jefe, rather than with the three mestizos as in the novel. Why, do you suppose?

15. The film makes some significant changes in the plot in regard to Cody (Lacaud): how do you react to them?

16. Harvey R. Greenberg, in *The Movies on Your Mind:*

One has noted the striking absence of women in the film. . . . Prior to Cody's appearance, they have been treated as degraded objects, treasure to be gotten with treasure, recipients of animal lust, nothing more. . . . Cody lays down his life for these alienated men who would have gunned him down. His bequest to them is the richness of his relationship with his wife. Although we never meet her, she is as crucial a character as her husband.

17. In one section of the film, when the bandits come into the village, not a single word of English is heard for over five minutes. Does that mean we do not comprehend everything that goes on? Should Huston have supplied English subtitles?

18. James Agee, in his review for *The Nation*:

The Treasure is one of very few movies made since 1927 which I am sure will stand up in the memory and esteem of qualified people alongside the best of the silent movies. . . .

. . . I doubt we shall ever see a film more masculine in style; or a truer movie understanding of character and of men. . . .

There is not a shot-for-shot's sake in the entire picture, or one too prepared-looking, or dwelt on too long. The camera is always where it ought to be, never imposes on or exploits or over-dramatizes its subject, never for an instant shoves beauty or special meaning at you. This is one of the most visually alive and beautiful movies I have ever seen. (*Agee on Film*)

19. "Agee was . . . wrong about Huston . . . but Huston is still coasting on his reputation as a wronged individualist with an alibi for every bad movie." (Andrew Sarris, *The American Cinema*)

20. Compare the prospects for Curtin at the end of the film and the novel.

Further Readings

BACHMANN, GIDEON. "John Huston." In *Interviews with Film Directors*. Ed. Andrew Sarris. New York: Avon, 1969, pp. 253–73. Originally published in *Film Quarterly* 19 (Fall 1965): 3–13.

BAUMANN, MICHAEL L. *B. Traven: An Introduction*. Albuquerque: University of New Mexico Press, 1976.

CHANKIN, DONALD O. *Anonymity and Death: The Fiction of B. Traven*. University Park: Pennsylvania State University Press, 1975.

GREENBERG, HARVEY R. *"The Treasure of the Sierra Madre*—There's Success Phobia in Them Thar Hills!" In his *The Movies on Your Mind*. New York: Saturday Review Press, 1975.

KAMINSKY, STUART. *John Huston: Maker of Magic*. Boston: Houghton Mifflin, 1978.

KONINGSBERGER, HANS. "From Book to Film—via John Huston." *Film Quarterly* 22 (Spring 1969): 2–4.

NOLAN, WILLIAM F. *John Huston: King Rebel*. Los Angeles: Sherbourne, 1965. A biography.

PRATLEY, GERALD. *The Cinema of John Huston*. South Brunswick, N.J.: A. S. Barnes, 1977. Consists chiefly of comments by Huston, in some general chapters and in discussions of individual films. Pratley summarizes the story of each film.

THE THIRD MAN

BACKGROUND

On the Novel and the Film

The Third Man is a complicated example of adaptation, and thereby an especially interesting one for anyone studying the relationships between written literature and film discussed in chapters 3 and 4. It began as an idea for a film but was nevertheless first written as a short novel; only then did Graham Greene go on to write the screenplay. In his almost apologetic Preface to the novel (published in 1950; the movie had appeared in 1949), Greene begins by insisting that "*The Third Man* was never written to be read but only to be seen." He explains the novel's

FIG. 24. The Museum of Modern Art/Film Stills Archive. Copyright 1949 Selznick Releasing Orgn.

existence by saying: "To me it is almost impossible to write a film play without first writing a story. Even a film depends on more than plot, on a certain measure of characterisation, on mood and atmosphere; and these seem to me almost impossible to capture for the first time in the dull shorthand of a script. . . . One must have the sense of more material than one needs to draw on." In essence, he says, the novel "was never intended to be more than the raw material for a picture."

Graham Greene (b. 1904) is a British novelist who was educated at Oxford (where he served as the film critic for the literary magazine he edited); he became a Roman Catholic in his early twenties. His first novel was *The Man Within* (1929), and he has continued to publish novels regularly ever since. (During the late 1930s, he also went back to writing film criticism.) For many years, Greene separated his works of prose fiction between his "novels" and his "entertainments," in an attempt to distinguish his more serious works of art from the rest of his work (such as his "thrillers"). The distinction was often unclear and misleading, and in later years he has discontinued it. In addition to *The Third Man*, among his most famous "entertainments" are *The Confidential Agent*

(1939) and *Our Man in Havana* (1959); among his most important "novels" are *Brighton Rock* (1938), *The Power and the Glory* (1940), *The Heart of the Matter* (1948), *The End of the Affair* (1951), and *The Quiet American* (1955). All the books mentioned as well as others have been the bases for film adaptations; for some, such as *Brighton Rock* (1947) and *Our Man in Havana* (1959), Greene wrote the screenplays himself.

The Third Man, which received the Grand Prix at the Cannes Film Festival in 1949, is widely regarded as Greene's most successful film, as well as the most fruitful of his several collaborations with its director. Greene dedicated the published novel "to Carol Reed in admiration and affection and in memory of so many early morning Vienna hours at Maxim's, the Casanova, the Oriental," and he describes in his Preface how they "worked closely together, covering so many feet of carpet a day, acting scenes at each other."

Carol Reed (1906–1976) began as an actor and directed his first film in 1934 (*Midshipman Easy*). Few of his films attracted much attention until the superb *Odd Man Out* (1947); in 1948 came his first collaboration with Greene, on *The Fallen Idol*. They also worked together on *Our Man in Havana*. Other films by Reed include *An Outcast of the Islands* (1951), *The Agony and the Ecstasy* (1965), and *Oliver!* (1968).

The producers were Alexander Korda and David O. Selznick. Korda's first great success was *The Private Life of Henry VIII* (1933); others of his productions include *Things To Come* (1936), *The Fallen Idol,* and *Richard III* (1955). (The art director for *The Third Man* was his brother, Vincent Korda.) Selznick was a major American producer whose other credits include *David Copperfield* (1934), *Gone with the Wind* (1939), *Duel in the Sun* (1946), and *Tender Is the Night* (1962).

Robert Krasker received an Academy Award for his cinematography for *The Third Man*. He had already photographed Laurence Olivier's *Henry V (1944) and David Lean's *Brief Encounter* (1945); later he worked on Peter Ustinov's *Billy Budd* (1962) and William Wyler's *The Collector* (1965). The music was composed and played on a zither by Anton Karas, whom Reed had discovered playing for coins in a Vienna restaurant. The melody associated in the film with Harry Lime—"The Third Man Theme"—became a great success and has been coupled with Orson Welles ever since.

Other credits: associate producer, Hugh Perceval; production manager, T. S. Lyndon-Haynes; editor, Oswald Hafenrichter; camera operators, Edward Scaife and Denys Coop; sound, John Cox; makeup, George Frost; wardrobe, Ivy Baker.

In the cast, *The Third Man* once again paired Joseph Cotten and Orson Welles, as in *Citizen Kane*. (They had also collaborated on a screenplay for *Journey into Fear,* 1942.) Here, Cotten played Holly Martins; his many other films include Hitchcock's *Shadow of a Doubt* (1943) and several produced by Selznick, including *Duel in the Sun.* Welles played Harry Lime. (For the films directed by Welles, see the sections on *Citizen Kane* and *The Trial,* pages 118 and 250.) One occasionally reads that Welles wrote most of his own role for *The Third Man;* that is not true, but he did write the most famous bit of dialogue in the film—Lime's speech about the cuckoo clock (see below, topic 17).

Alida Valli (Anna Schmidt) had been in Italian films during the 1930s; her first movie in English was Hitchcock's *The Paradine Case* (1948). Other films include Antonioni's *Il Grido* (1957) and Bertolucci's *1900* (1976). Major Calloway was Trevor Howard, who has also been in Reed's *An Outcast of the Islands,* David Lean's *Brief Encounter* (1945) and *Ryan's Daughter* (1971), and Jack Cardiff's *Sons and Lovers* (1960).

Other members of the cast: Bernard Lee (the "M" of the James Bond films) as Sergeant Paine; Paul Hoerbiger as the porter and Annie Rosar as his wife; Ernst Deutsch as Kurtz; Sigfried Breuer as Popescu; Erich Ponto as Dr. Winkel; Wilfrid Hyde-Whyte as Crabbit; Hedwig Bleibtreu as Anna's landlady; Herbert Halbik as the boy, Hansl; Alexis Chesnakov as Brodsky; Paul Hardtmuth as the hall porter at Sacher's. In the version released in the United States, the opening narration is by Joseph Cotten, while in British prints the voice is that of Carol Reed.

Running time varies with different prints, between 93 and 104 minutes. Distributors include Budget and Kit Parker (the longer version); Select; Twyman; University of California Extension Media Center; Walter Reade.

TOPICS TO THINK ABOUT

1. *The Third Man* is a work of suspense. Consequently *you may wish to postpone looking at the Topics To Think About until you have either read the novel or seen the film.*

2. There are of course notable differences between the novel and the published version of Greene's original script (for example, the novel is narrated by Calloway, while there is no narrator in the script). But there are even more important shifts between the script and the actual film, which, according to Greene, in his Preface to the novel, "is better than the story because it is in this case the finished state of the story."

Martins is British in both the novel and the script, but with the casting of Joseph Cotten in the role he was made an American (and his name was changed, since Cotten objected to "Rollo," although Holly was chosen as also "an absurd one"). That meant that an American also had to be cast as Lime, since the two men had been friends at school. (Some of the villains were then changed to Europeans; the filmmakers did not want all of them to be American.) The screenplay was also tightened—for example, the cultural officer Crabbit in the film is a composite of two characters in the script. And some incidents changed in significant ways: in the script, Anna does not figure in the scene entrapping Lime.

3. The film takes place in an Austria occupied after World War II by Allied forces. As Calloway puts it in the novel, "If you are to understand this strange, rather sad story you must have an impression at least of the background—the smashed dreary city of Vienna divided up in zones among the four powers; the Russian, the British, the American, the French zones, regions marked only by notice-boards, and in the centre of the city, surrounded by the Ring with its heavy public buildings and its prancing statuary, the Inner Stadt under the control of all four powers." (Chapter 1)

Later, Calloway observes, in regard to Anna's arrest, that "there is a lot of comedy in these situations if you are not directly concerned. You need a background of central European terror, of a father who belonged to a losing side, of house searches and disappearances, before the fear outweighs the comedy." (Chapter 12)

4. *The Third Man* was one of the first important British films to be shot on foreign location. Try to imagine the film as it would have been had it been shot on studio sets.

5. CALLOWAY, in the script: "Miss Schmidt, Vienna is a closed city. A rat would have more chance in a closed room without a hole and a pack of terriers loose."

6. Vernon Young, in *On Film:* "The deficiencies are simple to note: there's padding in this film and often glibness rather than facility, and there is rather more characterization than character. All the same, it casts a spell—the spell of heartbreak in an hour and half that enshrines the end of Europe more indelibly than any film I know." What might Young mean—in an essay written in 1969—by "the end of Europe"?

Young goes on: "Holly Martins, the nice American, is a tourist, no more equipped to understand Anna than Europe, in ruins around him, or Lime, when he finds out how rotten a man can be. . . . The nice American helps clean up the aftermath and Europe leaves him standing there with his packed suitcase and walks on past in its raincoat."

As we saw above, in the original version Martins was British rather than American: how much does the change affect the story that is told about him, and the reverberations of that story?

7. Notice how many shots in the movie are filmed with a slightly tilted camera, so that the angles of vision are slightly off. What is the effect of that device?

8. At the start of the novel, Calloway quotes from a note he had made for his file on Martins: "In normal circumstances a cheerful fool. Drinks too much and may cause a little trouble. Whenever a woman passes raises his eyes and makes some comment, but I get the impression that really he'd rather not be bothered. Has never really grown up and perhaps that accounts for the way he worshipped Lime."

In the film, shortly after Lime says to him, "We aren't heroes . . . The world doesn't make heroes outside your books," Martins echoes an earlier comment of Anna's about Lime by saying, "You've never grown up, Harry."

9. The film is more than half over by the time Lime appears, yet many people believe that he dominates the film. Indeed, some feel that he becomes *too* dominant, spoiling the balance. How do you feel about these reactions?

10. Even before he appears, we have been given many indications of Lime's charm and ability to captivate people, through the feelings of both Martins and Anna. Then, just before we see him, we learn that even the disagreeable cat "only liked Harry"—a remark which is soon followed by the striking visual of the cat nuzzling at the shoe of the mysterious figure hidden in the dark doorway.

What are the bases of Lime's appeal? Is it cogently conveyed to the audience? If so, how?

11. As Anna seems to be ignoring all that Lime has done—"He was Harry," and that seems all she cares about—Martins responds, "You make it sound as if his manners were occasionally bad. . . . I hate the way you talk."

Like the cat, Anna only likes Lime and will not respond to Martins. But Lime betrays her; in the novel, it is especially clear that he has informed on Anna. "The price of living" in the Russian zone, he tells Martins, is giving "them a little information now and then." (Chapter 14)

How much of a villain is Lime? Is he "evil"? (Welles has said that he hates the figure of Lime, and he has compared him to Lucifer—"the fallen angel.")

12. Characterize the relationship that has existed—and now exists—between Martins and Lime.

13. More than once, Anna absent-mindedly calls Holly "Harry," and of course the names do sound alike. Indeed, near the start of the film Holly, half-drunk, says, "I guess there's nobody knew Harry like he did . . . like I did." What impressions are conveyed by such instances of confusion, however momentary?

14. If you know *Citizen Kane, compare the roles played by Cotten and Welles, and their relationship, in that film and this one.

15. Graham Greene reports his surprised and perturbed reaction when, during a conference about the film, David O. Selznick objected to the idea of a movie about one man going to search for another as "sheer buggery" (a British term for sodomy): "It's what you learn in your English schools?" (*Graham Greene on Film*)

16. Explore the motives for Holly's decision to "betray" Harry.

17. Harry, to Holly: "Don't be so gloomy. . . . After all, it's not that awful—you know what the fellow said. . . . In Italy for thirty years under the Borgias they had warfare, terror, murder, bloodshed—they produced Michaelangelo, Leonardo da Vinci and the Renaissance. In Switzerland they had brotherly love, five hundred years of democracy and peace, and what did that produce . . . ? The cuckoo clock."

18. Holly Martins, the innocent abroad, is surrounded by cynicism. When Crabbit observes that his coming to Vienna to see a man who has apparently died is "awkward," Martins replies: "Is that what you say to people after a death? Goodness, that's awkward!" Later, Calloway urges him to give up his quest: "Death's at the bottom of everything, Martins. Leave death to the professionals."

19. In two important instances in the film, we are given information which the chief characters are not given: that the porter is in danger, and that the cat who only liked Harry is nuzzling the shoe of a man in a doorway. Does our knowledge lessen or increase our tension and suspense?

20. Contrast the final chase in the sewers under the streets of Vienna with what is probably the penultimate climactic moment in the film—the conversation between Martins and Lime high above Vienna, on the Prater Wheel.

21. In the novel, Martins and Anna leave the cemetery arm in arm, and that is how Greene wanted to end the film, causing what he calls in his Preface "one of the very few major disputes" between him and Reed; for in a reversal of the usual cliché situation of the relationship between the novelist and the filmmaker, it was the director who argued that they did not need a "happy ending." Greene observes that Reed "has been proved triumphantly right." Do you agree?

Further Readings

DeVitis, A. A. *Graham Greene.* New York: Twayne, 1964.

Gomez, Joseph A. "The Theme of the Double in *The Third Man.*" *Film Heritage* 6 (Summer 1971): 7–12, 24.

Greene, Graham. *Graham Greene on Film: Collected Film Criticism 1935–1940.* Ed. John Russell Taylor. New York: Simon and Schuster, 1972.

―――. *The Portable Graham Greene.* Ed. Philip Stratford. New York: Viking, 1973. Includes stories and essays by Greene, as well as the complete novels *The Heart of the Matter* and *The Third Man.*

―――. *The Third Man and The Fallen Idol.* London: Heinemann, 1950. Includes a Preface to each novel.

―――, and Carol Reed. *The Third Man: A Film.* New York: Simon and Schuster, 1968. Most of the differences between·the original script and final film are indicated in notes.

Phillips, Gene D. *Graham Greene: The Films of His Fiction.* New York: Teachers College Press, 1974. Quotes extensively from interviews with Greene.

Samuels, Charles Thomas. "Sir Carol Reed." In his *Encountering Directors.* New York: Putnam's Sons, 1972, pp. 163–78. Interview.

Wolfe, Peter. *Graham Greene the Entertainer.* Carbondale: Southern Illinois University Press, 1972.

RASHOMON

BACKGROUND

On the Stories

Ryunosuke Akutagawa (1892–1927) was the author of many short stories especially admired both for their prose style in the original Japanese and for their special kind of irony—a kind which seemed to some of his compatriots too "Western." Nevertheless, he was a very popular as well as critically esteemed writer when he committed suicide at the age of thirty-five.

Since the two stories upon which Kurosawa has based his *Rashomon* may not be readily available to readers of this volume, their relationship to the film can be briefly summarized here.

One story, "Rashomon," provides the title and the basic tone and situation of the "frame" tale—even the pouring rain—although not the same characters. The title refers to a large and famous gate built in the eighth century in Kyoto, when that city was still the capital of Japan. In later centuries Kyoto declined in power and wealth (the film takes place in the twelfth century, not the ninth as some prints indicate), and the gate came into disrepair. (Its remnants had to be constructed for the film.) In the story, a dismissed servant is pondering whether he could ever become a thief to prevent himself from starving, when he comes upon an old woman who is stealing hair from the corpses left in the gate. Confronted with his accusations, she defends herself by saying that she has no choice if she is to live. He agrees—and uses her logic to become a thief, stealing her clothes as his first act in his new career.

The second story, "In a Grove" ("Yabu no Naka"), presents the accounts by various witnesses of the crime which also provides the core of the film. We get, in order: the "testimony" of a woodcutter, a traveling Buddhist priest, a policeman, and an old woman (the mother of the wife); the "confessions" of Tajomaru the bandit and "a woman who has come to the Shimizu temple" (the wife); and the "story" of "the murdered man, as told through a medium."

On the Film

Rashomon (1950), which won the Grand Prix at the Venice Film Festival in 1951 and then became an international success, was a revelation to Western audiences who had not until then seen any Japanese films, but its triumphs were also a surprise in Japan, where critics had not been favorably impressed. (It was selected for submission to Venice only at the insistence of an Italian woman then living in Japan.)

After studying to be a painter, Akira Kurosawa (b. 1910) began working in films as an assistant director, directing his first film on his own in 1943 (*Sanshiro Sugata*). *Rashomon* was his twelfth; like a number of his other works, it showed his interest in written literature and its influence on him. Among his later films are adaptations of Shakespeare [*Throne of Blood,* a version of *Macbeth* (*Kumonosu-jo*), 1957], Dostoevsky [*The Idiot* (*Hakuchi*), 1951], Gorky [*The Lower Depths* (*Donzoko*), 1957], and the American mystery writer Ed McBain [*High and Low,* an adaptation of the novel *King's Ransom* (*Tengoku to Jigoku*), 1963]. Aside from *Rashomon*

FIG. 25.   The Museum of Modern Art/Film Stills Archive. Courtesy Janus Films.

and *Throne of Blood,* his most famous films are probably *Ikiru* (1952) and *The Seven Samurai* (*Shichinin no Samurai,* 1954).

Kurosawa has been both receptive to and appreciated by Occidental culture, and he has been especially interested in Western painting, literature, and of course films. He has testified to having been particularly influenced by John Ford, so it is fitting that a number of Kurosawa's "period" movies have been remade by Western filmmakers as, indeed, "Westerns": *The Seven Samurai* by John Sturges as *The Magnificent Seven* (1960), with Yul Brynner; and *Yojimbo* (1961) as *For a Fistful of Dollars* (1964), with Clint Eastwood. *Rashomon* itself was remade by Martin Ritt as *The Outrage* (1964), with Paul Newman (in the role corresponding to that of the bandit), Laurence Harvey (the husband), Claire Bloom (the wife), Edward G. Robinson (a "con man" corresponding to the commoner), Howard Da Silva (a prospector: the woodcutter), and William Shatner (the "preacher"); the film was not received well. It was based on a Broadway play (1959) by Fay and Michael Kanin which had kept the title *Rashomon* and which had starred Rod Steiger and Claire Bloom.

Kurosawa works as his own editor, and he also serves as co-screenwriter. He wrote *Rashomon* with one of his most frequent collaborators, Shinobu Hashimoto; their other films together include *Ikiru, The Seven Samurai, Throne of Blood,* and *Dodesukaden* (1970). Hashimoto has also acknowledged the influence of John Ford.

And like Ford and other directors (notably Ingmar Bergman), Kurosawa likes to work with a core of people who have been with him on other films and with whom he feels comfortable. He felt an especially close friendship with Fumio Hayasaka, who wrote the music for most of Kurosawa's films until his death; for *Rashomon,* Kurosawa requested something on the order of Ravel's *Boléro,* which results for the film that many find distracting.

The cinematography was by Kazuo Miyagawa in his first assignment for Kurosawa; he later worked on *Yojimbo,* as well as on Mizoguchi's *Ugetsu* (1953). The art direction was by So Matsuyama, who had first served Kurosawa in that capacity in 1948, for *Drunken Angel* (*Yoidore Tenshi*).

Toshiro Mifune (Tajomaru, the bandit) had appeared in other Kurosawa films, but it was *Rashomon* that made him a star. They have made fifteen movies together, and while Mifune has appeared in films by other directors—such as *Grand Prix* (1966), *Hell in the Pacific* (1968), and *Midway* (1976)—and has directed one film himself (*Legacy of the Five Hundred Thousand,* 1963), he has testified in regard in Kurosawa that "I have never as an actor done anything that I am proud of other than with him."

Takashi Shimura (the woodcutter) has also been in many Kurosawa movies: he was the leader of the samurai in *The Seven Samurai*. Masago, the wife, was played by Machiko Kyo, who has been in many other Japanese films (notably *Ugetsu*) and in the American film *The Teahouse of the August Moon* (1956). Takehiro, the samurai-husband, was the first film role for Masayuki Mori; he has continued his stage career but has also been in numerous films, including *Ugetsu* and Kurosawa's *The Idiot*. Both Minoru Chiaki (the priest) and Kichijiro Ueda (the commoner) have been in a number of other Kurosawa films.

Running time: 83 minutes. Distributors: Audio Brandon; Janus.

TOPICS TO THINK ABOUT

1. Kurosawa has said that he has been influenced in his frame composition by the simplicity of modern painting. Can you discern that influence here? (See the discussion of *mise en scène* in chapter 2, pages 37–38 and 49.)

2. A frequently noted element of *mise en scène* in *Rashomon* is the use of triangular composition, especially employing three people—such as the three in the grove or the three in the Rashomon. Keep alert for the variations on such triads, and their possible significance.

3. *Rashomon* alternates between energetic, occasionally even frenetic movement (by the camera or the actors) and static composition of stationary objects or people. And it employs both dynamic cutting (with numerous short shots) and extended takes. Consider how these approaches are played against one another, and the ways in which each is dominant or subordinate at various times—in the Rashomon or in the grove, in one version of the tale or another.

4. How possible or impossible is it to determine the truth of what happened in the forest? In terms of artistic as distinct from legal needs, how desirable or necessary is it?

5. Seeing is believing.

6. THE WOODCUTTER: "It's a lie. They're all lies. Tajomaru's confession, the woman's story—they're lies!"

THE COMMONER: "Well, men are only men. That's why they lie. . . . They can't tell the truth, not even to themselves."

THE PRIEST: "That may be true. But it's because men are so weak.

That's why they lie. That's why they must deceive themselves."

7. See the discussions of point of view in written literature and in film, in chapters 1 and 2, pages 9–11 and 38–41.

Can you discern significant ways in which the camera is used in *Rashomon* to enhance the sense of subjectivity within each tale?

8. Who is recounting to us and to the commoner in the Rashomon the various eye-witness reports? Is it the woodcutter? the priest? the two of them together? If any of these, do we assume that we are getting an accurate transcription of what each person actually said at the inquiry? Or is it the film itself that provides the flashbacks to the testimony? If our source is the film rather than one of its characters, do we assume a fidelity that we might not otherwise take for granted? If we make that latter assumption, are we wise to do so?

9. We get only the testimony of each witness, without the questions or responses of the examining magistrate, who is neither seen nor heard. Why, do you suppose?

10. If you know Welles's *Citizen Kane,* compare and contrast the presentation of eye-witness accounts in that film with what is being done in *Rashomon.*

11. Parker Tyler, in "*Rashomon* as Modern Art": "Chagall with his levitated fantasy world and childhood symbols, Picasso with his creative analysis of psychological movements translated into pictorial vision, . . . each, in the static field of the painting, reveals multiple aspects of a single reality, whether literally or in symbols. *Rashomon*, as a time art, cinema, corresponds with multiple-image painting as a space art."

12. Geoffrey Wagner, in *The Novel and the Cinema:*

> Being a selective presence itself, inevitably a point of view, the camera simply cannot combine several, often conflicting, centres of consciousness. . . . It would be too self-defeating to do so. *Rashomon* tried, but could not possibly reproduce the simultaneity available to such cross-functioning in fiction. In a film the director cannot fuse the temporal elements properly. . . . So Kurosawa had to continue with each story in *Rashomon* until it was exhausted. But the human self is interpenetrated with a whole variety of perplexing and disparate elements that have to be handled at once; the self unifies all these experiences under the *I*.

13. Apparently, the various versions of what happened in the grove are in fundamental agreement until the conclusion of the rape: the most basic contradictions center on the death of the husband. Each of the three major participants insists on his or her own responsibility for that death, when we might naturally have supposed that all of them would deny it. How could one explain these unexpected claims?

14. To have denied responsibility would have been, at least on the surface, more self-serving than to have claimed it. But could one argue that, for the three major figures in the grove, their versions of what happened are after all defenses—perhaps indeed self-exalting and ennobling ones?

15. The woodcutter's version, flattering to no one and making no one seem especially evil either, is not in Akutagawa's original story. What does it add?

16. If one were to take the cynical view that the version that is deflating for everyone must be the "truest," then presumably one would believe the woodcutter's story. Should one? How relevant is it that his new account can only be true if he has been lying all along about what he saw?

Is there any way in which his removal of all heroic dimensions from what happened in the woods can be seen as a self-aggrandizing "defense" of sorts?

17. "Truth as it appears to others. This is one of the themes, perhaps the main one of this picture. No one—priest, woodcutter, husband, bandit, medium—lied. They all told the story the way they saw it, the way they believed it, and they all told the truth. Kurosawa therefore does not question truth. He questions reality." (Donald Richie, *The Films of Akira Kurosawa*)

18. "*Rashomon* is a simple-minded proof of an idea that informs most films . . . as obvious as it sounds in synopsis." (David Thomson, *A Biographical Dictionary of Film*)

19. From "Tajomaru's Confession," in Akutagawa's "In a Grove":

> To me killing isn't a matter of such great consequence as you might think. . . . Am I the only one who kills people? You, you don't use your swords. You kill people with your power, with your money. Sometimes you kill them on the pretext of working for their good. It's true they don't bleed. They are in the best of health, but all the same you've killed them. It's hard to say who is a greater sinner, you or me. (An ironical smile.)

20. Kurosawa, in an interview with Donald Richie: "We were staying in Kyoto, waiting for the set to be finished. While there we ran off some 16mm prints to amuse ourselves. One of them was a Martin

Johnson jungle film in which there was a shot of a lion roaming around. I noticed the shot and told Mifune that that was just what I wanted him to be."

21. The wife, at the end of her testimony in the film: "What should a poor helpless woman like me do?"

Is there an answer to her question? If so, is it within the film?

22. How does the "frame" story—all that takes place in the Rashomon—function within the film? Does it relate to the tales of what happened in the woods, and does it contribute to our comprehension of those tales?

23. THE PRIEST: "But it's horrible. If men don't trust one another then the earth becomes a kind of hell."

THE COMMONER: "You are right. The world we live in is a hell."

THE PRIEST: ". . . But I don't want to believe that this world is a hell."

THE COMMONER: ". . . Which one of these stories do you believe?"

THE WOODCUTTER, interposing: "I don't understand any of them. They don't make any sense."

THE COMMONER: "Well, don't worry about it. It isn't as though men were reasonable."

24. At the end, the priest says that because of the woodcutter's last action in taking responsibility for the baby, he is able to keep his faith in humanity. Considering the film as a whole, does such faith seem justified?

25. "Having asked what truth is, and where it can be found, *Rashomon* turned its back on intellectual complexity in favour of sentimental affirmation." (Penelope Houston, *The Contemporary Cinema*)

26. "Akutagawa is content to question all moral values, all truth. Kurosawa, obviously, is not. Neither anarchist nor misanthrope, he insists upon hope. . . . Like the priest he cannot believe that men are evil—and, indeed, if Kurosawa has a spokesman in the film it is probably the priest: weak, confused, but ultimately trusting." (Richie, *Films of Kurosawa*)

27. THE COMMONER: "I don't mind a lie. Not if it's interesting."

Further Readings

AKUTAGAWA, RYUNOSUKE. *Rashomon and Other Stories*. Trans. Takashi Kojima. New York: Liveright, 1970.

KUROSAWA, AKIRA. *Rashomon: A Film*. Consulting ed. and trans. Donald Richie. New York: Grove, 1969. In addition to the script, reprints the two Akutagawa stories, essays by Parker Tyler, James F. Davidson, and Richie, and the first sequence from the screenplay by Michael Kanin for Martin Ritt's remake, *The Outrage*.

RICHIE, DONALD. "Akira Kurosawa." In *Interviews with Film Directors*. Ed. Andrew Sarris. New York: Avon, 1969, pp. 287–308. Originally published in *Sight and Sound* 33 (Summer and Autumn 1964).

———. *The Films of Akira Kurosawa*. A fine, comprehensive study by a critic to whom all students of Kurosawa are indebted.

———, ed. *Focus on Rashomon*. Englewood Cliffs, N.J.: Prentice-Hall, 1972. A useful collection of reviews and critical essays; also reprints the two Akutagawa stories.

WILD STRAWBERRIES

BACKGROUND

The Swedish director Ingmar Bergman (b. 1918) is one of the major figures in contemporary cinema, and many people believe that he has already earned an assured and honored place in film history. After a background in the theater (where in fact he has remained active as a director of stage productions), he began writing film scripts and working as an assistant director in the early 1940s; he directed his own first film, *Crisis* (*Kris*) in 1945. His movies were successful in Sweden, and some— like *Smiles of a Summer Night* (*Sommarnattens Leende*, 1955)—attracted attention outside that country; but it was *The Seventh Seal* (*Det Sjunde Inseglet*, 1957), an enigmatic parable of death, love, and faith set in the middle ages, that first brought him international critical acclaim. *Wild Strawberries* (*Smultronstället*, 1957) assured his fame and respect, winning awards all over the world.

Bergman has been a prolific director; among his later films have been: *The Virgin Spring* (*Jungfrukällen*, 1960)—the only film mentioned which Bergman did not also write; *Through a Glass Darkly* (*Såsom i en Spegel*, 1961); *The Silence* (*Tystnaden*, 1963); *Persona* (1966); *Cries and Whispers* (*Viskingar och Rop*, 1972); and *The Serpent's Egg* (*Ohmens Ägg*,

1977). In 1974 he directed a six-part television series, *Scenes from a Marriage* (*Scener ur ett Aektenskap*).

Perhaps no director in history has made such well-known use of a "repertory" company of technicians and actors as has Bergman, and most of the people who worked on *Wild Strawberries* have been involved in others of his films as well. The director of photography, for example, Gunnar Fischer, served in the same capacity for *Smiles of a Summer Night*, *The Seventh Seal*, and *The Magician* (*Ansiktet*, 1958; in England, *The Face*). The assistant director, Gösta Ekman, also worked on *The Magician*.

Other credits: the screenplay of *Wild Strawberries* was of course by Bergman; production supervisor, Allan Ekelund; assistant cameraman, Björn Thermenius; music, Erik Nordgren; sets, Gittan Gustafsson; costumes, Millie Ström; sound, Aaby Wedin and Lennart Wallin; editor, Oscar Rosander.

The central role of Isak Borg was played by Victor Sjöström (1879–1960), who had himself long been an important figure in Swedish film, both as a director and as an actor: he directed his first film in 1913. Among his most famous Swedish pictures are *The Outlaw and His Wife* (*Berg-Ejvind och hans Hustru*, 1918) and *The Phantom Carriage* (*Körkalen*, 1921), but during the 1920s he also spent several years in Hollywood, directing for example *The Scarlet Letter* (1926) with Lillian Gish. On many occasions, Bergman has testified to his personal gratitude toward Sjöström, who encouraged the younger director at some difficult periods early in his career.

Ingrid Thulin (Marianne) has been in a number of Bergman films (notably *The Silence* and *Cries and Whispers*), as well as other Swedish and international productions, including Alain Resnais' *La Guerre est finie* (1966) and Luchino Visconti's *The Damned* (1969). Bergman has said that what was needed for her role was "a person of firm, strong character . . . who knew how to express it. . . . Not anyone would have done to play against so overwhelming a personality as Victor" (*Bergman on Bergman*).

The two Saras were both played by Bibi Andersson, who first worked with Bergman when she was a teen-ager, appearing in a commercial he made for television; she has been in *Smiles of a Summer Night*, *The Seventh Seal*, *Persona*, and other Bergman films.

Gunnar Björnstrand (Evald, Borg's son) first acted for Bergman in 1946, and he has appeared in *Smiles of a Summer Night*, *The Seventh Seal*, and *Winter Light* (*Nattvardsgästerna*, 1963). Another major figure in a number of Bergman films, Max von Sydow (*The Seventh Seal, The Virgin*

FIG. 26.   The Museum of Modern Art/Film Stills Archive. Courtesy Janus Films.

Spring, and others), appeared here in a minor role as Akerman, the gas station proprietor.

Other members of the cast: Jullan Kindahl as Agda, Borg's housekeeper; Folke Sundquist and Björn Bjelvenstam as Anders and Viktor; Naima Wifstrand as Isak's mother; Gunnar Sjöberg and Gunnel Broström as Mr. and Mrs. Alman; Gertrud Fridh as Isak's wife and Ake Fridell as her lover; Sif Ruud as the aunt; Yngve Nordwald as Uncle Aron; Per Sjöstrand as Sigfrid; Gio Petré as Sigbritt; Gunnel Lindblom as Charlotta; Maud Hansson as Angelica; Anne-Mari Wiman as Mrs. Akerman; Eva Norée as Anna; and Lena Bergman and Monica Ehrling as the twins.

Running time: 90 minutes. Distributor: Janus.

TOPICS TO THINK ABOUT

1. "My impulse has nothing to do with intellect or symbolism; it has only to do with dreams and longing, with hope and desire, with pas-

sion. . . . So when you say that a film of mine is intellectually complicated, I have the feeling that you don't talk about one of my pictures." (Bergman, in an interview with Charles Thomas Samuels)

2. Bergman, in "Bergman Discusses Film-making," printed as an introduction to the screenplay of *Wild Strawberries:*

> Film has nothing to do with literature; the character and substance of the two art forms are usually in conflict. This probably has something to do with the receptive process of the mind. The written word is read and assimilated by a conscious act of the will in alliance with the intellect; little by little it affects the imagination and the emotions. The process is different with a motion picture. When we experience a film, we consciously prime ourselves for illusion. Putting aside will and intellect, we make way for it in our imagination.

3. *"Wild Strawberries* is a film in novel form. It . . . frees film art from a conventional dramatic structure and a naturalistic development of events . . . [and] presses ahead to insights with which literature has been familiar since the beginning of the century." (Jörn Donner, *The Films of Ingmar Bergman*)

4. Bergman has often spoken of the importance to him of the work of the Swedish dramatist August Strindberg, about whom he wrote his undergraduate thesis and whose plays he has made a specialty of directing. In regard to *Wild Strawberries,* he acknowledges that an important and obvious influence was Strindberg's *A Dream Play* (1901–2), a complex drama in the form of a dream.

5. In the published script of *Wild Strawberries,* in which Isak's narration is even more extensive than in the film, he tells us that "I have found that during the last few years I glide rather easily into a twilight world of memories and dreams which are highly personal." And in regard to his first vision of the Sara out of his youth, he says: "Mental image or dream or whatever this was, she looked just as I remembered her."

What word might best describe Isak's "dreams"—memories? hallucinations? visions? mental images? daydreams? dreams, indeed? How important is it that we be able to categorize them?

6. "A dream does not want to say anything to anyone. It is not a vehicle for communication; on the contrary, it is meant to remain ununderstood." (Sigmund Freud, *Complete Introductory Lectures on Psychoanalysis*)

7. "We can begin by saying that happy people never make phantasies, only unsatisfied ones. Unsatisfied wishes are the driving power behind phantasies; every separate phantasy contains the fulfillment of a wish, and improves on unsatisfactory reality." (Freud, "The Relation of the Poet to Day-dreaming")

8. Isak, in the published script: "I have never been particularly enthusiastic about the psychoanalytic theory of dreams as the fulfillment of desires in a negative or positive direction. Yet I cannot deny that in these dreams there was something like a warning, which bore into my consciousness and embedded itself there with relentless determination."

9. Freud says that "the most interesting" achievement of "the dream-work . . . consists in transforming thoughts into visual images." (*Introductory Lectures*)

10. "You know, somebody studying sleep discovered that if they prevent you from dreaming, you go crazy." (Bergman, interview with Richard Meryman)

11. *Wild Strawberries* makes carefully discriminating use of cuts (especially match cuts) and dissolves. (See the discussions of those terms in chapter 2, pages 45–46.) Consider for example the various modes of transition between the here and now (the "present," or "reality") and the visionary (the "past," or "fantasy").

12. Compare and contrast the shifts from the present to the envisioned past in *Wild Strawberries* to the more immediately comprehensible and logical "flashbacks" of traditional films and novels.

If you know Arthur Miller's play *Death of a Salesman* (or the film adaptation of it), or such films as Fellini's *8½*, Lumet's *The Pawnbroker*, or Resnais' *Last Year at Marienbad*, consider the similarities and differences between their temporal shifts and those in *Wild Strawberries*.

13. Jörn Donner, on *Wild Strawberries*: "This film never begins, never ends, but is a short segment of the unceasing stream of consciousness."

See the discussion in chapter 3 (pages 57–58) of stream of consciousness, and of the depiction of mental states in both film and written literature.

14. Consider the effect of Isak's being the narrator, and of the consequent fact that we get everything through him and *his* vision. (See the discussions of point of view and narration in chapters 1 and 2, pages 9–11 and 38–41, and of the voice-over in chapters 3 and 4, pages 58 and 83.)

15. Notice the use of low-angle and high-angle shots to determine our views (literally and figuratively) of various figures in certain scenes. Consider, for example, the scene of Isak and his mother, with Marianne looking on; the dream-sequence in which Isak is "examined" by Alman; the formal procession.

16. "In the close-up lies the great suggestive power of the film medium." (Bergman, interview with Birgitta Steene)

17. ALMAN [during the fantasy-Examination]: ". . . you are guilty of guilt."

ISAK: "Guilty of guilt?"

ALMAN: "I have noted that you don't understand the accusation."

Do you understand it? What might it mean, to be "guilty of guilt"?

18. "I chose the name Isak because he seemed icy." (*Bergman on Bergman*)

We are told in several ways of Isak's aloofness and coldness: Marianne says that he had refused to listen to anything about her troubles with his son Evald. Plaintively, the Sara out of the past tells Charlotta that "he likes to kiss only in the dark and he talks about sinfulness. I think he is extremely intellectual and morally aloof and I feel so worthless . . ." Bitterly, his wife says that "he doesn't care about anything because he's completely cold."

19. How sympathetic or unsympathetic is Isak? Vernon Young feels that in a sense he seems *too* sympathetic: "The man, Isak Borg, whom we see, does not bear out the accumulated impression given by his accusers; he is a sweet, troubled old gentleman who in context seems to be the victim of an unreasonable amount of abuse from people who are mostly less attractive than he and inordinately self-righteous." (*Cinema Borealis*)

20. Isak says that Mr. and Mrs. Alman remind him of his own marriage. What then is suggested by the fact that it is Mr. Alman who conducts the Examination (which Isak fails) in the dream-vision, and who is then the guide to the scene between Isak's wife and her lover?

21. After Marianne has demanded that the Almans leave the car, Mrs. Alman sadly requests, "Forgive us if you can."

During the Examination conducted by Mr. Alman, Isak fails to remember that "a doctor's first duty is to ask forgiveness."

That evening, Isak says to Agda, "I'm sorry for this morning." Her response is to ask if he is sick—to which he replies, "Is it so unusual for me to ask forgiveness?"

22. Why is everyone in the envisioned past dressed so immaculately in white?

After her encounter with Sigfrid, Sara spills the basket of strawberries and stains her apron. Is that stain "symbolic"? (See the discussion of symbols in chapter 1, pages 17–18, and Bergman's remark on symbolism quoted above, in topic 1).

23. What *do* the wild strawberries of the title suggest, refer to, or represent?

24. Carl Gustav Jung, in "Psychological Aspects of the Mother Archetype":

> Like any other archetype, the mother archetype appears under an almost infinite variety of aspects. I mention here only some of the more characteristic. First in importance are the personal mother and grandmother, stepmother and mother-in-law; then any woman with whom a relationship exists—for example, a nurse or governess or perhaps a remote ancestress. Then there are what might be termed mothers in a figurative sense. To this category belongs the goddess, and especially the Mother of God, the Virgin, and Sophia. . . . Other symbols of the mother in a figurative sense appear in things representing the goal of our longing for redemption, such as Paradise, the Kingdom of God, the Heavenly Jerusalem. Many things arousing devotion or feelings of awe, as for instance the Church, university, city or country, heaven, earth, the woods, the sea or any still waters, matter even, the underworld and the moon, can be mother-symbols. The archetype is often associated with things and places standing for fertility and fruitfulness: the cornucopia, a ploughed field, a garden.

(Also, see the section on *$8^{1}/_{2}$*, topics 23 and 24, page 265.)

25. SARA: "My name is Sara. Silly name, isn't it?"
    ISAK: "My name is Isak. Rather silly too."
    SARA: "Weren't they married?"
    ISAK: "Unfortunately not. It was Abraham and Sara."
(The Biblical Sarah was Isaac's mother.)

26. What do we learn from Isak's visit to his mother?

27. "Evald and I are very much alike," Isak asserts, and Marianne agrees.

From what we see of Evald, can we feel that there are in addition ways in which he is *not* like his father? What might those ways be, and how significant do they seem?

28. "Philosophically, there is a book which was a tremendous experience for me: Eiono Kaila's *Psychology of the Personality*. His thesis that man lives strictly according to his needs—negative and positive—was shattering to me, but terribly true." ("Bergman Discusses Film-making," in the published edition of *Wild Strawberries*)

EVALD: "There is nothing which can be called right or wrong. One functions according to one's needs; you can read that in an elementary-school textbook."

MARIANNE: "And what do we need?"

EVALD: "You have a damned need to live, to exist and create life. . . . My need is to be dead. Absolutely, totally dead."

29. That conversation is recalled by Marianne because Isak has said, about his dreams, that "it's as if I'm trying to say something to myself which I don't want to hear when I'm awake. . . . That I'm dead, although I live."

30. Marianne then reflects that "there is only coldness and death, and death and loneliness, all the way. Somewhere it must end."

Is there promise among the young? They are clearly associated in Isak's visions with those who used to be young, and the two Saras are even played by the same actress. Do the associations suggest sterility, or renewal? A hopeless cycle, or a hopeful one? Death, or rebirth? Or are the effects more complicated than those alternatives allow?

31. Can we associate Isak's mother as we have seen her with the idyllic vision of his parents at the very end? And why does his father not appear until that moment, and then only distantly?

Robin Wood, in *Ingmar Bergman:* "Whether his parents really were like that is unimportant; what matters is that Isak can at last *see* them like that." Do you agree?

32. Does Isak change or develop through the day in which we follow his journey?

33. ". . . the only true paradise is always the paradise we have lost." (Marcel Proust, *The Remembrance of Things Past*)

Further Readings

BERGMAN, INGMAR. *Four Screenplays: Smiles of a Summer Night, The Seventh Seal, Wild Strawberries, The Magician.* Trans. Lars Malmström and David Kushner. New York: Simon and Schuster, 1960.

––––––. *Wild Strawberries: A Film.* Trans. Lars Malmström and David Kushner. New York: Simon and Schuster, 1960. Identical to the script in the above volume, but with some additional materials (including an Appendix containing a technical shot-by-shot cutting continuity). In the screenplay the narration by Isak is even more detailed and extensive than the voice-overs in the film, and Isak's words provide the equivalents of scene directions.

BJÖRKMAN, STIG, TORSTEN MANNS, and JONAS SIMA. *Bergman on Bergman: Interviews with Ingmar Bergman.* Trans. Paul Britten Austin. New York: Simon and Schuster, 1973.

DONNER, JÖRN. *The Films of Ingmar Bergman.* Trans. Holger Lundbergh. New York: Dover, 1972. A re-issue of the 1964 translation, which had the title *The Personal Vision of Ingmar Bergman.* (The Swedish edition appeared in 1962.) Donner is himself a film director.

KAMINSKY, STUART M., with JOSEPH HILL, eds. *Ingmar Bergman: Essays in Criticism.* New York: Oxford University Press, 1975. Reprinted essays by various critics.

MERYMAN, RICHARD. "I Live at the Edge of a Very Strange Country." *Life* 71 (October 15, 1971): 60–74. Includes interviews with Bergman, Bibi Anderson, Max von Sydow, and others.

SAMUELS, CHARLES THOMAS. "Ingmar Bergman." In his *Encountering Directors.* New York: Putnam's Sons, 1972, pp. 179–207. Interview.

STEENE, BIRGITTA. *Ingmar Bergman.* New York: Twayne, 1968. Takes a "literary" approach to Bergman's work.

————. "Words and Whisperings: An Interview with Ingmar Bergman." In *Focus on The Seventh Seal.* Ed. Birgitta Steene. Englewood Cliffs, N.J.: Prentice-Hall, 1972.

WOOD, ROBIN. *Ingmar Bergman.* New York: Praeger, 1969. A good short study, stressing the image of the journey in Bergman's films.

YOUNG, VERNON. *Cinema Borealis: Ingmar Bergman and the Swedish Ethos.* New York: David Lewis, 1971. Young dislikes *Wild Strawberries,* and indeed much of Bergman's other work as well.

■ ■ ■ ■ ■ ■ ■ ■ ■ ■ ■ ■ ■ ■ ■ ■ ■ ■ ■ ■
CAT ON A HOT TIN ROOF
■ ■ ■ ■ ■ ■ ■ ■ ■ ■ ■ ■ ■ ■ ■ ■ ■ ■ ■ ■

BACKGROUND

On the Play

Cat on a Hot Tin Roof was presented on Broadway in 1955, directed by Elia Kazan and starring Barbara Bel Geddes as Maggie, Ben Gazzara as Brick, Burl Ives as Big Daddy, and Mildred Dunnock as Big Mama. The play was a commercial success and was also awarded both the Pulitzer Prize and the Drama Critics' Circle Award. It was considerably revised for a 1974 production, and the new version has been published; Williams has said in his *Memoirs* that this revision is "my favorite among the plays I have written."

Tennessee Williams was born Thomas Lanier Williams in 1911 (not

1914, although that date is frequently given in reference books) in Mississippi. His first successful play was *The Glass Menagerie* (1945); and *A Streetcar Named Desire* (1947) assured his fame. He followed those plays with *Summer and Smoke* (1948) and *The Rose Tattoo* (1951). Some critics regard the late 1950s as the period of his greatest achievements, starting with *Cat on a Hot Tin Roof* in 1955 and including *Orpheus Descending* (1957), *Suddenly Last Summer* (1958), and *Sweet Bird of Youth* (1959). Other plays include *The Night of the Iguana* (1961) and *The Milk Train Doesn't Stop Here Anymore* (1964).

Williams was a writer for MGM during the 1940s, but none of his screenplays were produced. He did co-author the script for the first of his plays to be filmed, *The Glass Menagerie* (1950), as well as those for *The Rose Tattoo* (1955), *Suddenly Last Summer* (1959), and *The Fugitive Kind* (1960; an adaptation of *Orpheus Descending*). Alone, he wrote the scripts for *A Streetcar Named Desire* (1951), *Baby Doll* (1956; a re-working of two short plays), and *Boom* (1968; adapted from *The Milk Train Doesn't Stop Here Anymore*).

He has also published volumes of poems and short stories, and a novel, *The Roman Spring of Mrs. Stone* (1950), filmed in 1961.

On the Film

The film of *Cat on a Hot Tin Roof* (1958) was directed and co-written by Richard Brooks (b. 1912), who began as a novelist and screenwriter. His first novel, *The Brick Foxhole* (1945), was adapted as the movie *Crossfire* (1947); a homosexual in the book, the victim of violent prejudice, became a Jew instead in the film. His other novels are *The Boiling Point* (1948) and a book about Hollywood, *The Producer* (1951). Brooks wrote the scripts for such films as Dassin's *Brute Force* (1947) and Huston's *Key Largo* (1948) before directing his own first picture, *Crisis* (1950). Since then, he has both written and directed most of his films, and he has specialized in adaptations of novels, as in *The Blackboard Jungle* (1955), *Elmer Gantry* (1960; he received an Academy Award for his screenplay), *Lord Jim* (1964), *In Cold Blood* (1967), and *Looking for Mr. Goodbar* (1978). He has also adapted another Williams play, *Sweet Bird of Youth* (1961).

The co-author of the screenplay was James Poe, who has also written *Around the World in Eighty Days* (1956) and *Lilies of the Field* (1964), as well as the adaptation of Williams' *Summer and Smoke* (1961). The producer was Lawrence Weingarten. William Daniels had been a distinguished cinematographer ever since working with Erich von Stroheim on *Foolish Wives* (1921) and *Greed* (1923); he photographed several

FIG. 27.   Courtesy MGM.

Garbo films, including *Queen Christina* (1933), and he received an
Academy Award for *The Naked City* (1948). (He was nominated for *Cat on
a Hot Tin Roof*.)

Other credits: assistant director, William Shanks; art directors, William H. Horning and Urie McCleary; wardrobe, Helen Rose; editor,
Ferris Webster.

Elizabeth Taylor and Paul Newman are of course among the major
stars of Hollywood history. Beginning as a child actress in films like *Jane
Eyre* (1943) and *National Velvet* (1944), Taylor went on to mature dramatic roles in *A Place in the Sun* (1951) and *Giant* (1956). She was nominated for an Academy Award for her performance in *Cat*, but the two
films for which she actually received the award are *Butterfield 8* (1960)
and *Who's Afraid of Virginia Woolf* (1966). Among her numerous other
films are *Cleopatra* (1962), *The Taming of the Shrew* (1967), and two adaptations of plays by Tennessee Williams: *Suddenly Last Summer* and *Boom*.

Paul Newman came to films from the theater and the famous Actors' Studio. After *Somebody Up There Likes Me* (1956), he was for a time
known as "another Marlon Brando," but he eventually overcame that
restrictive image. His many films include *The Hustler* (1961), for which he

received the British Film Academy Award, the adaptation of Williams' *Sweet Bird of Youth* (repeating the role he had played in the original Broadway production in 1959), *Cool Hand Luke* (1967), *Butch Cassidy and the Sundance Kid* (1969), and *Buffalo Bill and the Indians* (1976). He has also been a director: of *Rachel, Rachel* (1968) and *The Effect of Gamma Rays on Man-in-the-Moon Marigolds* (1972), in neither of which he acted, and of *Sometimes a Great Notion* (1971; later called *Never Give an Inch*), in which he did.

Burl Ives repeated the role of Big Daddy that he had played in the original production; he received an Academy Award for best supporting actor that year, but for a different film, *The Big Country*. Jack Carson (Gooper) was in no less than ten feature films during his first year in the movies (1937), and he was to appear in numerous films in the years to come, attaining some prominence as a comedian in Warner Brothers films of the 1940s—pictures with names like *Two Guys from Milwaukee* (1946) and *Two Guys from Texas* (1948)—and settling into character roles after that. Judith Anderson (Big Mama) has had an especially prominent stage career but has also had important roles in such films as *Rebecca* (1940), *Laura* (1944), and *A Man Called Horse* (1970).

Other members of the cast: Madeleine Sherwood as Mae; Larry Gates as Dr. Baugh; Vaughn Taylor as Deacon Davis (Reverend Tooker in the play); Vince Townsend, Jr., as Lacey; Zelda Cleaver as Sookey; Brian Corcoran as the boy; Hugh Corcoran as Buster; Rusty Stevens as Sonny; Patty Ann Gerrity as Dixie; Deborah Miller as Trixie.

Running time: 108 minutes. Distributor: Films Inc.

TOPICS TO THINK ABOUT

1. From Brooks Atkinson's review in *The New York Times* of the original Broadway production of the play:

> It seems not to have been written. It is the quintessence of life. It is the basic truth. . . . It is not only part of the truth of life: it is the absolute truth of the theatre. . . .
> . . . "Cat on a Hot Tin Roof" is a delicately wrought exercise in human communication. His characters try to escape from the loneliness of their private lives into some form of understanding. The truth invariably terrifies them. That is the one thing they cannot face or speak.

2. From the review in *Time* of the play:

There is no question how hard Williams can hit, or how vividly he can write, or that, in a theater full of feigned and borrowed emotions, his are honestly hot and angry. But his own feelings, often intemperate, work against him.

. . . Too much explodes, too little uncoils; much more is highlighted than truly plumbed.

3. From the review in *Newsweek* of the film: "In . . . the transition from play to shadow play . . . the four-letter words have gone the way of all four-letter words, the reference to homosexuality is no more, and the ending is a few degrees more upbeat. It has not, however, lost a bit of dramatic punch."

4. From Stanley Kauffmann's review of the film:

Cat on a Hot Tin Roof . . . is Williams' least worthy long play to date. It seems to me to abuse the license he has earned by past work, like a planter despoiling his own fields; it lacks resonance beneath its action; its writing is sometimes stilted, some of its motivations are insufficient, and its resolution is feeble.

These faults are all italicized in the current film of the play. (*A World on Film*)

5. Among his reasons for preferring *Cat on a Hot Tin Roof* to all his other plays Williams mentions:

That play comes closest to being both a work of art and a work of craft. It is really very well put together, in my opinion, and all its characters are amusing and credible and touching. Also it adheres to the valuable edict of Aristotle that a tragedy must have unity of time and place and magnitude of theme.

The set in *Cat* never changes and its running time is exactly the time of its action, meaning that one act, timewise, follows directly upon the other, and I know of no other modern American play in which this is accomplished.

Actually, the "edict" which stressed the so-called "unities" of time (one day), place, and action (or plot) was not Aristotle's but rather was instituted by some of his later followers. In any case, do you agree with Williams that *Cat* gains from adhering to them?

6. In his "Notes for the Designer" in the published version of the play, Williams describes the set (for example, the "big double bed" should be made "a functional part of the set as often as suitable") and then says:

The set should be far less realistic than I have so far implied in this description of it. I think the walls below the ceiling should dissolve mysteriously into air; the set should be roofed by the sky; stars and moon suggested by traces of milky pallor, as if they were observed through a telescope lens out of focus.

Is any of that also conveyed or suggested in the film?

7. The world of the film "opens out" from that of the single set of the play. Is anything gained—or lost—by that change?

8. Edward Murray, in *The Cinematic Imagination,* on the opening scene in the film, in which Brick jumps the hurdles:

> Although the stadium is empty, Brick hears (through a subjective use of sound) the cheers that, in the sober light of day, he will never hear again. This scene invented by Brooks does more than merely *show* us how Brick broke his ankle, for if that was all it accomplished it would scarcely justify the time and trouble to shoot it. . . . The filmic virtue of the scene, in terms of structure, character and theme, is that it transports us directly and immediately into Brick's inner world of crippling neuroticism.

Do you agree that the addition of the scene is beneficial? Or would you argue that it is a mistake, or a distraction?

9. The film rearranges some elements of the play; for example, Maggie's near-monologue in the first act is broken up by the insertion of bits and pieces from other parts of the play. Why, do you think? And with what effect?

10. "It is simple enough: a movie has to be a good movie *first*. It has to be a good adaptation of a novel, story, play, or whatnot, *second*. Any compromise of these principles means the conscientious movie-maker has forsaken his prime obligation." (Richard Brooks, "A Novel Isn't a Movie")

Does Brooks's own film of *Cat on a Hot Tin Roof* work as "a good movie *first*," as distinct, say, from seeming merely a good adaptation or a well-photographed play?

11. Elizabeth Taylor and Paul Newman are among the select number of so-called superstars whose periods of stardom extend over more than a few years and a few pictures. How is your response to *Cat* affected by all the other Taylor and Newman roles you have either seen or heard about? (See the discussion of the star system in chapter 2, pages 32–33.)

12. Maggie tells Brick how she:

Always had to suck up to people I couldn't stand because they had money and I was poor as Job's turkey. . . .

And my poor Mama, having to maintain some semblance of social position, to keep appearances up, on an income of one hundred and fifty dollars a month . . .

So that's why I'm like a cat on a hot tin roof!

What is the role of money in *Cat on a Hot Tin Roof*?

13. From Williams' scene descriptions during the second act: "The bird that I hope to catch in the net of this play is not the solution of one man's psychological problem. I'm trying to catch the true quality of experience in a group of people, that cloudy, flickering, evanescent—fiercely charged!—interplay of live human beings in the thundercloud of a common crisis."

What sorts of interrelationships do we sense in the play and in the film? What picture do we get of marriage? the family? friendship?

14. BIG MAMA: "Brick never liked bein' kissed or made a fuss over, I guess because he's always had too much of it!"

15. MAGGIE: "Brick, I used to think that you were stronger than me and I didn't want to be overpowered by you. But now, since you've taken to liquor—you know what?—I guess it's bad, but now I'm stronger than you and I can love you more truly!"

16. "We are in a flight from eros—and we use sex as the vehicle for the flight." (Rollo May, *Love and Will*)

17. Within the world depicted in *Cat on a Hot Tin Roof*, Brick's proper function is to be the heir of the plantation, to manage it and oversee it, while Maggie's is to procreate: to produce the heir of the third generation (presumably a son).

What do you sense are Williams' underlying attitudes toward those assumptions about sex roles? What might Maggie's be? What are yours?

18. Is Maggie "liberated"? Or is she perhaps a perpetuator and/or victim of stereotyped sexual roles? Or does asking such questions bring in terminology that seems irrelevant to, or intrudes upon, the 1950s world of the play and the film?

19. In regard to the play, just how important do you suspect homosexual elements may have been in the feelings Skipper had for Brick, and Brick for Skipper?

20. From the scene directions in Act Two, during the conversation between Brick and Big Daddy:

The thing they're discussing, timidly and painfully on the side of Big Daddy, fiercely, violently on Brick's side, is the inadmissible thing that Skipper died to disavow between them. The fact that if it existed it had to be disavowed to "keep face" in the world they lived in, may be at the heart of the "mendacity" that Brick drinks to kill his disgust with. It may be the root of his collapse. Or maybe it is only a single manifestation of it, not even the most important.

What is Brick disgusted with, then? What must he disavow? Is it perhaps that he refused to acknowledge homosexual feelings in Skipper or otherwise help his friend? Or is it that he is also afraid of the possible sources of his own love for Skipper? If the latter, do you believe that he has cause to be afraid?

21. How much is lost because the film—given the taboo nature of the subject on the Hollywood screen in the 1950s—so scrupulously avoids explicitly dealing with the theme of homosexuality?

22. BRICK: "One man has one great good true thing in his life. One great good thing which is true!—I had friendship with Skipper.—You are naming it dirty!"

MAGGIE: "I'm not naming it dirty! I am naming it clean."

23. As Chance Wayne in Brooks's film of Williams' *Sweet Bird of Youth*, Paul Newman speaks of "the enemy, time." How is time an enemy to Brick, too? or to Maggie? to Big Daddy?

24. "Death is the unavoidable eventuality which in most cases we avoid as long as we can, but which, finally, when all the possible options have expired, we must attempt to accept with as much grace as there remains in our command." (Williams, *Memoirs*)

25. *"Nous mourrons tous, moi aussi peut-être."* (Attributed to an anonymous French preacher: We must all die, maybe even me.)

26. The epigraph to the published version of *Cat on a Hot Tin Roof* is the last stanza of Dylan Thomas' "Do Not Go Gentle into That Good Night" (1952):

> And you, my father, there on the sad height,
> Curse, bless, me now with your fierce tears, I pray.
> Do not go gentle into that good night.
> Rage, rage against the dying of the light.

27. Williams has repeatedly said that his belief that *Cat on a Hot Tin Roof* is his best play rests above all on what he calls in his *Memoirs* "the kingly magnitude of Big Daddy."

28. "Go to, they are not men o' their words. They told me I was everything. 'Tis a lie—I am not ague-proof." (Lear, in William Shake-speare, *King Lear,* Act IV, Scene vi)

29. BIG DADDY: "Life is important. There's nothing else to hold onto."

He is afraid of death. Is his son afraid of life? Maggie wants life, indeed to create life. Does her husband wish for death?

30. Brick feels disgusted with "mendacity." Maggie closes the play with a lie—though one she regards as a life-saving lie and which she is determined to turn into truth. What do you think of her lie, and of the way she proceeds to get Brick to come to bed with her?

31. What seem to be the prospects for Maggie and Brick at the end of the play? of the film?

32. BRICK: "Who *can* face truth? Can *you?*"

Who among the characters in *Cat on a Hot Tin Roof* can? Are there any characters with greater self-awareness at the end than at the start? If so, what have they learned? Are there any important characters who have failed to achieve a greater self-knowledge? If so, what have they *not* learned?

33. From the scene directions for Act Two:

> Some mystery should be left in the revelation of character in play, just as a great deal of mystery is always left in the revelation of character in life, even in one's own character to himself. This does not absolve the playwright of his duty to observe and probe as clearly and deeply as he *legitimately* can: but it should steer him away from "pat" conclusions, facile definitions which make a play just a play, not a snare for the truth of human experience.

Further Readings

BROOKS, RICHARD. "A Novel Isn't a Movie." In *Hollywood Directors: 1941–1976.* Ed. Richard Koszarski. New York: Oxford University Press, 1977, pp. 179–85. Originally published in *Films in Review* 3 (February 1952): 55–59.

NELSON, BENJAMIN. *Tennessee Williams: The Man and His Work.* New York: Ivan Obolensky, 1961.

WEALES, GERALD. *Tennessee Williams.* Minneapolis: University of Minnesota Press, 1965. A pamphlet.

WILLIAMS, TENNESSEE. *Cat on a Hot Tin Roof.* New York: New Directions, 1975.

———. *Memoirs.* New York: Doubleday, 1975.

YACOWAR, MAURICE. *Tennessee Williams and Film.* New York: Ungar, 1977.

■ ■ ■ ■ ■ ■ ■ ■ ■ ■ ■ ■ ■ ■ ■ ■ ■ ■ ■

PSYCHO

■ ■ ■ ■ ■ ■ ■ ■ ■ ■ ■ ■ ■ ■ ■ ■ ■ ■ ■

BACKGROUND

On the Novel

The novel *Psycho* (1959) is a mystery thriller by Robert Bloch (b. 1917). He did not have any connection with writing the film, but he has gone on to write his own screenplays, including a remake of *The Cabinet of Dr. Caligari* (1962) and *The Nightwalker* (1964). Few critics of the film have paid much attention to the novel, and ultimately there may be little reason to do so; yet those who have dismissed the book as merely a sensational "pot-boiler" do it an injustice, for it starts with an ingenious premise and does some interesting things with it. Still, the movie *Psycho*, while no less "sensational," is an achievement in film that is unmatched by Bloch's achievement in prose fiction.

On the Film

Psycho appeared in 1960, since which time it has achieved a reputation as the most effective horror film ever made. Moreover, it is often regarded as the most complete artistic success of one of the major filmmakers in the history of the cinema: Alfred Hitchcock (b. 1899).

Hitchcock is one of the very few directors whose careers extend from the silent films of the 1920s into the 1960s and, in his case, even into major productions of the 1970s. Born in England, he began his work in films as a title artist in 1920, eventually working as a script writer, art director, and assistant director. His first important picture as a director was *The Lodger* (1927). He made the first British sound feature film, *Blackmail* (1929), and in the 1930s came his major British achievements, such as *The Man Who Knew Too Much* (1934; he also made a later version in 1956), *The Thirty-Nine Steps* (1935), and *The Lady Vanishes* (1938).

He came to Hollywood in 1939, and his first American film, *Rebecca* (1940), received the Academy Award as the best picture of the year. Other films of the 1940s include *Shadow of a Doubt* (1943), *Notorious* (1946), and *Rope* (1948). Many critics believe that his most important achievements are those of the 1950s and early 1960s, especially *Strangers on a Train* (1951), *Rear Window* (1954), *North by Northwest* (1959), of

FIG. 28.   The Museum of Modern Art/Film Stills Archive.   Courtesy Paramount Pictures.

course *Psycho*, and *The Birds* (1963). Later films include *Frenzy* (1972) and *The Family Plot* (1976).

Hitchcock's influence on younger filmmakers has been immense; among the first to take him fully seriously were the French critics of *Cahiers du Cinéma:* Eric Rohmer and Claude Chabrol collaborated on a book on Hitchcock in 1957, before either one had directed a feature film, and François Truffaut has published a volume of his conversations with Hitchcock, whom he calls in the Introduction "the most complete filmmaker of all."

Although Hitchcock is not given a credit for helping to write the screenplay by Joseph Stephano for *Psycho*, as always the director was from the start intimately involved with the creation of the script. He also produced the film. The cinematographer was John L. Russell, who had worked on the television series *Alfred Hitchcock Presents;* this was his first feature film with Hitchcock, but he had directed the photography for Orson Welles's *Macbeth* (1948). Another person who had worked with Welles was Bernard Hermann, who had composed the music for **Citizen Kane* and now created the extraordinarily effective music—restricted to strings—for *Psycho;* he had already worked with Hitchcock on such films as *The Man Who Knew Too Much* (1956) and *North by Northwest*. George Tomasini, the editor, had also been with Hitchcock for years. Saul Bass, who created the titles, had also done that for *Vertigo* (1958) and *North by Northwest;* in addition, he served on *Psycho* as pictorial consultant, helping to create a number of the visual concepts in some key sequences, such as that in the shower.

Other credits: special effects, Clarence Champagne; art direction, Joseph Hurley and Robert Clatworthy; sets, George Milo; sound, Waldon Watson and William Russell; assistant director, Hilton Green; costumes, Helen Colvig.

Heading the cast as Norman Bates was Anthony Perkins, in the role for which he will probably always be most remembered, but he has also given sensitive performances in *Fear Strikes Out* (1957), Welles's **The Trial* (1963), *Pretty Poison* (1968), and *Catch-22* (1970). He also wrote the screenplay for the suspense film *The Last of Sheila* (1973). Janet Leigh, who was nominated for an Academy Award for her role as Marion Crane in *Psycho*, has been in many films since *The Romance of Rosy Ridge* (1947), including Welles's *Touch of Evil* (1958) and Frankenheimer's *The Manchurian Candidate* (1962).

Other members of the cast: Vera Miles as Lila Crane; John Gavin as Sam Loomis; Martin Balsam as Milton Arbogast; John McIntire as

Sheriff Chambers; Laureen Tuttle as Mrs. Chambers; Frank Albertson as Cassidy; Vaughn Taylor as Mr. Lowery, Marion's employer; Simon Oakland as the psychiatrist; Mort Mills as the state policeman; John Anderson as the car salesman. Caroline, the other secretary in Marion's office, was played by Pat Hitchcock, the director's daughter. Hitchcock himself appears briefly, as he does in all his films; here he is outside the real estate office when Marion returns from seeing Sam, and he is wearing a Stetson cowboy hat.

Running time: 109 minutes. Distributors: Swank; Twyman; Universal.

TOPICS TO THINK ABOUT

1. *If you have not yet seen the film, in this instance do not read the Topics to Think About until you have.* Psycho is a suspense film—indeed, a "shocker"—and there is no point in diluting that element of the experience of viewing it for the first time.

2. John McCarten, in his review in *The New Yorker:* "Hitchcock does several spooky scenes with his usual éclat, and works diligently to make things as horrible as possible, but it's all rather heavy-handed and not in any way comparable to the fine jobs he's done in the not so distant past."

3. The film follows the novel—which I assume most readers of this volume will not be reading—in many particulars as well as in regard to the basic situation and plot, but it also makes significant departures. For example, in the book Norman is forty years old and fat; and all the background involving the theft of the $40,000 and leading up to the arrival at the motel of Marion (called Mary) is dealt with in a single chapter of ten pages, after a first chapter in which we have already met Norman—and his mother. (The novel was apparently based on newspaper stories about a man who preserved at home the dead body of his mother.)

We have also been given the first of a number of "conversations" between Norman and his mother, without our realizing their actual nature. But Bloch does not quite cheat, since her words are never explicitly attributed to her: there are no phrases like "said Mother," or "she replied." Or is that cheating anyway?

For that matter, is it also accurate to say—as Hitchcock said in an interview with Charles Thomas Samuels—that "it was a bit of a cheat" for him to have used a woman's voice, instead of Perkins' disguised voice, for the words of the mother except at the very end? In either case, do you mind?

4. As indicated above, the film greatly expands the role of Marion Crane and the plot of the stolen money. Why? "In fact, the first part of the story was a red herring," Hitchcock told Truffaut, echoing the sentiments of many viewers and critics (and of Janet Leigh, who good-naturedly told an interviewer, "The interesting thing to me was that my whole story really had nothing to do with the film"). What is your reaction to these views? Does the first third work with or against the rest of the film?

5. "*Psycho* begins with the normal and draws us steadily deeper and deeper into the abnormal." (Robin Wood, *Hitchcock's Films*)

6. For audiences seeing the film today fully to comprehend the original surprising impact of Marion's death, they must be aware of the fact that Janet Leigh was after all the biggest *star* in the film (a bigger star than Anthony Perkins)—and you just do not kill off the star one third of the way through the movie. What you do is give her the Vera Miles role of Lila. "Of course," Hitchcock remarked to Peter Bogdanovich, "this is idiot thinking. The whole point is to kill off the star, that is what makes it so unexpected."

7. There are many parallels and echoes in the film of earlier situations, visual images, or phrases which did not convey their full relevance when they were first encountered.

Consider, for example, just some of those contained in the superbly performed interior monologue at the end. Norman is sitting, alone and tight-lipped, the blanket wrapped around him, as we hear the voice-over of "Mother." "She" says that they should "put him away now, as I should have years ago." (In his conversation with Marion, we may recall, Norman had bridled at her suggestion in regard to his mother that it might "be better . . . if you put her . . . someplace.") At the end, again, we hear Mother's assuring voice, saying "As if I could do anything but just sit and stare like one of his stuffed birds" ("Why," Norman had similarly assured Marion, "she's as harmless as one of those stuffed birds")—at last the whole relevance of Norman's hobby of taxidermy finally becomes clear. To show how harmless she is, the voice of the Mother says that she will not even "swat that fly. I hope that they are watching. They will see, they will see, and they will say, 'Why she wouldn't even harm a fly.' " (The first words we hear after Marion has been murdered and her car has been sunk into the swamp are those of the woman in Sam's hardware store, who wants assurance that the insect killer is "painless" before she will buy it.)

8. A more complex visual mode of parallelism has occurred when Norman has removed the picture from the wall to reveal a hole through which he can spy on Marion. The picture is of a "classical"-looking scene in which two men seem about to rape a woman, in a sly visual counter-part to Norman's psychic motivation for peeping. What he does at that moment is of course contemptible; but are you entirely glad, or do you feel disappointed or even annoyed, when the film cuts from Janet Leigh's impressive body to Norman's eye—the eye that is seeing what you (we) would wish to see?

Is the possible sense that *we* are also implicated in Norman's voy-eurism supported by the opening of the film? The camera begins with long shots of Phoenix, Arizona, and pans along a single building; it seems to hesitate before it chooses the slightly open window to peep through, at half-naked bodies in a depressing hotel room. (Hitchcock had already played with associations between cinema audiences and a voyeur in *Rear Window*.)

9. The murder that follows Norman's peeping is one of the most famous sequences in film history, and probably the most famous horror scene of all. (It was censored after being shot, so as not to show too much naked flesh; hence the masking of the frame during the sequence.)

What makes it so effective? Is it the horror of the violence itself? It is certainly a violent scene, yet compared to the blood baths which have since become commonplace in movies clearly influenced by *Psycho*, made by people who try to copy Hitchcock's boldness but who do not have his technical skill, discipline, or cleverness, the shower scene may seem a model of restraint and good taste. Does it? Or does it seem to you to be regrettably sensational and crude?

10. How important in our experience of the shower sequence is the element of surprise? Certainly there is no comprehensible reason for Marion to be killed. Does the shock derive from that arbitrariness itself? Or from what?

11. The sequence is extraordinarily complicated for one so brief. Hitchcock has said that it took seven days to film. (Understandably, no doubt, Janet Leigh's memory is that it took even longer—"at least two weeks.") The result was a masterpiece of montage (for a discussion of montage, see chapter 2, pages 47–49), in which we actually *see* hardly anything at all in any given shot. James Naremore has carefully analyzed this sequence, between the ripping aside of the curtain and the long final shot, and says that "there are between fifty-five and sixty-five cuts, de-pending on where you start counting," and that "the average number of frames per shot is around fifteen; the briefest shot runs for eight frames, and the longest for thirty-five." (Keep in mind that motion pictures run at twenty-four frames per second.)

12. "You can do anything you want with montage. Cinema is simply pieces of film put together in a manner that creates ideas and emotions." (Hitchcock, interview with Charles Thomas Samuels)

13. Andrew Sarris, in *The American Cinema:*

> Hitchcock requires a situation of normality, however dull it may be on the surface, to emphasize the evil abnormality that lurks beneath the surface. Hitchcock understands, as his detractors do not, the crucial function of counterpoint in the cinema. You cannot commit a murder in a haunted house or dark alley, and make a meaningful statement to the audience. The spectators simply withdraw from these bizarre settings, and let the décor dictate the action. It is not Us up there on the screen, but some play actors trying to be sinister. However, when murder is committed in a gleamingly sanitary motel bathroom during a cleansing shower, the incursion of evil into our well-laundered existence becomes intolerable.

14. Another mode of what Sarris calls "counterpoint" involves a balance of visual cinematic approaches. Hitchcock had long been known as a master of montage; during the 1940s, he also became increasingly intrigued with the possibilities of the moving camera, even experimenting in *Rope* (1948) with long, continually mobile shots, only cutting when it was necessary to reload the camera every ten minutes or so.

Here the frenetic montage of a series of very brief shots during the murder is immediately counterpointed by lengthy shots of Marion's eye and face. Then (to the diminishing sound of the running water) there is a slow tracking shot leading out of the bathroom, into the main room, pausing at the newspaper we know is rolled around $40,000, and then to the window, through which we see the old house up on the hill.

15. Again in terms of what Sarris calls "counterpoint," what is the effect of the subsequent scene, in which Norman discovers the murder, and then cleans up the mess it has caused?

16. Truffaut, not in the specific context of a discussion of *Psycho:* "I believe you film emotions you feel very deeply—fear, for instance."

Hitchcock: "Absolutely. I'm full of fears and I do my best to avoid difficulties and any kind of complications. I like everything around me to be clear as crystal and completely calm. . . . I get a feeling of inner peace from a well-organized desk. When I take a bath, I put everything neatly back in place. You wouldn't even know I'd been in the bathroom. My passion for orderliness goes hand in hand with a strong revulsion toward complications."

17. Suddenly, a film that has seemed to be about Marion Crane centers on Norman Bates. At this point, what is the attitude of an audience toward Norman likely to be?

18. In one of the "conversations" between Norman and his mother in the novel, she is shocked when he suggests that perhaps it would be best if they openly confronted "what they call the Oedipus situation." In regard to the film, to what degree would you say we are led to suspect that Norman's problems with his mother may include "the Oedipus situation"?

The reference of course is to Sigmund Freud's concept that the love that a male child feels for his mother is much more sexual—more "erotic"—than was formerly thought. Inevitably allied to those feelings, according to the Freudian pattern, will be sensations of envy and jealousy in regard to the father, the son's chief—and formidable— "rival." (The name "Oedipus" refers to the Greek figure who, though unknowingly, killed his father and married his mother.) In the normal course of things, a boy eventually grows out of or beyond the Oedipus complex, although its influence is never totally eradicated; but sometimes it may persist longer than, or be more intense than, what is regarded as "normal" or "healthy" by society—or by the son, perhaps. "Well," Norman tells Marion in the film, "a son is a poor substitute for a lover."

19. Another psychological concept which may or may not strike you as helpful in thinking about Norman is *dissociation,* which refers to the "splitting off" of certain aspects or processes of the mind from others, or even from the rest of the personality; possible results include amnesia, somnambulism ("sleepwalking"), or even the extreme of "multiple personalities."

In literature, a similar concept entails what critics refer to as "doubles" or *"doppelgängers,"* terms which can refer to two different though related phenomena. First, there is the case of the "split personality," in which one person has two or more distinct personalities, the most famous example being the extreme one of Robert Louis Stevenson's *The Strange Case of Dr. Jekyll and Mr. Hyde.* Or, the doubles may be two different people whose personalities seem so identified with one another that the two characters become connected in some sort of twinship, whether symbolic, psychological, moral, or metaphysical. Often, a protagonist is illuminated by means of a double who serves as a "foil." An especially famous example occurs in Joseph Conrad's "The Secret Sharer."

20. The first kind of "doubling" mentioned above is clearly relevant to Norman. Is the second? How suggestive is the physical resemblance between Anthony Perkins and John Gavin, who plays Sam Loomis? Is there any significance in Sam's being resentful of his dead father for loading him with debts? or in his joking question to Marion, "And after the steak, do we send Sister to the movies? Turn Mama's picture to the wall?"

21. In any case, the first kind of doubling—involving an ostensibly single but split personality—*is* surely present in Norman. As the psychiatrist puts it at the end of the film, "at times he could be both personalities, carry on conversations."

Does the fact that his other personality is a woman—his mother— make us suspect that Norman may be a latent homosexual? The notion that Norman is a "transvestite" seems to be rejected by the psychiatrist in the film, although not by his counterpart in the novel. In any case, however, the latter explains that "transvestites aren't necessarily homosexual, but they identify themselves strongly with members of the other sex."

22. Is it homosexuality that Norman has repressed, do you think? Or might it be sexuality itself? Do his slightly "effeminate" traits signify less a possible homosexuality than his having been, in more general terms, deprived of his "manhood"? (The term is Arbogast's, when he assures Norman that he did not mean one of his remarks as "a slur on your manhood.")

What do Lila and we see in Norman's room?

23. In an interview with Ian Cameron and V. F. Perkins, Hitchcock referred—not specifically in regard to *Psycho*—to a famous line in Oscar Wilde's poem, "The Ballad of Reading Gaol":

> What's that old Oscar Wilde thing? "Each man kills the thing he loves . . ." That I think is a very natural phenomenon, really.
> *You don't find it somewhat perverted?*
> Well, everything's perverted in a different way, isn't it?

24. "You have to remember that *Psycho* is a film made with quite a sense of amusement on my part. To me it's a *fun* picture. . . . After all it stands to reason that if one were seriously doing the *Psycho* story, it would be a case history. . . . Probably the real *Psycho* story wouldn't have been emotional at all; it would've been terribly clinical." (Hitchcock, interview with Ian Cameron and V. F. Perkins)

Some critics have felt that in many remarks during his interviews Hitchcock is unfair to the full seriousness of some of his own films.

Would you regard the above comment as such as instance? Or does it strike you as pertinent?

25. In his review of *Psycho* in *Sight and Sound*, Peter John Dyer asserts that "a thriller which, by its very nature, stands or falls by its action, is merely exposing its debility when it comes to depend on a complex, last-minute explication: a movie-psychiatrist's explication at that." And James Naremore, in his later full-length study of the film, says that "there is no question that the psychiatric explanations in *Psycho* are flat, dull, and pompously acted."

Robin Wood, in contrast, argues: "The psychiatrist's 'explanation' has been much criticized, but it has its function. It crystallises for us our tendency to evade the implications of the film, by converting Norman into a mere 'case,' hence something we can easily put from us. The psychiatrist, glib and complacent, reassures us. But Hitchcock crystallises this for us merely to force us to reject it." (*Hitchcock's Films*)

Is Wood's explanation convincing? Is it needed?

26. "A boy's best friend is his mother." (Norman Bates)

27. "We are what we pretend to be, so we must be careful about what we pretend to be." (Kurt Vonnegut, Jr., in his novel *Mother Night*)

Further Readings

BLOCH, ROBERT. *Psycho*. New York: Award, 1975. Originally published 1959.

BOGDANOVICH, PETER. *The Cinema of Alfred Hitchcock*. New York: Museum of Modern Art Film Library, 1963. Interviews.

CAMERON, IAN, and V. F. PERKINS. "Alfred Hitchcock." In *Interviews with Film Directors*. Ed. Andrew Sarris. New York: Avon, 1969, pp. 241–52. Originally published in *Movie* 6 (January 1963): 4–6.

DURGNAT, RAYMOND. *The Strange Case of Alfred Hitchcock: Or, The Plain Man's Hitchcock*. Cambridge, Mass.: MIT Press, 1974.

HITCHCOCK, ALFRED. *Psycho*. Ed. Richard J. Anobile. New York: Universe, 1974. Valuable shot-by-shot record of the film; over 1300 frame stills.

LaVALLEY, ALBERT J., ed. *Focus on Hitchcock*. Englewood Cliffs, N.J.: Prentice-Hall, 1972. A good collection of essays by various critics; includes a 1937 essay by Hitchcock entitled "Direction."

NAREMORE, JAMES. *Filmguide to Psycho*. Bloomington: Indiana University Press, 1973. Excellent, detailed analysis.

NOGUEIRA, RUI. "*Psycho*, Rosie and a Touch of Orson." *Sight and Sound* 39 (Spring 1970): 66–70. Interview with Janet Leigh.

SAMUELS, CHARLES THOMAS. "Alfred Hitchcock." In his *Encountering Directors*. New York: Putnam's Sons, 1972, pp. 231–50. Interview.

TRUFFAUT, FRANÇOIS, with HELEN G. SCOTT. *Hitchcock*. New York: Simon and Schuster, 1967. The most extensive interviews with Hitchcock yet published, and all in all the best, with added interest because of Truffaut's own stature as a film director (of, for example, **Jules and Jim*).

WOOD, ROBIN. *Hitchcock's Films*. 3d ed. Cranbury, N.J.: A. S. Barnes, 1978.

■ ■

THE INNOCENTS
(THE TURN OF THE SCREW)
■ ■

BACKGROUND

On the Novel

The Turn of the Screw (which is variously described as a short novel or a long short story; see the discussion of such distinctions in chapter 1, pages 13–15) was published as a serial in *Collier's Weekly* in 1898 and revised for the collected edition of James's works in 1908. Henry James (1843–1916) says in a Preface to that edition that his tale originated in a conversation during which someone told of once hearing about "a couple of small children in an out-of-the-way place, to whom the spirits of certain 'bad' servants, dead in the employ of the house, were believed to have appeared with the design of 'getting hold' of them."

James was one of the most important novelists of the late nineteenth and early twentieth centuries; an American, he settled in England in his thirties. His first novel was *Roderick Hudson* (1875), but it was *Daisy Miller* (1879) that brought him international fame, although *Portrait of a Lady* (1881) was the first of his truly major works. Other novels include *The Spoils of Poynton* and *What Maisie Knew* (both 1897), and the ambitious and complex novels of his later years, *The Wings of the Dove* (1902), *The Ambassadors* (1903), and *The Golden Bowl* (1904). Besides *The Turn of the Screw*, works by James that have been adapted for the movies include *Daisy Miller* (by Peter Bogdanovich, 1974), *Washington Square* (1881; by William Wyler as *The Heiress*, 1949), *The Aspern Papers* (1888; by Martin

FIG. 29.   The Museum of Modern Art/Film Stills Archive. Copyright © 1961 20th
Century-Fox. All rights reserved.

Gabel as *The Lost Moment,* 1947), and *The Sense of the Past* (1917, unfinished; by Frank Lloyd as *Berkeley Square,* 1933, and by Roy Baker as *I'll
Never Forget You,* 1951).

The *Turn of the Screw* has given rise to voluminous and vociferous
controversies, the central issues of which are indicated in the Topics To
Think About, below (which the reader may wish to postpone looking at
until after reading the novel or seeing the film).

On the Film

The Innocents (1961)—which Pauline Kael called in her review "the
best ghost movie I've ever seen"—was based on a play of the same title by
William Archibald, which had been produced in New York in 1950.
Archibald also served as one of the screenwriters for the film. Another
was Truman Capote, who is best known for his novels, the first of which
was *Other Voices, Other Rooms* (1948); two of his books that have been
adapted as films are *Breakfast at Tiffany's* (1958; film, 1961) and *In Cold
Blood* (1966; film, 1967). He also wrote the script for John Huston's *Beat
the Devil* (1953). "Additional scenes and dialogue" were contributed by
John Mortimer, whose screenplays include *Bunny Lake Is Missing* (1965).

The film was directed by Jack Clayton (b. 1921), a British filmmaker who had been an assistant producer before directing *The Bespoke Overcoat* (1955), a short film based on a story by Gogol; it attracted a great deal of attention and won a prize at the Venice Film Festival. His first feature film, *Room at the Top* (1958), was also a critical and popular success; like all his subsequent films, such as *The Pumpkin Eater* (1964) and *Our Mother's House* (1967), it was based on a novel—as of course was *The Great Gatsby* (1974).

The cinematography was by Freddie Francis, who had also worked on *Room at the Top* and won an Academy Award for *Sons and Lovers* (1960). He went on to become a director, specializing in horror films like *The Evil of Frankenstein* (1964) and *Tales from the Crypt* (1971). Georges Auric composed the music, as he had thirty years before for René Clair's *À Nous la Liberté* (1931); he also wrote scores for *Caesar and Cleopatra* (1945) and *The Wages of Fear* (1953). For *The Innocents,* he and Paul Dehn (a screenwriter) wrote the song, "O Willow Waly."

Other credits: cameraman, Ron Taylor; art director, Wilfred Shingleton; editor, James Clark; sound, A. G. Ambler and John Cox; costumes, Sophie Devine; makeup, Harold Fletcher.

Deborah Kerr, who played the governess (called Miss Giddens in the film) has been in movies since *Major Barbara* (1941). She went from England to Hollywood, where she appeared in *Julius Caesar* and *From Here to Eternity* (both 1953), *The King and I* and *Tea and Sympathy* (both 1956), and *The Night of the Iguana* (1964), as well as many other films.

Michael Redgrave (the uncle) has been especially associated with the British theater, although he has also appeared in films since Hitchcock's *The Lady Vanishes* (1938), including *1984* (1956), *The Loneliness of the Long Distance Runner* (1962), *Young Cassidy* (1964—as William Butler Yeats), and *The Go-Between* (1971).

Megs Jenkins (Mrs. Grose) has been maternal and understanding in *The History of Mr. Polly* (1949), *Bunny Lake Is Missing,* and *Oliver!* (1968). Flora was Pamela Franklin's first role; she has since been in Clayton's *Our Mother's House,* and in *The Prime of Miss Jean Brodie* (1969) and *The Legend of Hell House* (1973). Martin Stephens (Miles) was one of the mysterious menacing chidren in *Village of the Damned* (1962) and has also appeared in other films, including *The Battle of the Villa Fiorita* (1964).

Other members of the cast: Peter Wyngarde as Peter Quint; Clytie Jessop as Miss Jessel; Isla Cameron as Anna; Eric Woodburn as the coachman.

In *The Nightcomers* (1972), directed by Michael Winner, Marlon Brando and Stephanie Beacham played Peter Quint and Miss Jessel in a film conjecturing what happened *before* the start of *The Turn of the Screw*, and ending with the arrival of the new governess.

Running time of *The Innocents:* 99 minutes. Distributor: Films Inc.

TOPICS TO THINK ABOUT

1. Since *The Turn of the Screw* and *The Innocents* are works of mystery and suspense, *you may not wish to read the Topics to Think About until you have read the novel or seen the film.*

2. "The story and the novel, the idea and the form, are the needle and thread, and I never heard of a guild of tailors who recommended the use of the thread without the needle, or the needle without the thread." (James, "The Art of Fiction")

For some of James's important views on prose fiction, see chapter 1, page 8, and chapter 3, page 66.

3. James, in the Preface to the 1908 edition, on *The Turn of the Screw:* "It is a piece of ingenuity pure and simple, of cold artistic calculation, an *amusette* to catch those not easily caught (the 'fun' of the capture of the merely witless being ever but small), the jaded, the disillusioned, the fastidious."

4. *The Turn of the Screw* has a relatively complex framework, with a story within a story (the manuscript, as introduced by Douglas) within a story (that of the first-person narrator). Why does James devise such a framework? Why do you suppose the film discards it?

5. What would you guess were the reasons for changing the title? How do you interpret the title *The Innocents?* To whom does it refer? In what respect are they "innocent," and of what?

6. "I now saw that I had been asked for a service admirable and difficult; and there would be a greatness in letting it be seen—oh, in the right quarter! that I could succeed where many another girl might have failed." (Chapter 6)

7. Douglas, in the Prologue: "She was the most agreeable woman I've ever known in her position; she would have been worthy of any whatever."

Do you feel that by the end of her story the governess has shown herself to deserve this praise?

8. "I had the view of a castle of romance inhabited by a rosy sprite, such a place as would somehow . . . take all colour out of storybooks and fairy-tales." (Chapter 1)

9. "Only make the reader's general vision of evil intense enough . . . and his own experience, his own imagination, his own sympathy (with the children) and horror (of their false friends) will supply him quite sufficiently with all the particulars." (James, Preface)

Who in the tale is *not* among "the innocents"? Who are the "false friends"?

10. James, in his Preface:

> Good ghosts, speaking by book, make poor subjects, and it was clear that from the first my hovering prowling blighting presences, my pair of abnormal agents, would have to depart altogether from the rules. They would be agents in fact; there would be laid on them the dire duty of causing the situation to reek with the air of Evil. . . .
> This is to say . . . that Peter Quint and Miss Jessel are not "ghosts" at all, as we now know the ghost, but goblins, elves, imps, demons as loosely constructed as those of the old trials for witchcraft; if not, more pleasingly, fairies of the legendary order, wooing their victims forth to see them dance under the moon.

11. "Henry James's ghosts have nothing in common with the violent old ghosts—the blood-stained sea captains, the white horses, the headless ladies of dark lanes and windy commons. They have their origin within us." (Virginia Woolf, "Henry James's Ghost Stories," 1921)

12. Most people have always read *The Turn of the Screw* as a straightforward ghost story, but many readers have felt that doing so produces problems of interpretation. To mention only one instance, they cite the last scene, in which the frightened Miles pants, "Is she *here?*"—and the governess is "staggered" by "his strange 'she,'" since until now Miles has invariably been associated with visions of Peter Quint, not Miss Jessel. How might this apparent discrepancy be resolved? Consider of course the context of the entire scene.

13. In "The Ambiguity of Henry James," a famous and controversial essay first published in 1934, the critic Edmund Wilson argued that *The Turn of the Screw* is not a straightforward ghost story at all, but a psychological tale about a deluded and ultimately dangerous young woman: "The theory is, then, that the governess who is made to tell the story is a neurotic case of sex repression, and that the ghosts are not real ghosts but hallucinations of the governess." (The argument was not completely original with Wilson, but he was the first to develop it fully in print, and while others have expanded upon it, his essay remains among the most lucid—and extreme—statements of his basic positions.)

In terms of your own reading of the novel, what is your initial reaction to that contention, presumably without having heard the evidence that Wilson cites to support it?

Of course, you may wish to read Wilson's essay and a selection of the many arguments that have been published attacking or supporting it, in one of the liveliest and most long-lasting critical controversies of the century. (See the list of Further Readings, below.)

14. Keep in mind that Wilson is really making a *dual* argument, and that while we can either agree or disagree with both his contentions, we can also accept one without the other—that is, we can believe that the ghosts are hallucinations, but not necessarily that they reflect "sex repression," or that the governess is indeed sexually repressed, but that the ghosts are nevertheless real ghosts.

15. Among the traits for which James's fiction is especially famous is his handling of the limited point of view. (See the discussions in chapters 1 and 2, pages 9–11 and 38–41, of point of view in written literature and film.) Sometimes by means of a direct first-person narration, as here, or sometimes through a third-person narrative which nevertheless presents information or views as if filtered through the perceptions of one of his characters, James provides a fascinating and subtly controlled angle of vision with a single sensibility acting as a "reverberator." (*The Reverberator* is the title of one of James's novels, 1888.) We may or may not fully go along with the perceptions of the given character, but it is through his or her eyes that we see everything—even those aspects of a story which may make our view vastly different from that of the character who is our only (or, perhaps, our major) source of information and awareness.

In *The Turn of the Screw*, how one feels about the issues of the reality of the ghosts and the psychology of the governess will depend on the degree to which we can feel that her narrative is one upon which we can rely. If, for example, we conclude that she is mad, we must arrive at that conclusion both through and in spite of what she herself tells us, for she is our only source of facts about her, except for the little we find out in the prologue from Douglas.

16. In the film, although there are a few voice-overs (of words recalled or imagined by Miss Giddens), there is no narration. What is the effect of that change? Does the film nevertheless somehow restrict itself to Miss Giddens' point of view?

17. One of the things within the novel that lead some readers to *reject* the view that the ghosts are only in the governess' mind is the fact that after she has seen Peter Quint for the second time, she is able to describe him accurately to Mrs. Grose. See the relevant passage in the short chapter 5. Is there any way in which we can see that she could have learned about the details of Quint's physical appearance without having seen his ghost?

18. One of the things within the novel that leads some readers to *accept* the view that the ghosts are only in the governess' mind is the fact that no one else ever admits seeing them. Does that seem to you a major or perhaps even decisive consideration, or a minor one?

Of course it is one of the favorite tricks of ghosts (in literature, anyway) to appear to one person but not another; you may recall the appearance of Duncan in *Macbeth,* or of the dead king in Gertrude's chamber in **Hamlet.* On the other hand, there are reasons for the selective appearance in each of those cases, and we may wonder why—if they have the ability—Quint and Miss Jessel do not hide themselves from the governess. Could you explain why?

19. "Miss Jessel stood before us on the opposite bank exactly as she had stood the other time, and I remember, strangely, as the first feeling now produced in me, my thrill of joy at having brought on a proof. She was there, and I was justified; she was there, and I was neither cruel nor mad." (Chapter 20)

Do you find it anomalous or ironic that she cites seeing a ghost as evidence of her sanity?

20. On Quint: "He was absolutely, on this occasion, a living, detestable, dangerous presence. But that was not the wonder of wonders; I reserve this distinction for quite another circumstance: the circumstance that dread had unmistakeably quitted me and that there was nothing in me that didn't meet and measure him." (Chapter 9)

21. What might one point to in the novel as evidence that the governess, either instead of or in addition to the ghosts, is a danger to her charges?

22. Miles confesses at the end that he had been sent home from school because he "said things," presumably sexual or "dirty" things that disturbed the other boys or shocked their Victorian schoolmasters. Does his having done so thereby indicate that he is not an "innocent"? (Could it suggest that he *is?*)

23. ". . . there had come to me out of my very pity the appalling alarm of his being perhaps innocent. It was for the instant confounding and bottomless, for if he *were* innocent, what then on earth was *I?*" (Chapter 24)

24. Why does Miles want to go back to school?:

"You know, my dear, that for a fellow to be with a lady *always*—!" . . .

. . . I remember that, to gain time, I tried to laugh, and I seemed to see in the beautiful face with which he watched me how ugly and queer I looked. "And always with the same lady?" I returned.

He neither blenched nor winked. The whole thing was virtually out between us. "Ah, of course, she's a jolly, 'perfect' lady; but, after all, I'm a fellow, don't you see? that's—well, getting on." (Chapter 14)

Why is the governess reluctant to let him return to school? Would not sending him away be a relatively safe or simple solution? Why does she eventually send Flora away with Mrs. Grose, leaving herself almost alone with Miles?

25. Which view of the novel—the one that sees the governess as reliable and even heroic, or the one that sees her as deluded and even a menace—seems to you to make the novel itself more effective? Which makes what we hear and what happens to the various characters more frightening? Or is the novel most effective and frightening if we remain uncertain?

26. Is there any way in which the view that questions the reliability of the governess can resolve the apparent discrepancies mentioned in topic 12 in regard to the last scene of the novel?

27. What seems to you to have been the approach of the filmmakers to the central controversies brought up above?

28. Spectators and critics of the film often feel that a shot supporting the reality of the ghosts is the one of the tear on the desk at which Miss Jessel has been seen sitting. Yet an added scene which may point in the opposite direction is the one in which Miss Giddens finds the photograph of Quint. That occurs after her first long-distance vision of his ghost, but just before she and we see a close-up of his face in the window; it is after that that she describes him to Mrs. Grose.

29. ". . . in *The Innocents*, Truman Capote had adapted James' narrative into post-Freudian terms. The ghosts are no longer demons from the pit as the author intended . . . but the products of the sick imagination of a spinster and the horror (if horror there be, since a more accurate word would be tension) derives from the fact that a neurotic woman comes to be responsible for the traumatization or death of her infant and sensitive charges." (Carlos Clarens, *An Illustrated History of the Horror Film*)

Do you agree that the viewpoint of the film is so clearly defined?

30. The uncle, in the first bit of direct dialogue in the film: "Do you have an imagination?"

31. In the film, Miles kisses Miss Giddens on the lips after she has found the dead pigeon under his pillow. What connections are suggested in that scene? When is the next time one of them kisses the other on the lips?

32. Deborah Kerr seems older than the young girl in the novel. Is anything lost because of that fact? Is anything gained? Does her age tend to support any particular approach toward the controversies raised?

33. The film makes extensive use of dissolves (see chapter 2, page 46). With what effect?

34. Jeanne Thomas Allen, in *"Turn of the Screw* and *The Innocents"*:

> By far . . . the best approximation of the novella's essential ambiguity—that of whether the reality of the governess's experience has been a subjective or objective one—is carried by the eerie, often unidentifiable soundtrack. The viewer's uncertainty goes beyond the difficulty of identifying a peculiar sound to knowing what the sound signifies within a code system that the film develops for music, echo effects, exaggerated volume, and electronic sound. . . .
>
> Several natural sounds are amplified frequently at points when Quint and Jessel appear to Miss Giddens: the plopping of the scissors in the water, the buzzing of flies in the tower and in the schoolroom, etc. This exaggeration may imply either the governess's heightened perception that enables her to apprehend Quint and Jessel, or it may suggest a neurotic hypersensitivity that makes her hallucination-prone.

35. In the film, Miss Giddens asks Mrs. Grose: "To wake a child out of a bad dream—is that a cruelty?"

36. "I don't want, you know, to say absolutely what the picture means. There should be an area of uncertainty; that's what I think James intended. I want the audience to exercise its intelligence." (Jack Clayton, quoted by James W. Palmer)

Further Readings

ALLEN, JEANNE THOMAS. *"Turn of the Screw* and *The Innocents:* Two Types of Ambiguity." In *The Classic American Novel and the Movies.* Ed. Gerald Peary and Roger Shatzkin. New York: Ungar, 1977, pp. 132–42.

ARCHIBALD, WILLIAM. *The Innocents.* New York: Coward-McCann, 1950. The script of the play.

CRANFILL, THOMAS M., and ROBERT L. CLARK, JR. *An Anatomy of The Turn of the Screw.* Austin: University of Texas Press, 1965. Favors the psychological view.

JAMES, HENRY. *The Art of the Novel.* New York: Charles Scribner's Sons, 1936. Prefaces.

———. *The Portable Henry James.* Ed. Morton Dauwen Zabel. New York: Viking, 1951. Contains three short novels (not including *The Turn of the Screw*), short stories, critical essays, and other materials.

———. *The Turn of the Screw.* Available in many editions. Easily accessible paperbacks are: *Great Short Works of Henry James* (Perennial); *The Turn of the Screw and Daisy Miller* (Dell); *The Turn of the Screw and Other Short Novels* (Signet); *The Turn of the Screw: An Authoritative Text and Background and Sources: Essays in Criticism* (Norton, 1966), ed. Robert Kimbrough; has annotations. Also, see Willen, below.

PALMER, JAMES W. "Cinematic Ambiguity: James's *The Turn of the Screw* and Clayton's *The Innocents.*" *Literature/Film Quarterly* 5 (Summer 1977): 198–215. A detailed examination.

SHEPPARD, E. A. *Henry James and The Turn of the Screw.* London: Oxford, 1974. An extended scholarly study.

SIEGEL, ELI. *James and the Children: A Consideration of Henry James's The Turn of the Screw.* Ed. Martha Baird. New York: Definition Press, 1968. Opposes Wilson's position.

WILLEN, GERALD, ed. *A Casebook on Henry James's "The Turn of the Screw."* 2d ed. New York: Thomas Y. Crowell, 1969. Includes the novel itself, James's Preface and some letters and a notebook entry, and many essays by various critics. A valuable collection.

WILSON, EDMUND. "The Ambiguity of Henry James." In his *The Triple Thinkers.* Rev. ed. New York: Oxford University Press, 148. Originally published in *Hound and Horn* 7 (April–June 1934): 385–406. Reprinted in Willen, above.

LAST YEAR AT MARIENBAD

BACKGROUND

Alain Resnais (b. 1922) started as a film editor and then began directing documentaries with a series of films on the painters Van Gogh, Gauguin, and Picasso in the late 1940s. His first feature film, *Hiroshima*

Mon Amour (1959), provided a great impetus for the "new wave" ("*nouvelle vague*") of French filmmakers when it received the International Critics' prize at Cannes, but because Resnais was never connected with the magazine *Cahiers du Cinéma,* he is often not considered a "member" of the new wave like François Truffaut, Jean-Luc Godard, Eric Rohmer, Claude Chabrol, and Jacques Rivette.

Hiroshima Mon Amour began the experiments with images of time, memory, and fantasy that Resnais continued in his second film, *Last Year at Marienbad* (*L'Année dernière à Marienbad,* 1961), which attracted a great deal of attention and became a center of many critical controversies. His later films include *Muriel* (1963), *La Guerre est finie* (1966), *Je t'aime, je t'aime* (1968), *Stavisky* (1974), and *Providence* (1977).

In contrast to many other important directors, Resnais takes a relatively inactive part in the composition of his screenplays, yet he regards them as the core of the completed films. He has a special fondness for working with writers of some fame outside the world of cinema, together with an uncanny ability to choose ones who turn out to have a genuine affinity for that world. Indeed, several of the novelists whose scripts he has filmed have themselves gone on to direct their own movies, such as Marguerite Duras (who wrote *Hiroshima Mon Amour*), Jean Cayrol (the author of *Muriel*), and Alain Robbe-Grillet (the writer of *Last Year at Marienbad*).

Alain Robbe-Grillet (b. 1922) had already become a prominent figure in French literature by the time he and Resnais met (although Resnais had not at that time read any of his novels). As both a novelist and critic, Robbe-Grillet has been at the center of the so-called "new novel" ("*nouveau roman*"), a movement also variously called the "anti-novel," or "*chosisme*" (that is, "thingism"), or "*l'école de l'objet*" ("the school of the object"). The writers associated under these classifications include Marguerite Duras, Nathalie Sarraute, Claude Simon, Michel Butor, and others. While they are less intimately connected than is sometimes assumed, many of their books do tend to share certain specific characteristics, several of which seem at least relevant to aspects of *Last Year at Marienbad* as well: undependable or seemingly undependable narration; disruption of "normal" temporal chronology; an apparent absence of traditional "plot"; a lessening of emphasis on character and character analysis; a great stress on visual description; and an extraordinary use of constant repetition.

Robbe-Grillet's first novel was *The Erasers* (*Les Gommes,* 1953). His

FIG. 30.   The Museum of Modern Art/Film Stills Archive

next four novels all had titles that could have served for *Last Year at Marienbad* as well: *The Voyeur* (*Le Voyeur*, 1955), *Jealousy* (*La Jalousie*, 1957), *In the Labyrinth* (*Dans le Labyrinthe*, 1959), and *La Maison de Rendez-vous* (1965). Other works include *Project for a Revolution in New*

York (Projet pour une Révolution à New York, 1970) and *Topology of a Phantom City (Topologie d'une Cité Fantôme,* 1976). In addition, he has directed a number of films for which he has also written the screenplays (*Marienbad* was his first script), including *L'Immortelle* (1963), *Trans-Europ-Express* (1966), and *Les Gommes* (1972).

Resnais and Robbe-Grillet were brought together for the idea of making a film by the producers Pierre Courau and Raymond Froment. Resnais' assistant on the film, Jean Léon, has worked with him on most of his films, as have the director of photography, Sacha Vierny (who also worked on Buñuel's *Belle de Jour,* 1967), and the cameraman, Philippe Brun.

Many of the interiors in the palace are actually studio sets designed by Jacques Saulnier, whose other credits include *Muriel* and *What's New Pussycat?* (1965). Resnais is very active during editing; he worked on *Marienbad* with the husband and wife team of Henri Colpi and Jasmine Chasney, who had also edited *Hiroshima Mon Amour;* Colpi has become a director, his first feature film being *Une Aussi Longue Absence* (1961). The sound engineer was Guy Villette; the organ music was by Francis Seyrig.

The woman (called for convenience "A" in the screenplay) was played by Delphine Seyrig; this was her first major part, and she has also appeared in Resnais' *Muriel,* as well as in Losey's *Accident* (1967), Truffaut's *Stolen Kisses* (1968), and Buñuel's *The Discreet Charm of the Bourgeoisie* (1972). The man who narrates most of the film and who talks about their having met last year at Marienbad (called "X") was the Italian actor Giorgio Albertazzi; American audiences without a special familiarity with the French language will not realize that he speaks with a slight Italian accent. The other chief male character was played by Sacha Pitoeff; that character is called "M" in the script, perhaps to suggest *"mari"* (husband).

The external locations for shooting were at several castles in the Munich area (those of Nymphenburg, Schleissheim, and Amalienburg).

Running time: 93 minutes. Distributor: Audio Brandon.

TOPICS TO THINK ABOUT

1. "As an academic joke has it, one sophomore to another, 'Have you seen *Last Year at Marienbad?*' The other slowly, thoughtfully, 'I— don't know.'" (Norman N. Holland, *The Dynamics of Literary Response*)

2. Robbe-Grillet, in the Introduction to *Last Year at Marienbad:*

The essential characteristic of the image is its presentness. Whereas literature has a whole gamut of grammatical tenses which makes it possible to narrate events in relation to each other, one might say that on the screen verbs are always in the present tense (which is what is so strange, so artificial about the "novelized films" which have been restored to the past tense so dear to the traditional novel!): by its nature, what we see on the screen *is in the act of happening,* we are given the gesture itself, not an account of it.

3. According to St. Augustine, " 'There be three times: a present of things past, a present of things present, and a present of things future.' For these three do exist in some sort, in the soul, but otherwise do I not see them; present of things past, memory; present of things present, sight; present of things future, expectation." (*Confessions*)

Do these "presents" cover the possibilities suggested in *Marienbad*?

4. T. S. Eliot, from "Burnt Norton":

> What might have been and what has been
> Point to one end, which is always present.
> Footfalls echo in the memory
> Down the passage which we did not take
> Towards the door we never opened. . . .

5. X, to A: "And you asked me to allow you a year, thinking perhaps that you would test me that way . . . or wear me out . . . or forget me. . . . But time, time doesn't count."

6. Robbe-Grillet has said that he was pleased at the prospect of working with Resnais because:

> . . . I saw Resnais' work as an attempt to construct a purely mental space and time—those of dreams, perhaps, or of memory, those of any affective life—without worrying too much about the traditional relations of cause and effect, or about an absolute time sequence in the narrative.
>
> Everyone knows the linear plots of the old-fashioned cinema, which never spare us a link in the chain of all-too-expected events. . . . In reality, our mind goes faster—or sometimes slower. Its style is more varied, richer and less reassuring: it skips certain passages, it preserves an exact record of certain "unimportant" details, it repeats and doubles back on itself. And this *mental time,* with its peculiarities, its gaps, its obsessions, its obscure areas, is the one that interests us since it is the tempo of our emotions, of our *life.*
> (Introduction, *Last Year at Marienbad.*)

7. In an interview, Resnais spoke in similar terms about *Marienbad:* "For me the film is also an attempt, still very crude and primitive, to approach the complexity of thought and its mechanism. . . . I believe that, in life, we don't think chronologically, that our decisions never correspond to an ordered logic."

Yet in the same interview he explains that in preparing for shooting, he made "a complete chronology on graph paper," showing the "actual" order of the scenes despite the order in which they were shot or in which they appear in the film: "For example, all costume changes naturally correspond to different pieces of time. This is certainly not the key to the film, if indeed there is one. But it is true that we could re-edit the film so as to restore the chronological order of the scenes."

Do you find any contradictions within Resnais' statements? Or between them and those quoted from Robbe-Grillet?

8. In the film, how are the shifts from one scene to another, and from one moment of time to another, similar to or different from the more fully announced "flashbacks," say, of traditional films and novels?

If you know Arthur Miller's *Death of a Salesman,* compare and contrast the abrupt temporal shifts in that play (or the film adaptation of it) to those in *Last Year at Marienbad.* Or if you have seen Bergman's *Wild Strawberries,* Fellini's *$8^1/2$,* or Lumet's *The Pawnbroker,* consider the similarities and differences between *Marienbad* and one or more of those films in the use of cuts from one visual, visionary, or temporal world to another.

9. See the discussion in chapter 3 (pages 57–58) of the depiction of mental states—and of the "interior monologue" and "stream of consciousness"—in film and written literature.

10. X: "Hadn't you ever noticed all this?"

A: "I never had such a good guide."

X: "There are lots of other things to see here, if you want to."

11. ". . . if I say, 'The world is man,' I shall always gain absolution; while if I say, 'Things are things, and man is only man,' I am immediately charged with a crime against humanity." (Robbe-Grillet, "Nature, Humanism, Tragedy," in *For a New Novel*)

12. "Things are entirely what they appear to be and *behind them* . . . there is nothing." (Roquentin, in Jean-Paul Sartre's novel, *Nausea*)

13. Béla Balázs, in *Theory of the Film:*

On the stage the living, speaking human being has a far greater significance than dumb objects. They are not on the same plane and their intensity is different. In the silent film both man and object were equally pictures, photographs, their homogeneous material was projected on to the same screen, in the same way as in a painting, where they are equally patches of colour and equally parts in the same composition. In significance, intensity and value men and things were thus brought on to the same plane.

Even in the talkie the speaking human being is still only a picture, a photograph. The word does not lift him out of the community of the common material.

14. In a prefatory note, Robbe-Grillet warns the reader of his novel *In the Labyrinth* that "it is subject to no allegorical interpretation. The reader is therefore requested to see in it only the objects, actions, words, and events which are described, without attempting to give them either more or less meaning than in his own life, or his own death."

Would applying that restriction to *Last Year at Marienbad* enhance or needlessly limit one's comprehension and appreciation of the film, do you think?

15. Was there a last year at Marienbad? If so, what happened? In either case, what is happening now?

16. "In *Marienbad,* at first we believe that there was no last year and then we notice that last year has crept in everywhere: there you have it, entirely." (Robbe-Grillet, interview with Andre A. Labarthe and Jacques Rivette)

Does that help you, entirely?

17. ". . . we have decided to trust the spectator, to allow him, from start to finish, to come to terms with pure subjectivities." (Robbe-Grillet, Introduction, *Last Year at Marienbad*)

18. If you know Kurosawa's *Rashomon,* compare and contrast the ways in which that film and this one provide varying and contrasting presentations of what is ostensibly a single incident.

19. Consider *Last Year at Marienbad* in relation to the discussions of narrative structure, plot, and story in chapter 1.

20. At one point in the film, A moves along the wall of her room toward an open door, while we hear X's voice—"in a desperate struggle against the images seen on the screen," according to the script—saying "The door was closed now. No! No! The door was closed. . . . Listen to me. . . ."

21. "It is a film about greater and lesser degrees of reality. There are moments when the 'reality' is completely invented, or interior, as when the image corresponds to the conversations. The interior monologue is never on the sound track: it is always in the image, which, even when it represents the past, always corresponds to what is present in the character's mind." (Resnais, interview)

22. "In 1928 Eisenstein and Pudovkin published a manifesto on the future sound film which advocated 'an orchestral counterpoint of visual and aural images' and 'the distinct non-synchronization' of sound and picture. This is the norm in *Marienbad.*" (Dwight Macdonald, in *Dwight Macdonald on Movies*)

(See chapter 2, page 26, for a discussion of that manifesto.)

23. Most critics and spectators remain fundamentally uncertain about much of what is happening or has happened in this film, but here is an analysis by one critic who is an exception:

> A year ago a man X met a woman A at Marienbad in a château where they were both guests. Under the nose of her husband M, he began an affair with her. After trying several times to persuade A to leave with him, X is warned off by M. Finally M kills A and X is left alone to mourn. . . .
> The story of *Marienbad* is told (i.e., remembered) . . . by X. It is one long interior monologue. (John Ward, *Alain Resnais*)

In a footnote to the last sentence, Ward writes: "Resnais' and Robbe-Grillet's statements to the contrary are not relevant."

24. "Symbolically the broken glass corresponds appropriately to the fact that A's grasp on reality is breaking down, i.e., she begins to doubt her own memory while at the same time fantasy images of rape, murder, and suicide begin to intrude on her consciousness." (Ben F. Stoltzfus, *Alain Robbe-Grillet and the New French Novel*)

25. "*Marienbad* is a film which, for my part, presents neither allegory nor symbol." (Resnais, interview)

(See the discussion of symbols in chapter 1, pages 17–18.)

26. M: "I know a game I always win. . . ."

X: "If you can't lose, it's not a game!"

M: "I can lose. . . . But I always win."

Who wins, in the end? Who loses?

(M's game, incidentally, is a variation on the ancient Chinese game of Nim.)

27. The statue in the formal garden was especially sculpted for the film. What functions are served by it, and by the discussions X and A have about it?

28. "A man's erotic activity in relation to a woman always represents a kind of violation." (Robbe-Grillet, interview with Pierre Démeron)

29. The woman, A, seems often afraid: of what, or of whom?

30. Saying that if we accept "Truffaut's formula [that] 'any film must be able to be recapitulated in one word,'" Resnais remarks in an interview: "I want very much for people to say: *Last Year at Marienbad* or 'persuasion.' It's a solution. But there are others."

31. Roy Armes, in *The Cinema of Alain Resnais,* on the differences he perceives in the conceptions of *Marienbad* by its screenwriter and its director:

> It is clear that approaching the film from literature, Robbe-Grillet has conceived his film in terms of a verbal persuading, that the narrator's words are half the film, its backbone as it were. Absorbing them we imagine from his point of view, while [in the script] the images, being described but not actually seen, are much less forceful. . . .
>
> The director, on the other hand, being primarily concerned with the images, was largely dealing with the woman's side of the affair, for the images belong to her principally, representing her thoughts and her relation to the man. From her point of view, and hence from the director's, there is no single certainty, rather the essence of the film lies in its ambiguity. Among the many explanations of the film put forward by Resnais, persuasion is only one of the possibilities.

32. How do you interpret A's final decision and action? Do they seem to lead to greater freedom, or less—or to neither? Is she a free person, whether with M or X, or is she somehow bound to either or both of them? Or do you regard such terms as irrelevant to this film?

33. At several points in the film—including the very beginning—X's voice refers to his wandering through these corridors "once again."

The actress on the stage closes the play at the start of the film with the words, "Very well. . . . Now I am yours." That play may well be the one also being performed at the end, as A waits.

Is there a sense of an endless cyclical pattern in the events of the film, or do things come to some sort of resolution after all?

Further Readings

ARMES, ROY. *The Cinema of Alain Resnais.* New York: A. S. Barnes, 1968.
A valuable short book.

DÉMERON, PIERRE. "A Voyeur in the Labyrinth: An Interview with Alain

Robbe-Grillet." Trans. Richard Howard. *Evergreen Review* 10 (October 1966): 46–49, 90–92.

Labarthe, André S., and Jacques Rivette. "Alain Resnais." Trans. Rose Kaplin. In *Interviews with Film Directors*. Ed. Andrew Sarris. New York: Avon, 1969, pp. 434–52. Originally published in *Cahiers du Cinéma* 123 (September 1961). Almost exclusively on *Marienbad*. Partially with Resnais alone, but then with Robbe-Grillet as well.

Morrissette, Bruce. *Alain Robbe-Grillet*. New York: Columbia University Press, 1965. A pamphlet.

———. *The Novels of Robbe-Grillet*. Ithaca, N.Y.: Cornell University Press, 1965. By a critic who has had a great influence on studies of Robbe-Grillet.

Nogueria, Rui. "The Lily in the Valley." *Sight and Sound* 38 (Autumn 1969): 184–87. Interview with Delphine Seyrig.

Robbe-Grillet, Alain. *For a New Novel: Essays on Fiction*. Trans. Richard Howard. New York: Grove, 1965.

———. *Last Year at Marienbad*. Trans. Richard Howard. New York: Grove, 1962. The script as Robbe-Grillet gave it to Resnais; there are some discrepancies between it and the completed film. Includes a great deal of description and even commentary: it reads almost like a Robbe-Grillet novel. Some stills.

Stoltzfus, Ben F. *Alain Robbe-Grillet and the New French Novel*. Carbondale: Southern Illinois University Press, 1964. Argues that Resnais' film works against Robbe-Grillet's script.

Ward, John. *Alain Resnais, or the Theme of Time*. Garden City, N.Y.: Doubleday, 1968. Stresses the importance to Resnais of the philosophy of Henri Bergson.

JULES AND JIM

BACKGROUND

On the Novel

Henri-Pierre Roché (1879–1961) published his first novel, *Jules and Jim* (*Jules et Jim*), in 1953, when he was a retired art dealer in his seventies. It was a largely autobiographical book, by a man who had lived a full life and had known such artists as Picasso and Brancusi, and such literary figures as Apollinaire and Gertrude Stein.

The novel covers the years 1907 to 1930. Since the English translation is out of print and may not be readily available, we can point out here that in spirit and tone the film follows the book quite closely, although important details are also changed: in the novel Jules is Jewish; Catherine is called Kathe (Kate in the English translation) and is Prussian; in the movie she is given some of the dialogue and traits of a couple of other women in the novel (just as Albert in the film is also a composite of several of her lovers); she and Jules have two children, not just one.

On the Film

This book by an old man had captivated the young François Truffaut, who was to write in his Introduction to a new edition that it "formed me professionally as a cinéaste. I was 21 years old and a film critic. The book overwhelmed me and I wrote: if ever I succeed in making films I will make *Jules et Jim*." In 1955 he mentioned the novel in a review as promising material for a film; the review came to the attention of Roché, and the two men began a correspondence and friendship that lasted until Roché died, just before the completion of the film *Jules and Jim* (1961). Years later, Truffaut reaffirmed his admiration for Roché by also adapting his second and only other novel, *Les Deux Anglaises et le Continent*, in 1971 (it was called *Two English Girls* in the United States, *Anne and Muriel* in England).

As in the case of the older Roché, François Truffaut (b. 1932) produced in his first major work of art a semi-autobiography. Antoine Doinel, the young protagonist of *The Four Hundred Blows* (*Les Quatre Cents Coups*, 1959), is modeled in part on Truffaut's own troubled childhood. Antoine's detention in a reformatory is based on Truffaut's own experiences, although the causes are different: at the age of fifteen, Truffaut had started his own film society, and financial troubles in its management led to his arrest. But through that society he had also met the critic André Bazin, who befriended him and now came to his aid. In his Foreword to the second volume of Bazin's *What Is Cinema?* Truffaut says, "I became his adopted son. Thereafter, every pleasant thing that happened in my life I owed to him."

Bazin's magazine *Cahiers du Cinéma* started publication in 1951. Truffaut began writing reviews for it in 1953, and his first important article—a controversial piece on adaptations, attacking a number of prominent figures while defending Bresson's *Diary of a Country Priest* (see the discussion in chapter 4, page 83)—appeared in 1954; from then on he had the reputation of being one of the most demanding and even at times vicious film critics in France. A number of the critics associated with *Cahiers du Cinéma* went on, like Truffaut, to be directors and came to be known as the "new wave" (*"nouvelle vague"*) of filmmakers in France. They included Jacques Rivette, Eric Rohmer, Claude Chabrol, and Jean-Luc Godard (whose *Breathless,* 1960, came from a story idea by Truffaut), as well as others not connected with *Cahiers,* such as Alain Resnais. The emergence of these new talents received a tremendous boost in 1959 when Resnais' *Hiroshima Mon Amour* won the International Critics' prize, and Truffaut won the prize for direction (for *The Four Hundred Blows*), both at Cannes—the festival which Truffaut the critic had often attacked and from which indeed he had been banned in 1958.

Stolen Kisses (*Baisers volés,* 1968) and *Bed and Board* (*Domicile Conjugal,* 1970) continued the story of Antoine of *The Four Hundred Blows,* still played by Jean-Pierre Léaud. Other Truffaut films include *Shoot the Piano Player* (*Tirez sur le Pianist,* 1960), *Fahrenheit 451* (1966)—his first English language film—and *The Story of Adele H.* (*L'Histoire d'Adele H.,* 1975). In *The Wild Child* (*L'Enfant Sauvage,* 1970) and *Day for Night* (*La Nuit Américaine,* 1973), he acted in important roles, as he has sometimes done in films for other directors, such as Steven Spielberg's *Close Encounters of the Third Kind* (1977).

Truffaut wrote the script for *Jules and Jim* with Jean Gruault, who also collaborated with him on *The Wild Child* and *Two English Girls.* The cinematography was by Raoul Coutard, who had already worked on *Shoot the Piano Player* and with Godard on *Breathless;* he has continued to photograph many of Godard's films. Georges Delerue wrote the music for *Jules and Jim* as well as for several of Truffaut's other films; he had already composed for Resnais' *Hiroshima Mon Amour.* The song "Le Tourbillon" ("The Whirlwind") was by Boris Bassiak (who also played Albert in the film); Jeanne Moreau's recording of the song became a big hit in France in the early 1960s.

Other credits: assistant directors, Georges Pellegrin and Robert Bober; editor, Claudine Bouche; costumes, Fred Capel.

Truffaut had Jeanne Moreau in mind for the role of Catherine for some time, and she also helped to finance the film. She has been in numerous films, including Vadim's *Les Liaisons Dangereuses* (1959), Antonioni's *La Notte* (1961), Welles's **The Trial* (1962), and Truffaut's *The Bride Wore Black* (*La Mariée était en Noir,* 1967). Oskar Werner (Jules) is an Austrian who has also been in *Decision Before Dawn* (1951), *Ship of Fools*

FIG. 31.   The Museum of Modern Art/Film Stills Archive. Courtesy Janus Films.

(1965), Truffaut's *Fahrenheit 451*, and *Voyage of the Damned* (1976). Jim
was Henri Serre, whose background had been in the Paris theater. Marie
Dubois (Thérèse) had been in *Shoot the Piano Player*.

Other members of the cast: Boris Bassiak as Albert (see above on his
composition of "Le Tourbillon"); Vanna Urbino as Gilberte; Sabine
Haudepin as Sabine; Jean-Louis Richard and Michel Varesano as the
first and second customers in the café, and Pierre Fabre as the drunkard;
Danielle Bassiak as Albert's friend; Bernard Largemains as Merlin (the
anarchist); Ellen Bober as Mathilde; the narrator was Michel Subor.

Running time: 105 minutes. Distributor: Janus.

TOPICS TO THINK ABOUT

1. For the views of the *Cahiers* critics on the *auteur* principle, see
chapter 2, pages 30–32. (Truffaut capsulized them in a 1962 interview as
"primarily the idea . . . that the man who has the ideas must be the same
as the man who makes the picture.")

2. Truffaut, in an interview with Charles Thomas Samuels:

I have often been asked to direct great novels, like Camus'
L'Étranger, Fournier's *Le Grand Meaulnes*, Céline's *Voyage au bout de la
nuit*, and [Proust's] *Du côté de chez Swann*. In each case my admiration
for the book prevented me from making it into a film. *Jules and Jim*
was an exception because it was so little known, and I wanted to
increase its popularity by calling it to the attention of a large
audience. However . . . I have never used a trash novel or a book I
did not admire.

(For Truffaut's views on adaptations, see chapter 4, page 83.)

3. *Jules and Jim* is filled with cinematic devices used by (and for)
lovers of movies. In addition to all the unobtrusive techniques which the
film employs, consider the uses (or, you may perhaps feel, the abuses) of
the following, all of which tend quite deliberately to call attention to
themselves: rapid cutting; masking; irises; freeze frames; rapid swish
pans (sometimes to a full 360 degrees); hand-held camera movement;
and the distortion of images by stretching normal frames to fill a wide
screen (in the newsreel of the war).

4. Another notable device is one that some critics would argue is
*un*cinematic: the use of a narrator, who in fact probably speaks at least as
many words as any single character, even the three leads.

What function or role does the narrator have? *Is* he "uncinematic"?
Often, his words are not really necessary as such, as when he tells us that
"the photographs showed a crudely sculptured woman's face wearing a
tranquil smile which fascinated them," or "Catherine was waiting for Jim
at the exit of the little station with her daughter." Why would Truffaut
go out of his way to employ the narrator in such instances?

See the discussion of voice-overs in chapter 3 (page 58), as well as
Truffaut's defense of Bresson's use of them (for *Diary of a Country Priest*)
in chapter 4 (page 83).

5. Consider the importance in this film of *words*—either written (in
letters, poems, Jim's own novel as well as the books the characters read)
or spoken (in the voice-over narration, the characters' arguments or
discussions, and the stories they tell one another, including the long one
Jim tells, about the soldier who had written to the girl he had met on a
train, during which story a static camera focuses on him for several
minutes).

See the discussions of sound and words in film in chapters 2 and 3
(pages 25–29 and 55–56).

6. Truffaut, asked by Charles Thomas Samuels if he has "a special
feeling for books," replied: "No. I love them and films equally, but how I
love them!"

7. "In general, the chance of happiness in *Jules et Jim* always seems most likely in an outdoor setting—on the beach, in the meadows and forests. It tends to recede in the more confining interiors—the chalet, the hotel room, the house near Paris: an observation pinpointed by the film's strongly contrasted black and white photography." (Don Allen, *François Truffaut*)

8. "As for myself, I am a nostalgic; I am not tuned in on what is modern, it is in the past that I find my inspiration." (Truffaut, Introduction to *The Adventures of Antoine Doinel*)

How well, and in what ways, does Truffaut evoke a sense of the past in *Jules and Jim*? Would you characterize the film as "nostalgic"? As "modern," perhaps, in spite of what Truffaut says above? As both?

9. The film begins, according to the narrator, "about 1912," and it ends (judging by the newsreel of the Nazis burning books) in the early 1930s, yet the characters hardly seem to age in their physical appearance over those twenty years or so. Obviously an impression of their getting older could easily have been conveyed through makeup, but Truffaut avoided that: why, do you think? What effect does that have? If they do not seem to "age," do they change? develop? mature?

10. An irony which can easily be missed by audiences whose knowledge of French is minimal or nonexistent is that as Jules boasts of his pure accent by singing *"La Marseillaise,"* his German accent becomes in fact increasingly pronounced—until we cut to scenes of World War I.

11. In the second half of the film, after the war, there is a noticeable change of pace, as the use of such techniques as striking camera movement or frenetic cutting is greatly subdued. Why, or to what effect? Are there comparable changes in the lives and personalities of the three leading characters?

12. What relationship do these characters have to the history of the world around them? What is evoked toward the end of the film by the clip of the Nazis burning books? (Incidentally, in *Fahrenheit 451* Oskar Werner starred for Truffaut as a man whose duty it is to burn all books, in a society where reading is forbidden.)

Why is Jules a Jew in the novel but not, presumably, in the film?

13. According to the narrator, the three leading characters are known to the people in the village as "the three lunatics." Why should that be?

14. How are Jules and Jim similar? How are they different? How can their respective characters be illumined by considering the relationship each has with the other, and with Catherine?

15. In the novel, Jules, Jim, and Kate—that is, the Catherine of the film—come upon a stream with a waterfall: "They decided that the mass of falling water was like Kate, the uneven surges were like Jim, and the succeeding calm stretch was like Jules."

16. The narrator of the film says that Jim "was not surprised" to see Catherine "ready to take flight at any moment," for "he remembered Jules's mistakes with Thérèse, with Lucie, with all the others." What sorts of mistakes? Does Jim make his own mistakes, whether similar or different?

17. "The esthetic tension of the film is not, as one might suppose, between Jules and Jim but rather between their passive, observant natures and the active will and concrete sympathies of Catherine." (James Monaco, *The New Wave*)

18. JIM: "I understand you, Catherine."

CATHERINE: "I don't want to be understood."

19. When Jules asks if Jim approves of his wanting to marry Catherine, Jim replies: "She is an apparition for all to appreciate, perhaps, but not a woman for any one man."

Why not? Or is Jim "romanticizing"?

Later, after the marriage, Jules tells Jim, "Catherine is neither particularly beautiful, nor intelligent, nor sincere, but she is a real woman . . . and she is a woman we love . . . and whom all men desire."

20. The origin of the fascination Catherine holds for Jules and Jim is in a work of art (the statue). How accurate (or, on the other hand, how much of an oversimplification) would it be to assert that Catherine herself becomes their creation—their work of art?

21. Jules, Jim, and Catherine go to a play by "a Swedish author"— one thinks of August Strindberg (1849–1912), a number of whose works deal with the rise of the "new woman." Afterward, Catherine says that "the girl appeals to me. She wants to be free. She invents her life every moment."

Jules responds by quoting the poet Charles Baudelaire: "Woman is natural, therefore abominable. . . . I have always been astonished that women are allowed in churches. What can they have to say to God?" Catherine then jumps into the Seine. How do you interpret that act? How do you feel about it?

22. Catherine is a "modern woman." Is she a "liberated" one?

23. Why is it so important to Catherine that she bear Jim's child?

24. Seeing Catherine dressed as a man, the narrator says, "Jules and Jim were moved, as if by a symbol which they did not understand." Does seeing the entire film help *us* to understand it?

25. Toward what does Catherine's jump into the Seine, and her nightgown catching fire, turn out to look forward?

26. Truffaut, quoted in C. G. Crisp, *François Truffaut:* "You must always try to see things from other people's points of view, because 'everyone has his reasons' [a phrase from Jean Renoir's film *The Rules of the Game* (1939), and one of Truffaut's favorite quotations]. . . . For me, the man can and must judge. The artist, never."

Do you agree with that view of art? Does the film live up to it by not judging Jules, Jim, and Catherine? Do we judge them? If so, how?

27. Pauline Kael, in her review:

> When the Legion of Decency condemned *Jules and Jim,* the statement read: the story has been developed "in a context alien to Christian and traditional natural morality." It certainly has . . . and yet, *Jules and Jim* is not only one of the most beautiful films ever made, and the greatest motion picture of recent years, it is also, viewed as a work of art, exquisitely and impeccably *moral.* (*I Lost It at the Movies*)

28. Jim, to Catherine: "Like you, I think that, in love, the couple is not ideal. One has only to look around one. You wanted to construct something better, refusing hypocrisy and resignation. You wanted to invent love from the beginning . . . but pioneers should be humble, without egoism."

29. "Once a picture is finished I realize it is sadder than I meant it to be. This happens with every picture." (Truffaut, Introduction to *The Adventures of Antoine Doinel*)

Further Readings

ALLEN, DON. *François Truffaut.* New York: Viking, 1974.

CRISP, C. G. *François Truffaut.* New York: Praeger, 1972. Makes extensive use of Truffaut's many interviews.

FRANCHI, R. M., and MARSHALL LEWIS. "François Truffaut." In *Interviews with Film Directors.* Ed. Andrew Sarris. New York: Avon, 1969, pp. 520–27. Originally published in *New York Film Bulletin* 3 (1962).

KLEIN, MICHAEL. "The Literary Sophistication of François Truffaut." *Film Comment* 3 (Summer 1965): 24–29. Reprinted in *Film And/As Literature.* Ed. John Harrington. Englewood Cliffs, N.J.: Prentice-Hall, 1977, pp. 327–35.

Monaco, James. *The New Wave: Truffaut, Godard, Chabrol, Rohmer, Rivette.* New York: Oxford University Press, 1976.

Petrie, Graham. *The Cinema of François Truffaut.* New York: A. S. Barnes, 1970. Structured by critical topics and approaches rather than chronologically or film by film.

Roché, Henri-Pierre. *Jules and Jim.* Trans. Patrick Evans. New York: Avon, 1963. Preface by Truffaut.

Samuels, Charles Thomas. "François Truffaut." In his *Encountering Directors.* New York: Putnam's Sons, 1972, pp. 33–55. Interview.

Truffaut, François. *The Adventures of Antoine Doinel: Four Screenplays.* Trans. Helen G. Scott. New York: Simon and Schuster, 1971.

_____. *The Films in My Life.* Trans. Leonard Mayhew. New York: Simon and Schuster, 1978. Reprinted reviews and essays.

_____. *Jules and Jim: A Film.* Trans. Nicholas Fry. New York: Simon and Schuster, 1968. The screenplay, with some stills.

_____, with Helen G. Scott. *Hitchcock.* New York: Simon and Schuster, 1967. Includes many of Truffaut's own comments on films and filmmaking.

LOLITA

BACKGROUND

On the Novel

Vladimir Nabokov (1899–1977) was born in Russia, which he left after the Revolution of 1917. As he once said, "I am an American writer, born in Russia and educated in England where I studied French literature before spending fifteen years in Germany" (*Strong Opinions*). An exile in Europe, he wrote novels and poetry in his native Russian language until the 1940s, when he settled in the United States, became an American citizen, and began to write fiction in English. Besides *Lolita*, his novels in English include *Bend Sinister* (1947), *Pnin* (1957), *Pale Fire* (1960), and *Ada* (1969).

Lolita was written while Nabokov was a professor at Cornell University. Despite his respectable reputation, the book was turned down by a

FIG. 32.   The Museum of Modern Art/Film Stills Archive. Courtesy MGM.

number of publishers as too daring; it was eventually accepted by the Olympia Press, a Paris firm which specialized in pornography, a fact of which Nabokov was unaware at the time. This French edition appeared in 1955 and soon overcame the context set up by its publication; it received a great deal of attention when the important British novelist Graham Greene chose it as one of the best books of the year. Finally, an American edition appeared in 1958 and was a huge success. Years later, in an interview, Nabokov remarked, *"Lolita* is famous, not I. I am an obscure, doubly obscure novelist with an unpronounceable name." (Try "Nah-BOH-koff.")

On the Film

The credits for *Lolita* (1962) give Nabokov as the screenwriter, but the facts are not that simple. He had indeed written a script, but the first version was too long. After consultation with the director, Stanley Kubrick, Nabokov wrote a much shorter version. However, although Kubrick used some of Nabokov's ideas, he basically created his own script.

As Nabokov has put it, he discovered when he saw the completed film:

> . . . that Kubrick was a great director, that his *Lolita* was a first-rate film with magnificent actors, and that only ragged odds and ends of my script had been used. The modifications, the garbling of my best little finds, the omission of entire scenes, the addition of new ones, and all sorts of other changes may not have been sufficient to erase my name from the credit titles but they certainly made the picture as unfaithful to the original script as an American poet's translation from Rimbaud or Pasternak.

These comments are from the Foreword to the published version of Nabokov's own (revised) screenplay, which did not appear until 1974; he also says there that he is publishing it "not in pettish refutation of a munificent film but purely as a vivacious variant of an old novel."

Stanley Kubrick (b. 1928) began his career as a still photographer. His first feature films, including *Killer's Kiss* (1955) and *The Killing* (1956), were produced independently of major studios; then came *Paths of Glory* (1957) and *Spartacus* (1960). The film which followed *Lolita* was the highly praised *Dr. Strangelove, or How I Learned to Stop Worrying and Love the Bomb* (1963). His next work did not appear until five years later: *2001: A Space Odyssey* (1968). On both the latter films Kubrick collaborated with the authors of the novels upon which they were based; for his next adaptations, he bore the entire responsibility for the screenplays: *A Clockwork Orange* (1971) and *Barry Lyndon* (1975).

The producer was James B. Harris, a friend who had produced earlier Kubrick films as well, and who also helped on the script of *Lolita:* he has since directed his own films, including *The Bedford Incident* (1965). The cinematography was by Oswald Morris, who has also directed the photography for *Moby Dick* (1956), *The Pumpkin Eater* (1964), and *Oliver!* (1968). Music was by Nelson Riddle; his other scores include those for *El Dorado* (1966) and *The Great Gatsby* (1974); the "Lolita" theme was by Bob Harris. Anthony Harvey, the editor, later became a director, notably of *The Lion in Winter* (1968).

Other credits: assistant directors, Rene Dubpont, Roy Millichip, and John Danischewsky; art director, William Andrews; set design, Andrew Low; sound, H. L. Bird and Len Shilton.

James Mason (Humbert Humbert) began in British films in the

1930s, although he did not achieve widespread notice until some exceptional performances in the 1940s, especially in *Odd Man Out* (1947). He has been in many films through a long career; some of them are *Madame Bovary* (1949; as the author of the novel, Gustave Flaubert), *Julius Caesar* (1953; as Brutus), *A Star Is Born* (1954), and *Lord Jim* (1965).

Sue Lyon (Lolita) was fourteen years old while the movie was being shot; her other pictures include *The Night of the Iguana* (1964) and *Evel Knievel* (1972). Shelley Winters (Charlotte Haze) started as a blond Hollywood starlet but soon attracted attention for her acting abilities in *A Double Life* (1948) and *A Place in the Sun* (1951). She has received Academy Awards for her supporting roles in *The Diary of Anne Frank* (1959) and *A Patch of Blue* (1965).

Quilty was played by Peter Sellers, who began his career in British radio and then went into films such as *The Ladykillers* (1955) and *I'm All Right Jack* (1959). His most famous film is probably still the next one he did for Kubrick, *Dr. Strangelove*, in which he played the title role and two other important parts as well. Another role with which he has become identified is that of Inspector Clouseau in *The Pink Panther* (1963) and its sequels.

Other members of the cast: Marianne Stone as Vivian Darkbloom (the silent brunette); Diana Decker and Jerry Stovin as Jean and John Farlow; Gary Cockrell as Dick Schiller; Cec Linder as the physician; Lois Maxwell (the Miss Moneypenny of the James Bond films) as Nurse Mary Lord; William Greene as Swine.

Running time: 135 minutes. Distributor: Films Inc.

TOPICS TO THINK ABOUT

1. You may wish to read Nabokov's "On a Book Entitled *Lolita*," printed at the end of the novel as an epilogue of sorts, before you read or finish the novel itself.

2. It may help to get some fictional dates straight: Humbert was born in 1910, Lolita on January 1, 1935. Humbert begins to live in the Haze home in 1947. He and Lolita move to Beardsley at the end of the summer of 1948. Lolita disappears in 1950. Humbert lives and travels with Rita from the summer of 1950 until the summer of 1952. He speaks of writing his narrative in September 1952. The Foreword says that he dies on November 16, 1952, and that Mrs. Richard F. Schiller dies on December 25, 1952. (In some editions of the novel there is no date at the end of the Foreword, but in others Dr. Ray dates it August 5, 1955.)

3. "Turning one's novel into a movie script is rather like making a series of sketches for a painting that has long ago been finished and framed." (Nabokov, interview, 1964)

4. In answer to an interview's question about what scenes he would have liked to have filmed, Nabokov in 1965 supplied the following list:

Shakespeare in the part of the King's Ghost.
The beheading of Louis the Sixteenth, the drums drowning his speech on the scaffold.
Herman Melville at breakfast, feeding a sardine to his cat.
Poe's wedding. Lewis Carroll's picnics.
The Russians leaving Alaska, delighted with the deal. Shot of a seal applauding.

5. In his review in the *Village Voice* of Nabokov's *Lolita: A Screenplay,* Dennis Delrogh declared that in publishing his version, "Nabokov has done Kubrick a service. . . . For the most part, Kubrick edited out what was over-drawn, unworkable, gratuitous, and condescending. When a scene had possibilities, Kubrick usually left it in and embellished it. For example, Kubrick added the entire ping-pong scene to the baroque homicide and reinstated the T. S. Eliot parody from the book."

You may of course wish to read Nabokov's screenplay in order to make your own comparisons, both with Kubrick's film and Nabokov's novel.

6. "I am probably responsible for the odd fact that people don't seem to name their daughters Lolita any more." (Nabokov, interview, 1964)

7. While filming *Lolita* in 1961, Kubrick published a short essay entitled "Words and Movies," in which he wrote:

The perfect novel from which to make a movie is, I think, not the novel of action but, on the contrary, the novel which is mainly concerned with the inner life of its characters. . . .
It's sometimes said that a great novel makes a less promising basis for a film than a novel which is merely good. I don't think that adapting great novels presents any special problems which are not involved in adapting good novels or mediocre novels; except that you will be more heavily criticised if the film is bad, and you may be even if it's good.

And for Kubrick's views on adapting a book with so notable a "prose style" as *Lolita*, see chapter 4 (page 80).

8. In the same article, Kubrick wrote that it is the director's "duty to be one hundred per cent faithful to the author's meaning and to sacrifice none of it for the sake of climax or effect."

Do you agree? In any case, does Kubrick succeed in that "duty" in *Lolita?*

9. "I never worry about the main titles. I have seen some very clever ones which I have admired, but I think that clever main titles are just a waste of money and a disservice to the film. I have a very simple-minded point of view, in that the first shot of the film should be the most interesting thing that the audience has seen since it sat down." (Kubrick, interview with Alexander Walker)

Yet consider the impressions conveyed by the image of the polishing of the toenails during the titles of *Lolita*.

10. When the film appeared, a widespread although not universal criticism was that it leaves out a good deal of the eroticism of the novel. What is your reaction to the accusation?

Given the censorship of films during the early 1960s, Kubrick had no choice (although by the latter half of the 1970s times had changed enough for child *prostitutes* to be important characters in such films as *Taxi Driver,* 1976, and *Pretty Baby,* 1978). But Kubrick has since said that he does feel that because Humbert's "sexual obsession was only barely hinted at, it was assumed too quickly that Humbert was in love. Whereas in the novel this comes as a discovery at the end." (Interview with Gene Phillips, 1971)

11. In the film, what is the effect of our meeting Quilty at the start, rather than very gradually, distantly, and uncertainly, as in the novel? Indeed, at the beginning of the novel we only know that Humbert is a murderer, but not the identity of his victim. What effect does that uncertainty have?

12. Some critics have felt that the screenplay and Sellers' performance combine to make Quilty too prominent—that, in effect, he almost "steals" the picture. Do you agree that that is a problem? Is anything gained, on the other hand, from Quilty's greater prominence?

13. "I'm not really with someone," Quilty assures Humbert in the film, "I'm with you."

14. Although Humbert's narration is not totally discarded in the film, its role is relatively slight. What is the effect of that difference from the novel? (See the discussions of narration and point of view in chapters 1 and 2, pages 9–11 and 38–41.)

15. Near the end of the film, Lolita says to Humbert, about Quilty:

"He wasn't like you and me. He wasn't a normal person."

What are the various possible implications of her remark? Do you agree with them?

16. In the film, we hear a voice-over of words from Humbert's diary which correspond quite closely to the following from the novel: "What drives me insane is the twofold nature of this nymphet—of every nymphet, perhaps; this mixture in my Lolita of tender dreamy childishness and a kind of eerie vulgarity." (Part One, chapter 11)

17. The second paragraph of Humbert's narrative reads: "She was Lo, plain Lo, in the morning, standing four feet ten in one sock. She was Lola in slacks. She was Dolly at school. She was Dolores on the dotted line. But in my arms she was always Lolita."

How complex a person is Lolita?

18. From Nabokov's *Lolita: A Screenplay:*

QUILTY: Say, didn't you have a little girl? Let me see. With a lovely name. A lovely lilting lyrical name—
CHARLOTTE: Lolita. Diminutive of Dolores.
QUILTY: Ah, of course: Dolores. The tears and the roses.

19. Allusions are made at several points in the novel (especially in regard to Humbert's childhood love for the girl Annabel) to Edgar Allan Poe's poem, "Annabel Lee" (1850). You will probably wish to read the entire poem, but in the meantime here are the first ten lines:

> It was many and many a year ago,
>   In a kingdom by the sea,
> That a maiden there lived whom you may know
>   By the name of Annabel Lee;—
> And this maiden she lived with no other thought
>   Than to love and be loved by me.
>
> *She* was a child and *I* was a child,
>   In this kingdom by the sea,
> But we loved with a love that was more than love—
>   I and my Annabel Lee—

20. Who is responsible for Humbert and Lolita's having sexual relations together in the novel? in the film?

21. Dr. Ray says in the Foreword that Humbert is "abnormal." In a famous scene in Kubrick's *Dr. Strangelove,* Colonel Bat Guano says he thinks Group Captain Lionel Mandrake is "some kind of deviated preevert." Is Humbert some kind of "deviated preevert"? Is one's answer the same for the film as for the novel?

22. According to Stanley Kauffmann's review, the film takes from Lolita "her nymphet precocity" and "changes her from twelve to an unspecified midadolescent age, fifteen or so (a bigger jump than from fifteen to thirty)," and thus "eliminates Humbert's sexual particularity and makes him more like the usual middle-aged fool." (*A World on Film*)

As if in reply, Pauline Kael asked in her own review, "Have the reviewers looked at the schoolgirls of America lately? The classmates of my fourteen-year-old daughter are not merely nubile: some of them look badly used." (*I Lost It at the Movies*)

23. "Oh, my Lolita, I have only words to play with!" (*Lolita,* Part One, chapter 8)

24. Humbert ironically remarks of Quilty's play *The Enchanted Hunters* that its "profound message" is "that mirage and reality merge in love." (Part Two, chapter 13)

25. What is the impact of the last visual image in the film—of the painting, over which we see the words "The End"?

Further Readings

APPEL, ALFRED, JR. *Nabokov's Dark Cinema*. New York: Oxford University Press, 1974. On Nabokov's relations with film.

————, and CHARLES NEWMAN, eds. *Nabokov: Criticism, Reminiscences, Translations and Tributes*. Evanston, Ill.: Northwestern University Press, 1970.

FIELD, ANDREW. *Nabokov: His Life in Part*. New York: Viking, 1977. Biography.

KAGAN, NORMAN. *The Cinema of Stanley Kubrick*. New York: Grove, 1972.

KUBRICK, STANLEY. "Words and Movies." In *Hollywood Directors 1941– 1976*. Ed. Richard Koszarski. New York: Oxford University Press, 1977, pp. 305–9. Originally published in *Sight and Sound* 30 (Winter 1960–61): 14.

NABOKOV, VLADIMIR. *The Annotated Lolita*. Ed. Alfred Appel, Jr. New York: McGraw-Hill, 1970. Contains extensive notes, and a long Introduction.

————. *Lolita*. New York: Capricorn, 1972.

————. *Lolita: A Screenplay*. New York: McGraw-Hill, 1974.

————. *Strong Opinions*. New York: McGraw-Hill, 1973. A collection of Nabokov's interviews, "letters to editors," and articles.

PHILLIPS, GENE. "Kubrick." *Film Comment* 7 (Winter 1971–72): 30–35. Interview.

———. *Stanley Kubrick: A Film Odyssey*. New York: Popular Library, 1975. Frequently quotes from Kubrick.

WALKER, ALEXANDER. *Stanley Kubrick Directs*. New York: Harcourt Brace Jovanovich, 1971. Based on extensive interviews with Kubrick.

■■■■■■■■■■■■■■■■■■■■

THE TRIAL

■■■■■■■■■■■■■■■■■■■

BACKGROUND

On the Novel

Franz Kafka (1883–1924) was born in Prague (which is now part of Czechoslovakia but was then under the Austrian empire), of a German-speaking Jewish family. At the university he received a law degree—a fact obviously relevant to *The Trial*—but he never practiced law and worked instead for an insurance firm and then for the workmen's compensation office of the Austrian government. However, tuberculosis forced him to retire, and for much of his short life he was in ill health; he died at the age of forty in a sanatorium near Vienna.

Kafka had been writing a great deal—novels, stories, parables, as well as diaries—for many years, but he had published very little (some stories, but none of his novels); and he even asked his friend Max Brod, who later wrote a biography of Kafka, to burn all his manuscripts upon his death, but Brod refused. In a terrible irony, the fate that was spared his manuscripts was not spared members of his family: as Kafka's writings were published after his death, his work attained fame, so that by the Nazi take-over his entire family was marked for extermination, and his three sisters died in Auschwitz. *The Trial* (*Der Prozess*), which Kafka never completed, had been published in 1925.

Other works by Kafka include the novels *The Castle* (*Das Schloss*, 1926) and *Amerika* (1927), and a number of extraordinarily powerful stories, such as "The Judgment," "The Metamorphosis," "In the Penal Colony," and "A Report to an Academy."

FIG. 33.   The Museum of Modern Art/Film Stills Archive

On the Film

At the age of twenty-five, Orson Welles (b. 1915) directed one of the greatest and most important movies ever made, *Citizen Kane* (1941), a fact which has sometimes so obscured the rest of his career as a director that his later achievements have not received their due. It is true of course that his work after *Kane* was uneven—hardly a shocking or unusual circumstance in itself, surely—and beset by difficulties, especially in regard to financing and controlling his own films. In fact, *The Trial* (1962) was his first picture since *Kane*, over twenty years earlier, to be released under Welles's complete artistic control. Nevertheless, some of the films he made during that period are superb, and none are less than fascinating: *The Magnificent Ambersons* (1942), *The Stranger* (1946), *The Lady from Shanghai* and *Macbeth* (both 1948), *Othello* (1951), *Confidential Report* (or *Mr. Arkadin*, 1955; based on his own novel, *Mr. Arkadin*), and *Touch of Evil* (1958). Since *The Trial* his films have included *Chimes at Midnight/Falstaff* (1960) and *F for Fake* (1973). His most famous role in another director's film was probably that of Harry Lime in Carol Reed's *The Third Man*. Welles received the Life Achievement Award of the American Film Institute in 1975.

Although, with *The Trial,* Welles was again able to control all aspects of production, he did have to work under severe financial restrictions. ("Only people with nothing to lose could make such a film," he told an interviewer; "the producers have no money, and I'm an outcast.") Shooting took place at various locations, but most of the picture was made in Zagreb, Yugoslavia, and in Paris—notably in the abandoned railroad station, the Gare d'Orsay.

The producers were Alexander and Michael Salkind. The director of photography was Edmond Richard, who served in the same capacity on *Chimes at Midnight/Falstaff*. Music was by Jean Ledrut, using the *Adagio* of Tommaso Albinoni (1671–1750).

Other credits: editing, Yvonne Martin; assistant directors, Marc Maruette and Paul Seban; camera, Adolphe Charlet; art direction, Jean Mandaroux; the pin screen images, Alexandre Alexeïeff and Claire Parker; special effects, Denise Baby; sound, Guy Villette.

Joseph K. was played by Anthony Perkins, whose many other films include *Friendly Persuasion* (1956), *Psycho* (1960), *Pretty Poison* (1968), and *Catch-22* (1970). Welles played the Advocate (Hastler), although he did not originally intend to—and had in fact shot scenes in which he played the priest but which then had to be scrapped. In addition, he dubbed the voices of many of the other speaking parts, including those of Titorelli (William Chappell), the Deputy Manager (Maurice Teynac), and the Examining Magistrate (Max Buchsbaum).

Jeanne Moreau (Miss Bürstner) had already starred in *Les Liaisons Dangereuses* (1959), *La Notte* and **Jules and Jim* (both 1961); among her many roles since *The Trial* is that of Doll Tearsheet in *Chimes at Midnight/Falstaff*. Bloch was Akim Tamiroff, who had also appeared in Welles's *Touch of Evil,* as well as in such films as *The Great McGinty* (1940) and *For Whom the Bell Tolls* (1943).

Other members of the cast: Romy Schneider as Leni; Elsa Martinelli as Hilda; Arnoldo Foà as the Inspector; Suzanne Flon as Miss Pittle; Madeleine Robinson as Mrs. Grubach; Wolfgang Reichmann as the courtroom guard; Thomas Holtzmann as Bert, the law student; Maydra Shore as Irmie; Max Haufler as Uncle Max; and Michael Lonsdale as the priest. Katina Paxinou and Van Doude appear in the credits, but their roles were cut from the final version of the film.

Running time: 119 minutes. Distributors: Audio Brandon; Budget; Kit Parker.

TOPICS TO THINK ABOUT

1. Kafka, "A Little Fable":

"Alas," said the mouse, "the world is growing smaller every day. At the beginning it was so big that I was afraid, I kept running and running, and I was glad when at last I saw walls far away to the right and left, but these long walls have narrowed so quickly that I am in the last chamber already, and there in the corner stands the trap that I must run into." "You only need to change your direction," said the cat, and ate it up.

2. "All these parables really set out to say merely that the incomprehensible is incomprehensible, and we know that already. But the cares we have to struggle with every day: that is a different matter." (Kafka, "On Parables")

In the case of *The Trial,* how different?

3. Kafka, in a letter:

If the book we're reading doesn't wake us up with a blow on the head, what are we reading it for? So that it will make us happy, as you write? Good Lord, we would be happy precisely if we had no books, and the kind of books that make us happy are the kind we could write ourselves if we had to. But we need the books that affect us like a disaster, that grieve us deeply, like the death of someone we loved more than ourselves, like being banished into forests far from everyone, like a suicide. A book must be the axe for the frozen sea inside us.

4. Near the start of the film, Welles's voice tells us that "it has been said that the logic of this story is the logic of a dream . . . of a nightmare."

Once, when a friend remarked to Kafka that his story "The Metamorphosis" is a "terrible dream," Kafka replied that "the dream reveals the reality, which conception lags behind."

5. Franz Kafka is widely regarded as one of the greatest writers of the century, but not everyone agrees. The poet Wallace Stevens, for example, wrote: "The exploits of . . . Kafka in prose are deliberate exploits of the abnormal. It is natural for us to identify the imagination with those that extend its abnormality. It is like identifying liberty with those that abuse it." (*The Necessary Angel*)

6. Based on *The Trial* and any other Kafka works you may know, how would you define the term "Kafkaesque"?

7. What do you make of K.'s actions and reactions the morning of the first interrogation, in the novel and the film?

8. Is K. guilty? Is he innocent? Guilty of what? Innocent of what? The proceedings against him are a farce, and he is in no way given a "fair trial." Does that fact in itself tell us anything about his guilt or innocence?

9. "And psychological truth is contained in this; even though man has repressed his evil desires into his Unconscious and would then gladly say to himself that he is no longer answerable for them, he is yet compelled to feel his responsibility in the form of a sense of guilt for which he can discern no foundation." (Sigmund Freud, *General Introduction to Psychoanalysis*)

Does such a concept seem to you relevant—or not—to the case of Joseph K.?

10. Near the end of the discussion with the priest in the film, K. remarks, "Of course, I'm responsible." Is he being ironic, or does he mean it?

11. Asked in a 1965 interview why he had said that he considers Joseph K. "guilty," Welles replied: "Who knows? He belongs to something that represents evil and that, at the same time, is part of him. He is not guilty as accused, but he is guilty all the same."

12. "See, Willem, he admits that he doesn't know the Law and yet he claims he's innocent." (Franz, in *The Trial,* chapter 1)

13. K. [in the film]: "I am sane. I am innocent. I have commited no crime."

MISS BÜRSTNER: "Three cheers for you."

14. The film has a fairly close parallel to the following passage in the novel:

> "But I am not guilty," said K.; "it's a mistake. And, if it comes to that, how can any man be called guilty? We are all simply men here, one as much as the other." "That is true," said the priest, "but that's how all guilty men talk." (Chapter 9)

15. The tale of the man from the country and the doorkeeper, which the priest tells K. in the novel, was published separately by Kafka, under the title "Before the Law." How do you interpret it? The comments on it by K. and the priest—which may remind one of Jewish scholars ruminating over the significance of every possible interpretation of the Talmud (which, incidentally, means "Law")—were not published separately. How do you interpret them?

Do you approve of Welles's decision to begin his film with this tale?

16. "The right perception of any matter and a misunderstanding of the same matter do not wholly exclude each other." (The priest, in chapter 9)

17. Broadly speaking, critics have tended to stress one of three general ways of interpreting this novel: (1) they look at it as a *social* document, examining its political, legal, and economic implications; (2) they take a *psychological* approach, looking at its central characters and situations from various psychological perspectives, including of course psychoanalytic ("Freudian") ones; or (3) they stress *philosophical* concerns, including religious and metaphysical ramifications.

The approaches need not be mutually exclusive, to be sure. In any case, which, if any, seems most (or least) promising and relevant to you?

18. According to John Simon (who alludes to "three levels" similar to those sketched above in topic 17), Welles, "with typical oversimplification," makes his version "purely political." (*Private Screenings*)

Do you agree? Geoffrey Wagner, apparently, would not. Although he calls the film "courageous" and "on the whole faithful," he feels that by stressing, for example, the parable of the man before the Law, Welles "obscures" the sense that *The Trial* remains a uniquely realistic novel, obviously reminiscent of the political arrests of this age." (*The Novel and the Cinema*)

19. Is it possible that K. is a victim of delusions, or that he is "insane"?

20. Kafka once intended to collect all his works under the general title, *The Attempt to Escape from Father.*

In the film, K. tells Miss Bürstner: "I can remember my father looking at me—you know, straight in the eye. 'Come on boy,' he'd say, 'exactly what have you been up to?'—and even when I hadn't been up to anything at all, I'd still feel guilty. You know that feeling?"

Later, his last words to the priest, just before the executioners come for him, are, "I'm not your son."

21. In his review, Stanley Kauffmann attacked this film because "everything sexual in the book is heavily amplified and a good deal is added" (*A World on Film*). Do you agree? If so, do you mind?

22. "In reality, I am a man of ideas; yes, above all else—I am even more a man of ideas than a moralist, I suppose." (Welles, interview, 1965)

23. Albert Camus associates Kafka with the philosopher Sören Kierkegaard, seeing them both as men who "embrace the God that consumes them" (*The Myth of Sisyphus*). The film in turn seems to allude to terms made famous by Camus when K. says to the Advocate, "Yes, that's the conspiracy. To persuade us all that the whole world's crazy. Formless, meaningless, absurd. That's the dirty game."

24. "Atlas was permitted the opinion that he was at liberty, if he wished, to drop the Earth and creep away; but this opinion was all that he was permitted." (Kafka, notebook)

25. Early in the proceedings against him, K. tells the Examining Magistrate that "it is only a trial if I recognize it as such." (Chapter 2)

Is that true?

26. The Advocate in the film tells K., "To be in chains is sometimes safer than to be free."

27. "Freedom! Certainly such freedom as is possible today is a wretched business. But nevertheless freedom, nevertheless a possession." (The dog, in Kafka, "Investigations of a Dog")

28. For Thomas Mann, Kafka was best characterized as "a religious humorist." In a 1965 interview, Welles said that his film of *The Trial* "is full of humor, but the Americans are the only ones to understand its amusing side." Why might that be so?

In his review of the film for *Film Quarterly*, Ernest Callenbach observed: "*The Trial* abounds in comic scenes, and would be obviously quite a cut-up movie if audiences did not come prepared for High Culture—prepared, that is, for polite despair."

Do you find much humor in *The Trial*—the film and the novel?

29. Peter Cowie, on the film of *The Trial:*

It was hailed as a masterpiece by a majority of continental critics. With few exceptions, it was dismissed as a boring failure by the British and American press. To my mind, *The Trial* remains Welles's finest film since *Kane* and, far from being a travesty of Kafka's work, achieves an effect through cinematic means that conveys perfectly the terrifying vision of the modern world that marks every page of the original book. (*A Ribbon of Dreams*)

30. What might some of the "cinematic means" be to which Cowie refers, above? For example, do any particular visual images or scenes strike you as especially effective?

31. How would you compare K.'s character in the novel and the film? In each work, how passive or active (even rebellious) is K.? Is he like or unlike the man from the country in the parable, "Before the Law"? Is he like or unlike the Franz Kafka suggested by the diary entry, "If I am condemned, then I am not only condemned to die, but also condemned to struggle till I die"?

32. Some people have felt that Anthony Perkins is miscast—that he is too "American," or too "boyish," for the role. Do you agree?

33. "The biggest mistake we have made is to consider that films are primarily a form of entertainment. The film is the greatest medium since the invention of movable type for exchanging ideas and information, and it is no more at its best in light entertainment than literature is at its best in the light novel." (Welles, "The Third Audience")

34. How might you account for the differences in the endings of the novel and the film? The end of the film has seemed to many viewers ambiguous, and it has aroused a great deal of controversy. For example, critics have disagreed about why Welles changed the mode of execution, and what it might be that K. picks up and throws, and whether or not the explosions at the end seem to form nuclear mushroom clouds, and what it would suggest if they do.

35. "I believe you must say something new about a book, otherwise it is better not to touch it." (Welles, interview, 1965)

36. "Say what you will, but *The Trial* is the best film I have ever made." (Welles, interview, 1965)

Further Readings

BAUER, JOHANN. *Kafka and Prague.* Trans. P. S. Falla. Photographs Isidor

Pollak. New York: Praeger, 1971. A good brief introduction to Kafka's life, with illustrations and evocative photographs.

BROD, MAX. *Franz Kafka: A Biography.* Trans. G. Humphreys Roberts. New York: Schocken, 1947. By Kafka's friend, but very limited as a biography.

CAMUS, ALBERT. "Hope and the Absurd in the Work of Franz Kafka." In his *The Myth of Sisyphus and Other Essays.* Trans. Justin O'Brien. New York: Vintage, 1955.

COBOS, JUAN, MIGUEL RUBIO, and JOSE ANTONIO PRUNEDA. "Orson Welles." Trans. Rose Kaplin. In *Interviews with Film Directors.* Ed. Andrew Sarris. New York: Avon, 1969, pp. 528–57. Originally published in *Cahiers du Cinéma* 165 (April 1965).

COWIE, PETER. *A Ribbon of Dreams: The Cinema of Orson Welles.* South Brunswick, N.J.: A. S. Barnes, 1973. An intelligent and useful general study.

GRAY, RONALD. *Franz Kafka.* Cambridge: Cambridge University Press, 1973.

———, ed. *Kafka: A Collection of Critical Essays.* Englewood Cliffs, N.J.: Prentice-Hall, 1962.

GREENBERG, MARTIN. *The Terror of Art: Kafka and Modern Literature.* New York: Basic Books, 1968.

HIGHAM, CHARLES. *The Films of Orson Welles.* Berkeley: University of California Press, 1970. Often surprisingly negative in its evaluations.

KAFKA, FRANZ. *The Complete Stories.* Ed. Nahum N. Glatzer. New York: Schocken, 1972.

———. *Dearest Father: Stories and Other Writings.* Trans. Ernst Kaiser and Eithne Wilkins. New York: Schocken, 1954.

———. *Letters to Friends, Family, and Editors.* Trans. Richard and Clara Winston. New York: Schocken, 1977.

———. *The Trial.* Trans. Willa and Edwin Muir, with additional material trans. E. M. Butler. New York: Schocken, 1968.

NAREMORE, JAMES. *The Magic World of Orson Welles.* New York: Oxford University Press, 1978. Excellent.

POLITZER, HEINZ. *Franz Kafka: Parable and Paradox.* Ithaca, N.Y.: Cornell University Press, 1962.

SOKEL, WALTER H. *Franz Kafka.* New York: Columbia University Press, 1966. A brief introduction.

WELLES, ORSON. "The Third Audience." *Sight and Sound* 23 (January–March 1954): 120–22. Reprinted as an appendix in Cowie, above.

_____. *The Trial: A Film.* Described by Nicholas Fry. New York: Simon and Schuster, 1970. Includes some stills.

BACKGROUND

The title of *8¹/₂* (1963) is like an "opus" number in music. Federico Fellini (b. 1921) playfully calls it his "eighth and a half" film because before it he had directed six feature films, and had collaborated on one and directed portions of two others; counting these last three as half a film each produces a total of seven and a half. *8¹/₂* is a clearly personal, even openly autobiographical statement, yet it was a huge success both commercially and critically. It received many awards, including both the Academy Award and the New York Film Critics Award as the best foreign language film, the Grand Prize at the Moscow Film Festival, and a record number (seven) of silver ribbons, the Italian equivalent of Oscars.

Fellini began in films as a writer, notably for Roberto Rossellini's *Open City* (1945) and *Paisan* (1947). He co-directed (with Alberto Lattuada) *Variety Lights* (*Luci del Varietà*, 1950) and then on his own directed *The White Sheik* (*Lo Sciecco Bianco*, 1952). He first attracted attention with *I Vitelloni* (1953) and *La Strada* (1954), the latter making a star of his wife, Giulietta Masina. It was the great success of the controversial *La Dolce Vita* (1959)—an episodic depiction of "decadence" in contemporary Rome—that made Fellini genuinely famous internationally. He followed that work with *8¹/₂*—and then with *Juliet of the Spirits* (*Giulietta degli Spiriti*, 1965), which he regarded as a counterpart for the woman of what *8¹/₂* had been for the man, and which starred his wife. Since then his films have included *Fellini Satyricon* (1969), *Roma* (1971), *Amarcord* (1974), and *Casanova* (1976).

Fellini wrote the screenplay with three other writers: Ennio Flaiano, Tullio Pinelli, and Brunello Rondi (who also receives credit for "artistic collaboration"). All of them worked on other films with him; indeed the full team of four had already written *La Dolce Vita,* and they all worked again on *Juliet of the Spirits.* Angelo Rizzoli produced both *8¹/₂* and *Juliet of the Spirits.* The director of photography was Gianni di Venanzo (who received an Italian silver ribbon); he performed the same role for *Juliet of the Spirits* as well as for Antonioni's *La Notte* (1960) and *The Eclipse* (1962). The cameraman was Pasquale De Santis, who later directed the photography for Visconti's **Death in Venice* (1971). Nino Rota (another silver ribbon recipient) has written the music for almost all of Fellini's films, as well as for Visconti's *The Leopard* (1963) and Coppola's *The Godfather* (1971). The scenery and wardrobe were by Piero Gherardi, who received an Academy Award for costume design.

Other credits: assistant director and casting, Guidarino Guidi; editor, Leo Catozzo; sound effects, Mario Faraoni and Alberto Bartolomei; production supervisor, Clemente Fracassi.

Like the director Guido Anselmi in *8¹/₂,* Fellini has a compulsion to find the right "faces and heads" for his cast—"the human landscape of the film." He is quoted in *Fellini on Fellini* as saying, "I am likely to see up to five or six thousand faces, and it is precisely these faces which suggest to me the behavior of my characters, their personalities, and even some narrative sections of the film."

Marcello Mastroianni (Guido Anselmi) became an international star after appearing in *La Dolce Vita;* his many major films include Antonioni's *La Notte,* Pietro Germi's *Divorce Italian Style* (1961), and Visconti's *The Stranger* (1967).

Anouk Aimée (Luisa) was also in *La Dolce Vita,* and in such films as Jacques Demy's *Lola* (1960), Claude Lelouch's *A Man and a Woman* (1966), and George Cukor's *Justine* (1969). Sandro Milo won a silver ribbon as supporting actress for her role as Carla, Guido's mistress. Claudia was played by Claudia Cardinale, who has also been in Visconti's *The Leopard,* Blake Edwards' *The Pink Panther* (1963), and Richard Brooks's *The Professionals* (1966).

Other members of the cast: Madeleine Lebeau as the French actress; Mario Pisu as Mario Mezzabotta, Guido's friend; Barbara Steele as Gloria Morin, Mario's young mistress; Caterina Boratto as the unidentified fashionable woman at the spa; Guido Alberti (a wealthy industrialist who has gone on to act in other films as well) as Pace, the producer; Mario Conocchia as Conocchia, Guido's older friend and assistant; Jean Rougeul as Daumier, the writer; Edra Gale as La Saraghina (whose name, which means "sardines" in the Rimini area, comes from the fact that during Fellini's childhood a comparable woman used to sell herself to the local fisherman for loads of sardines); Annibale Ninchi as

FIG. 34. The Museum of Modern Art/Film Stills Archive. Courtesy Embassy Pictures.

Guido's father (he had already played Mastroianni's father in *La Dolce Vita*); Giuditta Rissone as Guido's mother; Tito Masini (a man Fellini had spotted leaving a library) as the Cardinal; and many others. All the cast and the technical staff participated in the dance at the end of the film.

Running time: 135 minutes. Distributor: Audio Brandon.

TOPICS TO THINK ABOUT

1. "I hazard that *8¹/₂* is Fellini's masterpiece precisely because it is about the two subjects he knows most about: himself and the making of movies." (*Dwight Macdonald on Movies*)

2. John Francis Lane, in his review in *Sight and Sound:*

At the end of *La Dolce Vita*, the young girl on the beach, the symbol of innocence, fails to communicate to Marcello. Fellini, plagued by reporters about his next film, said he would make a picture which explained what the girl with the Umbrian smile was trying to say to Marcello as he stumbled back to the orgies. Instead of making *that* film, Fellini has in fact made a film about a director who wants to make that film—and who fails.

3. Fellini, in conversation with Angelo Solmi: "I realize that *8½* is such a shameless and brazen confession . . . that it is futile to try and make people forget that it is about my own life. But I try to make a film that pleases me, first of all, and then the public. In *8½* the boundary line between what I did for myself and what I created for the public is very subtle." (*Fellini*)

Is it *too* subtle, do you think? (Or might you argue the opposite—that it is too emphatic, or brazen?) Does the combination of private and public expression succeed in *8½* or not?

4. During the shooting of *8½*, Fellini placed a note next to the camera: "Remember that this is a comic film."

5. From *Fellini on Fellini:*

Improvisation becomes merely a certain form of sensitivity to the demands of the particular moment; for instance, when it is a case of altering something at the last minute. In other words, it is concerned only with detail. The complete work must be carried out with mathematical precision. . . . Having said this, it must also be said that mathematical precision does not mean a dead plan. A film is a living reality: sometimes its orders must be obeyed, sometimes one must recall it to its own internal rhythm. I don't want to make a mystery of my work, but I should like to say that my system is to have no system. I go to a story to discover what it has to tell me.

6. Christian Metz, in *Film Language:*

Like those paintings that show a second painting within, or those novels written about a novel, *8½* with its "film within the film" belongs to the category of works of art that are divided and doubled, thus reflecting on themselves. . . .

. . . *8½*, one should be careful to realize, is a film that is *doubly doubled.* . . . It is not only a film about the cinema, it is a film about a film that is presumably itself about the cinema; it is not only a film about a director, but a film about a director who is reflecting himself onto his film. . . .

It is therefore not enough to speak of a "film within the film": *8½* is the film of *8½* being made; *the "film in the film" is, in this case, the film itself.*

7. As a particularly complicated example of his point, Metz mentions the scene in which Guido, his wife Luisa, and others watch the screen tests of actors and actresses who might play roles obviously corresponding to people we have been seeing in Guido's own life.

Just how involuted is that scene, and how do you respond to it? For example, Luisa reacts to an actress who is portraying her (that is, an actress playing the role of an actress in a screen test). Meanwhile, the role of *Luisa* is also being played, by an actress. The audience aware of autobiographical elements will further perceive that Luisa's role is similar to that of Giulietta Masina, Fellini's own wife (who moreover is herself an actress).

Are all these convolutions merely clever or gimmicky, or do they have important functions and significance?

8. *"Cinéma-vérité?* I prefer 'cine-mendacity.' A lie is always more interesting than the truth. Lies are the soul of showmanship and I adore shows. Fiction may have a greater truth than everyday, obvious reality." (*Fellini on Fellini*)

9. Guido says that in his film "everything happens. I put in everything." And he tells Claudia that the chief character in the film "wants to possess and devour everything."

Yet the accusation against him throughout the film is that—as the American woman shouts near the end—"He's lost! He has nothing to say!" (Orson Welles has said of Fellini that "he shows dangerous signs of being a superlative artist with little to say.") Oddly, perhaps, Guido agrees: "I have nothing to say, but I want to say it just the same."

Is the presentation of an artist with such a compulsion and in such a situation itself a sufficient "statement"?

10. Would you agree with Christian Metz that "the paradoxical and startling thing about *8½*" is that "it is a powerful and creative meditation on the inability to create"?

11. "I never go to the cinema. But if I happen to go, all that interests me is the story. I never take any notice of the camera movements, the sets, the technical side of it." (1971, *Fellini on Fellini*)

Yet in 1965 he had said (quoted by Lillian Ross, in the context of a discussion of *Juliet of the Spirits*): "The story is nothing. . . . Movies now have gone past the phase of prose narrative and are coming nearer and nearer to poetry. I am trying to free my work from certain constrictions—a story with a beginning, a development, an ending. It should be more like a poem, with metre and cadence." See the discussion of developments in modernism within written literature and film in chapter 3, pages 75–76.

12. Consider *8¹/₂* in relation to the discussions of narrative structure, plot, and story in chapter 1.

13. How could one label the scenes which depart from the reality of the here and now? Are they Guido's dreams, or daydreams, or nightmares? Or are they fantasies? wish fulfillments? memories? hallucinations? Are some of them perhaps his mental images of scenes in the film he is contemplating? Could they be actual scenes from that film?

14. See the discussion, in chapter 3 (pages 57–58), of stream of consciousness, and of the depiction of mental states in both film and written literature.

15. When many viewers of *8¹/₂* wondered if Fellini had been influenced by *Last Year at Marienbad* (1961) in the presentation of sudden shifts from one time to another, or from present reality to illusion or fantasy, he said that in fact he had never seen Resnais' film. Questions of influence aside, if you have seen *Marienbad*, or such films as Bergman's *Wild Strawberries* or Lumet's *The Pawnbroker*, compare and contrast their cuts from one visual world to another with those in *8¹/₂*.

16. Daumier, the writer, argues that Guido's "childhood memories . . . mean nothing for the film." Presumably, both Guido and Fellini would disagree. What *is* the function of the childhood memories in *8¹/₂*?

17. Ted Perry, on "the dollying and trucking" in *8¹/₂*:

> Guido is trapped by a camera that moves with him constantly, caging him by its frame no matter where he moves, while unfriendly people freely enter and exit from off-screen space, making demands on him, accosting him. This camera technique is particularly evident in the outdoor scene at the spa, in the lobby of the spa hotel, in the steam baths of the spa when it is announced that the Cardinal will see Guido, and at the press conference. In all these instances, Guido is revealed as trapped and surrounded; and this feeling is in some cases accentuated by the camera's assuming his point of view almost entirely as people stare toward him (the camera).

See the discussions of camera movement and of *mise en scène* in chapter 2 (especially pages 37–38 and 49).

18. Mario's mistress Gloria says that her university thesis is on "the solitude of modern man as reflected in the contemporary theater." Is Guido representative of the solitude of modern man as reflected in the contemporary film?

19. Luisa's friend Rosella refers to Guido as Pinocchio. What are the various connotations in her calling him that?

20. As Guido describes to her the protagonist of his film, Claudia persistently remarks that "he doesn't know how to love."

21. How would you characterize Guido's relationships (actual, remembered, and imagined) to the various women in his life (actual, remembered, and imagined)?

What do you make of the harem sequence and "the house rules" (which Luisa defines and defends by saying, "my husband does exactly as he pleases")?

22. "I have complete faith in [Carl Gustav] Jung, and total admiration for him." (*Fellini on Fellini*)

23. There seems to be a veiled reference to one of Jung's most famous psychological concepts when the magician Maurice reads Guido's mind and comes up with the enigmatic phrase—"the magic word"—out of Guido's childhood, "asa nisi masa." The phrase is reported to derive from a children's language game in which the vowel of each syllable in every word is followed by "s" and then repeated. Thus, "asa nisi masa" would be a code term for *anima*.

In Jung, the anima is the inner part of a man which represents or personifies woman (as well as the analogue in Jung's thought to what others might term the "soul"). In a woman, the counterpart is the *animus*, which represents all that is male within her psyche. (Both the anima and the animus are *archetypes*: images or "memories" out of the *collective unconscious*—the inherited psychological past shared by all humanity.)

24. Jung, in *Aion*, says that in each man's

> . . . psyche there exists an image of the mother and not only of the mother, but also of the daughter, the sister, the beloved, the heavenly goddess, and the earth spirit. . . . Every mother and every beloved is forced to become the carrier and embodiment of this omnipresent and ageless image which corresponds to the deepest reality in a man. It is his own, this perilous image of Woman; she stands for the loyalty which in the interests of life he cannot always maintain; she is the vital compensation for the risks, struggles, sacrifices which all end in disappointment; she is the solace for all the bitterness of life. Simultaneously, she is the great illusionist, the seductress who draws him into life—not only into its reasonable and useful aspects but into its frightful paradoxes and ambivalences where good and evil, success and ruin, hope and despair counterbalance one another.
> . . . Whenever she appears in dreams, visions, and fantasies, she takes on personified form, thus demonstrating that the factor she embodies possesses all the outstanding characteristics of a feminine being. She is not the invention of the conscious mind, but a spontaneous production of the unconscious.

(See also the section on *Wild Strawberries*, topic 24, page 195.)

25. What role in Guido's life—past and present—is played by La Saraghina?

Compare and contrast that role with the one fulfilled (or not fulfilled?) by Claudia and Guido's visions of her. Why does she say, as she lies next to him in bed, that she has come to bring order and cleanliness?

26. Many critics and viewers (some of whom otherwise admire the film) feel disappointment in the ending, which they believe presents not so much a resolution of Guido's conflicts as a dismissal of them. How do you respond to such an accusation?

27. At the end, in his final vision, Guido asks Luisa to "accept me as I am," and, at least in his vision, she agrees to try.

To some, his request is egotistical, selfish, and sexist, and his redemption—if such indeed it is—is unearned, as man or as artist. To others, it is a moving if inevitably temporary sign of renewed life and courageous affirmation. What is your reaction?

28. Throughout the film, people constantly direct questions at Guido, and almost all of them remain unanswered. How might you reply to the very early one, just after his opening nightmare: is the film Guido is working on (and the one in which he appears) "another film without hope"?

29. A member of the Cardinal's retinue, to Guido: "I don't believe the cinema is the proper medium for certain subjects."

30. ". . . there is a path that leads back from phantasy to reality— the path, that is, of art." (Sigmund Freud, *Complete Introductory Lectures on Psychoanalysis*)

Further Readings

BONDANELLA, PETER, ed. *Federico Fellini: Essays in Criticism*. New York: Oxford University Press, 1978. Reprinted essays by various critics.

FELLINI, FEDERICO. *Fellini on Fellini*. Ed. Anna Keel and Christian Strich. Trans. Isabel Quigley. New York: Delta, 1976. A valuable collection of statements by Fellini, many of which are otherwise difficult to locate.

KAST, PIERRE. "Federico Fellini." Trans. Rose Kaplin. In *Interviews with Film Directors*. Ed. Andrew Sarris. New York: Avon, 1969, pp. 175–92. Originally published in *Cahiers du Cinéma* 164 (March 1965).

METZ, CHRISTIAN. "Mirror Construction in Fellini's *8½*." In his *Film Language: A Semiotics of the Cinema*. Trans. Michael Taylor. New York: Oxford University Press, 1974, pp. 228–34.

MURRAY, EDWARD. *Fellini the Artist*. New York: Ungar, 1976.

PERRY, TED. *Filmguide to 8¹/₂.* Bloomington: Indiana University Press, 1975. A detailed study, showing special awareness at all times of the camera and its role.

Ross, LILLIAN. "Profile." *The New Yorker* 41 (October 30, 1965): 63–107. On Fellini, mostly *Juliet of the Spirits.*

SAMUELS, CHARLES THOMAS. "Federico Fellini." In his *Encountering Directors.* New York: Putnam's Sons, 1972, pp. 117–41. Interview.

SOLMI, ANGELO. *Fellini.* Trans. Elizabeth Greenwood. London: Merlin, 1967.

THE PAWNBROKER

BACKGROUND

On the Novel

The Pawnbroker (1961) was published the year before its author, Edward Lewis Wallant (1926–1962), died at the untimely age of thirty-six. He had published his first novel, *The Human Season,* in 1960. Two others appeared posthumously: *The Tenants of Moonbloom* (1963) and *The Children at the Gate* (1964). All the books were written within a period of six years, despite the fact that he was also working full-time as an art director for an advertising agency in New York City.

Wallant was born and grew up in New Haven, Connecticut. His family was Jewish, and one relative operated a pawnshop in Harlem, which Wallant often visited; he also knew survivors of the Nazi concentration camps. After service in the Navy (1944–46), he attended the Pratt Institute in New York and then, while making his living as a graphic artist, took writing courses at the New School for Social Research. He was awarded a Guggenheim Fellowship in 1962, and he took his wife and children to Europe; it was shortly after their return that he died of a stroke in December of that year. He left behind a great many unpublished writings which are now in the library at Yale University.

On the Film

Sidney Lumet (b. 1924) began directing in television, and his first feature film, *Twelve Angry Men* (1957), was adapted from a television play. His other films have included *The Fugitive Kind* (1959), *Long Day's Journey into Night* (1962), and—after *The Pawnbroker* (1965)—*The Seagull* (1968), *Serpico* (1974), *Murder on the Orient Express* (1974), and *Equus* (1977). Almost all of Lumet's films have been adaptations—notably "faithful"—of novels, plays, or non-fiction books. An exception is *Network* (1976).

The Pawnbroker was made by the production company of Ely Landau, who had produced *Long Day's Journey into Night* and who went on to film the presentations of the American Film Theatre (1972–74). The producers were Philip Langner and Robert H. Lewis. David Friedkin and Morton Fine wrote the screenplay.

Boris Kaufman (cinematography) has worked on many other Lumet films, as well as with other important directors—for example with Jean Vigo on *Zéro de Conduite* (1933), where uses of slow motion look forward to some key shots in *The Pawnbroker*. For Elia Kazan's *On the Waterfront* (1954), Kaufman received an Academy Award.

The editor was Ralph Rosenblum, and the production design was by Richard Sylbert, who has also worked on *The Graduate* (1967) and *Catch-22* (1970). Quincy Jones composed the music; he has also been an actor, for example in Lumet's *The Anderson Tapes* (1971).

Other credits: executive producer, Worthington Miner; associate producer, Joseph Manduke; costumes, Anna Hill Johnstone; assistant director, Dan Eriksen.

The cast was headed by Rod Steiger as Sol Nazerman. He was nominated for an Academy Award and received the British Film Academy Award; he later received both those awards for his performance in *In the Heat of the Night* (1967). His first important film role had been in *On the Waterfront*, directed by Elia Kazan, one of the founders of the Actors' Studio, of which Steiger was a member. He has also been in *The Sergeant* (1968), *Waterloo* (1970), and *W. C. Fields and Me* (1976).

Geraldine Fitzgerald (Marilyn Birchfield) has been in movies since the 1930s, with roles in *Wuthering Heights* (1939), *Watch on the Rhine* (1943), *Rachel, Rachel* (1969), *Harry and Tonto* (1974), and many other films. Jesus Ortiz was played by Jaime Sanchez. Rodriguez (the counterpart to Murillio in the novel) was Brock Peters, who has also been in *To Kill a Mockingbird* (1962) and *Major Dundee* (1965). Tangee was Raymond St. Jacques, whose films include *Uptight* (1968) and *Lost in the Stars* (1973).

Other members of the cast: Thelma Oliver as Mabel Wheatly; Baruch Lumet as Mendel; Juano Hernandez—whose other films include

FIG. 35.   The Museum of Modern Art/Film Stills Archive. Courtesy Allied Artists.

Intruder in the Dust (1948)—as George Smith; Marketa Kimbrell as Tessie; Linda Geiser as Ruth; Nancy R. Pollock as Bertha; John McCurry as Buck; Ed Morehouse as Robinson; Eusebia Cosme as Mrs. Ortiz; Warren Finnerty as Savarese; Jack Ader as Morton; E. M. Margolese as Selig; Marianne Kanter as Joan.

Running time: 114 minutes. Distributor: Audio Brandon.

Historical Background

We are told that Sol Nazerman was an instructor at the University of Cracow, in Poland, before his experiences in the Nazi concentration camps. The Germans invaded Poland September 1, 1939, starting World War II. The Russians invaded from the east shortly afterward, and by the end of the month Germany and Russia had divided Poland, the war in that country being "over."

Under the government set up by the Germans, Jews had to wear Star of David armbands and were subject to terror, hunger, and forced labor, and then (in 1940) were imprisoned within walled ghettos. By 1942, the mass transfer of Jews to the concentration and extermination camps had begun. Before the war, about 3,300,000 Jews lived in Poland; despite resistance against the Nazis—for example, the Warsaw uprising of April 1943—about 3 million of them, or 90 percent, were killed by the Germans. Altogether, out of the 9 million Jews of prewar Europe, about 6 million were killed in the Holocaust—that is, in "the final solution," the Nazi term for their plan of annihilation as the "solution" to "the Jewish problem."

The Germans developed their skills at large-scale extermination starting in 1939 with a "euthanasia" program called T-4, in which the mentally ill, the retarded, and the physically deformed were gassed to death. (The organization in charge of this program was called the "Reich Committee for Scientific Research of Heredity and Severe Constitutional Diseases.") By the time of the mass murders of Jews in the extermination camps, the numbers involved were staggering; according to the postwar testimony of the commandant of Auschwitz, "We were required to carry out these exterminations in secrecy, but of course the foul and nauseating stench from the continuous burning of bodies permeated the entire area and all of the people living in the surrounding communities knew that exterminations were going on at Auschwitz."

In *The War Against the Jews: 1933–1945,* Lucy S. Dawidowicz describes how Jews arriving at camps such as those at Auschwitz, Belżec, and Treblinka—and others—"encountered a standard procedure":

> At camps maintaining labor installations, like Auschwitz, 10 percent of the arrivals—those who looked fittest—were selected for work. The remainder were consigned to the gas chambers. They were instructed to undress; the women and girls had their hair cut. They were then marched between files of auxiliary police (Ukrainians usually) who hurried them along with whips, sticks, or guns, to the gas chambers. As in Operation T-4, these were identified as shower rooms. The Jews were rammed in, one person per square foot. The gassing lasted from ten to thirty minutes, depending on the facilities and techniques used. In Belżec, according to an eyewitness, it took thirty-two minutes and "finally, all were dead," he wrote, "like pillars of salt, still erect, not having any space to fall." To make room for the next load, the bodies were right away tossed out, "blue, wet with sweat and urine, the legs covered with feces and menstrual blood." Later the bodies were burned, either in the open air or in crematoria. Himmler complained about the slowness of the proceedings. But no quicker or more secret method could be found. A worker at Auschwitz said that "the stench given off by the pyres contaminated the surrounding countryside. At night the red sky over Auschwitz could be seen for miles."

Sometimes, special deaths were arranged; at Buchenwald, Ilse Koch, the wife of the commandant and the "Bitch of Buchenwald," arranged for some prisoners (such as those with tattoos) to be killed by injections and their skins specially treated and made into lamp shades or other items of houseware.

The doctors who helped prepare Frau Koch's lamp shades were only a few among the many who participated in acts such as the "scientific" experiments Sol Nazerman recalls going through on an operating table, in *The Pawnbroker*—experiments which lead the doctor examining Mendel, Tessie's father, to observe (in chapter 19) that "the man's body is a crime." According to William L. Shirer in *The Rise and Fall of the Third Reich:*

> It is a tale of horror of which the German medical profession cannot be proud. Although the "experiments" were conducted by fewer than two hundred murderous quacks—albeit some of them held eminent posts in the medical world—their criminal work was known to thousands of leading physicians of the Reich, not a single one of whom, so far as the record shows, ever uttered the slightest public protest.

One of the "murderous quacks" had been a member of the faculty of the Harvard Medical School.

TOPICS TO THINK ABOUT

1. Rosalie L. Colie, in "Literature and History":

> Sometimes what is interesting is that great events are *not* worthily represented in the arts—the literature of the European Resistance is usually technically inept, and concentration-camp literature and art, though extremely moving, is rarely so for its aesthetic success. If we take the example of Tolstoy [in *War and Peace*] as normative, then we can expect to wait a long time before the significance of an overwhelming historical event, such as the Second World War, can be proportioned into art.

Do you agree? Does *The Pawnbroker* tend to support or deny this assertion?

How much does either the novel or the film come somewhere close to being an adequate attempt at conveying even a minimal sense of the experiences of the Holocaust victims?

2. How do history and the present relate in this novel? In the film?

3. See the discussion in chapter 3 (pages 57–58) of the depiction of mental states (and of the "interior monologue" and "stream of consciousness") in film and written literature.

4. In the novel, most of Sol's dreams seem to re-present for him accurate reconstructions of his life in the concentration camp, while some of the dreams graft onto that world the inhabitants of the present, such as Jesus Ortiz, Morton, or even Murillio. Which dreams also occur in the film? On what bases do they seem to have been selected?

5. What is the effect of having the "flashbacks" in the film occur while Sol is awake, rather than while he is dreaming, as in the novel?

6. Often in movies, flashbacks are introduced by slow dissolves, or by ripples across the screen, or other visual announcements. The technique in *The Pawnbroker* is strikingly different: the scenes out of Sol's past are first introduced in a few frames, in a fraction of a second, as if to attain an almost subliminal effect. (Notice the similarly quick cuts between Sol and Rodriguez during their scene in the latter's apartment.) Even when presented at length, a scene out of the past is introduced with a sudden cut, never a dissolve or fade. What sorts of relationships between past and present are suggested in such an approach?

7. In the editing of the film, particularly in the use of the "subliminal" frames, Lumet has clearly been influenced by Alain Resnais, especially *Hiroshima Mon Amour* (1959) and **Last Year at Marienbad* (1961). If you know those films, or Fellini's **8½*, or Bergman's **Wild Strawberries* (or such a play as Arthur Miller's *Death of a Salesman*), compare and contrast their shifts from present to past with those in *The Pawnbroker*.

8. "Pictures have no tenses. They show only the present—they cannot express either a past or a future tense." (Béla Balázs, *Theory of the Film*)

9. From an unpublished journal by Edward Lewis Wallant:

Frustrated suddenly today. . . . how little I live as a writer—how little miserable time I have to work.

. . . Maybe inside I'm chaos? Can some order come from it? I *know* there are much bigger things down deeper. Stop caring about results. Think about what you want to do. There must be words—clear, understandable words which—in proper sequence —can make solid shapes of my feelings.

About what? Life, death, love, responsibility, mystery, God, lust, fear, guilt, compassion, beauty—

10. From Wallant, "The Artist's Eyesight":

Seeing is my key word, seeing with the heart, with the brain, with the eye. I suggest that most people are nearsighted, myopic in their inability to perceive the details of human experience. . . .

I believe that, for the writer and subsequently for the reader, things must be magnified. Call reading, then, a sort of magnifying lens, a pair of aesthetic spectacles.

11. Keep aware of the imagery of sight and seeing throughout the novel. For example, on the first page Sol is described as having "heedless dark eyes, distorted behind the thick lenses of strangely old-fashioned glasses." Compare those "heedless" eyes with what we are later told in a flashback about his duties in the concentration camp:

As he tugged at a corpse, something bright and delicate tumbled at his feet. He bent down quickly. It was a pair of spectacles, remarkably unbroken. He put them on, and the whole vast spectacle leapt into horrid clarity. He clenched his jaws as though to break the bone there and went back to his work, inflicting the cleared vision on himself. It was the very least he could do. (Chapter 20)

12. From Wallant, "The Artist's Eyesight":

A writer . . . is obsessed by the vividness of life. Those [esthetic] spectacles again! There are times when he yearns to cast them aside because they burn his eyes with color, make him subject to a constant assault of sensation and mystery. And of course he cannot take the spectacles off because they have become his very eyes. His eyesight may have become his curse but it is also his life.

13. "Perhaps with some small talent for graphic art, I was sensitive to the cinematographic." (Wallant, "The Artist's Eyesight")

Can you discern in the novel signs of influence by the cinema?

14. In the context of a discussion of "the bad good movie, the movie with serious intentions and pretensions that turns its back haughtily on the box-office in order to make a Meaningful Statement," Dwight Macdonald calls *The Pawnbroker* "the bad good film that has everything: alienation, anomie, neurosis, inability to love or communicate, the inhumanity of the metropolis, and the two great traumatic experiences of our age, the Jewish and the Negro, Harlem and the Nazi death camps." (*Dwight Macdonald on Movies*)

15. Raney Stanford wonders, in "The Novels of Edward Wallant," if in this case "the film was perhaps even more dramatically convincing than the novel, because the striking variety of cinematic effects compensated for weakness of script."

16. Few people who have ever seen actual photographs of the Jews in the concentration camps will not immediately realize that the Rod Steiger of the flashbacks is simply too heavy. Is his performance nevertheless one that can make us forget or ignore that fact, or does what we *see* overcome everything else in this instance?

17. Much of importance is conveyed through dialogue in the film, but in other ways as well it is unmistakably a "sound" movie. What role for example is played by music? By *noise?*

18. Sol, to Marilyn Birchfield: "I have some respect for fear. Love I will not talk about; it is too offensive—the obscenities committed in its name. But fear . . ." (Chapter 14)

What does Sol fear?

19. Sol, to Tessie: "Don't think, don't feel. Get through things—it is the only sense. . . . Don't suffer, don't fear. . . . Don't pay attention, don't cry!" (Chapter 23).

20. All of Wallant's other protagonists similarly withdraw from life and involvement. In a comic variation, *The Tenants of Moonbloom,* Norman Moonbloom is a rent-collector for several buildings in a slum neighborhood, and through his job he meets in his tenants a panorama of human misery, rather as Sol does in his work. The difference is that in Moonbloom's case his own suffering has been mild, and the horrors he witnesses have no parallels in his personal existence; as if because of that, Moonbloom is not a whole human being: " 'I'm not more than half alive,' he thought cheerfully, never considering that the state of being fully alive might be impending. 'God forbid,' he would have said to that suggestion, not believing in God or the threat."

21. The British psychologist R. D. Laing, in *The Divided Self:*

> It seems to be a general law that at some point those very dangers most dreaded can themselves be encompassed to forestall their actual occurrence. Thus, to forgo one's autonomy becomes the means of secretly safeguarding it; to play possum, to feign death, becomes a means of preserving one's aliveness. . . . To turn oneself into a stone becomes a way of not being turned into a stone by someone else.

22. From chapter 7:

> "It happen Jesus Christ hisself was a Catholic," Jane Ortiz threw in as a clincher.

"It happen he was a Jew," Mrs. Mapp answered.
"Why, Mrs. Mapp, what a awful thing to say!"

23. How would you characterize the relationship between Sol Nazerman and Jesus Ortiz. In the novel? In the film?

24. Ortiz thinks a good deal about Sol's "secret." Is there one? If so, does Ortiz ever learn it? Do we?

25. In a conversation about the customers of the pawnshop that also occurs in the film, Ortiz asks Sol:

"Why you call them creatures? Because they niggers?"
"No, no," Sol denied with a harsh chuckle. "I am nonsectarian, nondiscriminatory. Black, white, yellow are all equally abominations. . . ." (Chapter 10)

26. Sol's sister reflects on her family: "You wouldn't even guess they were Jews, Bertha thought proudly." (Chapter 2)

Ortiz' mother reflects on her husband: "In her own dark skin and simple ways, she had felt she perhaps hadn't deserved that handsome, facile man. He had been too *white!*" (Chapter 24)

27. In 1938, in order to plan for the expropriation of all Jewish property, the Nazis found it necessary to define what was meant by a "Jewish" company. They issued a decree that "a business enterprise is considered Jewish if its owner is a Jew" or "when it is under the dominant influence of Jews." Is the pawnshop a Jewish firm?

28. What is Murillio's role? In the novel? In society? What is made of Sol's relationship to him? Why does the film transfer Murillio's role to a black man, Rodriguez?

29. Marilyn Birchfield is the one major WASP in the novel and the film. How significant is that fact? What is your reaction to her?

30. Why is so little made of Morton in the film, do you think?

31. When it seems as if Robinson is about to kill him:

. . . Sol felt a sudden outrage. That his whole vast collection of experience should elude him now! He became incensed that his beginning and ending had no more depth and breadth than this shabby, littered shop. Suddenly he yearned for the drowning man's cliché, for some great distillation of everything. (Chapter 28)

Does the revelation ever come for Sol?

32. Why does Ortiz do what he does at the end? Does his motivation seem identical, similar, or different in the film version? Regardless of his motivation, what *effects* does his act have? Are they different in the film?

33. Compare and contrast the endings of the novel and the film. In particular, how would you compare what occurs or does not occur after the scene of violence?

34. "So maybe I love all of them, does it do any good? Doesn't that make it worse?" (Chapter 28)

How might you answer those questions?

35. In Wallant's *The Children at the Gate,* a character tells a friend how he has been beaten by the police and has confessed to a crime he did not commit:

> "Did I suffer? Yeah, sure I did, but that was all right. I'd be afraid *not* to suffer. . . . Let me tell you the worst dreams of all for me. I dream like I'm God, up on top of everything with nothing higher. All I have to do is wave my hand and I got what I want. I got no pains, no problems. . . . you know, it's the worst, worst feeling I ever have. It's so lonely not to suffer, so *lonely.* Who would want it if they knew? I don't say I *like* to suffer or *not* like to suffer. But *not* to!"

Further Readings

AYO, NICHOLAS. "The Secular Heart: The Achievement of Edward Lewis Wallant." *Critique* 12 (1970): 86–94.

BAUMBACH, JONATHAN. "The Illusion of Indifference: *The Pawnbroker* by Edward Lewis Wallant." In his *The Landscape of Nightmare: Studies in the Contemporary American Novel.* New York: New York University Press, 1965, pp. 138–51.

LORCH, THOMAS F. "The Novels of Edward Lewis Wallant." *Chicago Review* 19 (1967): 78–91.

LYONS, JOSEPH. *"The Pawnbroker:* Flashback in the Novel and Film." *Western Humanities Review* 20 (Summer 1966): 243–48.

PETRIE, GRAHAM. "The Films of Sidney Lumet: Adaptation as Art." *Film Quarterly* 21 (Winter 1967–68): 9–18.

RABINOWITZ, DOROTHY. *New Lives: Survivors of the Holocaust Living in America.* New York: Knopf, 1976. A non-fiction account of people whose lives are often in great contrast to Sol Nazerman's, even as in part they may be reminiscent of it.

STANFORD, RANEY. "The Novels of Edward Wallant." *Colorado Quarterly* 17 (Spring 1969): 393–405.

WALLANT, EDWARD LEWIS. "The Artist's Eyesight." *Teacher's Notebook in*

English (Fall 1963): 1–5. Distributed by the School Department Research Division of Harcourt.

_____. *The Children at the Gate.* New York: Harcourt Brace Jovanovich, 1964.

_____. *The Human Season.* New York: Berkley Medallion, 1964.

_____. *The Pawnbroker.* New York: Manor, 1973.

_____. *The Tenants of Moonbloom.* New York: Popular Library, 1963.

_____. Unpublished journal, quoted from an office memorandum, "The Unpublished Papers of Edward Lewis Wallant" (dated April 12, 1968), by Dan Wickenden, one of Wallant's editors at Harcourt.

BLOW-UP

BACKGROUND

On the Short Story

Julio Cortázar was born in Brussels, Belgium in 1914, grew up in Argentina, and now lives in Paris. His first volume of short stories, *Bestiario,* was published in 1951; *The Winners* (*Los premios*), his first novel, appeared in 1960. Cortázar's most famous book is the novel *Hopscotch* (*Rayuela,* 1963), an "open" work which the reader is invited to read in either "chronological" order or the order suggested by the narrator, the effect of each choice being quite different from the other.

The Spanish title of the story "Blow-Up" is "Las babas del diablo," or the devil's drool; the reference is to a Spanish saying about being in the devil's drool, or just escaping him, having a close call, and so on. The story was published in the volume *The Secret Weapons* (*Las armas secretas,* 1964).

On the Film

Blow-Up (1966; called *The Blow-Up* in England) won the Grand Prize at the Cannes Film Festival and was named the "Best Film" of the year by the National Society of Film Critics. It was directed by the Italian director Michelangelo Antonioni (b. 1912). He also co-wrote the screenplay with Tonino Guerra, with whom he has collaborated on many of his films; they worked on the English dialogue with Edward Bond.

Antonioni began making films in the 1940s, and his first feature film (*Cronaca di un Amore*) appeared in 1950; other movies include *Le Amiche* (1955) and *Il Grido* (1957), but he did not achieve international notice until the ambiguous and controversial *L'Avventura* (1960). That was followed by *La Notte* (also 1960), *The Eclipse* (*L'Eclisse,* 1962), and *Red Desert* (*Deserto rosso,* 1964), his first color film and a striking one. *Blow-Up* was his first picture to be shot entirely outside Italy; others are *Zabriskie Point* (1969) and *The Passenger* (1975).

The producer was Carlo Ponti, who has been responsible for many other international productions as well, including King Vidor's *War and Peace* (1956) and David Lean's *Doctor Zhivago* (1966). The director of photography was Carlo di Palma, who had worked with Antonioni on *Red Desert;* the camera was operated by Ray Parslow. Herbie Hancock wrote the music; the group doing "Stroll On" was the Yardbirds.

Other credits: executive producer, Pierre Rouve; editor, Frank Clarke; art director, Assheton Gorton; assistant director, Claude Watson; sound recordist, Robin Gregory; sound editor, Mike le Mare; photographic murals, John Cowan; wardrobe, Jackie Breed.

David Hemmings played the photographer (called Thomas in the published screenplay, although the chief characters are not named within the film itself). Hemmings had been in films for several years, but *Blow-Up* was his first genuinely important role; his other pictures include *The Charge of the Light Brigade* (1968) and *Alfred the Great* (1969); he directed *Running Scared* (1972).

The girl (Jane) was played by Vanessa Redgrave, who has also been in *Morgan* (1966), *Isadora* (1968), *The Devils* (1971), and *Julia* (1977). Sarah Miles (Patricia) had been in *The Servant* (1963); her first major starring role came in *Ryan's Daughter* (1970).

Other members of the cast: Peter Bowles as Ron; John Castle as the painter (Bill); Verushka as the first model; Jane Birkin and Gillian Hills as the blond and brunette teen-agers.

Running time: 111 minutes. Distributor: Films Inc.

TOPICS TO THINK ABOUT

1. "The idea for *Blow-Up* came to me while reading a short story by Julio Cortázar. I was not so much interested in the events as in the

FIG. 36.   The Museum of Modern Art/Film Stills Archive. Courtesy MGM.

technical aspects of the photographs. I discarded the plot and wrote a new one, in which the technical aspects took on a different weight and significance." (Antonioni, foreword to the Italian edition of the published screenplay)

2. "The shooting script is never definitive for me. It's notes about the direction, nothing more." (Antonioni, interview with Pierre Billard)

3. While filming *Blow-Up*, Antonioni remarked to Nadine Liber, "I have never felt salvation in nature. I love cities above all." Would you guess that from *Blow-Up*?

4. The narrator in Cortázar's story "Blow-Up":

I know that the most difficult thing is going to be finding a way to tell it, and I'm not afraid of repeating myself. It's going to be difficult because nobody really knows who it is telling it, if I am I or what actually occurred or what I'm seeing (clouds, and once in a while a pigeon) or if, simply, I'm telling a truth which is only my truth.

5. Antonioni, an Italian, has taken a story in Spanish by an expa-

triate Argentine writer, which is set in France, and has adapted it to take place in England. Why, do you suppose? What is the effect of the London setting? What sort of world does the film depict? What sort of society?

6. Our first glimpse of the photographer occurs as he is leaving the doss-house (a hostel for tramps and down-and-outs): what context is set up by that scene?

7. Carey Harrison, in the review of *Blow-Up* in *Sight and Sound:*

> *Blow-Up* is unconsciously an appeal to the worst kind of intellectual sentimentality. It is a lesson in how to take the easy way out. It could become the handbook of those words-don't-ever-really-communicate and you-can't-ever-really-know-what-I'm-feeling merchants who settle for these half-truths the moment a discussion becomes demanding, in the impermeable conviction that they are bravely confronting a more challenging and subtle reality than you.

8. *"Blow-Up* is like the latest copy of *Vogue.* It commandeth the eye but sticketh not in the memory." (Vernon Young, *On Film*)

9. Arthur Knight, in "Three Encounters with *Blow-Up":*

> I suspect that future historians will recognize it as important and germinal a film as *Citizen Kane, Open City* and *Hiroshima, Mon Amour*—perhaps even more so. For in a curious, complex way, Antonioni is getting back to first principles. Like Griffith, he wants to make you *see,* to absorb quickly, intuitively, the visual symbols that are semaphored from the screen.

10. Antonioni, in an interview with Pierre Billard:

> What people ordinarily call the "dramatic line" doesn't interest me. . . . And I don't believe that the old laws of drama have validity any more. Today stories are what they are, with neither a beginning nor an end necessarily, without key scenes, without a dramatic arc, without catharsis. They can be made up of tatters, of fragments, as unbalanced as the lives we lead.

11. What happens in the park?

12. The girl, to the photographer: "Why don't you say what you want?"

13. What roles do women have in the world of *Blow-Up?* In the photographer's work? In his life?

14. Jonas Mekas, on Antonioni, in 1962, before the appearance of

Blow-Up: "His films are about people, about *us,* who don't have anything to communicate, who don't feel a need to communicate, whose human essence is dying. Antonioni's films are about the death of the human soul."

15. In 1964, before he made *Blow-Up,* Antonioni told Jean-Luc Godard: "What interests me now is to place the character in contact with things, for it is things, objects and materials that have weight today."

16. The photographer to the girl in the park: "It's not my fault if there's no peace."

17. In the film, the Yardbirds sing:

> . . . it's all gone
> Treat you right
> You make me cry
> You're tellin' me
> You didn't see . . .

18. In few films is the act of *seeing* itself, the process of vision, so central. As Antonioni said in a 1967 interview reprinted with the script of *Blow-Up:* "I'm really questioning the nature of reality. This is an essential point to remember about the visual aspects of the film, since one of its chief themes is 'to see or not to see properly the true value of things.'"

19. In the film, the photographer tells the girl in the park: "I'm only doing my job. Some people are . . . bull-fighters. Some people are politicians. I'm a photographer." Does that say or imply anything about him other than that is the way he makes his living?

When do we see him without his camera?

20. "*Blow-Up* is in fact a series of photographs about a series of photographs and so constitutes what might be called a metalinguistic metaphor, a highly self-conscious and self-reflexive meditation on its own process." (John Freccero, *"Blow-Up:* From the Word to the Image")

21. Bill talks about his paintings to the photographer: "They don't mean anything when I do them—just a mess. Afterwards I find something to hang onto—like that—like—like . . . that leg. . . . And then it sorts itself out. It adds up. It's like finding a clue in a dectective story."

22. All along, Thomas is a photographer. In the scene in which he closely examines the blow-ups he becomes in effect an editor as well, arranging his shots as if in a process of editing and montage. (See the discussion of montage in chapter 2, pages 47–49.)

How would you react to the proposition that, ultimately, the subject of this movie is the movies?

23. In his studio, the photographer assures the girl from the park that there is "nothing like a little disaster for sorting things out." Is there such a disaster in this film? Are things sorted out?

24. What functions are served by the young mimes who appear at both the start and the end of the film?

25. There has been a great deal of controversy about the final scene of the film, but most interpretations tend to fall into one of two broad categories: either they agree with Robin Wood, in his and Ian Cameron's *Antonioni,* that "Thomas' retrieving of the 'ball' marks his final surrender" and shows that "his grasp of objective reality" is "fatally undermined," or they agree with Arthur Knight that "when the hero joins their game, one has the feeling of a final affirmation, that he is aligning himself with people who are joyfully alive and not part of his shadowy black-and-white world of photographs." Does either approach match your own?

Further Readings

ANTONIONI, MICHELANGELO. *Blow-Up: A Film.* New York: Simon and Schuster, 1971. Includes the screenplay, some stills, several interviews, and Antonioni's short essay, "Reality and *Cinéma-Vérité.*"

BILLARD, PIERRE. "An Interview with Michelangelo Antonioni." In Antonioni, *Blow-Up,* above.

CAMERON, IAN, and ROBIN WOOD. *Antonioni.* New York: Praeger, 1969.

FERRUA, PIETRO. *"Blow-Up* from Cortázar to Antonioni." *Literature/Film Quarterly* 4 (Winter 1976): 68–75.

FRECCERO, JOHN. *"Blow-Up:* From the Word to the Image." *Yale/Theatre* 3 (Fall 1970): 15–24. Reprinted in Huss, ed., *Focus on Blow-Up,* below.

GODARD, JEAN-LUC. "Michelangelo Antonioni." Trans. Rose Kaplin. In *Interviews with Film Directors.* Ed. Andrew Sarris. New York: Avon, 1969, pp. 21–32. Originally published in *Cahiers du Cinéma* 160 (November 1964).

HUSS, ROY, ed. *Focus on Blow-Up.* Englewood Cliffs, N.J.: Prentice-Hall, 1971. Includes an "Outline" of the film, Cortázar's story, and essays and reviews. A useful collection.

KNIGHT, ARTHUR. "Three Encounters with *Blow-Up." Film Heritage* 2 (Spring 1967): 3–6. Reprinted in Huss, ed., *Focus on Blow-Up,* above.

LIBER, NADINE. "Michelangelo Antonioni Talks about His Work." In Antonioni, *Blow-Up,* above.

SAMUELS, CHARLES THOMAS. "Michelangelo Antonioni." In his *Encountering Directors.* New York: Putnam's Sons, 1972, pp. 15–32. Interview.

2001: A SPACE ODYSSEY

BACKGROUND

On the Story and the Novel

The germ of the idea for the film was a short story, "The Sentinel," originally written in 1948 and published in 1950, by Arthur C. Clarke (b. 1917), a British writer of science fiction whose books have become among the most famous in that genre; especially notable are the novels *Childhood's End* (1952), *Rendezvous with Rama* (1976), and of course the novel that came out of the film, *2001: A Space Odyssey* (1968).

"The Sentinel" is about an expedition to the moon in 1996 which discovers a "roughly pyramidal structure." Apparently it is a warning system (a "sentinel") designed to relay to the extraterrestrial beings who have placed it there—perhaps millions of years before—the information that the inhabitants of Earth are now able to reach the moon; the story does not go much beyond that basic concept. In 1964, Stanley Kubrick contacted Clarke with the idea of collaborating on a science fiction film, and eventually Clarke recalled his short story, and from then on the history of the writing of the film and the novel that resulted was quite unusual. At Kubrick's urging, they agreed to work together on writing a prose treatment—which in effect was the draft of a novel—before writing a script. Actually, as Clarke has since testified, the process turned out to be much more complicated, and "toward the end, both novel and screenplay were being written simultaneously, with feedback in both directions. . . . After a couple of years of this, I felt that when the novel finally appeared it should be 'by Arthur Clarke and Stanley Kubrick; based on the screenplay by Stanley Kubrick and Arthur Clarke'—whereas the movie should have the credits reversed." Clarke dedicated the published version of the novel "To Stanley."

While "The Sentinel" provided the core situation, others of Clarke's works provided a number of the situations or themes that would be developed in both the novel and the film, and over the years the treatment/novel went far beyond the original short story; it became much fuller and more detailed (although the novel, for good or ill, is also much fuller and more detailed—and less mysterious—than the film).

FIG. 37.   The Museum of Modern Art/Film Stills Archive. Courtesy MGM.

On the Film

2001: A Space Odyssey (1968) was produced, directed, and co-written by a man who refuses to travel by airplane, Stanley Kubrick (b. 1928). After having made several films independently, including *Killer's Kiss* (1955) and *The Killing* (1956), he worked with studio backing on *Paths of Glory* (1957), which starred Kirk Douglas, and then on Douglas' own production of the epic *Spartacus* (1960)—an experience which made Kubrick resolve that he would no longer work on any film over which he did not retain complete artistic control. His next film was **Lolita* (1962), and then came one which many critics feel is one of the great films of all time (although *2001* makes even more "ten best" lists), *Dr. Strangelove, or How I Learned to Stop Worrying and Love the Bomb* (1963). After *2001* he made **A Clockwork Orange* (1971) and *Barry Lyndon* (1975).

In addition to directing, co-writing, and producing (which in his case especially means overseeing *everything*), Kubrick was also in charge of special effects (the only category for which *2001* received an Academy

Award). The film is a landmark in the history of special effects. They were immensely expensive and complicated; shooting with the actors took about four and a half months, while work on the 205 separate shots needing special effects took a year and a half.

Four major breakthroughs are usually cited in discussions of the technical achievements of *2001:*

1. The quality of the models of the spacecraft. Most were only a foot or two, and even the cavernous moon landing site was only fifteen feet high, yet the details were so fine that even close-ups were both possible and impressive.

2. The delicacy and complexity of the matte shots. (*Mattes* are masking devices by which certain areas of the frame are blacked out during takes, so that in subsequent takes other scenes can be superimposed upon those portions of the frame.) For example, the windows through which we see crew members in the space stations entail superimposed takes on blacked-out windows no larger than a few inches.

3. The perfection of the technique of *front projection,* in the Dawn of Man sequences. In front projection, scenes shot elsewhere are projected in a studio onto a huge special screen behind the actors, in a method leading to results that are both preferable to and much larger than those possible with the older process, by which scenes are projected from behind the screen (back or rear projection).

4. The slit-scan machine used in the so-called light-show of the Star Gate sequence.

The latter device was the work of Douglas Trumbull, one of Kubrick's special effects supervisors; Trumbull was later in charge of visual effects for *Close Encounters of the Third Kind* (1977), and before that he had directed his own science fiction film, *Silent Running* (1973). The other special effects supervisors were Wally Veevers, Con Pederson, and Tom Howard.

Hardy Amies was in charge of wardrobe and costumes; Clarke has wondered if Amies failed to receive an Academy Award because no one realized that the apes were human actors. (The babies were in fact real baby chimps.) The editor was Ray Lovejoy, but Kubrick is always extensively involved with the editing process, which, as he is quoted as saying in *Stanley Kubrick Directs,* he regards as "the one and only aspect of films that is unique and unrelated to any other art form." The director of photography was Geoffrey Unsworth, whose other films include *A Night to Remember* (1958), *Cabaret* (1972), and *Murder on the Orient Express* (1974). Additional photography was by John Alcott, who went on to be the director of photography for *A Clockwork Orange and Barry Lyndon, receiving an Academy Award for the latter.

Other credits: assistant director, Derek Cracknell; art director, John Hoesli; sound editor, Winston Ryder; scientific consultant, Frederick I. Ordway III. Originally Kubrick planned to have music composed for the picture, and in fact Alex North did complete a score, but in the end Kubrick decided to use music by Aram Khatchaturian, György Ligeti, Johann Strauss, and Richard Strauss (see below, topics 11 and 12).

Dave Bowman was played by Keir Dullea, who has also been in *The Hoodlum Priest* (1961), *David and Lisa* (1962), and *The Fox* (1968). Gary Lockwood played Frank Poole; he was in *Splendor in the Grass* (1961) and has been active in television. Heywood Floyd was William Sylvester, an American actor who has been in many British films. The ape who discovers the use of the bone as a tool (he is of course nameless in the movie, but he was called Moon-Watcher in the treatment/novel) was Dan Richter. The voice of HAL was that of Douglas Rain, a Canadian stage actor who has been in major productions in both Canada and England. He was originally hired to read narration—which, however, Kubrick eventually scrapped; and he then replaced Martin Balsam, whose reading of HAL's lines Kubrick came to feel was too emotive; Rain was asked to be dry and matter-of-fact at all times.

Other members of the cast: Leonard Rossiter and Margaret Tyzack as Smyslov and Elena, the two Russians; Vivian Kubrick (the director's daughter, uncredited) as "Squirt," Floyd's daughter; Robert Beatty as Halverson; Sean Sullivan as Michaels; Frank Miller as Mission Control; Penny Brahms as the stewardess.

Running time: 141 minutes. Distributor: Films Inc.

TOPICS TO THINK ABOUT

1. With some notable exceptions, *2001* was not at first greeted enthusiastically by reviewers, although as the film came to cause a great deal of excitement and debate among audiences, a number of critics went to the trouble of recanting their previously tepid responses.

2. "The movie is so completely absorbed in its own problems, its use of color and space, its fanatical devotion to science-fiction detail, that it is somewhere between hypnotic and immensely boring." (Renata Adler, review in *The New York Times*)

3. "I think Stanley Kubrick's *2001: A Space Odyssey* is some sort of great film, and an unforgettable endeavor. . . . It is . . . a uniquely poetic piece of sci-fi, made by a man who truly possesses the drives of both science and fiction." (Penelope Gilliatt, review in *The New Yorker*)

4. "It is morally pretentious, intellectually obscure, and inordinately long. The concluding statement is too private, too profound, or perhaps too shallow for immediate comprehension." (Arthur Schlesinger, Jr., review in *Vogue*)

5. "The slab is never explained, leaving *2001*, for all its lively visual and mechanical spectacle, a kind of space-*Spartacus* and, more pretentious still, a shaggy God story." (John Simon, review in the *New Leader*)

6. "I have always enjoyed dealing with a slightly surrealistic situation and presenting it in a realistic manner. I've always liked fairy tales and myths, magical stories, supernatural stories, ghost stories, surrealistic and allegorical stories." (Kubrick, interview with Penelope Houston)

Kubrick called *2001* a "mythological documentary," and it was he who chose its final title over the earlier one, *Journey Beyond the Stars*. What are the effects of the echoes of Homer's *Odyssey*, and of the sense of "mythical" overtones in the film?

7. In a log he kept while working with Kubrick, Clarke records for September 26, 1964: "Stanley gave me Joseph Campbell's analysis of the myth *The Hero with a Thousand Faces* to study. Very stimulating." (*The Lost Worlds of 2001*)

Campbell's important book is, first, a study of the role of myth in human life:

> It would not be too much to say that myth is the secret opening through which the inexhaustible energies of the cosmos pour into human cultural manifestation. Religions, philosophies, arts, the social forms of primitive and historic man, prime discoveries in science and technology, the very dreams that blister sleep, boil up from the basic, magic ring of myth.

8. More specifically, *The Hero with a Thousand Faces* is a study of what Campbell calls (borrowing a term from James Joyce's *Finnegans Wake*) the "monomyth": the recurrent pattern evident in the adventures of major heroes of mythology in cultures all over the world, in all periods of history:

> The standard path of the mythological adventure of the hero is a magnification of the formula represented in the rites of passage: *separation—initiation—return:* which might be named the nuclear unit of the monomyth.

> A hero ventures forth from the world of common day into a region of supernatural wonder: fabulous forces are there encountered and a decisive victory is won: the hero comes back from this mysterious adventure with the power to bestow boons on his fellow man.

Is it illuminating to consider 2001 in light of the monomyth?

9. What is the role of the black monolith in the "Dawn of Man" section of the film? In the novel, it is a sort of audio-visual aid, showing the apes (particularly Moon-Watcher) pictures teaching the use of tool-weapons. Why does the film refrain from showing such scenes?

10. "As I see it, Kubrick's film is a study of various capacities for consciousness, an attempt to suggest through spectacle the possibilities and limitations of the powers of Mind for perception, intellection and feeling." (Don Daniels, "A Skeleton Key to 2001")

11. The music at the start and end of the film is from Richard Strauss's Also Sprach Zarathustra (Thus Spoke Zarathustra), a composition which was inspired by the philosopher Friedrich Nietzsche's book with the same title, in which he says that as ape seems to man, so will man seem to the Superman, as the evolution of humanity continues:

> Man is something that should be overcome. . . .
> All creatures hitherto have created something beyond themselves: and do you want to be the ebb of this great tide, and return to the animals rather than overcome man?
> What is the ape to men? A laughing-stock or a painful embarrassment. And just so shall men be to the Superman: a laughing-stock or a painful embarrassment.

12. Another striking musical association is that of Johann Strauss's The Blue Danube with the first scenes of spaceships as Floyd is taken to the moon. Carolyn Geduld regards that conjunction as "a classic example of what Eisenstein and Pudovkin call an orchestral counterpoint of visual and aural images" (Filmguide to 2001). (See the summary of their manifesto in chapter 2, page 26.)

Other juxtapositions are: Aram Khatchaturian's Gayané ballet suite with shots of the interior of the spaceship Discovery (as, for example, we see Poole jogging); Györgi Ligeti's Requiem and Lux Aeterna with the appearances of the monolith; and Ligeti's Atmospheres with the Star Gate sequence.

13. In the "Dawn of Man," a common transitional device is the fade, which makes all the more striking the famous sudden match cut from

the bone to the space station (see the discussion of fades and match cuts in chapter 2, pages 45–46). What is the effect of that cut?

14. There is no dialogue until we are well into the second part of the film, half an hour after its start (the hostess says to Floyd, "Here you are, sir"); and only about one third of the film as a whole has dialogue (about forty-six minutes out of 141).

Originally, there was to be some narration, but it was ultimately discarded. Presumably that decision did not come about as a result of some general objection by Kubrick toward voice-over narration (see the discussion of voice-overs in chapter 3, page 58). He had used it before (in *Lolita and *Dr. Strangelove) and would do so again—especially extensively in *A Clockwork Orange, but in *Barry Lyndon* too. So why do you think he chose to dispense with it here?

15. Unlike the other two films by Kubrick treated in this volume, then, *2001* has no narration and relatively little dialogue. Is it thereby almost like a "silent movie," or a purely visual experience? How important is what we hear (or what we do not)?

16. The novel Clarke published is always much clearer and more explicit than the film. Is that an advantage or not, do you think?

17. The narrator in "The Sentinel," on the pyramidal structure which is the equivalent of the monolith in the film:

> Perhaps you understand now why that crystal pyramid was set upon the Moon instead of on the Earth. Its builders were not concerned with races still struggling up from savagery. They would be interested in our civilization only if we proved our fitness to survive—by crossing space and so escaping from the Earth, our cradle. . . .
> . . . If you will pardon so commonplace a simile, we have set off the fire alarm and have nothing to do but to wait.
> I do not think we will have to wait for long.

18. Keir Dullea (quoted in *The Making of Kubrick's 2001*) has said that "HAL is more human than I am in the picture." That has been a common reaction not only to Bowman, but to Floyd and Poole as well; do you share it?

19. HAL's name stands for "*H*euristically programmed *AL*gorithmic computer, no less." (Clarke, *2001,* chapter 16)

Kubrick, in an interview with Alexander Walker:

> Once a computer learns by experience as well as by its original

programing, and once it has access to much more information than any number of human geniuses might possess, the first thing that happens is that you don't really understand it anymore, and you don't know what it's doing or thinking about. You could be tempted to ask yourself in what way is machine intelligence any less sacrosanct than biological intelligence, and it might be difficult to arrive at an answer flattering to biological intelligence.

20. HAL brings up in conversation with Bowman "those strange stories before we left about something being dug up on the moon," although he admits that "maybe I'm just projecting my own feelings." Later, as Bowman seems trapped in the pod outside the Discovery, HAL says, "This mission is too important for me to allow you to jeopardize it."

What are HAL's motives for what he does?

21. Cybernetics is a scientific discipline based on the premise that in both organic and inorganic systems (that is, animals and machines) the laws governing organization, control, and communication are the same. Ann Neel, in *Theories of Psychology*, explains that "the basic and single principle of cybernetics was the assumption that the function of every dynamic system, be it mechanical or living, was governed by the necessity of maintaining itself and, further, that all systems went about this in the same general way."

22. As in many tales, from that of the Golem through Frankenstein to Doctors Jekyll and Strangelove, humanity's wizardry or science has created in HAL a force it cannot then seem to control.

How would you describe what Bowman does to save himself when he is in the pod outside the ship? Is it clever, innovative, and creative, and therefore victorious over HAL, whose intelligence turns out to be limited after all? Or would you say instead that Bowman's act—submitting himself to the vacuum of space without a helmet—is an irrational one born of desperation; in other words, that what saves Bowman in his competition with HAL is not his ability to defeat him on HAL's own terms (by being "smarter"), but his humanity? (What kills the Frankenstein monster in the movies is not some scientific device, but the villagers: the irrational, antiscientific villagers with their primitive torches.)

23. What *is* the attitude toward science and its products in this film? Would you agree with either Norman Kagan (in his book on Kubrick) on the one hand, that "despite its beautiful images, *2001* is anti-scientific," or with Judith Shatnoff (in her review in *Film Quarterly*) on the other hand, that "*2001* is straight—and must be taken straight—in its celebration of technology"?

24. There are two depictions of "death" in this film unlike those in any other movie: the killing of the hibernating astronauts ("Computer Malfunction" . . . "Life Functions Critical" . . . "Life Functions Terminated") and the lobotomizing of HAL ("I'm afraid, Dave. My mind is going. I can feel it. . . . There is no question about it. I can feel it. . . . I'm afraid"); HAL then sings "Daisy, Daisy . . . I'm half crazy . . ."

25. HAL "is programmed to sound forever calm for the sake of the astronauts, right up to the horrifying moment in the 'logic memory center' when he pleads in even tones with Bowman, unable even to express the fear of his own death in any other way." (Geduld, *Filmguide*)

26. The image of Floyd, on a monitor, states in a prerecorded message that "now that you are in Jupiter space"—and now that "the entire crew is revived"—the purpose of the mission, which up to now has been known only by HAL, can be revealed:

> Eighteen months ago, the first evidence of intelligent life off the Earth was discovered. It was buried forty feet below the lunar surface, near the crater Tycho. Except for a single, very powerful radio emission aimed at Jupiter, the four-million-year-old black monolith has remained completely inert, its origin and purpose still a total mystery.

The word *mystery* is the last word spoken in the film.

27. The experience Bowman has as the film presents its psychedelic light show is identified in the novel as his passage through "the Star Gate"—"some kind of cosmic switching device, routing the traffic of the stars through unimaginable dimensions of space and time." (Chapter 41)

28. In most science fiction films about extraterrestrial beings, sooner or later we get to see them, as in *Close Encounters of the Third Kind*—and, in fact, as in the early plans for *2001*. Is the restraint of the final version of the film disappointing, or effective (or both)?

29. In the modernistic Louis XVI room, how—why—does Bowman see himself?

30. Of the fact that originally he and Kubrick planned to have others in the crew besides Bowman survive, Clarke writes, in an allusion to the ending of *Moby Dick:* "We should have taken a hint from Melville, who placed at the opening of his brief Epilogue the line from Job: 'And I only am escaped alone to tell thee.' " (*Lost Worlds*)

31. At the end, after extending his hand toward the monolith—like Moon-Watcher and Floyd before him—Bowman is transformed into what the novel calls a "Star-Child": the next step, as Kubrick has put it, in "man's evolutionary destiny." (Interview with Joseph Gelmis, in *The Film Director as Superstar*)

32. Clarke's Third Law: "Any sufficiently advanced technology is indistinguishable from magic." (*Lost Worlds*)

33. "Two-thirds of *2001* is realistic—hardware and technology—to establish a background for the metaphysical, philosophical, and religious meanings later." (Clarke, in Agel, *Making of 2001*)

34. Have the extraterrestrial beings "created" the human race—programmed it, as the humans themselves program computers like HAL?

If so, are those extraterrestrial beings God, or gods?

If you know Kubrick's *A Clockwork Orange,* compare and contrast the "conditioning" of Alex in that film with what Moon-Watcher and Bowman seem to undergo in *2001*.

35. "I think it was a prominent astronomer who wrote recently, 'Sometimes I think we are alone, and sometimes I think we're not. In either case, the idea is quite staggering.' " (Kubrick, interview with Eric Norden)

Further Readings

AGEL, JEROME, ed. *The Making of Kubrick's 2001.* New York: Signet, 1970. An extremely valuable collection of miscellanea about the film from its makers, critics, reviewers, and audiences.

American Cinematographer 49 (June 1968). The entire issue is devoted to *2001;* includes technical articles by Herb A. Lightman on front projection and Douglas Trumbull on special effects.

CLARKE, ARTHUR C. *The Lost Worlds of 2001.* New York: Signet, 1972. Clarke's account of the creation of *2001;* includes some chapters of early versions of the prose treatment that became the novel.

———. "The Sentinel." Reprinted in Agel, *Making of 2001*, and Clarke, *Lost Worlds,* above.

———, based on a screenplay by Stanley Kubrick and Arthur C. Clarke. *2001: A Space Odyssey.* New York: Signet, 1968.

DANIELS, DON. "A Skeleton Key to *2001." Sight and Sound* 40 (Winter 1970–71): 28–33.

GEDULD, CAROLYN. *Filmguide to 2001: A Space Odyssey.* Bloomington: Indiana University Press, 1973.

KAGAN, NORMAN. *The Cinema of Stanley Kubrick.* New York: Grove, 1972.

KUBRICK, STANLEY. "Words and Movies." In *Hollywood Directors 1941–1976.* Ed. Richard Koszarski. New York: Oxford University Press,

1977, pp. 305–9. Originally published in *Sight and Sound* 30 (Winter 1960–61): 14.

NORDEN, ERIC. "Playboy Interview: Stanley Kubrick." *Playboy* 15 (September 1968): 85–86+. Reprinted in Agel, *Making of 2001,* above.

PHILLIPS, GENE D. *Stanley Kubrick: A Film Odyssey.* New York: Popular Library, 1975. Frequently quotes from Kubrick.

WALKER, ALEXANDER. *Stanley Kubrick Directs.* New York: Harcourt Brace Jovanovich, 1971. Based on extensive interviews with Kubrick.

A CLOCKWORK ORANGE

BACKGROUND

On the Novel

The British novelist Anthony Burgess (b. 1917) published *A Clockwork Orange* in 1962; although he did not write his first novel until his late thirties, he has been notably prolific ever since. Among his most well-known novels are *The Doctor Is Sick* (1960), *The Wanting Seed* (like *A Clockwork Orange* set in the not-too-distant future and published in 1962), *Inside Mr. Enderby* (1963; the first of several volumes about the title figure), *Nothing Like the Sun* (1964; a novel about William Shakespeare), and *Napoleon Symphony* (1974), which had its source in Burgess' ideas for Stanley Kubrick's long-planned film about Napoleon.

In 1974, Burgess published a sardonically comic novel called *The Clockwork Testament, or: Enderby's End,* which despite its main title is not a sequel to *A Clockwork Orange* but rather the last Enderby novel. In it, Enderby, a British poet, becomes a sudden celebrity when a filmmaker produces a movie and gives Enderby credit for the original idea. The movie, supposedly an adaptation of Gerard Manley Hopkins' poem *The Wreck of the Deutschland,* features a great deal of sex and violence, and Enderby finds himself being regarded as an expert on both those topics—and also as someone who must respond to attacks upon himself, art, the movie he had nothing to do with, or all three.

In regard to the novel *A Clockwork Orange* itself, there is a major difference in the endings of the versions published in England and America (see topic 35, below).

On the Film

Stanley Kubrick (b. 1928) produced, directed, and wrote the screenplay for *A Clockwork Orange* (1971); he received the New York Film Critics Awards for the best picture and best direction. He made his first film, a documentary short, *Day of the Fight,* in 1951, while in his early twenties. Next came other shorts and some independently produced features, including *Fear and Desire* (1953). His first major production was *Paths of Glory* (1957), an antiwar film starring Kirk Douglas, for whose company Kubrick then directed *Spartacus* (1960). As a result of disappointments over the handling of that production, Kubrick resolved never again to relinquish artistic control of his films.

He then directed **Lolita* (1962); for that film, Kubrick consulted with and, in a complex way, collaborated with the author of the novel he was adapting (Vladimir Nabokov). He again collaborated with the original authors on *Dr. Strangelove, or How I Learned to Stop Worrying and Love the Bomb* (1963) and **2001: A Space Odyssey* (1968), two of the most widely praised movies in film history. For *A Clockwork Orange,* he wrote the screenplay alone for the first time since *The Killing* (1956); he did so again for *Barry Lyndon* (1975). In the case of *Clockwork,* he has said that the novel was a relatively uncomplicated one to adapt, since its scope did not necessitate oversimplification. In an interview with Philip Strick and Penelope Houston, Kubrick claimed that writing the screenplay "was principally a matter of selection and editing, though I did invent a few useful narrative ideas and reshape some of the scenes."

The executive producers were Max L. Raab and Si Litvinoff, and Bernard Williams was the associate producer. The director of photography was John Alcott, who had worked under Geoffrey Unsworth on *2001;* Alcott was again in charge of cinematography for *Barry Lyndon,* for which he received an Academy Award. But Kubrick often operates the camera himself—as he invariably does in hand-held shots, such as those in *Clockwork* of the beating and rape in the Alexander home, and of the violence in the Catlady's home. He also is very active in the process of editing, working closely with the editor, who in this case was Bill Butler.

The production design was by John Barry, who performed the same function for *Star Wars* (1977). Russell Hagg and Peter Shields were the art directors, with special paintings and sculptures by Herman Makkink, Liz Moore, Cornelius Makkink, and Christiane Kubrick (Stanley Kubrick's wife).

As in *2001* and *Barry Lyndon,* the music in *Clockwork* was not especially composed for the film, except for the electronic compositions and

FIG. 38.   The Museum of Modern Art/Film Stills Archive. Copyright © by Warner
Bros., Inc. 1972. (All rights reserved.)

variations (notably of Beethoven's Ninth Symphony) by Walter Carlos.
Beethoven's Ninth is featured in the second scene in the Korova
Milkbar, in the record shop, during the Ludovico treatment, at the
suicide attempt, and at the end. The opening music is from Henry
Purcell's *Music for the Funeral of Queen Mary;* during the fight with Bil-
lyboy's gang, we hear Gioacchino Rossini's *The Thieving Magpie;* the
fast-motion sexual play in Alex's room is to Rossini's familiar *William Tell
Overture;* the arrival of the Minister of the Interior at the prison is,
appropriately, to Edward Elgar's *Pomp and Circumstance;* the Biblical
daydreams are to Rimski-Korsakov's *Scheherazade.* The song "I Want To
Marry a Lighthouse Keeper" is by Erika Eigen, whose voice is heard
singing it. "Singin' in the Rain" is by Arthur Freed and Nacio Herb
Brown; the rendition by Gene Kelly over the final credits is of course
from the sound track of *Singin' in the Rain* (1952).

Other credits: sound editor, Brian Blamey; sound recording, John

Jordan; costumes, Milena Canonero; assistant directors, Derek Cracknell and Dusty Symonds.

Alex was played by Malcolm McDowell, whose first film was *If* . . . (1968); he has also been in *O Lucky Man* (1973; based largely on his own experiences) and *Royal Flash* (1975). Patrick Magee played Mr. F. Alexander (given the first name Frank in the film); he has been especially prominent in the theater (for example in Samuel Beckett's *Krapp's Last Tape*) and was in *Barry Lyndon*. Michael Bates (the Chief Guard) has been in *I'm All Right Jack* (1959), *Bedazzled* (1967), and *Patton* (1970).

Other members of the cast: Anthony Sharp as the Minister of the Interior; Warren Clarke as Dim; Carl Duering as Dr. Brodsky; James Marcus as Georgie; Miriam Karlin as the Catlady; Aubrey Morris as Mr. Deltoid; Godfrey Quigley as the prison chaplain; Adrienne Corri as Mrs. Alexander; Paul Farrell as the tramp; Philip Stone and Sheila Raynor as Alex's father and mother; Clive Francis as Joe, the lodger; Madge Ryan as Dr. Branom; John Clive and Virginia Wetherell as the stage actor and actress; Michael Gover as the prison governor; Dave Prowse as Julian, Mr. Alexander's assistant; Pauline Taylor as the psychiatrist in the hospital; Michael Tarn as Pete.

Running time: 137 minutes. Distributors: Swank; Warner.

TOPICS TO THINK ABOUT

1. Alex, in both the novel and the film, on the first movie shown during the Ludovico treatment: "It's funny how the colours of the like real world only seem really real when you viddy them on the screen." (Part 2, chapter 4)

2. "The people I first admired were not film directors but novelists. Like Conrad." (Kubrick, interview with Craig McGregor)

3. On the Nadsat words in the novel:

"Quaint," said Dr. Brodsky, like smiling, "the dialect of the tribe. Do you know anything of its provenance, Branom?"
"Odd bits of old rhyming slang," said Dr. Branom. . . . "A bit of gipsy talk, too. But most of the roots are Slav. Propaganda. Subliminal penetration." (Part 2, chapter 6)

What seems to be the function of Nadsat in the novel? of language?

4. You may wish to be aware of the "Glossary of Nadsat Language" at the back of the American paperback edition of the novel, but you should also realize that it is not by Burgess, who has expressed his disapproval of its presence.

5. "The cultural implications of language have, in our own society, been almost entirely neglected." (Burgess, "Word, World and Meaning," in *Urgent Copy*)

What do they seem to be in *A Clockwork Orange?*

6. How do the verbal pyrotechnics of the book—which, most readers and viewers agree, are preserved to a surprising degree—come off in the film?

If you know **2001: A Space Odyssey,* contrast the minimal role played by words in that film with their prominence here.

7. Few films make such extensive and important use of narration and voice-overs as *A Clockwork Orange.* Do they work effectively? (See the discussions of narration in written literature and film in chapters 1 and 2, pages 9–11 and 38–41, and of voice-overs in chapter 3, page 58.)

8. Dr. Brodsky, in the novel: "The sweetest and most heavenly of activities partake in some measure of violence—the act of love, for instance; music, for instance." (Part 2, chapter 6)

9. Much has been made of how "stylized" the violence often is in the film, and some viewers claim that the result is to distance us from it too much, making us feel its full horror much less acutely than we should. According to Christopher Ricks in his review for the *New York Review of Books,* for example, "The real accusation against the film is certainly not that it is too violent, but that it is not violent enough." And Geoffrey Wagner argues that the film "drained the book of ethos" by putting "a different emphasis on the main theme, how a society accommodates violence." (*The Novel and the Cinema*)

Do you agree with such accusations?

10. According to Burgess, Alex "has the three main human attributes—love of aggression, love of language, love of beauty." ("Juice from a Clockwork Orange")

11. How sympathetic is the presentation of Alex? Is there a basic shift in sympathy after the Ludovico treatment, or not? Is there a shift between the novel and the film?

12. Consider the difference in Alex's picking up the girls in the record shop. In the novel they "couldn't have been more than ten," and he rapes them.

13. "If Alex were a lesser villain, then you would dilute the point of the film. It would be like one of those Westerns which purports to be against lynching and deals with the lynching of innocent people. . . .

Obviously if Alex were a lesser villain, it would be very easy to reject his 'treatment' as inhuman. But when you reject the treatment of even a character as wicked as Alex, the moral point is clear." (Kubrick, quoted by Gene D. Phillips)

What *is* the moral point? According to the Minister of the Interior in both the film and the novel (part 2, chapter 7), "The point is . . . that it works." Presumably, Kubrick disagrees. Do you?

14. A remark of the Minister of the Interior, in the novel, commented on by Alex:

> ". . . This vicious young hoodlum will be transformed out of all recognition."
> And those hard slovos, brothers, were like the beginning of my freedom. (Part 2, chapter 2)

In the novel and the film, how would you characterize the sense one gets of freedom? Of dignity?

15. The chaplain, in both the novel and the film: "The question is whether such a technique can really make a man good. Goodness comes from within, 6655321. Goodness is something chosen. When a man cannot choose he ceases to be a man." (Part 2, chapter 1)

16. Samuel McCracken believes that the chaplain's argument is "undercut" in the novel (but not the film), and that he "has confused freedom and license." In essence, McCracken's position is at least partially a defense of the Ludovico technique: he says that "given the world of the novel, the State has pretty clearly opted for the best choice open to it." ("Novel into Film")

17. F. Alexander tells Alex that "you have no power of choice any longer. You are committed to socially acceptable acts, a little machine capable only of good." (Part 3, chapter 4)

Is Alex conditioned only to be capable of good—to be honest and truly gentle, and so on—or merely to *behave* as if he were? Is the distinction a significant one?

18. From a newspaper article which appeared under the headline, "U.S. Modifies Its Own Behavior, Ends Jail Study":

> The Federal Bureau of Prisons is discontinuing a behavior modification experiment that critics have charged is both unconstitutional and a failure, and that inmates and former inmates have described as "pavlovian" and reminiscent of "Clockwork Orange." . . .

. . . The techniques vary widely and include isolated confinement, the application of heavy stress or repeated pain (aversion therapy) and the use of drugs, electrodes, and even psychosurgery.

The prison project that is being abandoned involved the punishment-reward technique. . . .

In announcing last week that the project would be dismantled, Bureau of Prisons officials said they were not abandoning the concept of behavior modification. They cited "economic" reasons for the decision—few inmates were involved . . . and the ratio of staff to inmates was so high as to make it not "feasible" to continue. (*The New York Times,* "Week in Review," February 4, 1974)

19. "It is necessary for man to have choice to be good or evil, even if he chooses evil. Tó deprive him of this choice is to make him something less than human—a clockwork orange." (Kubrick, interview with Strick and Houston)

The title is never explained in the film, as it is in the novel, ironically, through the inflated rhetoric of F. Alexander's manuscript: "The attempt to impose upon man . . . laws and conditions appropriate to a mechanical creation, against this I raise my sword-pen—." (Part 1, chapter 2)

20. In the novel, Alex screams during the demonstration scene, "Me, me, me. How about me? . . . Am I just to be like a clockwork orange?"

But in the comparable scene in the movie, at least after he has passed his "test," Alex looks smug and complacent. What is the effect, on him and on the audience of the film, of this lack of awareness?

21. If you know *2001: A Space Odyssey,* compare and contrast, to the conditioning Alex undergoes in *Clockwork,* the way in which the extraterrestrial beings apparently may be said to have "programmed" humanity.

And where would HAL fit in? If the Ludovico technique shows the dangers of mechanizing human behavior (turning an orange into a clockwork), does the depiction of HAL suggest the dangers of humanizing machines (turning a clockwork into an orange)?

22. In the film as in the novel, Dr. Deltoid asks, "What gets into you all? We study the problem and we've been studying it for damn well near a century, yes, but we get no farther with our studies. You've got a good home here, good loving parents, you've not too bad of a brain. Is it some devil that crawls inside you?" (Part 1, chapter 4)

F. Alexander's answer would presumably center on Alex's being, like Alexander's wife, "a victim of the modern age." Would he be correct?

23. "The proposition that what is done to Alex is 'worse' than what he does is nonsense in any ordinary human terms." (Jackson Burgess, review in *Film Quarterly*)

24. Can you discern a political statement in the novel or the film?

25. F. Alexander, in the novel: "The tradition of liberty means all. The common people will let it go, oh yes. They will sell liberty for a quieter life. That is why they must be prodded, *prodded*—" (Part 3, chapter 5). (In the film, "they must be led, . . . driven, *pushed* . . .")

26. "There was . . . a copy of *A Clockwork Orange*, and on the back of the book, like on the spine, was the author's eemya—F. Alexander. Good Bog, I thought, he is another Alex." (Part 3, chapter 5)

In what ways is Alexander "another Alex"?

27. What significance do you see in Alex's love for classical music? More generally, what is the role of art within the novel and film (within these works of art)?

28. Notice the symmetry with which Alex's victims reappear after his release: the old man, the droogs, F. Alexander.

29. In the novel, in the fight with the Catlady it is Alex who uses the bust of Beethoven as a weapon, while in the film the woman does. Why, do you suppose? And why does Kubrick give Alex the particular weapon that he does?

30. For Kubrick's views on adaptations of novels, see chapter 4 of this volume (page 80) and the section on *Lolita, topic 7 (page 246).

31. "Kubrick finds brilliant cinematic equivalents for Burgess' gimmicks, but he is limited by the original's intellectual and emotional thinness." (Charles Thomas Samuels, "The Context of *A Clockwork Orange*")

32. Not surprisingly, perhaps, Anthony Burgess' views of the film are not always easy to pin down, although they seem generally to include a large measure of respect for its achievement and a certain amount of irritation at its notoriety.

Mostly, Burgess commends its fidelity. In "Juice from a Clockwork Orange" he says, "The plot of the film is that of the book, and so is the language, although naturally there's both more language and more plot in the book than in the film." Yet in an interview with C. Robert Jennings, while calling the film a "classic," he nevertheless claims that as an adaptation it "misses many of the main points of the book." What main points might he have in mind?

33. If you are familiar with other Kubrick films, you may notice here some of his distinctive cinematic traits. For example, even before the appearance of *A Clockwork Orange*, Alexander Walker called attention to what he called "Kubrick's often-repeated 'corridor' compositions." Instances in *Clockwork* of this particular trait are the shots of: Alex walking along the hall in the apartment, passing Deltoid in a side room (as is usual, we go along with Alex in a tracking shot); the Minister's visit to the prison; Alex being dragged through the woods to the clearing; and the final tracking shot along the hospital corridors to Alex's ward.

A sense of the frequency of some of the techniques and motifs which recall other Kubrick films can be reached by referring only to various sequences involving F. Alexander: his ominous role as a figure in a wheelchair clearly echoes Dr. Strangelove; the selective use of harshly bright lighting especially recalls a number of scenes in *2001*, as does the extraordinarily intensive use of wide-angle lenses, notably when placing people in a stark modernistic setting; the loud noises in an otherwise quiet scene (the spaghetti meal in *Clockwork* being in this respect as in others reminiscent of Bowman's meal in the strange room at the end of *2001*); unexpected but striking musical accompaniment—*The Blue Danube* in *2001*, "Singin' in the Rain" here.

The latter was an inspiration during shooting: Kubrick asked Malcolm McDowell to sing something, and that was the only song he could immediately recall to which he knew all the words. (For a discussion of the echoes of this scene elsewhere, and of its use of the counterpoint between sight and sound, see chapter 2, page 26.)

34. Compare and contrast Alex's visual imagery at the end of the novel to the last visual image of the playful sexual romp in the film. Do the different images convey a different meaning in Alex's words, "I was cured all right"?

35. At the suggestion of the American publishers, the U.S. edition of *A Clockwork Orange* leaves out the final chapter of the original British edition, in which Alex brings us to the time he is eighteen and says that he has decided to settle down and get married, so that he can have a son: "I knew what was happening, O my brothers. I was like growing up."

Stanley Kubrick did not find out about that chapter until late in the preparations for the film, but in any case he—like almost all the American critics who have commented on the different editions—preferred the American version. And Burgess himself has remarked, "I've been persuaded by so many critics that the book is better in its American form that I say, 'All right, they know best.' " (Interview with John Cullinan)

36. "The Johnsonian definition of a work of art is . . . meaningful to me, and that is that a work of art must either make life more enjoyable or more endurable. Another quality, which I think forms part of the definition, is that a work of art is always exhilarating and never depressing, whatever its subject matter may be." (Kubrick, interview with Strick and Houston)

Further Readings

BURGESS, ANTHONY. *A Clockwork Orange.* New York: Ballantine, 1965. The British edition with the additional chapter is published in London by Heinemann, 1962.

_____. *The Clockwork Testament, or: Enderby's End.* New York: Knopf, 1975.

_____. "Juice from a Clockwork Orange." *Rolling Stone* 10 (June 8, 1972): 52–53.

_____. "On the Hopelessness of Turning Good Books into Films." *The New York Times,* April 20, 1975, sec. 2, pp. 1, 15.

_____. *Urgent Copy: Literary Studies.* New York: Norton, 1968. Reprinted criticism and reviews.

CULLINAN, JOHN. "Anthony Burgess." *Paris Review* 56 (Spring 1973): 118–63. Interview.

DeVITIS, A. A. *Anthony Burgess.* New York: Twayne, 1972. An introductory study.

JENNINGS, C. ROBERT "Anthony Burgess: Candid Conversation." *Playboy* 21 (September 1974): 69–86.

KAGAN, NORMAN. *The Cinema of Stanley Kubrick.* New York: Grove, 1972.

KUBRICK, STANLEY. *A Clockwork Orange.* New York: Ballantine, 1972. The screenplay, with many stills.

_____. "Words and Movies." In *Hollywood Directors 1941–1976.* Ed. Richard Koszarski. New York: Oxford University Press, 1977, pp. 305–9. Originally published in *Sight and Sound* 30 (Winter 1960–61): 14.

McCRACKEN, SAMUEL. "Novel into Film; Novelist into Critic: *A Clockwork Orange* . . . Again." *Antioch Review* 32 (1973): 427–36.

McGREGOR, CRAIG. "Nice Boy from the Bronx?" *The New York Times.* January 30, 1972, sec. 2, pp. 1, 13.

MORRIS, ROBERT. *The Consolations of Ambiguity: An Essay on the Novels of Anthony Burgess.* Columbia: University of Missouri Press, 1971. A short book.

PHILLIPS, GENE D. *Stanley Kubrick: A Film Odyssey.* New York: Popular Library, 1975. Frequently quotes from Kubrick.

SAMUELS, CHARLES THOMAS. "The Context of *A Clockwork Orange.*" *The American Scholar* 41 (Summer 1972): 439–43.

STRICK, PHILIP, and PENELOPE HOUSTON. "Interview with Stanley Kubrick." *Sight and Sound* 41 (Spring 1972): 62–66.

WALKER, ALEXANDER. *Stanley Kubrick Directs.* New York: Harcourt Brace Jovanovich, 1971. Published before the appearance of *A Clockwork Orange,* but a valuable study of Kubrick's career before then, based on extensive interviews with him.

■■■■■■■■■■■■■■■■■■■
DEATH IN VENICE
■■■■■■■■■■■■■■■■■■■

BACKGROUND

On the Novel

Death in Venice (*Der Tod in Venedig,* 1911)—which is sometimes described as a long story rather than a short novel (see the discussion of such distinctions in chapter 1, pages 13–15)—was written when its author, like its protagonist, was already internationally famous and respected. But unlike Aschenbach, Thomas Mann (1875–1955) had many years, and many of his greatest achievements, ahead of him. Nevertheless, over twenty years later, Mann wrote in a letter that *Death in Venice* was one of his works in which he had "the most faith," in part because "the coherent and pregnant form of the novella has more durability than the loose, expansive form of the novel."

Although Mann's epic first novel, *Buddenbrooks* (1901), made him famous, he was known mostly for his stories and short novels until the major success of *The Magic Mountain* (*Der Zauberberg,* 1924), one of the most important novels of the century. He received the Nobel Prize in 1929. Other major works include the huge, four-part novel, *Joseph and His Brothers* (*Joseph und seine Brüder,* 1933–43), *Doctor Faustus* (*Doktor Faustus,* 1947), and *Confessions of Felix Krull, Confidence Man* (*Bekenntnisse des Hochstaplers Felix Krull,* 1954). In addition to *Death in Venice*, works by Mann that have been filmed include: *Buddenbrooks* (twice—by Gerhard

FIG. 39. The Museum of Modern Art/Film Stills Archive. Copyright © 1971 by Warner Bros., Inc. (All rights reserved.)

Lamprecht, 1923, and by Alfred Weidenmann in two parts, 1961); the 1903 short novel *Tonio Kroger* (by Rolf Thiele, 1964); and *Confessions of Felix Krull* (by Kurt Hoffman, 1958).

Death in Venice has also served as the basis for an opera by Benjamin Britten (1973).

On the Film

Death in Venice (1971), which won a Special Prize at the Cannes Film Festival, was also made in an Italian-language version (as *Morte a Venezia*). It was produced, directed, and co-written by Luchino Visconti (1906–1976), who began his career as an assistant to Jean Renoir. His own early movies—such as *Ossessione* (1942), *La Terra Trema* (1947), and *Senso* (1954)—made him one of the founders of the important Italian neo-realist movement of the 1940s; his later films went in new directions, although he always kept his passionate concern for naturalistic details. Other films include *Rocco and His Brothers* (*Rocco e i Suoi Fratelli*, 1960), *The Damned* (*La Caduta degli Dei*, 1969), *Ludwig II* (1972), and *Conversation Piece* (1975).

Several of the films mentioned are adaptations of novels—for example *Ossessione* is based on James M. Cain's *The Postman Always Rings*

Twice—and Visconti adapted a number of works by major literary figures: Mann's *Death in Venice* of course, but also Dostoevsky's *White Nights* (*La Notti Bianche*, 1957), Giuseppe Tomasi di Lampedusa's *The Leopard* (*Il Gattopardo*, 1963), and Albert Camus' *The Stranger* (*Lo Straniero*, 1967). But his interest in Mann was a special one: *Rocco and His Brothers* seems to have been influenced—as its title acknowledges—by *Joseph and His Brothers*, and *The Damned* by *Buddenbrooks* (while an important character in *The Damned* is also named Aschenbach).

Mann had based the character of Aschenbach on several figures, in addition to himself perhaps: the poet Goethe (1749–1832), and the musicians Richard Wagner (1813–1883)—who had in fact died in Venice—and Gustav Mahler (1860–1911), who died the year Mann wrote his short novel. In Mann, of course, Aschenbach is a writer; but Visconti carried further the correspondences with Mahler by making Aschenbach a famous conductor and composer and through other changes suggesting Mahler's life; for example, like Visconti's Aschenbach, Mahler was terribly stricken by the death of his little daughter. And Visconti was apparently told by the Mann family that Mann had once met Mahler, who told him that he had fallen in love with a young boy. Most importantly, Visconti used Mahler's own music throughout the film, especially the *Adagietto* movement of the Fifth Symphony ("The Giant"). The musical director was Franco Mannino.

Visconti collaborated on the script with Nicola Badalucco, as he had on *The Damned;* and one of the directors of photography for that film, Pasquale De Santis, served in that role here; he had been the cameraman for Fellini's *8¹/₂*. Piero Tosi designed costumes for most of Visconti's films. The editor, Ruggero Mastroianni, had worked on both *The Stranger* and *The Damned*. And the sound was the work of Vittorio Trentino, who also worked on many of Visconti's films.

Other credits: executive producers, Mario Gallo and Robert Gordon Edwards; production manager, Anna Davini; assistant director, Albert Cocco; art director, Ferdinanco Scarfiotti.

Dirk Bogarde (Gustave von Aschenbach) made his first film, *Esther Waters*, in 1947, and for many years he was largely restricted to romantic and comedy leads. But he received the British Film Academy Award for his performance in *The Servant* (1963), and then again for *Darling* (1965). Other films include *The Fixer* (1967) and Visconti's *The Damned*. Bogarde is a published poet and the author of a memoir of his childhood and youth, *A Postillion Struck by Lightning* (1977).

Tadzio was played by Björn Andresen. His mother was Silvana

Mangano, whose films include *Bitter Rice* (1949), *Teorema* (1968), and Visconti's *Conversation Piece*. Marisa Berenson (Aschenbach's wife) has also been in *Cabaret* (1972) and *Barry Lyndon* (1975). Mark Burns (Alfred) has appeared in such films as *The Charge of the Light Brigade* (1967) and *Juggernaut* (1974).

Running time: 130 minutes. Distributor: Warner.

TOPICS TO THINK ABOUT

1. Thomas Mann, in "On the Film":

And the film has, quite specifically, nothing to do with the drama. It is narrative in pictures. That these faces are present to your sight does not prevent their greatest effectiveness from being in its nature epic; and in this sphere, if in any, the film approaches literary art. It is much too genuine to be theatre. . . . The film possesses a technique of recollection, of psychological suggestion, a mastery of detail in men and in things, from which the novelist, though scarcely the dramatist, might learn much.

2. In the Preface to his *Stories of Three Decades,* Mann speaks of the importance of "music as a shaping influence in my art," and of his conception of "prose-composition as a weaving of themes, as a musical complex of associations." One "musical" technique for weaving together such associations which has come to be connected especially with Mann's work is the *leitmotif,* a term Mann borrowed from Wagner. In literature, it has come to refer to a recurrent image—one that reappears through a given work, or at least in several important contexts, and which does so in a meaningful or suggestive way.

What are some of the more notable leitmotifs within *Death in Venice?*

3. "Who shall unriddle the puzzle of the artist nature?" (Mann, *Death in Venice*)

To what extent does Aschenbach seem meant to represent a general picture of "the artist nature"? What seems to be said within the novel about the artist's relationship to the world and the rest of humanity? What approach does the film seem to take toward such questions?

4. William Butler Yeats, in "The Choice":

The intellect of man is forced to choose
Perfection of the life, or of the work,

> And if it take the second must refuse
> A heavenly mansion, raging in the dark. . . .

Would Aschenbach agree, do you think? Would Mann? Or Visconti? (Would you?)

5. In an essay entitled "Dostoyevsky—Within Limits," Mann speaks of "the religious greatness of the damned; genius as disease, disease as genius, the type of the afflicted and possessed, where saint and criminal become one."

6. Do you see any significant connections among the man at the cemetery, the dandy on the boat, the gondolier, and the street-singer? Why do they all appear in the film except the man at the cemetery?

7. Why does Aschenbach go away? Why does he go to Venice?

8. "His love of the ocean had profound sources: the hard-worked artist's longing for rest, his yearning to seek refuge from the thronging manifold shapes of his fancy in the bosom of the simple and vast; and another yearning, opposed to his art and perhaps for that very reason a lure, for the unorganized, the immeasurable, the eternal—in short, for nothingness." (Mann, *Death in Venice*)

9. In 1904, seven years before Mann wrote this short novel, the young Virginia Woolf, while on a trip through Italy, wrote to a friend back home in England: "Venice is a place to die in beautifully: but to live [in] I never felt more depressed—that is exaggerated, but still it does shut one in and make one feel like a Bird in a Cage after a time."

10. "Everything is what it is: the tramp is a tramp, the street-musician is a street-musician, the hotel is a hotel, and Venice is Venice. No attempt is made—say, in the manner of Kafka—to unsteady our trust in the reliability of everyday experience. Nevertheless the ordinary world is under notice of dismissal." (Erich Heller, *Thomas Mann*)

11. How would you describe Aschenbach's love for Tadzio?

12. In the novel, to what degree does Aschenbach's feeling for Tadzio seem to be that for a son he has never had?

In the film, when Aschenbach refrains from warning Tadzio's family about the epidemic, we go to a flashback of his grief over the death of his daughter. Is the connection gratuitous, or illuminating?

13. Few readers totally deny the presence of homosexual feelings in Aschenbach's passion for Tadzio, but there is far from total agreement over how important they are. How central or dominant do they seem to be to you?

14. At least one studio executive urged Visconti to change Tadzio to a girl; would the resulting obsession have been "healthier"?

15. Some people feel that the film greatly exaggerates the sexual aspects of Aschenbach's feelings for Tadzio, as well as of Tadzio's responses to Aschenbach's betrayal of those feelings. Do you agree?

Are the Aschenbach and Tadzio of the film a dirty old man and a young flirt? Whether they are or not, do they accurately reflect Mann's characters?

16. How do you interpret Aschenbach's "fearful dream" near the end of the novel? What is the significance of its omission from the film?

17. " 'He is delicate, he is sickly,' Aschenbach thought. 'He will most likely not live to grow old.' He did not try to account for the pleasure the idea gave him." (Mann, *Death in Venice*)

Could you?

18. What effects does Aschenbach's love for Tadzio have on him?

19. In her negative review in *Film Quarterly*, Joan Mellen says that "Visconti in truth cannot decide whether Aschenbach's desire for the boy is a liberation or a degradation." Can Mann? Can you?

20. Josef von Sternberg's film *The Blue Angel* (1930), with Emil Jannings and Marlene Dietrich, was adapted from *Professor Unrath* (1905), a novel by Heinrich Mann, Thomas Mann's brother. If you know that film, compare and contrast the professor's obsession with Lola to Aschenbach's with Tadzio.

21. How much is added by the flashbacks in the film? Do you discern any pattern to the ways in which they are introduced?

22. In the flashbacks, what are Alfred's accusations against Aschenbach's art? Are we meant to take them at face value? Are they supported or refuted by the music that we hear—Mahler's music?

23. Geoffrey Nowell-Smith, in *Luchino Visconti,* on Aschenbach in the film:

> He never speaks with his fellow guests, but only with people who are structurally in the position of servants or cast in a role of service and even servility. . . .
>
> Aschenbach comes to Venice alone and he dies there alone, but the sense of the event is given not by the emptiness but rather by the fullness of what surrounds him. The emptiness is between himself and the world, not in the world itself.

24. "Whether or not Visconti's assault on *Death in Venice* is a great film is open to opinion; but it surely succeeds in complementing its wonderful original, in the manner of some richly visual footnote." (Geoffrey Wagner, *The Novel and the Cinema*)

Film Distributors

The following are some of the major distributors of 16mm films. Catalogues with rental fees and ordering information are available from each firm.

AUDIO BRANDON   34 MacQuesten Parkway S., Mount Vernon, N.Y. 10550
  There are also several regional offices. A major resource which distributes a great many films.

BAUER INTERNATIONAL   119 North Bridge St., Somerville, N.J. 08876
  A small number of interesting recent foreign films.

BUDGET FILMS   4590 Santa Monica Blvd., Los Angeles, Calif. 90029
  As the name indicates, often less expensive than other distributors—but not invariably.

CORINTH FILMS   410 E. 62 St., New York, N.Y. 10021
  A good selection of foreign films.

FILMS INC.   440 Park Ave. S., New York, N.Y. 10016
  There are also several regional offices. A major distributor of a great many films.

GROVE PRESS FILMS   196 W. Houston St., New York, N.Y. 10014
  Specializes in avant-garde films.

INDIANA UNIVERSITY AUDIO-VISUAL CENTER   Bloomington, Indiana 47401
  Many excerpts from feature films available for study.

JANUS FILMS   745 Fifth Ave., New York, N.Y. 10022
   A major distributor of a number of important films, especially foreign ones.

KIT PARKER FILMS   Carmel Valley, Calif. 93924
   Often less expensive than other distributors. Its catalogues are detailed and interesting.

MUSEUM OF MODERN ART   Department of Film Circulating Programs, 11 W. 53 St., New York, N.Y. 10019
   A major source of a number of classic films.

NEW YORKER FILMS   16 W. 61 St., New York, N.Y. 10023
   Specializes in recent foreign films.

PARAMOUNT   5451 Marathon St., Hollywood, Calif. 90038

SELECT FILM LIBRARY   115 W. 31 St., New York, N.Y. 10001
   A large selection.

SWANK MOTION PICTURES   393 Front St., Hempstead, N.Y. 11550
   There are also several regional offices. A major source of many films.

TWYMAN FILMS.   329 Salem Ave., Boc 605, Dayton, Ohio 45401
   There are also offices in New York and Los Angeles. A major source of many films.

UNITED ARTISTS   729 Seventh Ave., New York, N.Y. 10019

UNITED FILMS   1425 S. Main, Tulsa, Okla. 74119
   A varied selection.

UNIVERSAL/16   445 Park Ave., New York, N.Y. 10022
   There are also several regional offices.

UNIVERSITY OF CALIFORNIA EXTENSION MEDIA CENTER   Berkeley, Calif. 94720

UNIVERSITY OF WASHINGTON   Audio Visual Services, Seattle, Wash. 98195

VIDEO COMMUNICATIONS   6555 E. Skelly Drive, Tulsa, Okla. 74145
   Specializes in British and American films.

WALTER READE   241 E. 34 St., New York, N.Y. 10016
   A small but excellent selection.

WARNER BROS.   4000 Warner Blvd., Burbank, Calif. 91522

WHOLESOME FILM CENTER   20 Melrose St., Boston, Mass. 02116
   Its catalogue is small, but more varied than the name of the firm might suggest.

Bibliography

This bibliography attempts to perform two major functions: first, to give bibliographical information for general works cited throughout this volume; and second, to provide a highly selective but useful list of works which will help readers explore for themselves additional aspects of film and literature. (Bibliographies for individual films, novels, stories, plays, filmmakers, and authors appear under the heading "Further Readings" for each section of part 2.)

AGEE, JAMES. *Agee on Film.* Vol. I. New York: Universal Library, 1969.

ALLEN, WALTER. *The English Novel: A Short Critical History.* New York: Dutton, 1958.

ANDREW, J. DUDLEY. *The Major Film Theories: An Introduction.* New York: Oxford University Press, 1976. Excellent.

ARMES, ROY. *French Film.* London: Studio Vista, 1970. A brief overview.

AUERBACH, ERICH. *Mimesis: The Representation of Reality in Western Literature.* Trans. Willard R. Trask. Princeton, N.J.: Princeton University Press, 1953. Very influential study; from Homer to Virginia Woolf.

AUGUSTINE, ST. *Confessions.* Trans. Edward B. Pusey. New York: Random House, 1949.

BALÁZS, BÉLA. *Theory of the Film: Character and Growth of a New Art.* Trans. Edith Bone. New York: Dover, 1970. A major work.

BAWDEN, LIZ-ANNE, ed. *The Oxford Companion to Film.* New York: Oxford University Press, 1976. An excellent reference book.

BAYER, WILLIAM. *The Great Movies*. New York: Grosset and Dunlap, 1973. Beautifully illustrated.

BAZIN, ANDRÉ. *What Is Cinema?* 2 vols. Ed. and trans. Hugh Gray. Berkeley: University of California Press, 1967, 1971.

BEJA, MORRIS. *Epiphany in the Modern Novel*. Seattle: University of Washington Press, 1971.

———, ed. *Psychological Fiction*. Glenview, Ill.: Scott, Foresman, 1971.

BENCHLEY, NATHANIEL. *Humphrey Bogart*. Boston: Little, Brown, 1975.

BLUESTONE, GEORGE. *Novels into Film*. Berkeley: University of California Press, 1957. An influential study of adaptations.

BOOTH, WAYNE C. *The Rhetoric of Fiction*. Chicago: University of Chicago Press, 1961.

BROOKS, CLEANTH. *The Well-Wrought Urn: Studies in the Structure of Poetry*. New York: Harvest, 1947.

BRYAN, MARGARET B., and BOYD H. DAVIS. *Writing About Literature and Film*. New York: Harcourt Brace Jovanovich, 1975.

CAMPBELL, JOSEPH. *The Hero with a Thousand Faces*. New York: Pantheon, 1949. A major study of myth.

CHASE, RICHARD. *The American Novel and Its Tradition*. Garden City, N.Y.: Anchor, 1957.

CLAIR, RENÉ. *Reflections on the Cinema*. Trans. Vera Traill. London: William Kimber, 1953.

CLARENS, CARLOS. *An Illustrated History of the Horror Film*. New York: Capricorn, 1968.

COLIE, ROSALIE L. "Literature and History." In *Relations of Literary Study: Essays on Interdisciplinary Contributions*. Ed. James Thorpe. New York: Modern Language Assoc., 1967

CORLISS, RICHARD. *Talking Pictures: Screenwriters in the American Cinema 1927–1973*. Woodstock, N.Y.: Overlook Press, 1974.

CROWTHER, BOSLEY. *The Great Films: Fifty Golden Years of Motion Pictures*. New York: Putnam's Sons, 1967.

DARDIS, TOM. *Some Time in the Sun*. New York: Charles Scribner's Sons, 1976. On the experiences of selected prominent writers in Hollywood: Fitzgerald, Faulkner, West, Huxley, Agee.

DAWIDOWICZ, LUCY S. *The War Against the Jews: 1933–1945*. New York: Bantam, 1976.

DE MARCO, NORMAN. "Bibliography of Books on Literature and Film." *Style* 9 (Fall 1975): 593–607.

DENITTO, DENNIS, and WILLIAM HERMAN. *Film and the Critical Eye*. New York: Macmillan, 1975.

DURGNAT, RAYMOND. *Films and Feelings.* Cambridge, Mass.: MIT Press, 1967.

EDEL, LEON. *The Modern Psychological Novel.* New York: Universal Library, 1964.

EIDSVIK, CHARLES. *Cineliteracy: Film Among the Arts.* New York: Random House, 1978.

EISENSTEIN, SERGEI M. *Film Form: Essays in Film Theory.* Ed. and trans. Jay Leyda. New York: Harcourt Brace Jovanovich, 1949. Among the most influential volumes on film ever published.

_____. *The Film Sense.* Ed. and trans. Jay Leyda. New York: Harcourt Brace Jovanovich, 1949.

_____. *Notes of a Film Director.* Trans. X. Danko. London: Lawrence and Wishart, 1959.

ELLMANN, RICHARD, and CHARLES FEIDELSON, JR., eds. *The Modern Tradition: Backgrounds of Modern Literature.* New York: Oxford University Press, 1965.

ENSER, A. G. S. *Filmed Books and Plays: A List of Books and Plays from Which Films Have Been Made, 1928–1974.* London: Andre Deutsch, 1975.

FELL, JOHN L. *Film and the Narrative Tradition.* Norman: University of Oklahoma Press, 1974.

FERGUSSON, FRANCIS. *The Idea of a Theater.* Garden City, N.Y.: Anchor, 1953.

FRANK, JOSEPH. *The Widening Gyre.* New Brunswick, N.J.: Rutgers University Press, 1963.

FREUD, SIGMUND. *The Complete Introductory Lectures on Psychoanalysis.* Ed. and trans. James Strachey. New York: Norton, 1966.

_____. *General Introduction to Psychoanalysis.* Trans. Joan Riviere. New York: Liveright, 1924.

_____. *The Interpretation of Dreams.* Ed. and trans. James Strachey et al. In *The Standard Edition of the Complete Psychological Works of Sigmund Freud.* Vol. IV. London: Hogarth, 1953.

_____. "The Relation of the Poet to Day-dreaming." In *On Creativity and the Unconscious.* Ed. Benjamin Nelson. Trans. Joan Riviere. New York: Harper and Row, 1958.

FRIEDMAN, MELVIN. *Stream of Consciousness: A Study in Literary Method.* New Haven: Yale University Press, 1955.

FRYE, NORTHROP. *Anatomy of Criticism.* Princeton, N.J.: Princeton Universtiy Press, 1957. Extremely important and influential.

GEDULD, HARRY M., ed. *Authors on Film.* Bloomington: Indiana University Press, 1972. A valuable collection of essays and comments about film by prominent literary figures.

———, and Ronald Gottesman. *An Illustrated Glossary of Film Terms.* New York: Holt, Rinehart and Winston, 1973.

Gelmis, Joseph. *The Film Director as Superstar.* Garden City, N.Y.: Doubleday, 1970.

Gerlach, John C., and Lana Gerlach. *The Critical Index: A Bibliography of Articles on Film in English, 1946–1973, Arranged by Names and Topics.* New York: Teachers College Press, 1974. Selected.

Gessner, Robert. *The Moving Image: A Guide to Cinematic Literacy.* New York: Dutton, 1970.

Godard, Jean-Luc. *Godard on Godard.* Ed. Jean Narboni and Tom Milne. New York: Viking, 1972.

Gifford, Denis. *British Cinema.* New York: A. S. Barnes, 1968.

Goldstein, Laurence, and Jay Kaufman. *Into Film.* New York: Dutton, 1976. An extensive, detailed textbook.

Graham, Peter, ed. *The New Wave.* Garden City, N.Y.: Doubleday, 1968.

Greenberg, Harvey R. *The Movies on Your Mind.* New York: Saturday Review Press, 1975. Essays on selected films from the perspective of psychoanalysis.

Graham, Sheilah. *College of One.* New York: Viking, 1967.

Griffith, Richard. "The Film Since Then." In Paul Rotha. *The Film Till Now: A Survey of World Cinema.* London: Spring Books, 1967.

Halliwell, Leslie. *The Filmgoer's Companion.* 6th ed. New York: Hill and Wang, 1977. A valuable source of data, especially on many lesser-known cinema figures.

Harrington, John, ed. *Film And/As Literature.* Englewood Cliffs, N.J.: Prentice-Hall, 1977. Excellent anthology.

Haskell, Molly. *From Reverence to Rape.* Baltimore: Penguin, 1974. On women in film.

Holland, Norman H. *The Dynamics of Literary Response.* New York: Oxford University Press, 1968. Psychoanalytic perspective.

Houston, Penelope. *The Contemporary Cinema: 1945–63.* Baltimore: Penguin, 1963.

Humphrey, Robert. *Stream of Consciousness in the Modern Novel.* Berkeley: University of California Press, 1958.

Hurt, James, ed. *Focus on Film and Theatre.* Englewood Cliffs, N.J.: Prentice-Hall, 1974. Collection of essays.

Jacobs, Lewis, ed. *The Emergence of Film Art.* New York: Hopkinson and Blake, 1969. Anthology of essays.

———. *The Rise of the American Film: A Critical History.* New York: Harcourt Brace Jovanovich, 1939.

JORDAN, THURSTON C., JR., ed. *Glossary of Motion Picture Terminology.* Menlo Park, Calif.: Pacific Coast Publishers, 1968.

JOYCE, JAMES. *James Joyce in Padua.* Ed. Louis Berrone. New York: Random House, 1977.

JUNG, CARL GUSTAV. *Aion.* In *Psyche and Symbol: A Selection from the Writings of C. G. Jung.* Ed. Violet S. de Laszlo. Garden City, N.Y.: Anchor, 1958.

————. "Psychological Aspects of the Mother Archetype." In his *The Archetypes and the Collective Unconscious.* Trans. R. F. C. Hull. Princeton, N.J.: Princeton University Press, 1959.

KAEL, PAULINE. *Deeper into Movies.* Boston: Little, Brown, 1972. Collected reviews, like the volumes below.

————. *Going Steady.* Boston: Little, Brown, 1970.

————. *I Lost It at the Movies.* Boston: Little, Brown, 1965.

————. *Kiss Kiss Bang Bang.* Boston: Little, Brown, 1968.

————. *Reeling.* New York: Warner, 1976.

KAUFFMANN, STANLEY. *A World on Film: Criticism and Comment.* New York: Delta, 1966. Collected reviews.

KNIGHT, ARTHUR. *The Liveliest Art: A Panoramic History of the Movies.* New York: Mentor, 1957.

KOSZARSKI, RICHARD, ed. *Hollywood Directors 1914–1940.* New York: Oxford University Press, 1976. A collection of articles by numerous filmmakers. See the companion volume below.

————. *Hollywood Directors 1941–1976.* New York: Oxford University Press, 1977.

KRACAUER, SIEGFRIED. *From Caligari to Hitler: A Psychological History of the German Film.* Princeton, N.J.: Princeton University Press, 1947.

————. *Theory of Film: The Redemption of Physical Reality.* New York: Oxford University Press, 1960. An important volume in the history of film theory.

LAING, R. D. *The Divided Self.* Baltimore: Penguin, 1965.

LAZARUS, ARNOLD, and H. WENDELL SMITH. *A Glossary of Literature and Composition.* New York: Universal Library, 1973.

LENNIG, ARTHUR. *The Silent Voice.* Troy, N.Y.: W. Snyder, 1969.

LEVIN, RICHARD, ed. *Tragedy: Plays, Theory, and Criticism.* New York: Harcourt Brace Jovanovich, 1960.

LINDGREN, ERNEST. *The Art of the Film.* New York: Macmillan, 1963.

LINDSAY, VACHEL. *The Art of Moving Pictures.* New York: Macmillan, 1922.

LUHR, WILLIAM, and PETER LEHMAN. *Authorship and Narrative in the*

Cinema: Issues in Contemporary Aesthetics and Criticism. New York: Capricorn, 1977.

MacCann, Richard Dyer, ed. *Film: A Montage of Theories.* New York: Dutton, 1966.

Macdonald, Dwight. *Dwight Macdonald on Movies.* Englewood Cliffs, N.J.: Prentice-Hall, 1969.

McLuhan, Marshall. *Understanding Media.* New York: McGraw-Hill, 1964. Extremely influential.

Magny, Claude-Edmonde. *The Age of the American Novel: The Film Aesthetic of Fiction Between the Two Wars.* Trans. Eleanor Hochman. New York: Ungar, 1972.

Manchel, Frank. *Film Study: A Resource Guide.* Rutherford, N.J.: Fairleigh Dickinson University Press, 1973. Useful.

Marcus, Fred H., ed. *Film and Literature: Contrasts in Media.* Scranton, Pa.: Chandler, 1971. Collection of reprinted essays.

Mast, Gerald. *Film/Cinema/Movie: A Theory of Experience.* New York: Harper and Row, 1977.

_____. *A Short History of the Movies.* 2d ed. Indianapolis: Bobbs-Merrill, 1976.

_____, and Marshall Cohen, eds. *Film Theory and Criticism: Introductory Readings.* New York: Oxford University Press, 1974.

May, Rollo. *Love and Will.* New York: Norton, 1969.

Mellen, Joan. *Women and Their Sexuality in the New Film.* New York: Horizon Press, 1973.

Metz, Christian. *Film Language: A Semiotics of the Cinema.* Trans. Michael Taylor. New York: Oxford Universtiy Press, 1974. An extremely influential and important study.

Monaco, James. *How to Read a Film: The Art, Technology, Language, History and Theory of Film and Media.* New York: Oxford University Press, 1977.

_____. *The New Wave: Truffaut, Godard, Chabrol, Rohmer, Rivette.* New York: Oxford University Press, 1976.

Murray, Eward. *The Cinematic Imagination: Writers and the Motion Pictures.* New York: Ungar, 1972. In two parts, on dramatists and novelists.

_____. *Nine American Film Critics: A Study of Theory and Practice.* New York: Ungar, 1975. A survey, from Agee to contemporary critics.

Nabokov, Vladimir. *Bend Sinister.* New York: Time, 1964.

Neel, Ann. *Theories of Psychology: A Handbook.* Cambridge, Mass.: Schenkman, 1969.

NICOLL, ALLARDYCE. *Film and Theatre*. New York: Thomas Y. Crowell, 1936.

NIETZSCHE, FRIEDRICH. *Thus Spoke Zarathustra*. Trans. R. J. Hollingdale. Baltimore: Penguin, 1976.

PANOFSKY, ERWIN. "Style and Medium in the Motion Pictures." In Harrington, ed. *Film And/As Literature*, above, pp. 283–94.

PEARY, GERALD, and ROGER SHATZKIN, eds. *The Classic American Novel and the Movies*. New York: Ungar, 1977. Reprinted essays on films based on novels, from *The Last of the Mohicans* to *The Sound and the Fury*.

PYNCHON, THOMAS. *Gravity's Rainbow*. New York: Bantam, 1974.

RICHARDSON, ROBERT. *Literature and Film*. Bloomington: Indiana University Press, 1969. A valuable short study.

RIIS, JACOB A. "How the Other Half Lives: Studies Among the Tenements." *Scribner's Magazine* 6 (December 1889): 643–62. Also published in book form: *How the Other Half Lives*. Cambridge, Mass.: Belknap Press, 1970.

ROSS, HARRIS. "A Selected Bibliography of the Relationship of Literature and Film." *Style* 9 (Fall 1975): 564–92.

ROSS, T. J., ed. *Film and the Liberal Arts*. New York: Holt, Rinehart and Winston, 1970. Anthology of essays.

SAGAN, CARL. *The Dragons of Eden: Speculations on the Evolution of Human Intelligence*. New York: Random House, 1978.

SAMUELS, CHARLES THOMAS. *Encountering Directors*. New York: Putnam's Sons, 1972. Interviews.

SARRIS, ANDREW. *The American Cinema: Directors and Directions 1929–1968*. New York: Dutton, 1968. A controversial volume by the leading American exponent of the *auteur* principle.

―――, ed. *Interviews with Film Directors*. New York: Avon, 1969. A valuable collection.

SCHOLES, ROBERT, and ROBERT KELLOGG. *The Nature of Narrative*. New York: Oxford University Press, 1966.

SCHORER, MARK, JOSEPHINE MILES, and GORDON McKENZIE, eds. *Criticism: The Foundations of Literary Judgment*. New York: Harcourt Brace Jovanovich, 1948. Anthology.

SCHULBERG, BUDD. *The Four Seasons of Success*. Garden City, N.Y.: Doubleday, 1972.

SHIRER, WILLIAM L. *The Rise and Fall of the Third Reich: A History of Nazi Germany*. New York: Simon and Schuster, 1960.

SIMON, JOHN. *Movies into Films*. New York: Dial, 1971. Collected reviews and essays.

————. *Private Screenings.* New York: Macmillan, 1967.

SOLOMON, STANLEY J. *Beyond Formula: American Film Genres.* New York: Harcourt Brace Jovanovich, 1976. On Westerns, musicals, detective and war films, etc.

————, ed. *The Classic Cinema: Essays in Criticism.* New York: Harcourt Brace Jovanovich, 1973.

SPIEGEL, ALAN. *Fiction and the Camera Eye: Visual Consciousness in Film and the Modern Novel.* Charlottesville: University Press of Virginia, 1976. Pays special attention to Flaubert and Joyce.

STEINBERG, COBBETT. *Reel Facts: The Movie Book of Records.* New York: Vintage, 1978.

STEVENS, WALLACE. *The Necessary Angel: Essays on Reality and the Imagination.* New York: Knopf, 1951.

STEVICK, PHILIP, ed. *The Theory of the Novel.* New York: Free Press, 1967. Anthology.

SUTTON, WALTER, and RICHARD FOSTER, eds. *Modern Criticism: Theory and Practice.* New York: Odyssey, 1963.

TAAFFE, JAMES G. *A Student's Guide to Literary Terms.* Cleveland: World, 1967.

TALBOT, DANIEL, ed. *Film: An Anthology.* New York: Simon and Schuster, 1967.

TAYLOR, JOHN RUSSELL. *Cinema Eye, Cinema Ear.* New York: Hill and Wang, 1964.

THOMSON, DAVID. *A Biographical Dictionary of Film.* New York: William Morrow, 1976. Short personal essays rather than biographies as such.

VAN GHENT, DOROTHY. *The English Novel: Form and Function.* New York: Harper and Row, 1961. Introductory essays on a number of classic novels.

WAGNER, GEOFFREY. *The Novel and the Cinema.* Rutherford, N.J.: Fairleigh Dickinson University Press, 1975.

WICKS, ULRICH. "Literature/Film: A Bibliography." *Literature/Film Quarterly* 6 (Spring 1978): 135–43.

WILSON, EDMUND. *The Boys in the Back Room: Notes on California Novelists.* San Francisco: Colt Press, 1941.

WINSTON, DOUGLAS GARRETT. *The Screenplay as Literature.* Rutherford, N.J.: Fairleigh Dickinson University Press, 1973.

WOOLF, VIRGINIA. *Collected Essays.* 4 vols. London: Hogarth, 1966–67.

————. *The Letters of Virginia Woolf, Volume I: 1888–1912.* Ed. Nigel

Nicolson, with Joanne Trautmann. New York: Harcourt Brace Jovanovich, 1975.

YOUNG, VERNON. *On Film: Unpopular Essays on a Popular Art.* Chicago: Quadrangle, 1972.